Collective and Mass Litigation in Europe

Collective and Mass Litigation in Europe

Model Rules for Effective Dispute Resolution

Edited by

Astrid Stadler

Professor and Chair in Civil Law, Procedural Law and Private International Law, and Comparative Law, University of Konstanz, Germany

Emmanuel Jeuland

Director, Sorbonne Institute of Legal Research and Professor of Private and Criminal Law, University of Paris I Pantheon-Sorbonne, France

Vincent Smith

Assistant Professor, ESCP Business School, UK and France; Visiting Fellow, British Institute of International and Comparative Law UK; Solicitor (England and Wales)

Edward Elgar PUBLISHING

Cheltenham, UK • Northampton, MA, USA

Published by
Edward Elgar Publishing Limited
The Lypiatts
15 Lansdown Road
Cheltenham
Glos GL50 2JA
UK

Edward Elgar Publishing, Inc.
William Pratt House
9 Dewey Court
Northampton
Massachusetts 01060
USA

A catalogue record for this book
is available from the British Library

Library of Congress Control Number: 2020942837

This book is available electronically in the **Elgar**online
Law subject collection
http://dx.doi.org/10.4337/9781789906059

Printed on elemental chlorine free (ECF)
recycled paper containing 30% Post-Consumer Waste

ISBN 978 1 78990 604 2 (cased)
ISBN 978 1 78990 605 9 (eBook)

Printed and bound in the USA

Contents

Contributors

Fernando Gascón Inchausti is a full Professor of procedural law at the Complutense University of Madrid, where he also obtained his PhD. He is interested in comparative and European procedural law. He was an active participant in the European Law Institute (ELI)/UNIDROIT Project on the European Rules of Civil Procedure (ERCP) (Co-Reporter of the Working Group on Access to Information and Evidence and member of the Working Groups on *Res Judicata and Lis Pendens* and Appeals).

Emmanuel Jeuland completed his master of laws at the University of Paris 1 – Panthéon-Sorbonne and holds an LLM from King's College (London). His PhD on the law of obligations focused on the procedural law relating to the substitution of persons in contractual and procedural matters. He is currently the Director of the Sorbonne Institute of Legal Research and the Director of the Master's Programme on Justice and Litigation at the University of Paris 1 – Panthéon-Sorbonne. He has published textbooks and essays on procedural law and legal theory. He has been a member of several sub-groups on the ERCP project and participated in the French version review.

Vincent Smith is Assistant Professor in law and ethics at ESCP Business School (London and Paris); he is also a solicitor in private practice (England), with an interest in collective actions. He is a visiting fellow at the British Institute of International and Comparative Law and was formerly Senior Director, Competition Enforcement at the UK Office of Fair Trading. His PhD (King's College, London) focused on collective alternative dispute resolution (ADR) in competition law. He was a member of the ELI/UNIDROIT Working Group on Parties and Collective Redress.

Astrid Stadler is a full Professor of civil law, procedural law, comparative law and private international law at University of Konstanz, Germany, where she also obtained her PhD. From 2011–15 she was part-time Chair in comparative mass litigation at Erasmus School of Law, Rotterdam. Her research focus is on European and international civil procedure and collective redress. In the ELI/UNIDROIT project 'From Transnational Principles to European Rules of Civil Procedure', she was a co-reporter in the Working Groups on Service of Documents and on Parties and Collective Redress.

Magne Strandberg is Professor at the Faculty of Law, University of Bergen.

He teaches civil procedure law and tort law, and is currently the Vice Dean for Education. He has been a member of two Working Groups under the ELI/UNIDROIT project 'From Transnational Principles to European Rules of Civil Procedure'.

Michael Stürner has been a Professor of civil law, private international law and comparative law at the University of Konstanz, Germany, since 2012. In 2019, he was elected Vice-Rector for Teaching and Curricular Affairs. He also serves as a part-time judge at the Regional Court of Appeals in Karlsruhe, Germany. His main research interests lie in the fields of cross-border dispute resolution, comparative law, conflict of laws and European private law. He was a member of the working group on evidence in the ELI/UNIDROIT project on the European Rules of Civil Procedure.

Ianika Tzankova has been studying mass claim dispute resolution since 2000 and has held a chair on that topic since 2007. She currently holds the Chair on Global Dispute Resolution and Mass Claims at Tilburg University, where she teaches the course on Civil Procedure and Global Dispute Resolution in the Global Law Programme. She combines her academic activities with work in practice and was also a member of the Working Group on Parties and Collective Redress in the ELI/UNIDROIT civil procedure project. She was a Fulbright Visiting Scholar at Stanford University and is a visiting Professor at Paris Dauphine University.

Stefaan Voet is a Professor of civil procedure at *Katholieke Universiteit Leuven* and a host Professor at the University of Hasselt. In 2011, he wrote his PhD thesis on complex litigation in Belgium, for which he received in 2014 the Belgian Triannual Prize of Civil Procedure. His research focuses on costs, ADR and online dispute resolution and complex litigation. He was a member of the ELI/UNIDROIT civil procedure project Working Group on Parties and Collective Redress and is also a substitute justice of the peace and a practising lawyer.

Nils von Hinten-Reed is a founder and Managing Director of CEG's European operations. He has provided expert advice in a wide range of competition and commercial litigation cases before competition authorities in Europe and Asia-Pacific, court proceedings and international arbitrations. He was included in *Global Competition Review*'s 2018 list of recommended competition economists and the *Expert Guide to the World's Leading Antitrust/Competition Lawyers and Economists*. He was also included in *WWL*'s *2019 List of Competition Thought Leaders*.

Foreign experts:

Peter Cashman is a practising barrister in Sydney, Australia and Adjunct Professor of Law at the University of New South Wales. Until recently, he was Professor of law (social justice) at the University of Sydney. He graduated from the University of Melbourne with a degree in law and a diploma in criminology, and subsequently completed a Master's in law and a PhD at the University of London (London School of Economics and Political Science). He was formerly Commissioner in charge of the civil justice review with the Victorian Law Reform Commission; Commissioner jointly in charge (with Justice John Basten) of the reference on class actions with the Australian Law Reform Commission; founding Director of the Public Interest Advocacy Centre; founder and senior partner of the firm Cashman & Partners, which merged with Melbourne firm Maurice Blackburn & Co to form the national firm Maurice Blackburn Cashman (now Maurice Blackburn Pty Ltd); Governor of the American Trial Lawyers' Association (now the American Association for Justice); and National President of the Australian Plaintiff Lawyers' Association (now the Australian Lawyers Alliance). He has practised law in the United Kingdom, the United States and Australia.

Choong-soo Han, an academic of civil procedure and bankruptcy law, is the author of several books and articles that cover civil procedure, class action and international litigation. He studied law at Yonsei University in Seoul and has been a member of the Seoul Bar Association since then. He later earned his postgraduate degrees at the same university, culminating in a PhD. He has been a faculty member of the Law School at Hanyang University in Seoul since 1997 and is honorary Chairman of the Korea Association of the Law of Civil Procedure.

Richard Marcus holds the Coil Chair in Litigation at University of California Hastings in San Francisco and is the author of leading books on civil procedure and civil litigation. Since 1996, he has served as Associate Reporter of the US Judicial Conference Advisory Committee on Civil Rules; and in 2003 and 2018 he was chief drafter of amendments to Rule 23, the American class action rule. He also serves as Vice President for North America of the International Association of Procedural Law.

Hermes Zaneti Jr is a tenured Professor of civil procedure at the Federal University of Espírito Santo, Vitoria, Brazil. He has a PhD in law (procedural law) from the Federal University of Rio Grande do Sul, Porto Alegre, Brazil (2005); and a PhD in law (legal theory and philosophy of law) from the Roma Tre University, Rome, Italy (2014). He is a member of the International Association of Procedural Law; and is a Public Prosecutor and Dean of the Public Prosecutors' School of the State of Espírito Santo. He has authored several essays and books on civil procedure and Brazilian collective redress.

1. General introduction

Astrid Stadler, Emmanuel Jeuland and Vincent Smith

1. EUROPEAN RULES OF CIVIL PROCEDURE

After several years of work by leading academics and practitioners from across Europe, UNIDROIT and the European Law Institute (ELI) adopted the European Rules of Civil Procedure 2020 (ERCP) in Autumn 2020. The project provides model rules for a European civil procedure code. Although followed by observers from the European Commission, the ERCP is not a blueprint for a potential European Directive or Regulation. The target of the project is a little less ambitious – to provide a model for national legislatures to use – because the political landscape in Europe is currently not much in favour of a complete harmonization of civil procedure law and the European legislature lacks the competence for such an advance. Therefore, the ELI/UNIDROIT project aimed mainly to identify converging tendencies in civil procedure across Europe and bring them together in the form of a code, to provide a basis for discussion and a 'best practice' template for national legislatures considering procedural reforms.[1]

The contributions in this book deal only with a specific part of the ERCP: the rules on parties and on collective redress (and their interplay). The contributions to this book were written based on a late (2019) draft of the ERCP model rules. The rules in Part XI (collective redress) are substantively the same as those finally adopted by the ELI and UNIDROIT. They explain and comment on these rules and provide a comparative context.

Rules on parties – such as joinder of parties, consolidation, representation and so on – are particularly important in the case of complex mass harm events. Policy makers can provide different options for litigants and courts to handle multi-party and collective proceedings. The 'traditional' class action

[1] Rolf Stürner, presentation at the German Association of International Procedural Law, March 2018, Hamburg.

model avoids procedural complexity by reducing the litigation to a one-on-one action, albeit with numerous procedural safeguards and modifications.

The implementation of collective redress instruments has been discussed at the European level since the beginning of the 2000s and a considerable number of Member States have enacted reforms of their procedural rules since then. As any set of rules on European civil procedure that did not take account of instruments on collective redress would be incomplete, the ERCP includes a chapter on collective proceedings in Part XI.

The European Commission presented a proposal for reform of EU consumer protection law in April 2018, which included a draft Directive on representative actions for consumers. This proposal draws a line under a controversial debate of many decades but was not foreseen when the ELI/UNIDROIT project started. Like the ERCP, the Directive is expected to be adopted in 2020

2. BACKGROUND TO THE ELI/UNIDROIT PROJECT

In 2004, the American Law Institute (ALI) and UNIDROIT (an intergovernmental agency based in Rome) completed a joint project and presented their Principles of Transnational Civil Procedure – a set of 31 principles – accompanied by some 36 more detailed rules (which were not formally adopted by ALI or UNIDROIT).[2] Work on the project had started in 1998, driven by the idea that – despite the differences of continental law and common law – it should be possible to draft common principles of civil procedure. The project had a quite limited scope of application and was intended to cover only commercial disputes in an international setting. The principles were meant to provide a valuable pattern for 'best practice' dispute resolution procedures.[3] The ALI/UNIDROIT principles contained no suggestions on collective redress.

A serious debate on strengthening the private enforcement of EU law in Europe by means of group or class actions had just started in Europe when the principles were adopted. Very few countries in Europe[4] had implemented rules on the collective enforcement of consumer rights which went beyond traditional representative actions for cease-and-desist (injunction) orders.

---

[2] ALI/UNIDROIT, *Principles of Transnational Civil Procedure*, CUP 2006.

[3] ALI/UNIDROIT, *Principles of Transnational Civil Procedure*, CUP 2006, Preface, p XXIX.

[4] Spain (Article 11 of the Civil Procedure Code 2001) and Portugal (Laws 83/95 and 24/96) were the first countries to implement collective actions for the recovery of damages, but the provisions did not gain much importance in practice. In 2002, Sweden was the first Member State to implement a mechanism that clearly followed the role model of the US class action, albeit with an opt-in mechanism.

In 2013/14, the ELI (a non-governmental organization based in Vienna) and UNIDROIT decided to launch a follow-on project, focusing on adapting the 2004 principles to European civil procedure and on regional implementation in Europe. The basic idea behind the new project was not to suggest the drafting of a legislative European code of civil procedure in order to harmonize civil procedure law within the European Union, but rather to provide a consistent set of procedural rules for debate.

The task of drafting the new model rules was given to recognized legal experts in civil procedure from across Europe. In 2016, when some groups had already more or less completed their drafts, the ELI and UNIDROIT decided to establish additional topics in order to cover all parts of civil procedure law. This included a group on 'parties'.[5] The remit of this group covered not only traditional rules on parties (eg, joinder, third-party notice), but also a separate chapter on collective redress. At that time, the European Commission had started to evaluate the implementation of Recommendation 396/2013 on collective redress: it eventually published the results of the evaluation in March 2018.[6]

In April 2018 the European Commission published its proposal for a New Deal for Consumers, including the draft Directive on collective redress (representative actions) in consumer law. The ELI/UNIDROIT 'parties' group referred to the proposal in the comments of its draft rules. Due to the coming into office of the new European Commission in October 2019, the European legislature was unable to finalize the draft Directive in Summer 2019 as intended. The EU institutional 'Trilogue' ended in June 2020 with a common position agreed between the European Council, Parliament and Commission. The new Directive is expected to be adopted by the end of 2020.

3. COLLECTIVE REDRESS IN THE ERCP

Although the ELI/UNIDROIT European Rules of Civil Procedure have the character of model rules only, the chapter on collective redress may gain some practical importance when the European legislature finally passes a binding Directive on consumer collective redress. Member States may consider the ERCP collective redress rules when implementing the Directive in national civil procedure law. The Directive will set out some basic building blocks of a new national collective redress instrument: the details will be for the Member States to design and the ERCP rules could provide a template.

---

[5] Emmanuel Jeuland and Astrid Stadler, co-reporters.

The scope of application of the ERCP covers domestic and cross-border civil proceedings; but family law, arbitration and insolvency proceedings are excluded. There are also no rules on jurisdiction, because the Brussels Ibis Regulation[7] covers questions of jurisdiction.

The ELI/UNIDROIT project has taken the ALI/UNIDROIT principles as a starting point only. It was clear from the outset that the principles would need to be adapted to the European context and traditions, and that the project should also try to present a set of more detailed rules than the earlier ALI/UNIDROIT project. In particular with respect to collective redress, the ALI/UNIDROIT principles were silent and the 'parties' group had to start without any guidance from that project.

The ELI/UNIDROIT project looked at the existing EU law relating to civil procedure ('*acquis communautaire*'), including EU Directives and Regulations, as well as the case law of the Court of Justice of the European Union. Another very important source of inspiration was, of course, national civil procedure law, and substantial comparative research was carried out in this regard. The research was not, however, intended to identify only the lowest common denominator; all groups had in mind to propose 'best practice' rules. Therefore, even where EU law existed, it was not taken as 'carved in stone', but subject to review and, within accepted limits, improvement.

4. OVERVIEW OF THIS STUDY ON PARTIES AND COLLECTIVE REDRESS

It is the objective of this book to explain the ERCP's rules on parties and on collective redress, taking into account the comparative context of their origin, and developments at the European level and outside Europe. The text of the rules can be found in the Appendix and the editors would like to express their sincere thanks to ELI and UNIDROIT for their permission to print the relevant rules. The ERCP is also available in full at https://www.unidroit.org/english/governments/councildocuments/2020session/cd-99-b/cd-99-b-10-rev-e.pdf (last accessed 4 October 2020).

The official comments on the ERCP had to be brief and could not cover all aspects that might be relevant for the implementation of the rules and their impact on court practice. Therefore, the chapters of this book go beyond the officially available comments and consider the rules on parties and collective redress in their European (and, in Chapter 14, global) context.

The first chapters of this book deal with the general rules on 'parties' in the ERCP. These include not only the traditional rules on legal standing, but

---

7 Regulation 1215/2012 [2012] OJEU L351/1.

also the capacity to be a party and litigation capacity. Chapter 2 (Emmanuel Jeuland) also analyses possible procedural ways in future to cope with mass harm situations – for example, in case of environmental disasters. The traditional continental European divide between public law and private law is not always very helpful in this respect and the handling of mass harm events must take both fields of law into consideration.[8] In the event that public regulators do not enforce environmental rules effectively, private enforcement (in a public interest) must step in to support the rule of law. Chapter 2 therefore explores ways to enforce environmental law, animal rights and so on by providing legal standing to 'entities' other than human beings and legal entities, or by legal representation.

Chapter 3 (Vincent Smith) deals with multi-party litigation in a contrast to collective redress actions. The ERCP opens the door to all kinds of ways to handle complex litigation. Joinder of parties, consolidation of proceedings and one-on-one test case litigation are possible ways to handle mass harm events; but the ERCP also provides a whole chapter on collective redress. Chapter 3 analyses the pros and cons of the various options.

Chapter 4 (Emmanuel Jeuland) goes into the detail of procedural settings in which the quite formal approach of defining the parties to litigation (Rule 29 of the ERCP) is not constructive. In order to finally solve a dispute that is pending in court, instruments such as substitution of parties might be necessary. The ERCP has – based on a comparative approach – implemented best practice solutions and not necessarily sought the 'middle ground'.

Chapters 5 to 12 deal with the most important issues in the context of collective actions and we have provided a separate introduction for this part in Chapter 5. In Chapter 6, Astrid Stadler starts by explaining the structure of collective redress proceedings in the ERCP and the requirements for certification. The chapter also describes the remedies available in collective redress actions and contrasts the ERCP with the European legislature's draft for a Directive on representative actions in the interest of consumers. The succeeding chapters walk along the course of a collective redress action and explain details on legal standing (Chapter 7, Ianika Tzankova); case management (Chapter 8, Magne Strandberg and Vincent Smith); the taking of evidence (Chapter 9, Fernando Gascón Inchausti); the calculation of damages (Chapter 10, Nils von Hinten Reed); collective settlements (Chapter 11, Astrid Stadler); and costs and funding (Chapter 12, Stefaan Voet). Mass harm events do not honour national

---

8 For a good example, see the project of the Visegrad Fund, 'Progress in collective redress mechanisms in environmental and consumer mass harm situations' 2018–19, www.ilaw.cas.cz/en/research-and-projects/research-projects/collectiveredress/info.html (last accessed 21 July 2020).

borders; today, they are mostly cross-border events. Thus, they inevitably raise questions of international jurisdiction and enforcement that are dealt with in Chapter 13 (Michael Stürner).

Our final chapter is a little different. In October 2019, the editors of this book invited leading foreign (non-European) experts in the field of collective redress to discuss Part XI of the ERCP, 'Collective Proceedings'. Peter Cashman (Barrister and Professor of Law at the University of Sydney Law School), Chongsoo Han (Professor of Law at Hanyang University, Seoul), Richard Marcus (Professor of Law at the University of Hastings, California) and Hermes Zaneti Jr (Federal University of Spirito Santo, Brazil) explained their views on the ERCP collective redress rules from their national perspectives. They provided short summaries of their contributions which became part of the final chapter of this book. The editors are grateful to them for their time and expertise.

From a global perspective, it became evident that the collective redress rules in Part XI of the ERCP are an attempt to establish a 'European way' of handling mass harm events through court action. Legal standing, the role of 'class counsel' and qualified entities, and costs and funding are just some of the issues on which the traditional class action countries, but also Brazil and South Korea, take different approaches. There is still widespread mistrust in Europe against lawyer-driven litigation and the risk that the economic interests of third parties such as lawyers or third-party funders may prevail over the legitimate interests of the class or group members. We hope, nevertheless, that the comments in Chapter 14 help to demonstrate that the ERCP rules on collective proceedings provide a firm foundation – particularly when viewed in the light of lessons learned outside Europe – for ensuring that European consumers and other victims of mass harm cause by breaches of both national and EU laws can obtain effective redress through proportionately managed court action following European principles.

2. The concept of 'party'

Emmanuel Jeuland

The General Part of the European Rules of Civil Procedure (ERCP) on parties takes into account the diverse traditions of Europe. It aims to open the doors of the court to all natural persons and legal person (1.1) and even entities, making room for natural and technological entities (1.2; 1.3) who have an interest in an action. This part takes into account mass litigation through tools dedicated to individual parties' cases. Individual actions are still the main tools readily available for mass claims in many EU Member States, with the exception of national class actions, which have yet to prove their effectiveness in many countries in Europe.

1. PARTIES TO THE PROCEEDINGS

A number of EU Member States provide basic rules on the question of who can be a party to civil proceedings. It is a common European concept to take a merely formal approach with respect to the definition of 'parties'. Irrespective of who is (under substantive law) the creditor or debtor to the disputed obligation, a 'party' is anybody who has brought an action or against whom an action has been brought. Proceedings may be seen as a procedural relationship so that it could be said that the notion of party is relational. In other words, parties are the persons bound by the procedural relationship.

Outside the field of procedure, the relationist approach to law was initiated by Savigny,[1] who considered the legal relationship – '*Rechtsverhältnis*' – as *the* key concept in law. By the mid-nineteenth century, Bülow affirmed that litigation was a legal relationship distinct from the substantive legal relation at stake – for example, a contract or a tort situation.[2] For this reason, he is considered the founder of procedural science, since his analysis led him to show that procedure was distinct from substantive law. A debate subsequently took

---

[1] F.C. von Savigny, System *des heutigen römischen* Rechts (8 vols, 1840–1849); F.C. von Savigny, *System of the Modern Roman Law*, William Holloway (translator) (Gale, 2013); *Système de droit romain*, available at: Gallica. https://gallica.bnf.fr/ark:/12148/bpt6k5826822p.texteImage (last accessed 10 September 2020).

[2] O. Bülow, *Die Lehre von den Prozesseinreden* (Verlag Emil Roth, 1868), § 1 p 3.

place in Germany concerning procedural relationships. Bülow thought that procedural relationships were those between a judge and the parties, so that there was a public bond between them. At the end of the nineteenth century, Bülow was criticized by Kohler, who suggested that procedural relationships consisted in the relations between the parties under the aegis of the judge.[3]

At the outset of the twentieth century, Goldschmidt said that this situation was irrelevant,[4] since parties had no obligations in procedural relationships, but rather 'charges'. The distinction between obligations and charges has been used in the European Law Institute (ELI)/UNIDROIT project, albeit not plainly, together with a principle of cooperation: the concept of procedural relationship has hence been preserved. As a result of this debate, it seems that in Germany, some professors have a relationist approach to procedure; while others consider that it is not useful and that litigation is simply a legal 'situation' (ie, a legal state of affairs).

This debate also influenced Italian scholars: for example, Chiovenda developed the idea of procedural relationships, describing litigation as a relationship mainly between parties under the aegis of the judge. In France, Vizioz was in turn influenced by Chiovenda and created the idea of the procedural bond between parties, coining the term '*lien d'instance*', or instance bond.

It is easy under this approach to define parties as members of a procedural relationship. But this is, in a way, too easy and not satisfactory, since a party to a procedural relationship may well not have a good reason to be a party; it might be due, for example, to a simple mistake made by the claimant.[5] Conversely, a person or entity may have a right or an interest at stake in a civil litigation, but feel reluctant to bring the action in court. Such is the case of substitutive actions.[6] From that perspective, how can we know who should be a party to include in this procedural relationship? A further concern is a certain lack of content to the procedural relationship, which must be elaborated: what is its object; what are the applicable rules and so on? Last but not least, what is the balance between public procedural relations (ie, between judges and parties) and private relations (ie, between parties under the aegis of the judge)?

Apart from the procedure itself, Savigny's relationist approach has been updated and revisited by different authors:[7] Jennifer Nedelsky did so for Canada in 2011 and Alexander Somek for Austria in 2017. I tried to contribute

---

[3] O. Bülow, *Der Process als Rechtsverhältnis* (Mannheim, 1888).

[4] J. Goldschmidt, *Der Prozess als Rechtlage* (Berlin, 1925).

[5] L. Veyre, *La notion de partie en procédure civile*, PhD University Paris 1, France, 2016.

[6] See Chapter 3.

[7] See J.F. Braunstein and E. Jeuland, *Law and Relations* (IRJS pub, 2018).

my share to the French tradition.[8] For example, Nedelsky suggests[9] adopting a three-step relationist method when assessing human rights:

1. What are the legal relationships and interests at stake?
2. What are the conflicting values?
3. Which solution best enhances the parties' autonomy?

Alexander Somek suggests that it is worth considering law, first, as a set of legal relationships, and then as norms, rights and institutions. He adds that in a relationship, one can imagine standing in for another person to solve a dispute. That is the role of procedural relationships.[10]

1.1 Public and private relationships

We have noted that there are two sets of relationships in procedure: the public (between parties and judges) and the private (between parties). The point is that in each type of relationship, different duties, obligations, powers and rights coexist. Over the twentieth century, the idea emerged that the well-known principle of cooperation is a consequence of the Franz Klein reform (the Austrian Code of Civil Procedure introduced by Klein, who served as minister of justice around 1900), as well as of the relationist approach.[11] This set of duties (rights of the parties and powers of the judge) must be balanced, which is the exact definition of the principle of cooperation.[12] It appears to be the main principle of the ERCP, along with proportionality and respect for the rights of defence.

Procedural relationships are tangible, not abstract in the Kantian way. Following this line of thinking, we must take into account the care approach, which means that weak people or entities that have litigation capacity, but cannot bring an action themselves must be protected by civil procedure rules.

If we want to be as realistic as possible, we should consider not only the parties, but also their rationality and emotions. This is what is called the 'emotional turn' in philosophy and law. An American line of scholarship actually

---

8 *La théorie relationiste du droit* (LGDJ pub, 2016).

9 J. Nedelsky, *Law's Relations: A Relational Theory of Self, Autonomy, and Law* (Oxford University Press, 2011).

10 A. Somek, *The Legal Relations* (Cambridge University Press, 2017).

11 B. Hahn, *Kooperationsmaxime im Zivilprozess?* (Carl Heymanns, 1983), p 1; see also R. Wassermann, *Der soziale Zivilprozess* (Berlin, 1978), p 97 ff – the paragraph is entitled: '*Der Zivilprozess als Arbeitsgemeinschaft*' ('Civil litigation as teamwork').

12 R van Rhee, *Principe de coopération Cooperation principle*, in E Jeuland and S Lalani (eds), *Recherche lexicographique en procédure civile Lexicographical research in civil procedure* (IRJS Editions, 2017), pp 207–14.

focuses on 'law and emotion', with Martha Nussbaum and Peter Goodrich among the leading academics.[13]

The main idea of this trend is not only that judicial reasoning involves emotion as much as reason, but also that we need to take into account emotion in order to reach the best possible decision. However, emotions fluctuate depending on time and place, which means in practical terms that they vary depending on the country and the period of time in question. In ancient times, the goal of litigation procedure may have been to calm down the judge, who might have felt upset by the dispute. The cultural approach of procedure should take into account the cultural construction of emotions. Tests in the United States have shown that female witnesses who get angry while under examination appear less convincing than male witnesses experiencing the same feelings. Consequently, it may also be said that emotion is gendered.

Emotions are channelled during the procedure by the procedural relationships – not only to keep them in check, but also to reach the best possible solution to the dispute. Channelling emotions implies that a procedural process must be adhered to, such as a courtroom, courtroom decorum, lawyers and judges' robes. This remark will prove of interest when we come to discuss the possibility for natural and technical entities to be parties.

A legal bond is not a physical rope: much to the contrary, it is a symbolic space between the parties. The goal is to have autonomous parties, or at least to help parties to be autonomous in their interdependence. Some legally capable people are too weak and dependent, such as minors, consumers and certain vulnerable employees – not to mention 'other' natural beings. Hence, the representation device – in the strict sense of someone bringing an action on behalf of another – is not always sufficient.

The capacity to sue or to be sued is to be clearly distinguished from the capacity to act during proceedings (litigation capacity – see ERCP Rule 30). Both questions are almost always closely linked to substantive law and reflect the idea that the capacity to sue or to be sued corresponds to the general ability under substantive law to hold rights or obligations. The parties to the action are the persons with the capability to possess or claim a right under substantive law (ERCP Rule 29). Moreover, they must have the capacity to exercise their right before court. If they do not have this litigation capacity themselves, they must be represented (Rule 30).

---

[13] For example: R Grossi, 'Understanding Law and Emotion', *Emotion Review*, 2015 January 5–60, online https://journals.sagepub.com/doi/abs/10.1177/1754073914545792?journalCode=emra (last accessed 10 March 2020); M Nussbaum, 'Emotion in the Language of Judging', *St John's Law Review*, 1996, 70, 23–30.

However, individual actions are not always sufficient to solve mass litigation. For example, in the '*Dieselgate*' case in France,[14] nine buyers and owners of Volkswagen vehicles sued Volkswagen France to demand the delivery of vehicles in accordance with their contracts, since the cars they received did not match those they bought when they signed the order form. The Soissons High Court dismissed the complaints of four of these customers, who were seeking an interim injunction against their distributor to exchange their vehicles. The court simply ruled that the importer of the vehicles – in this case, the French subsidiary – could not be held liable in place of the manufacturer based in Europe. This validates www.weclaim.com's strategy in its class action engaging Volkswagen AG's liability in Germany. The consumer association *UFC Que Choisir* explained:

> There is no proven financial prejudice for the consumer since they recognized cheating concerns above all NOx, information that does not seem to have been communicated to consumers. For the time being, it is therefore difficult to argue that the consumer has suffered harm that could be the subject of real compensation.[15]

In France, Italy and Spain, the attempts of Volkswagen customers to obtain replacement vehicles through civil proceedings have all failed thus far. In Germany, many individual actions were settled by Volkswagen before reaching the level of a final appeal in order to avoid a High Court decision. A law firm working with several claimants might consider filing a civil suit with the Paris Public Prosecutor's Office as part of the judicial investigation for aggravated deception, in the hope that it would be referred to the court. Unlike in the United States and Australia, it has been very difficult for diesel car owners in Europe to get compensation from Volkswagen.

In the meantime, each claimant must therefore undertake this legal battle on an individual basis. This is done through what is called joint legal action. There are as many legal actions as there are claimants – a dispersion that probably

---

[14] S Mandard, '"*Dieselgate": première action collective en France contre Volkswagen*', *Le Monde*, 23 Jan 2020, www.lemonde.fr/planete/article/2020/01/23/dieselgate-une-action-collective-europeenne-lancee-contre-volkswagen_6026899_3244.html (last accessed 10 March 2020). See Laurent Posocco, 'French Report', in Marco Frigessi di Rattalma (ed), *The Dieselgate, A Legal Perspective* (Springer 2017) 3–26; Emmanuel Jeuland, 'Enforcing Consumer and Capital Market Law in France', in Thomas Möllers, *Enforcing Consumer and Capital Market Law*, Intersentia, forthcoming 2020.

[15] Website UFC Que Choisir, '*Dieselgate, Premiers conseils sur l'affaire Renault*', 16 March 2017, www.quechoisir.org/actualite-dieselgate-premiers-conseils-sur-l-affaire-renault-n25596/ (last accessed 10 March 2020).

does not allow for pressure similar to that which Volkswagen experienced in the United States.

1.2 Capacity to possess a right

At first sight, the concept of party to proceedings seems to be simple and obvious. It should be enough to look at who brings the action against whom. However, it may happen that a party to a particular proceeding should not in fact be a party. So, there is a need for further conditions. The definition of parties is both descriptive and prescriptive in the ELI/UNIDROIT project.

According to Rule 29, paragraph 1: 'Parties to civil proceedings are all the persons by and against whom the proceedings are brought.' The parties are the plaintiff, who brings the action; the defendant, against whom the action is brought; and thereafter, the intervenors. However, this descriptive approach does not suffice, as mistakes may be made. For example, where one of the parties should not have been a party, the judge has the power to substitute a person who should be a party (see Chapter 4). Or it may be that parties to the proceedings ought not to be parties, since they do not have the capacity to possess a right. This is why paragraph 2 provides: 'Anybody who has the capacity to possess a right under substantive law may be a party to civil proceedings.' This principle may be found in the Bulgarian Civil Procedure Code (Article 26 [1]) and the Swiss Federal Civil Procedure Code (Article 66).[16]

This is a prescriptive approach to the concept of 'party': a 'party' is one who has a capacity to possess a right under substantive law. In the French version of the ELI/UNIDROIT Rules, the phrase 'capacity to possess a right' in this context is rendered by the traditional concept of '*capacité de jouissance*'. There is a tiny nuance between having a right and being able to take benefit of a right ('*jouissance*').[17]

This rule does not mean that plaintiffs must have a right grounding their claim, but only that they have the capacity to possess a right. As a matter of fact, the lawsuit will recognize (or even create) the right which is in dispute as a result of the claim. The word 'action' in the English version is translated as 'proceedings' in the French version, since the concept of 'action' has the

---

[16] '*Toute personne capable d'ester en justice peut se faire représenter au procès*', translated freely: 'any person able to bring an action may be represented in court.'

[17] Article 29: '*Parties à la procédure: (1) Les parties à la procédure sont les personnes par lesquelles et contre lesquelles une action en justice est engagée. (2) Toute personne qui a la capacité de jouissance en vertu du droit matériel peut être partie à la procédure.*'

specific meaning of a right to bring a lawsuit in French law (Article 30 of the *Code de Procedure Civile*), and not the meaning of proceedings.[18]

Legal persons (eg, corporations, registered associations) may be parties. This solution was discussed in many countries before being accepted.[19] According to Rule 31, 'Legal persons and other entities that are parties must exercise their rights through those natural persons who are entitled to represent them according to the substantive law.'[20] Each European state defines what constitutes a 'legal person' ('*personne morale*' in French).

A group or entity that does not have the capacity to possess a right cannot be a party, and this depends on substantive law. Usually, a family, a tribe or an unregistered corporation does not have the capacity to possess a right (under French case law). All natural and legal persons have that ability; but it may also be extended, for example, to unborn children and entities that are not legal persons, such as trade unions, trusts and associations that have no legal capacity (Section 50(2) of the German Civil Procedure Code). This is an interesting solution, since procedural law is more flexible than substantive law to admit parties in proceedings.

1.3 Litigation capacity

> Rule 30 Litigation Capacity of Natural Persons
> (1) Litigation capacity is the capacity to exercise rights in civil proceedings.
> (2) Anybody who has the capacity to exercise rights or obligations in their own name under the substantive law shall be deemed to have litigation capacity.[21]

Terminology in national rules varies – 'legal standing', 'litigation capacity', 'capacity to proceed', 'capacity to conduct proceedings' or 'procedural legal capacity' – but all expressions describe the same phenomenon. Rule 30 adopts the concept applicable in numerous EU Member States, which simply refers to the decisions made in substantive law with respect to the ability to act on one's

---

[18] See E. Jeuland and S. Lalani (eds), *Lexicographical Research in Civil Procedure* (IRJS 2017), 'Action' and 'Proceedings'.

[19] *Trustees of Darmouth College v Woodward*, 17 US (4 Wheat) 518 (1819); in France, Fruehauf case: Cass 2° civ, 28 January 1954, JCP 54, II, 7958 concl Lemoine.

[20] Article 31: '*Représentation des personnes morales et autres entités. Les personnes physiques habilitées à représenter une personne morale ou autre entité exercent les droits de celle-ci conformément au droit applicable.*'

[21] Article 30: *Capacité d'agir en justice des personnes physiques: (1) La capacité d'agir en justice est l'aptitude à exercer des droits dans le cadre d'une procédure juridictionnelle. (2) Toute personne ayant la capacité d'exercer ses droits et obligations en son propre nom, selon le droit applicable, est considérée comme ayant la capacité d'agir en justice.*

own account (sub-paragraph 2). The 'capacity to exercise rights' in particular means the capacity to enter into contracts and, more generally, act with legal effect.[22] As some Member States have different rules for the capacity to enter into contracts and for becoming liable under tort law, depending on the age of the persons and their ability to consider the legal consequences of their acts, a rather general wording for Rule 30(2) seemed to be appropriate.

In principle, a person with legal capacity has litigation capacity, but there are exceptions. The German Civil Procedure Code expresses this clearly:

> Sec 50 Capacity to be a party to court proceedings
> (1) Any person having legal capacity shall also have the capacity of being a party to court proceedings.[23]

This solution also exists in Croatian law,[24] Hungarian law[25] and Latvian law,[26] among others. There are no explicit rules in this respect in Austria, Sweden[27] or Belgium. Similarly, outside Europe, there is no specific rule in the Code of Civil Procedure in Quebec, for example. The Brazilian Code of Civil Procedure (2015) refers only to the 'capacity to exercise rights' – that is, it refers to litigation capacity.[28]

1.4 Parties in the public interest

A person who is authorised by law to act in the public interest may act as a party (Rule 35). That person will not represent a public body in this context, but will rather be a complete party (whether initially or as intervenor). It could

---

[22] Van der Kaaij, *The Juridical Act*, Springer, 2019, p 31 using the expression 'ability to perform an act' as a functional term translating different approach in comparative law (competence, power, capacity, etc).

[23] '*Parteifähig ist, wer rechtsfähig ist.*'

[24] Civil Procedure Code, Section 77(1).

[25] Civil Procedure Code, Section 48.

[26] Civil Procedure Code, Section 71 ('capacity to have civil-procedural rights and duties'), Section 74(1).

[27] Civil Procedure Code, Chapter 11, Section 1 ('Any person may be a party to litigation'); Chapter 11, Section 2 (special rule on corporations, partnerships and cooperatives that can acquire substantive rights and assume legal liabilities).

[28] Section 70: '*Toda pessoa que se encontre no exercício de seus direitos tem capacidade para estar em juízo*' ('Everyone who finds himself in the exercise of his rights has the capacity to be in court').

be said that this person acts on behalf of society as a whole. As society is not a legal person, it is not a matter of simple representation.

Rule 35 Public Interest
A person who is authorised by law to act in the public interest, may act as a party or intervene in any proceedings.[29]

In some European countries,[30] public prosecutors or public regulators may intervene in civil proceedings in order to protect a relevant public interest. This will often apply in family proceedings, which are beyond the scope of these rules; but may also become necessary in civil litigation. For example, at the appellate level, legal issues are often at stake that are of general public interest. In such circumstances, it may become necessary for a representative of the public interest to be joined as a party to the proceedings and (for example) ensure that the appellate court can issue a final judgment, notwithstanding the fact that the actual parties to the proceedings have abandoned the appeal. More generally, intervention may be permitted in order to enable issues of public interest to be properly raised in the proceedings. The extent to which this form of intervention can be used will depend on the substantive law of the forum.

For example, in France, Article 421 of the Civil Procedure Code provides that: 'The public prosecutor may act as a main party or intervene as joining party.' According to Article 422, the public prosecutor acts *sua sponte* in matters prescribed by law; and according to Article 423, he or she may act to defend the public order where the facts alleged may amount to an infringement of it. According to Article 425, the public prosecutor must be informed of matters relating to parentage, to the organization of a guardianship and to personal bankruptcy. Article 426 provides that 'The public prosecutor may be informed of such other matters in relation to which he judges that he must intervene'; and Article 427 that 'The judge may *sua sponte* decide to inform of a matter to the public prosecutor'. Mass litigation is concerned, since the public prosecutor or the judge may consider that it is necessary to defend public order. The public prosecutor may have notice of a request to get an approval order of the settlement which could prove to be important for mass settlement.

Outside Europe, public prosecutors may play an important role in civil matters, and in mass litigation in particular. For example, in Brazil, the public prosecutor may initiate a collective redress action. The person acting in the public interest may be the ombudsman in Scandinavian countries.

---

[29] Article 35: *Défense de l'intérêt public: Une personne autorisée par la loi à agir dans l'intérêt public peut être partie principale à la procédure ou y intervenir.*

[30] France – Code of Civil Procedure, Articles 421, 422; Belgium, Netherlands, Greece, Norway, Sweden, Finland, England.

The ERCP rules do not provide for the 'popular action', since it seems quite dangerous (eg, it is prohibited in France), although this action exists in certain European states (eg, Portugal) and may ground the collective redress action in such countries. This action may be useful to protect natural entities and is used for this purpose in South America (see below).[31]

1.5 Prospective parties

I shall add another concept: the concept of 'prospective party'. In other words, a specific person should be part of a lawsuit because his or her rights are at stake. In a representative action (in a civil law sense), a party may be represented in court and remain a party to the procedural relationship. In a substitutive action, a prospective party who has rights at stake in a litigation does not become a party to the procedural relationship, but only to the relationship under substantive law (eg, to the compensation decided on the merits). A group member is not a procedural party, but will receive compensation through the qualified entity. Even an animal or a robot could be characterized as a prospective party.

2. DO NATURAL ENTITIES HAVE LITIGATION CAPACITY?

Animals have feelings[32] (so-called 'sentience' – they feel pain) and some of them have mirror neurons, so that humans may be aware of their feelings. Animals may also be aware of humans' feelings. In this situation, however, there may be issues of interpretation of their feelings. Sentience is controversial for plants; and almost nobody claims that mountains and rivers have feelings, even though for certain people a relationship may exist with them (eg, Maoris consider rivers as their ancestors).

---

[31] Hermes Zaneti in Chapter 14.

[32] French law: the new Article 515-14 of the Civil Code (2015) reads as follows: 'Animals are living beings endowed with sensitivity. Subject to the laws protecting them, animals are subject to the property regime.' In German law, animals have rights – Article 20a of the German Basic Law says: 'Mindful also of its responsibility towards future generations, the state shall protect the natural foundations of life and animals by legislation and, in accordance with law and justice, by executive and judicial action, all within the framework of the constitutional order.'

As a consequence, it could be said that natural entities such as animals, plants[33] and rivers should be considered as having legal capacity.[34] Several countries outside Europe have recently adopted this approach.[35] A kind of legal relationship should be acknowledged between natural entities and humans. As a result, these natural entities should be introduced in the field of civil procedure.

Can natural entities (eg, animals, plants, rivers, mountains) take legal action? Is it necessary to admit, for this purpose, that these natural entities are qualified as legal persons? And if so, is the procedural regime for legal persons perfectly adapted to natural beings? The question of animal rights is widely debated, but the procedural consequences are still uncertain. There are criminal offences in case of mistreatment of animals, but the natural entity is not considered as a party.

There are three conditions in common law to admit that an entity is a legal person: (1) the entity can institute legal actions at its behest;[36] (2) in determining the grant of legal relief, the court takes injury to it into account; and (3) the relief granted is to the benefit of it.[37] It may well be that in civil law (where the question is more substantive than procedural), the condition does not involve legal standing, which is more a consequence of 'personification'. For example, in France, there is a general requirement that a legal person be represented by

---

[33] C.D. Stone, 'Should Trees Have Standing?' *Law, Morality, and the Environment* (Oxford University Press, 3rd Edition, 2010). He wrote: 'The fact is, that each time there is a movement to confer rights onto some new "entity", the proposal is bound to sound odd or frightening or laughable.'

[34] For example: D. Shelton, 'Nature as a legal person', VertigO - la revue électronique en sciences de l'environnement, *Hors-série* 22 September 2015, http://journals.openedition.org/vertigo/16188 (last accessed 15 February 2020); and S. Donaldson and W. Kymlicka, *Zoopolis, A Political Theory of Animal Rights* (Oxford University Press, 2011).

[35] See Catherine Jorns Magallanes, 'Nature as an Ancestor: Two Examples of Legal Personality for Nature in New Zealand', VertigO - la revue électronique en sciences de l'environnement, *Hors-série* 22 September 2015, http://journals.openedition.org/vertigo/16199 (last accessed 15 February 2020): 'Te Awa Tupua as a legal entity with standing in its own right.'

[36] The natural entities need a 'friend' (guardianship approach) to bring the action, for example. In a US Supreme Court action concerning sequoia brought by Sierra Club, *Sierra Club v Morton* – 405 US 424 (1972), Mr Justice Douglas, dissenting, said: 'I am quite seriously proposing that we give legal rights to forests, oceans, rivers, and other so-called 'natural objects' in the environment – indeed, to the natural environment as a whole.'

[37] C.D. Stone, 'Should Trees Have Standing? Toward Legal Rights for Natural Objects', *Southern California Law Review*, 45 (1972) p 458.

its board or similar body, and as such the board may bring an action on behalf of the legal person.

Animal trials have existed for 1000 years in Europe. A dog was sentenced to death as recently as in 1906 in Macedonia. Criminal trials against domestic animals could lead to the death penalty; while ecclesiastical-civil trials against animals that were not entirely attainable (eg, vermin, caterpillars, rats) could lead to a curse and allow for their extermination if they harmed crops. These trials were criticized as irrational and gradually disappeared. They led to excommunication based on the parable of the excommunication of the snake in Genesis I-28.[38]

The question today is no longer whether trials can be conducted against animals, but rather whether a possible claim may be brought by natural entities – not just animals – against humans. The theories of legal persons and subjective rights (even if their origins date back to the Middle Ages) have been developed mainly since the nineteenth century.

The animal trials of the past were symbolic, to make peasants understand that they had to feel guilty and say prayers.[39] Therefore, perhaps we should make a suggestion for our times and admit natural entities as plaintiffs, to reintroduce them into the relationship of the trial and remove us from our anthropocentric perspective – not to 'excommunicate' ourselves, but from a non-religious perspective. We must not pretend to be angelic and deny the existence of a power relationship between human beings and other natural entities. Dominance exists and can be positive – as is the case when one trains a dog or a horse, or when one cultivates roses.

---

[38] Genesis 1, 28: 'And God blessed them; and God said unto them: "Be fruitful, and multiply, and replenish the earth, and subdue it; and have dominion over the fish of the sea, and over the fowl of the air, and over every living thing that creepeth upon the earth."' Rachi in his commentary considered that the verb '*hébreux*'/'*weyirdou*' means both dominating and falling from the present situation to a situation below animals if humans do not behave themselves. Maybe we should reinterpret this verse and understand it as: 'And God blessed them; and God said unto them: "Be fruitful, and multiply, and replenish the earth, and subdue it; and come up at the level of the fish of the sea, and at the level of the fowl of the air, and at the level of every living thing that creepeth upon the earth"' (see T.T. Houmach and B. Rachi, translation into French. J Kohn (Gallia, 1998)).

[39] E. Leavitt, *Animals and their Legal Rights* (Animal Welfare Institute, 1st edition Washington 1968, 1978); M. Rousseau, *Les procès d'animaux* (Wesmael- Chalier, 1964), p 40.

In 1868, E. Osenbrüggen wondered whether natural entities have legal personality (ie, the ability to possess a right).[40] As long as legal personality and subjective rights were not conceived as part of a structured legal theory, animal trials were possible. One might therefore still wonder today whether the difficulty of classifying natural entities could not be avoided. We could speak of a legal relationship that would comprise only 'rights' in the vague sense or differentiated interests (not to be mistreated, in particular; and not the whole panoply of *human* rights) and duties on the side of humanity. Environmental justice can then appear as justice between humans and natural 'others' which have standing in acting *vis-à-vis* humans, who in turn have duties towards them in the event of damage (and – especially for the purposes of this book – damage caused by mass harms). In such cases, alternative methods should be provided for, so that the interests of natural entities can be taken into account before the courts without them being 'persons' in the legal sense.

The legal scheme seems to be the simplest and most robust solution: the natural entity is qualified as a legal person for lack of being a natural person and becomes subject to rights and obligations; it can therefore take legal action.[41] If we consider the concept of a 'legal person' as a plastic one that can accommodate anything that is likely to have legitimate interests, then it will suffice to decide that natural beings are legal persons. Ethical and philosophical debates also lead to such proposals today. Differences in treatment between natural entities and human beings would then be risky: for example, it would become difficult to justify laboratory tests on natural entities when one refrains from performing them on human beings. The qualification as a legal person has the advantage of being able to maintain a *summa divisio* between human beings and natural or even artificial entities (eg, robots). But is it convincing?

The theory of the legal person is based on a realistic approach which supposes an autonomous body endowed with a system of representation. Natural entities are often collectives of individuals. The entity would still need to be endowed with a mode of representation. The law could provide for this. But as long as the law is properly engaged, anything is possible – although at the price of a distortion of legal categories. The entity would no longer be within a realistic theory of the legal person, but under a legalistic and artificialist approach. The family, the company, the joint ownership could then claim the

---

[40] *Studien zur deutschen und schweizerischen Rechtsgeschichte* (Schaffhausen, 1868), p 139.

[41] See in particular: C.R. Sunstein, 'The Rights of Animals: A Very Short Primer' (August 2002) https://web.archive.org/web/20120220134847/www.law.uchicago.edu/files/files/157.crs_.animals.pdf (last accessed 15 February 2020); M.A. Hermitte, '*La nature, sujet de droit?*' Annales. Histoire, Sciences Sociales, no 1 (2011), 173; J.P. Marguénaud, F. Burgat and J. Leroy, '*La personnalité animale*' (D 2020), 28.

status of a legal person. The danger to our legal categories would be quite high. However, it is not certain that a simple and robust solution would be found. Nothing in theory, therefore, could prevent the law (philosophical theory) or even the judge (realistic theory) from granting legal personality to a natural entity, except the overall coherence of the legal construction. The law is constructed; but it is not constructed in any way, because it must also be convincing. In common law, a trust may play this role, since the trust can act through the trustees, but is not a legal person. The English judge can imply a trust relationship over a right in favour of a beneficiary – usually, but not always, human – without upsetting the coherence of the common law. There are now fiduciary mechanisms in civil law systems (in Quebec and France) which are close to a trust. The substitution mechanism might come close to a trust. For different reasons in common law (no need) and civil law (disruption), it seems debatable whether legal personality should be given to natural entities.

The masters of domestic animals, or even associations for the defence of animals in the event of abuse, would be the bodies representing the animals. The disadvantage of this thesis is that it does not lead to wild animals and other natural entities (eg, rivers, mountains, wild plants) being automatically recognized as subjects of law. A natural entity would have to be already integrated into human life to become a subject of law.

In order to circumvent these doctrinal oppositions, which risk locking everyone into their own position, it may be interesting to consider the most concrete currently available rules – those of procedure.

If one turns to the rule in relation to legal persons, the document instituting proceedings should include the place of the registered office and the representatives of the legal person (Rule 31). This compulsory requirement of a writ makes it possible to determine the competent court and the place where the document must be served. The law must therefore not simply appoint a guardian for natural entities, but must also establish a registered office. Certainly, case law could recognize the master of the domestic animal or a defence association as a 'friend' of the animal legal person; their domicile would therefore be the equivalent of a registered office.

However, there is a practical difficulty when the natural entity in question cannot be apprehended. Where is the head office of a swarm of bees or of a mountain? Should a few hives or a whole region be retained in the event of a nuisance caused by pollution? The law may well decide that the registered office is that of the legal guardian of the natural entity. The disadvantage is that this distorts the category of legal personality a little more from a procedural point of view. The same difficulty arises if one considers the question of the appearance of the parties and their possible presence during an expert's inspection.

On the merits, it seems easy in law to grant rights to natural entities that have become legal persons; but what about their procedural duties? How can the principles of adversarial proceedings and cooperation be enforced? Can we hear natural entities; make them speak; ask them to communicate documents spontaneously? Admittedly, one could resolve this through appointing a guardian, as if the natural entities were minor children. But this analogy also has its limits, because a child has the right to be heard under the United Nations Convention on the Rights of the Child (which entered into force on 2 September 1990) and has the capacity to enjoy rights. An Argentine judge decided that a chimpanzee should be released from a zoo since she had no companion. The judge considered that this animal was a legal person and could be represented by a non-governmental organization (NGO).[42]

Qualifying a natural being as a legal person is perhaps basically a 'false good' idea, based on an individualistic approach to law (determining subjects of rights); all the more so as the procedure offers solutions that are less disruptive of legal dogma, which presuppose conceiving law in more relational terms. Natural entities could fall within the concept of 'other entities' provided by Rule 31.[43]

Civil procedure must constantly play with categories. One can thus bring an action against a dissolved society in order to prevent the dissolution from being used to avoid a lawsuit. However, it is true that a company in formation, a business or a family cannot bring a lawsuit. It has been accepted, however, that an unincorporated tribe (in France) or a non-legal association (in Germany) can sue.[44]

It is therefore not enough to have an interest to sue. The trustee is admitted in person to act on behalf of a trust. The person acting has standing and the entity for which he or she is acting does not actually become a party. However, it is the interests of the entity that are brought before the courts. This is the pattern of substitution action.[45] A surrogate person acts in the interest of an entity,

---

[42] Tercer Juzgado de Garantías, Judicial Power Mendoza File P-72.254/15 'Presented by AFADA about the chimpanzee "Cecilia"' non-human individual', 3 November 2016, www.nonhumanrights.org/content/uploads/Chimpanzee-Cecilia_translation-FINAL-for-website-2.pdf (last accessed 10 March 2020). 'Animals must have fundamental rights and the applicable legislation in accordance with such fundamental rights to protect the particular situation they encounter, following the evolutionary degree that science has determined they can reach... The rights of incompetent persons are exercised by their legal representatives, that in the case of animals they could be represented by NGO or by any State organism or by any person who claims collective or diffuse interests' (last accessed 15 February 2020).

[43] For details see Chapter 3.

[44] German Civil Procedure Code, Section 50 (2).

[45] See Chapter 3.

which does not become a party. Group actions follow this pattern. The victims do not become a party to the proceedings, but may benefit from the right to reparation created by the judgment (see Chapter 3).

A procedural arsenal already exists in favour of the environment. Dozens of cases are pending all over the world. The Court of Justice of the European Union (CJEU) has indicated that the European Union may require Member States to ensure the protection of the environment by means of criminal sanctions.[46] Action is taken against the European Union of Member States when they have failed to comply with their obligations under international treaties. Several states have also been convicted by their own courts for failing to comply with international environmental conventions.[47] Proceedings are underway against the European Union,[48] the Netherlands,[49] France[50] and private companies.[51] Another solution could be the creation of national and international tribunals specialized in environmental matters. If the action in representation is not the appropriate tool because animals and plants are not autonomous legal persons, a substitute action might perhaps be possible, since it does not imply agreement. Several countries have thus considered the use of *actio popularis* in environmental matters (Costa Rica, Bolivia, Ecuador).

---

[46] CJEU (Grand Chamber), 13 September 2005, C-176/03, *European Commission v Council of the European Union* [2005] ECR-I 7879.

[47] Superior Court of the State of Washington for King County, 19 November 2015, 14-2-25295-1; in *Our Children Trust v Washington Department of Ecology*, Judge Hill declared that the youth's very survival depends upon the will of their elders to act now, decisively and unequivocally, to stem the tide of global warming…before doing so becomes first too costly and then too late'; http://ourchildrenstrust.org (last accessed 10 March 2020). See, in favour of the action against the government of United States based on the US Constitution, United States Court of Appeal for the Ninth Circuit, 17 January 2020, *Juliana v United States*, 18-36082, DC 6:15-cv -01517-AA.

[48] EU General Court, 24 May 2018, Case T-330/18 *Armando Ferrao Carvalho v European Parliament and Council.*

[49] Supreme Court of the Netherlands, Civil Div 19/00135, 20 December 2019, *The Netherlands (Ministry of Economic Affairs and Climate Policy) v Stichting Urgenda.* The Dutch Supreme Court, the highest court in the Netherlands, upheld the previous decisions in the *Urgenda Climate* case, finding that the Dutch government had obligations to urgently and significantly reduce emissions in line with its human rights obligations.

[50] Paris Administrative Court, 14 March 2019, *affaire du siècle (4 NGO: FNH; Greenpeace France; Notre Affaire à Tous; Oxfam France) v French State*, https://laffairedusiecle.net/ (last accessed 10 March 2020).

[51] *Lliuya v RWE AG*, Filing Date 2015, Case 2 O 285/15 Essen Regional Court, the case is admissible: 'The case will move forward into the evidentiary phase to determine whether the Lliuya's home is (a) threatened by flooding or mudslide as a result of the recent increase in the volume of the glacial lake located nearby, and (b) how RWE's greenhouse gas emissions contribute to that risk.'

The current limits of these procedures relate to the entities protected by these actions: human (and not other) beings in group actions in environmental matters or in actions against states.

Several countries have allowed actions in favour of natural entities (mountains and rivers in India; rivers in New Zealand; *Pachamama* in Colombia, Ecuador and Bolivia).[52] These provisions make natural entities parties to the lawsuit and they benefit from a representative. However, the concept of representation has a fairly broad meaning in common law and may cover actions in which the victims are not parties. Thus, the class action is qualified as a 'representative action' in common law without the victims whose interests are defended becoming parties.

In an Indian decision, it appears that the 'representative' (guardian of the river) has the margins of manoeuvre of a full party.[53] It is therefore possible that the mechanism used in common law may be translated into civil law as a substitute action. Similarly, in New Zealand, a river is described as being in trust (the river bed more than the water itself) and its representative a trustee (although the legal technique used here is rather complex and seems to be a statutory corporation). This solution became necessary because the Maori

---

52 The seventh chapter of Ecuador's new constitution is entitled 'Rights of Nature.' This document establishes Pachamama as a legal entity for the first time in history. María Valeria Berros, 'The Constitution of the Republic of Ecuador: Pachamama Has Rights'. *Environment & Society Portal* (Arcadia, 2015), No 11; Rachel Carson Center for Environment and Society, https://doi.org/10.5282/rcc/7131 (last accessed 10 March 2020). Bolivia's 2010 Law of Mother Nature was the first national-level legislation in the world to bestow rights on the natural world (Mother Earth is 'a collective subject of public interest'). Colombia, Bogota 9 August 2018, *Juan Carlos Alvarado Rodríguez y otros Accionad v Ministerio de Medio Ambiente y otros Expediente*: 15238 3333 002 2018 00016 01: '*Declarar que el Páramo de Pisba es sujeto de derechos, con los alcances señalados en la parte motiva de esta providencia, en consecuencia: – Se le aplicará el Convenio de Diversidad Biológica. – Se le concede estatus de protección auto ejecutiva*' ('Declare that the Páramo de Pisba (alpine tundra ecosystems) is a subject of rights, with the scope indicated in the reasoning of this provision, consequently: – The Convention on Biological Diversity will be applied to it. – It is granted self-executing protection status').

53 The High Court of Uttarakhand (*Modh Salim v State of Uttarakhand*, 126, 2014, 20 March 2017) held that two rivers – the Ganges and Yamuna – are living beings with rights: 'All the Hindus have deep Astha in rivers Ganga and Yamuna and they collectively connect with these rivers. Rivers Ganga and Yamuna are central to the existence of half of Indian population and their health and well-being.' The head of Namami Gange, the chief secretary of the state of Uttarakhand and the public prosecutor of the state of Uttarakhand are 'persons *in loco parentis*'.

tribes consider the river to be their ancestor and the government agreed to translate this cosmology into common law.[54]

According to Donaldson and Kymlicka, three stages marked the philosophy of animality with consequences for legal theory.[55] According to Tom Regan,[56] animals are subjects of a life and thus have rights. He is against speciesism: the existence of species does not justify the refusal to recognize rights. He rejects anthropocentrism and acknowledges that sentience can have several degrees (eg, between earthworms and dogs), which induces a kind of hierarchy in recognition.

Finally, an attempt has been made to reconstruct the duty to respect 'otherness'. According to Kymlicka and Donaldson, three types of relations between animals and humans must be distinguished: relations with the domestic animal, the liminal animal and the wild animal (which has the right to be left alone). Animals have feelings; agility; the power to express their needs and preferences, and to resist. In other words, they have interests to defend. They are ethical subjects: 'animal citizens'. The problem is that these authors do not qualify these relationships as legal relationships. It is true that this would be half a symbolic space and would include only differentiated rights (a concept derived from the law of minorities and transectionality). There is a sovereignty for wild animals, even if it is not organized – one can use the category of resident as with a human migrant.

If incentive mechanisms are put in place, one could imagine that this alternative action could be extended to environmental issues. Subsidies, insurance or funds could provide incentives for action.

These are forms of alternative action, such as class action, which might perhaps merit being created under European law for natural entities – for example, in the environmental field. That said, one cannot deny a technical obstacle: hitherto, all class actions have concerned victims who were human beings and a law has nevertheless been necessary, except for the few examples mentioned above concerning the trust or the competition authority. A law

---

54 New Zealand, 29 March 2017 Te Awa Tupua (Whanganui River Claims Settlement) Act 2017, 7, 12: 'Te Awa Tupua is an indivisible and living whole, comprising the Whanganui River from the mountains to the sea, incorporating all its physical and metaphysical elements'; 14: 'Te Awa Tupua declared to be legal person (1) Te Awa Tupua is a legal person and has all the rights, powers, duties, and liabilities of a legal person. (2) The rights, powers, and duties of Te Awa Tupua must be exercised or performed, and responsibility for its liabilities must be taken, by Te Pou Tupua on behalf of, and in the name of, Te Awa Tupua, in the manner provided for in this Part and in Ruruku Whakatupua—Te Mana o Te Awa Tupua.'

55 S. Donaldson and W. Kymlicka (n 34).

56 Tom Regan and Peter Singer, *Animal Rights and Human Obligations* (Englewood Cliffs, 1976).

would therefore be necessary and a certain disorder of existing legal categories would not be avoided. However, this may be the most efficient solution. It does not require natural entities to have full legal personality and does not upset the category of legal persons.

The environment is not around us, as this unfortunate term would suggest; it is rather among us in terms of legal relations. It is not a matter of facilitating the advances of an enemy that is encircling us – nature – by offering it procedural weapons, but rather of defending our own legal relationships, some of which are with natural entities. Christopher Stone wrote in 1972:

> A radical new conception of man's relationship to the rest of nature would not only be a step towards solving the material planetary problems; there are strong reasons for such a changed consciousness from the point of making us far better humans.[57]

Environmental justice is justice between humans and 'others' with an interest in acting, with the consequence that there is no damage to natural entities, because such damage would also result in harm to human beings.

Jacques Derrida wondered whether natural beings could respond to human beings.[58] Procedurally, one would speak of the principle of the adversarial process. In fact, natural entities should be included in the procedural symbolic scheme in such a way that fundamental principles are respected without distorting our legal categories. This undoubtedly leads to the recognition of natural entities as 'others' for which it is possible to substitute, and to the recognition of a new legal relationship between humans and non-humans.

This relationship would not be procedural, because the substitute – and not the natural entity – would be a party to the trial, but would be substantial because the judgment would have a substantive effect on animals (eg, end of pollution, restoration of biotopes or creation of new places that promote biodiversity). At the same time, this 'new' legal relationship with 'others' would be very old – for example, New Zealand's Maori tribes, at the origin of the recognition of the legal personality of two rivers, insisted on their deep relationship with these entities, which they consider to be their ancestors.

Finally, the relationship leads to recognition of the status of natural beings as potential parties, since they may have rights, but have no body to express

---

57 C.D. Stone (1972), 'Should Trees Have Standing? – Toward Legal Rights for Natural Objects', *Southern California Law Review*, 45, pp. 450–501, fn 28, n 240, 495 fn 28, n 240, 495.

58 J. Derrida, *L'animal que donc je suis* (Galilée, 2006), p 156; J. Derrida, *The Animal That Therefore I Am, Perspectives in Continental Philosophy*, 2008-04-15, M.L. Mallet (ed), D. Wills (trans) criticizes Levinas in that for the latter, the other can only be a man: 'For a thought of the other, of the infinitely other that looks at me, should on the contrary privilege the question and the demand of the animal.'

their interests. The genetic traits which allow us to know ourselves (self-love) in childhood constitute a breeding foundation for emotions (notably pity for animals) and symbols (serving to move emotions in order to transform them) in our relationships with other human beings.

3. DO ROBOTS AND OTHER 'ARTIFICIALLY INTELLIGENT' MACHINES HAVE CAPACITY TO LITIGATE?

Since natural entities may have standing or a least be substituted in court, the issue may also arise in relation to robots. 'Artificial intelligence' (AI) does not really exist outside of discourse. If we understand 'intelligence' to mean the combination of several modes of access to the world – namely reason, emotion, sensation and intuition, taking forms as different as emotional, relational and bodily intelligence – it seems difficult to admit that this can be artificially recreated. The European Commission for the Efficiency of Justice (CEPEJ) report indicates in this sense that the so-called 'strong' AI of science fiction does not exist: this type of AI – endowed not only with intelligence, but also with consciousness – remains purely fictional.[59] Machine learning systems currently under development are described as 'weak' AI and are capable of extracting complex patterns and learning from large amounts of data efficiently, and often with high levels of predictive accuracy. Legaltech businesses themselves admit that they have not yet integrated much AI into their programs that facilitate online procedures. On the other hand, sophisticated modes of calculation that exceed human capacity are now very real, allowing machines to integrate information by themselves through what is called 'machine learning'.

The proposal that machines could be parties to litigation, or even replace judges, is therefore a longstanding fantasy that reappears from time to time according to technical discoveries. Nonetheless, technical advances are making increasingly sophisticated decision-support tools available to the judiciary, which requires reflection and may lead to legal changes.

It seems that what characterizes the law is not so much defining what should be by means of rules (eg, there are non-legal norms in technical, managerial and nutritional matters) as symbolizing, by means of legal devices, human relationships and perhaps relationships with natural entities. These symbolic arrangements have been accompanied by rituals for millennia. However, it does not seem impossible to reconstruct symbolic forms with the help of

[59] European Ethical Charter on the Use of AI in Judicial Systems and their environment, CEPEJ https://rm.coe.int/ethical-charter-en-for-publication-4-december-2018/16808f699c (last accessed 15 February 2020).

digital technology. It may be noted that the duration of an acceptance click has been extended for online contracts beyond what is technically necessary, to give the impression of a real commitment. This is a form of ritual.

Robots are less sensitive to emotions than humans, but are also less intuitive and have no subconscious understanding of what is necessary to build institutions. Moreover, the ethical debate on whether robots should have rights has been shifted by one author towards a Levinassian-type relational approach.[60] The question is not so much whether robots should intrinsically and ontologically have rights (including the right to take legal action), but whether there are interactions between robots and humans which lead to a consideration of the robot as an 'other', in the same way as can be admitted for natural entities. This approach is based on the relational turn in ethics – an approach that we also call for in law.[61] In this case, the answer should rather be negative, insofar as there is no otherness in AI; such technologies are only man-made tools and it is quite possible that the famous autonomous vehicle will never be truly autonomous. It is true that two connected computers have started to create elements of a new language, but so far this has only been a kind of cryptographic key to protect their data from a third computer.[62]

The procedural framework for the different modes of access to the world, and thus to the case before the court, is comprised of sensations (to establish the facts through the senses), intuition (of the judge and the lawyers), reason (of the judge) and emotions.

This framework restrains (in the sense of regulating) the emotions of the judge (who must not express them, but must be aware of them) and of the parties (emotions regulated by the judge's procedural police power). The emotions of the judge – which must not imply a prejudice towards any party – serve to achieve a balanced solution as much as reason, intuition and sensations (the judge's sensations are limited by the prohibition against relying on his or her personal knowledge acquired outside the procedural framework). It could be said that the 'intelligent' machine has an advantage over a judge because it has no emotion and a disadvantage because it has no intuition.

---

[60] D.J. Gunkel, 'The other question: can and should robots have rights?', Vol (0123456789), *Ethics Inf Technol* (2018) 20:87–99, https://link.springer.com/content/pdf/10.1007%2Fs10676-017-9442-4.pdf (last accessed 9 March 2019); M Coeckelbergh, 'Robot rights? Towards a social-relational justification of moral consideration', *Ethics and Information Technology* 2010, 12 (3), 209–21, doi: 10.1007/s10676-010-9235-5.

[61] E. Jeuland, 'Theories of Legal Relations', *Encyclopedia of the Philosophy of Law and Social Philosophy* (Springer, 2020 online (forthcoming)).

[62] M. Abadi and D.G. Andersen, 'Learning to protect communications with adversarial neural cryptography', Google Brain, arXiv:1610.06918v1, last accessed 21 October 2016.

In his time, Bergson crowned intuition as dazzling reason.[63] It is now recognized that a decision taken without any emotion[64] may not be a good solution. The absence of emotion in the machine is therefore in reality a disadvantage; even though it is true that judges must be able to recognize their emotions, and even prevent old traumas or family histories from inappropriately affecting their emotions. From this point of view, the judge's unconscious is taken into account, and the distance taken from his or her personal and family history can help him or her to make a good decision. The adversarial principle can also be seen as a means of getting to the unconscious root of the dispute. Here again, the automaton seems quite limited compared to the parties and the judge. It is the absence of emotion and unconsciousness which makes the machine fallible from the point of view of justice. Today, online dispute resolution could be used to help in resolving mass litigation. Platforms are used in mass litigation based on joinder or class action (eg, in *Dieselgate*).

It is not impossible that in future, we may be able to combine an expert decision-support system and this 'AI'. Even if this were possible, the robot would still need to be equipped with intuitive and emotional faculties that can 'play' with an unconscious mind (emotions are by definition conscious). For the same reason, we can begin to admit the possibility that natural entities can be defended in a trial. It remains questionable, however, to consider robots as potential parties, even though this could resolve the difficulties of identifying the person responsible for the robot. It could be enough to have an insurance policy for the robot to cover the costs of a trial and the compensation of harm it causes; but who would pay the insurance premium (certainly the manufacturer)?

An American scholar writes as follows: 'autonomous vehicles must change from being a product to being a legal entity – an artificial person – with all the rights and duties of legal persons.'[65] She adds: 'This legal status would allow autonomous vehicles to sue or be sued in the event of an accident.'

---

[63] F. Worms, '*L'intelligence gagnée par l'intuition ? La relation entre Bergson et Kant*', in Les Études philosophiques 2001/4 (n° 59), paras 453–64, www.cairn.info/revue-les-etudes-philosophiques-2001-4-page-453.htm (last accessed 10 March 2020).

[64] A. Damasio, *Descartes' Error: Emotion, Reason, and the Human Brain* (Putnam, 1994; revised Penguin edition, 2005).

[65] M. Selliwood, 'The Road to Autonomy', *San Diego Law Review*, 12 January 2017, vol 54: 'Autonomous vehicles must evolve from being classified as products to being classified as legal entities – artificial persons – possessing the legal rights and duties of a corporation…'. See G. Loiseau, '*La voiture qui tuait toute seule*' (D, 2018), 793.

The concept of 'entity' used in Rule 31 could allow robots to be admitted as parties. The European Parliament recommended that an e-personality be created for robots:

> creating a specific legal status for robots in the long run, so that at least the most sophisticated autonomous robots could be established as having the status of electronic persons responsible for making good any damage they may cause, and possibly applying electronic personality to cases where robots make autonomous decisions or otherwise interact with third parties independently.[66]

The European Parliament has further suggested that certain very autonomous robots should be registered and insured.[67]

The European Economic and Social Committee (EESC) advocates a humanistic approach to issues relating to AI, which leads it to reject definitively the idea of giving legal personality to cognitive robots.[68] The concept it defends, known as 'human-in-command', is intended to guarantee responsible, safe and useful development of AI, in which machines remain machines, under the permanent control of humans.[69]

The EESC explains:

> There is a lot of discussion regarding the issue of who can be held liable when an AI system causes damage, particularly if the AI system is self-teaching and continues to learn after entering into use. The European Parliament has drawn up recommendations for civil law on robotics, including a proposal to explore an "e-personality" for robots so that they can incur civil liability for any damage they cause. The EESC is opposed to any form of legal status for robots or AI (systems), as this entails an unacceptable risk of moral hazard. Liability law is based on a preventive, behaviour-correcting function, which may disappear as soon as the maker no longer bears the liability risk since this is transferred to the robot (or the AI system). There is also a risk of inappropriate use and abuse of this kind of legal status. The comparison with the limited liability of companies is misplaced, because in that case a natural person is always ultimately responsible. In this regard, it should be examined to what extent the current national and EU laws, rules and case law in the area of product and risk liability provide an adequate answer to this question and, failing that, what kind of legal solutions can be put forward.[70]

---

66 Resolution of 16 February 2017 with recommendations to the Commission on Civil Law Rules on Robotics (2015/2103[INL]), paragraph 59(f).

67 See n 66.

68 Opinion of the EESC on 'Artificial intelligence — The consequences of artificial intelligence on the (digital) single market, production, consumption, employment and society' (own-initiative opinion), OJ C 288, 31.8.2017, p 1–9, adopted on 31 May 2017, reference: INT/806-EESC-2016-05369-00-00-AC-TRA.

69 See n 64 (1.6).

70 See n 64 (3.3.3).

In a letter to the European Commission, 156 AI experts from 14 European countries – including computer scientists, law professors and chief executives – warn that granting robots legal personhood would be 'inappropriate' from a 'legal and ethical perspective'.[71] The questions of the legal nature of the cognitive robot and the robot judge are linked, since if we admit that a robot is a person who can be a party to a trial, we are led to admit that a robot can also be a judge.

4. CONCLUSION

The concept of the 'party' may sound pretty easy to define. 'Parties' are those who exercise their rights. However, the victims of mass harm do not always have rights. That is the case of natural entities. Perhaps they should be recognized as legal persons, to be able to bring an action. They could be an 'entity' under the ERCP. However, natural entities do not really have the capacity to be a party. A more efficient solution would be to open collective redress action to natural entities as group members. The qualified claimant would bring the action on their behalf. Conversely, robots have no emotions and should not become party to proceedings, even as group members.

---

[71] J. Delcker, 'Europe divided over robot "personhood", in letter to Commission, 156 experts from 14 countries warn against adopting EU Parliament proposal', *Politico*, 4 November 2018: 'By adopting legal personhood, we are going to erase the responsibility of manufacturers, said *Nathalie Navejans*, a French law professor at the Université d'Artois, who was the driving force behind the letter. Noel Sharkey, emeritus professor of artificial intelligence and robotics at the University of Sheffield added that by seeking legal personhood for robots, manufacturers were merely trying to absolve themselves of responsibility for the actions of their machines.'

3. Joinder, consolidation and group claims

Vincent Smith

1. INTRODUCTION: WHAT THIS CHAPTER IS ABOUT

Most national civil procedure rules are based on the – usually implicit – assumption that the dispute to be decided is bilateral: between a claimant and a defendant. In practice, of course, much (perhaps most) significant litigation will have more than two parties, or at least more than two persons having some interest in its outcome.

This chapter considers these 'multi-party' proceedings and the rules which seek to address them – particularly in Part II of the European Law Institute (ELI)/UNIDROIT European Rules of Civil Procedure (ERCP).[1] It is also important to distinguish a multi-party proceeding of the type discussed in this chapter from a collective redress proceeding as described in Part XI of the ERCP. Collective redress proceedings are characterized by the use of a qualified entity approved by the court to conduct the proceedings commenced by the entity on behalf of a group of harmed persons.[2] In contrast, in multi-party proceedings – dealt with in this chapter – the (multiple) parties all retain their own rights of action and (at least in major part) conduct their own cases.

The concept of a 'qualified entity' approved to act for the group making a collective redress claim is discussed in more detail in Chapter 4. This chapter, in contrast, discusses the case management of claims where there is a multiplicity of parties or of other persons having an interest in the outcome of the dispute.

---

[1] European Law Institute/UNIDROIT European Rules of Civil Procedure (ERCP Rules) 29–46.

[2] *Ibid*, Rule 207.

Various techniques have been developed in a number of European countries (eg, the group litigation order (GLO) in England)[3] to manage cases with large numbers of parties on one side or another of the dispute. But, at the most basic level, where there may be more than one claimant or more than one defendant seeking to participate in the same claim, the reflex of the court will be to 'join' them and require them to proceed in the same way (and to the same timetable). More advanced group litigation techniques permit a greater degree of variation in case management according to the individual needs of the separate parties whose claims are being managed together in one proceeding.

This chapter therefore first considers the concept of 'joinder', where additional parties are added to an action that has already commenced. The ERCP deals separately with voluntary joinder (Rule 33) and compulsory joinder (Rule 35) of parties to an existing claim – whether as claimants or defendants. These mirror the requirements in most national civil procedure rules in Europe and are a well-developed part of civil procedure rules.

As a complement to the courts' powers to join non-litigating *parties* to a single existing claim, most civil procedure rules also address the situation where two *claims* have been commenced which are so closely related that they should be consolidated. Again, the ERCP addresses this possibility (Rule 34). However, there appears to be a greater degree of diversity in European practice on consolidation of claims – arising not only from different legal traditions, but also from the organization of the court system. Those European states which have a 'federal' structure of court organization (eg, Germany) necessarily require more complex consolidation (or stay) rules than countries having a unitary court system.[4]

Once the claim is underway, non-parties may wish to intervene in the proceedings. Some of them may wish to be (voluntarily) joined to the proceedings as parties; others may have an interest in the outcome of the proceedings, but not wish to claim a remedy. This will especially be the case for public bodies and other entities in a similar situation that wish to make observations to the court – for example, on matters of public policy – but not be directly involved in the conduct of the claim: *amici curiae*. The ERCP distinguishes between these intervenors (principal intervenors) and others who wish to intervene to support one or other side of the dispute which lies at the root of the action. Intervenors in support may, for example, wish to provide additional evidence to the defendant or claimant side. Section 4 of this chapter will examine this

---

[3] England and Wales, Civil Procedure Rules (SI 1998/3132) (CPR), Rules19.10–19.15.

[4] For example, in England and Wales in CPR Practice Direction (PD) 7A. Also, Adrian Zuckerman, *Zuckerman on Civil Procedure* 3 ed (Sweet & Maxwell, 2013) 170.

distinction and consider, in particular, whether intervenors become parties to the proceedings and how far intervenors can be bound by a decision of the court resolving the original claim(s).

Where the number of parties begins to outgrow what can be sensibly dealt with by 'traditional' joinder or consolidation rules, more sophisticated group litigation techniques may be used instead. As we have noted, unlike collective redress proceedings, group litigation is not conducted through a qualified entity acting for the group. In Section 5, we discuss the definition of 'collective redress proceeding' (Rule 207) in light of the European legislation on which it is mainly based and contrast it with group litigation. The diversity of group litigation techniques – in particular, the degree of closeness of the claims (or common issues) required for group litigation in key national procedure rules across Europe – will also be considered.

To continue the section on group litigation, national litigation techniques for group litigation in England and Germany will be measured against the requirements in EU legislation and guidance for collective redress. In particular, the 'baseline' in EU law, that collective redress mechanism should adopt an 'opt-in' approach, will be considered and the scope of the definition of 'opt-in' compared and contrasted with current group litigation techniques.

Also in Section 5 on group litigation, we take a closer look at the particular case management needs for multi-party claims of this kind (without an entity to organize the group's case) – with a particular reference to the English GLO rules[5] – in order to contrast them with the case management needs of the court to successfully control a collective redress proceeding conducted by a qualified entity.

In Section 6, we consider remedies in group litigation cases. In particular, we examine whether any remedies are available in collective redress proceedings – for example, 'skimming' remedies, such as account of profits – are not usually (or cannot) be claimed by group members in a group litigation procedure.

This chapter concludes by contrasting the simplicity of joinder of parties or consolidation of claims with more advanced group litigation procedures. We also offer some conclusions on the factors that courts might consider when deciding whether to use a group litigation case management tool in contrast to the even more advanced possibilities offered by collective redress proceedings envisage by Part XI of the ERCP.

---

[5] n 3.

2. JOINDER OF PARTIES TO AN ACTION

Joinder is a well-known instrument for adding further parties to an existing action by application to the court. The concept is common in European civil procedure rules.[6] This type of joinder should be contrasted with situations where a number of persons simultaneously bring a new claim together – although not all European civil procedure rules make this distinction expressly. Although the newly commenced claims will be 'joined', the court will not normally be required to consider whether each of the claimants should be a party to the proceedings at the time they are issued. However, the court may later be asked to consider whether the single action commenced by all of the joint parties should continue as such or should be divided (perhaps best described as 'disjoinder'). Nevertheless, the ERCP rules are intended to provide principles to apply to both situations.

Joinder should also be contrasted with a collective redress proceeding, where a single person (the 'qualified entity') brings a single claim on behalf of members of a defined group. Group members are not joined as, and do not become parties to, the collective redress proceeding.[7]

Although joinder is a well-known concept, the civil procedure rules that the court is required to follow show some quite significant differences across Europe. In particular, many (but not all) national rules distinguish between situations where a non-litigant wishes to be joined as a party ('voluntary joinder') and situations where another person must be joined against his or her will (either as claimant or, more usually, as defendant) to ensure that the action can proceed properly. We will consider the ERCP rules dealing with each of these scenarios below.

The other issue on which there is significant national divergence is the degree of connection between the person to be joined to the action and the original dispute. ERCP Rule 36 on voluntary joinder sets out only two requirements: (1) the claims of the parties to be joined must be 'closely connected'; and (2) the court must have jurisdiction over all of the persons to be joined.

---

[6] For example, Austria – Civil Procedure Code, Section 11; Belgium – Judicial Code, Article 701; Bulgaria – Civil Procedure Code, Article 215; England and Wales – CPR 19.3–19.4; France – Civil Procedure Code, Article 323 ('common interest'); Germany – Civil Procedure Code, Sections 59, 60; Greece – Civil Procedure Code, Articles 74, 78; Hungary – Civil Procedure Code, Sections 51(b) and (c); Italy – Civil Procedure Code, Section 103; Latvia – Civil Procedure Code, Section 75 (no particular requirements for joinder); Ireland – Rules of the Superior Courts, Order 14 I(1); detailed rules in Order 18 (joinder of causes of action); Switzerland – Federal Civil Procedure Code, Article 71.

[7] ERCP Rule 207.

At one end of the scale, the English rules on joinder of further parties are highly permissive: the court need only reach the view that it is 'desirable' to join the person as a party.[8] In Germany, the requirement is a slightly more restrictive 'similarity' test;[9] while the French Civil Code requires a 'sufficient link' between the joining (intervening) party and the claim.[10] However, it is clear from each of these formulations that in practice, the threshold test applied in Europe, on voluntary joinder at least, is usually relatively permissive.

The ERCP takes a slightly more restrictive stance, requiring a 'close' connection. While still offering courts significant flexibility, the 'close' element appears to better reflect the provisions of EU law on jurisdiction in cross-border situations.[11] A European civil court will have jurisdiction over joint defendants in different countries where 'the claims are so closely connected' that they ought to be heard together 'to avoid the risk of irreconcilable [separate] judgments'.[12] A similar requirement to avoid conflicting judgments is seen in the (connected) rules on *lis pendens*, permitting European civil courts to decline jurisdiction over related claims.[13] As the ERCP has a vocation to apply to cross-border situations within Europe on an equivalent footing to purely domestic actions, this slight restriction of the scope of the voluntary joinder rules appears appropriate.

The generally permissive stance to voluntary joinder is not necessarily repeated in the national rules on necessary joinder.[14] Persons may be compulsorily joined to an action only where they are jointly entitled to or liable for a remedy in the action (so that there is necessarily the closest of connections between them).[15] Again, this difference is reflected in the ERCP rules on necessary joinder (Rule 38), dealt with in Section 2.2 below.

---

[8] England and Wales CPR 19.2(2).

[9] German *Zivilprozess Ordnung* (ZPO) (5 December 2005, BGBl IS 3202 as amended), Section 60.

[10] France, *code de procedure civile* (French Civil Procedure Code), Article 325.

[11] Regulation EC 1215/12 [2012] OJEU L351/1, Article 8(1).

[12] *Ibid.*

[13] Regulation 1215/12, Article 30(3).

[14] For example, ZPO s 62.

[15] England and Wales CPR 19.3.

2.1 Voluntary joinder

Rule 36 on voluntary joinder provides as follows:

> (1) Multiple parties may bring or defend claims in a single proceeding. They may do so if
> (a) their claims are closely connected, and
> (b) the court has jurisdiction with respect to all parties.
> (2) The court may, where it is necessary for the purpose of properly managing the proceedings, order the claims to continue as separate proceedings.
> (3) Each of the joined parties acts on their own account. Their actions or omissions in the proceedings shall not prejudice the other joined parties.

As we have noted above, although this model rule expressly applies only to joint parties who commence an action together (or who form a group to defend one), these principles should also apply where the court is requested to join another person to an action already commenced.

The only substantive condition is that the claims of (or against) the person to be joined are closely connected with the existing claim. However, where the proceedings have already commenced, there may be additional considerations for the court in deciding whether further parties should be joined. In particular, if the proceedings have progressed so far that the joinder of additional parties would unnecessarily delay the resolution of the dispute, the court should be able to refuse a voluntary joinder application.[16] These more general case management powers of the court (discussed in Chapter 8) are a feature both of the ERCP and of many national civil procedure rules.

Where a person voluntarily applies to join the proceedings, his or her autonomy of procedural action should not be unduly compromised. But, perhaps more importantly, his or her procedural actions should not compromise the position of the existing parties in the proceedings he or she has joined. Of course, complete independence of action for joint parties on either the claimant or defendant side will be impossible as a practical matter: joining an existing proceeding inevitably implies some degree of restriction on procedural freedom, particularly if the proceedings have been running for some time.

From the court's case management perspective, joining additional persons as parties will put them within the procedural control of the court hearing the action and should make case management more efficient as a result. This is likely to be particularly true for gathering and (if necessary) hearing the evidence, organizing the trial and dealing with the costs of the claim. It may

---

[16] For example, under ERCP Rule 36(2). The court's general duty of fairness and active management (Rule 4) and the principles of proportionality and effectiveness (Rules 2 and 4) will also apply.

also make settlement easier by facilitating alternative dispute resolution. For the joining (and possibly the joined) parties, the possibility of economy in evidence gathering and participation in any settlement or similar steps is also likely to be attractive.

However, the continuing procedural autonomy of the joined parties is central to distinguishing 'simple' joinder from other forms of multi-party and representative litigation. Most more advanced forms of multi-party case management impose greater restrictions on the parties forming part of the 'mass' claim. The individual procedural freedom of the members of the group bringing (or defending) a more advanced multi-party claim may be either partially (eg, in relation to certain issues, as under the English GLO)[17] or entirely (as in the collective redress proceeding)[18] restricted. For a court, presented with a choice between using simple joinder or allowing an application for a more advanced form of procedure, the requirement (under simple joinder) to permit each joined party to act separately (eg, to be heard separately if he or she wishes) is the key case management consideration. The point at which the number of persons to be joined reaches a level where the individual proceedings will become difficult to manage together is the point at which a court can (and should) consider alternatives. This is likely to differ considerably from case to case.

The available procedural alternatives to joinder will, of course, also differ from state to state. The ERCP offers a court the option of a collective redress proceeding – on either an opt-in or (in appropriate cases) opt-out basis – in Part XI. Other alternatives to joinder may exist: one of the most prominent is the English GLO system, which permits the court to manage claims together in relation to certain common issues, leaving open the possibility of more freedom of action of parties in relation to individual elements of their cases. However, in view of the diversity of these 'mass' procedures, even in Europe, the ERCP does not attempt a 'middle-ground' multi-party procedure, instead preferring to allow the court substantial flexibility within the framework of the proposed model collective redress proceeding.

It is a common feature of civil procedure rules that a person does not have a *right* to be joined 'voluntarily' to a claim already commenced. The court will have a discretion whether to join them as a party. Similarly, the court will also have a discretion to remove parties who have commenced an action jointly.[19] We have noted that the ERCP provides only two criteria for the court to apply

---

17 For example, England and Wales CPR 19.11(3).

18 ERCP, Rule 207 onwards.

19 ERCP, Rule 36(2).

when exercising this discretion: that it has jurisdiction over the persons to be joined and that there is a close connection between their cases.

These two conditions are not exhaustive and the ERCP rules on general case management give the court a wide-ranging set of powers to ensure that cases are managed appropriately. The 'overriding objectives' set out at the beginning of the rules – in particular, the requirement on the parties and their lawyers to cooperate with the court (Rules 2 and 3) and the parallel responsibility of the court to ensure active and effective case management (Rule 4) – give the court the ability to take a range of factors into account when considering whether to join latecomers to a proceeding or to 'disjoin' superfluous joint parties.[20]

Parallels to these broad discretionary powers in national civil procedure rules in Europe are widely known. The English, French and German civil procedure rules, for example, have broad statements of purpose at or near the beginning of the code which give the court a broad discretion to take case management steps as required.[21] In addition, civil procedure rules usually contain more detailed provisions on persons joining the proceedings voluntarily.[22]

For example, under the English Civil Procedure Rules, the court may order a person to be added as a party either if it is desirable to do so to resolve all of the matters in dispute in the proceedings or if there is an issue between an existing party and that person, related to the proceedings, which makes it desirable to join him or her.[23] Where a person applies to join a proceeding, the court's permission is required if the claim form has already been served on the other parties.[24] In addition to considering the desirability of joining the new party, the court may give procedural directions concerning the management of the proceedings as a consequence of the joinder – this power is not limited to giving directions to the new party. Finally, the English rules have an express provision permitting the court to remove a party from the proceedings if it is no longer desirable for him or her to be party to that action.[25]

The French rules take a similar approach to voluntary joinder, although the Code of Civil Procedure does not specify the degree of proximity of the claims to be joined with the original civil action.[26]

---

20 See Chapter 8 for further discussion.

21 England and Wales CPR 1.4, French Civil Procedure Code, Article 3; German ZPO.

22 See n 5.

23 England and Wales CPR 19.2(2).

24 England and Wales CPR 19.4 (1).

25 England and Wales CPR 19.2(3).

26 French Civil Procedure Code, Article 66 ; Emmanuel Jeuland '*Droit processuel général*' 4 ed (Domat, 2018) para 416.

The German Civil Procedure Code also permits several persons to sue or be sued jointly if their dispute concerns similar claims or obligations, and those persons' claims are advanced on a similar factual and legal basis.[27] The code makes it clear that each of the joined parties proceeds on his or her own account, so that none of their procedural acts will either benefit or disadvantage the other parties to the proceedings.[28] And, like the English rules, there is an express power for the court to separate previously joined parties from the proceedings.[29]

In conclusion, ERCP Rule 36 on voluntary joinder – giving the parties broad freedom to join (or not) a pending proceeding and giving the court broad powers to allow a person to be joined as a party and to make appropriate case management orders – follows the lead given in European national civil procedure rules. However, in the (rarer) cases where a party *must* be joined due to the nature of the claim or his or her relationship with an existing party, there is greater procedural divergence in national rules, as we see in the next section.

2.2 Necessary joinder (Rule 38)

Rule 38 on necessary joinder provides as follows:

> (1) A proceeding must be brought by or against parties jointly where either the joint nature of the legal right or the substantive law requires a judgment to bind all of the joined parties in the same terms.
> (2) A procedural act carried out by one or more of the joined parties shall affect all such parties equally.
> (3) In the case of settlement, waiver of claim, or an admission, all the joined parties must consent to be bound by the act.

The essential function of Rule 38 is to require the court to deal with a situation where not all of the 'correct' parties are suing or (more commonly) have been sued. The court has the power to compel persons who must be parties to the proceedings (but have not agreed to join) to become parties, so that it can exercise its case management powers over them and so that any final decision on the substance will bind them.

Again, the principal issue is the closeness of the connection between the dispute (and hence the proceedings) and the interests of the party to be joined. The ERCP adopts a functional approach: if the final judgment necessarily has to bind persons who are not yet parties *in the same terms*, they must be joined

---

27 German ZPO, Section 60.

28 German ZPO, Sections 61, 63.

29 German ZPO, Section 145. The court may separate the jointly brought actions if there is a legitimate reason to do so.

as parties. As we shall see, most civil procedure rules in Europe adopt a varied and more abstract approach, and the terms used to describe the circumstances in which joinder is necessary vary significantly. However, the essence of these rules is that 'necessary' joinder occurs where a judgment must necessarily bind the additional parties in question.

The English civil procedure rules on necessary joinder are relatively narrow in scope – the drafters of the rules clearly wished to allow the court discretion as to when parties should be joined (rather than require joinder) in the majority of such cases. Where two or more claimants are jointly entitled to a remedy, they must all be made parties to the proceedings.[30] Since, in England, no one may be compelled to be a claimant in any proceeding (ie, without his or her consent),[31] if a person refuses to agree to become a claimant, he or she must instead be joined as one of the defendants. This appears sensible if that person disputes that he or she is jointly entitled to the remedy, but in other circumstances may lead to the person not taking an active part in the proceedings and having judgment given against them by default.[32]

There is no equivalent provision to compulsorily join defendants. Where several defendants are jointly liable, the claimant(s) may bring their proceeding against one (or some) of them only. If they are found liable, those 'active' defendants will have a cause of action against the non-litigating co-defendants for a contribution to the damages and costs they have been required to pay.[33] There is thus no need for jointly liable defendants to be compulsorily joined to the original proceeding.

It is apparent that the degree of connection for a person to be compulsorily joined to an English proceeding is a very close one: essentially, identity of interest is required. The focus in the English rules on the remedy (outcome) of the litigation is reflected in ERCP Rule 38, which also focuses on the outcome of the case (a judgment which must bind in the *same* terms).

The French civil procedure rules take a slightly different approach. They distinguish between necessary joinder and other situations, but appear to leave to the other parties to the proceedings the initiative of applying for a third person to be compulsorily joined.[34] A party who wishes to ensure that the outcome of the case will apply to another person may apply to have him or her bound by the same judgment in the action.[35] Again, this use of the outcome

---

30 England and Wales CPR 19.3(1).
31 England and Wales CPR 19.4(4) and PD 19A para 2.
32 Zuckerman (n 4), 657 (para 13.8 and fn 10).
33 Civil Liability (Contribution) Act 1978, Section 1.
34 French Civil Procedure Code, Article 331.
35 *Ibid*, second para.

of the proceedings as the nexus for a necessary joinder of the third person is mirrored in the formulation of the ERCP rule.

German practice is slightly different again. The section on necessary joinder requires joinder where the 'legal relationship' in dispute can only be established against the parties in a uniform manner (presumably by a judgment of the court), or if there are other special reasons for doing so.[36] However, if the relevant persons are not joined, rather than permitting a judge to compel them to court, the German rules provide that the proceedings will be deemed to have been conducted on their behalf by the parties who are litigating on their 'side', particularly if this is permitted by the legal rule under which the claim is made.[37]

To give compulsory effect to a necessary joinder, the ERCP also includes a rule (Rule 42) on how to join a person through a 'third-party' notice. The serving of a third-party notice on a non-party is intended to put that person on notice of the proceedings and allow him or her to raise any objections to joinder by applying to the court not to be joined. It will be for the court to decide whether the person must be necessarily joined because the judgment in the action will have to apply to him.

Similar (but not identical) rules are available in national civil procedure codes. The German Civil Procedure Code allows a party to serve a third-party notice where they believe that, if they lose, the third party will have a claim against them (or vice versa).[38] However, the consequences of a successful third-party notice are rather different in Germany than under the ERCP (Rule 35). German procedure only allows the 'noticed' third party to be an intervenor in support of the existing party, rather than being joined as a party in his or her own right.[39] As we will see later in this chapter,[40] this solution would limit the third party's freedom to raise issues in the proceedings: essentially, he or she must follow the procedural steps of the existing party that he or she is 'supporting'.[41] This may not be wholly desirable in many circumstances.

The English civil procedure rules require a 'third party' notice to be filed with the court and served on the third party and the other parties.[42] Unless all

---

36 German ZPO, Section 62.

37 For example, under the German company legislation (Section 248), the effect of a judgment obtained by a shareholder against the company may also be extended to other shareholders.

38 German ZPO, Section 72.

39 German ZPO, Section 74(1).

40 Section 4.2.

41 But this restriction is – at least under German law – compensated by the fact that the supporting party is bound by the outcome of the litigation only to the extent that he or she could influence the proceedings (ZPO, Section 68).

42 England and Wales CPR PD 19.A, para 1.4.

of the parties agree otherwise, a hearing will be held for the court to determine whether the third party should (or must) be joined as a party to the proceedings. There is no equivalent to the German procedure of treating the third party as an intervenor and, if the court allows the application, the person will be joined as a full party.[43]

In adopting a hybrid of German and English practice, the ERCP seeks to strike a balance between ensuring that the third-party notice procedure should be used only where there is a real issue where the 'third person' has a close connection with the proceedings and allowing him or her (if the application to join is successful) all procedural rights of a party to the proceedings. So, for example, if he wishes, the 'noticed' party could make a counterclaim against the party who originally applied to join him under the ERCP rules, which would not be possible if he were simply an intervenor in support. Necessary joinder in the rules is not intended to be used in a situation where it might simply be desirable for a third person to participate in the proceedings without becoming a party: here the court may exceptionally order them to be treated as a non-party intervenor.[44]

We have now looked at the situation where persons who have not yet commenced litigation may or must be joined to an ongoing proceeding. However, it is also possible that two or more separate proceedings already begun will need to be treated together, by consolidating them.

3. CONSOLIDATION OF EXISTING CLAIMS (RULE 37)

ERCP Rule 37 on consolidation of existing claims provides as follows:

> The court may order the consolidation of separate proceedings to enable them to be managed properly in a single proceeding.

Combining separate proceedings already started is a different procedural measure from adding or removing parties to a proceeding – in particular as the procedural status at the time of consolidation of the proceedings to be grouped will be of even greater significance.

The scope of the term 'consolidation' is also not well settled and does not appear to be well defined in most national civil procedure rules.[45] Proceedings which are consolidated will normally continue after consolidation as a single

---

43 *Ibid*, para 1.1; Zuckerman (n 4), 655–56.

44 ERCP Rule 39(2).

45 England and Wales CPR 3.1(2)(g); French Civil Procedure Code, Article 367; German ZPO, Section 147.

proceeding; but it is also possible that they will remain discrete proceedings, but simply be case managed together (eg, for the purposes of hearing evidence).[46] The English civil procedure rules distinguish between consolidation and this type of 'parallel' case management, although the distinction has been criticized as being redundant.[47]

The basis on which courts should exercise their discretion to consolidate varies in national civil procedure rules, but – as with joinder of parties – a substantial margin of discretion is given to the court. The English civil procedure rules give no express indication of the bases on which consolidation may be ordered. In contrast, both the French and German codes provide a little more guidance specifically relating to consolidation. The French code requires there to be a sufficient link as between the proceedings to be consolidated, so that it is in the interests of the good administration of justice for them to be judged together.[48] And the German code goes even further than this: there must be legal 'links' between the proceedings to be consolidated or they should contain claims which could have been commenced in a single proceeding.[49] It seems clear from these national examples that the required connection between proceedings to be consolidated is not as strong as those for a party to be compulsorily joined to proceedings. In the note to ERCP Rule 37, the indication is that the criteria for consolidating claims should be the same as those for voluntary joinder – that the court has jurisdiction over all of the claims to be consolidated and that there is a close connection between them.

Unlike the ERCP rules, both the French and German (but not the English) rules expressly permit the court to 'dis-consolidate' a single proceeding into two or more separate proceedings.[50] The German code notes simply that 'dis-consolidation' should occur only where justified on adequate grounds. But, even without express provision, it is difficult to see how 'dis-consolidation' of a party's action from that of others differs in practice from 'disjoinder' of the party from the proceedings (which, as noted above, is expressly allowed in England). The circumstances in which it should be allowed should therefore also be equivalent. In the ERCP rules, the possibility of either 'disjoinder' or 'dis-consolidation' might be implied from the general case management power of the court to ensure that the proceedings are effectively conducted and are not allowed to become unmanageable.[51]

---

[46] England and Wales CPR 3.1(2)(g) and (h).

[47] *Ibid*; Zuckerman (n 4), 658 (para 13.12).

[48] French Civil Procedure Code, Article 367.

[49] German ZPO, Section 147.

[50] German ZPO, Sections 145(1) and 150; French Civil Procedure Code, Article 367, 2e al.

[51] ERCP Rules 4-8 and Chapter 8 of this book.

4. INTERVENORS IN AN ACTION

The approach to (voluntary) intervention in the ERCP rules follows the practice in several European civil (Roman) law jurisdictions in classifying interventions into two kinds: 'principal' intervention and intervention in support of a party (sometimes 'accessory' intervention). There are a wide variety of approaches to intervention in Europe.[52] The German civil procedure code has relatively detailed rules on both kinds of intervenors; the French code has briefer rules on both kinds of intervention, but does not follow the detail of the German code. English procedure rules specifically relating to intervenors are non-existent: if necessary, the 'intervenors' are joined as parties to the proceedings.

4.1 Principal intervenors (Rule 39) and *Amici Curiae* (Rules 35 and 43)

ERCP Rule 39 on principal intervention provides as follows:

> Anyone not a party to proceedings who claims a right in its subject matter may bring a claim directly against one or more of the parties in the Court in which the dispute is pending at first instance or, if the Court so permits, on appeal.

Rule 39, derived from the similar provisions of the German Civil Procedure Code,[53] is intended to deal with the (fairly rare)[54] situation where a non-litigating person believes that the litigation relates to a right – usually a property right – where one of the parties has no interest and where the intervenor instead owns that right. The intervenor is in effect bringing his own claim against one or more of the parties, but using the intervention mechanism because (for example) the court seised of the pending litigation would not otherwise have jurisdiction over the separate claim.

Importantly, and in contrast to the mechanism of voluntary joinder of a party, both the ERCP and the German code permit (but do not require) the court to suspend the original litigation while the intervenor's claim is resolved.[55] In light of this discretion, the ERCP leaves open the question of whether the intervenor necessarily becomes a party to the original proceedings. If those proceedings are suspended (stayed), then there is in theory no necessary reason

---

[52] Jeuland (n 26), para 417.

[53] German ZPO, Section 64.

[54] Peter L. Murray and Rolf Sturner, *German Civil Justice* (Carolina Academic Press, 2004 reprinted 2015), 205.

[55] ERCP Rule 38(2); German ZPO, Section 65.

for the intervenor to become party to them. However, if they are continued 'in parallel', then the court should be in a position to join the intervenor as a party to the original proceedings rather than be forced to continue with two actions.

The French civil procedure code also distinguishes between principal and subsidiary intervenors.[56] A principal 'intervenor' is a person who voluntarily applies to become party to the original proceedings in which he or she has a cause of action and seeks a remedy.[57] This characterization of intervention appears identical to the concept of voluntary joinder of the applicant to the proceedings and indeed, the French code does not contain separate rules on joinder of parties and intervention, treating them together.

In contrast to the German code, the French rules require the court to give judgment in the original proceedings before turning to the claims of the intervenor if simultaneous judgment would excessively delay the proceedings.[58]

As noted above, the English civil procedure rules do not contain separate provision for (principal) intervenors, relying instead on the flexible rules on joinder of parties and the general discretion available to any court to stay (suspend) its proceedings, if necessary, in the interests of justice.[59]

The mechanism of principal intervention is available only where the intervenor has a cause of action related to the proceedings in which he wishes to intervene. Where he has no cause of action, but his legal interests may be affected by the outcome of the proceedings to which he is not party, he may be able to intervene in support of a party (see the next section). But if a 'disinterested' person with particular knowledge relating to the case, or a public interest body, wishes to make representations to assist the court in resolving the dispute, it may engage with the proceedings only as an *amicus curiae*. ERCP Rules 35 and 43 address this possibility.

Rule 35. Public Interest
A person who is authorised by law to act in the public interest, may act as a party or intervene in any proceedings.

Rule 43. Amicus Curiae

(1) Any legal or natural person, or other entity, may provide the Court with submissions concerning important issues in proceedings with the consent of the court. The court may also invite such submissions.
(2) Before giving its consent, or inviting submissions, under Rule 42(1) the Court must consult the parties.

---

56 French Civil Procedure Code, Article 328.
57 French Civil Procedure Code, Article 329.
58 French Civil Procedure Code, Article 326.
59 England and Wales CPR 3.1(f).

Although *amicus curiae* interventions are a prominent feature of litigation in several common law jurisdictions (notably the United States), they are considerably less widely used in European civil litigation. None of the English, French or German rules have express provisions relating to *amici curiae*, whose position to intervene in any case relies instead largely on case precedent.[60]

Although ERCP Rules 35 and 43 are generally applicable, it is likely that in practice they will be used more in multi-party proceedings (and in collective redress proceedings under the ERCP), as these may more frequently give rise to issues which are of public interest. For example, a group or collective proceeding where the common claim is based on an infringement of competition law may be an action where the national competition authority of the court concerned – or indeed, even the European Commission – might intervene.[61] ERCP Rule 35 gives an express right to 'authorised persons' to intervene in a case in the public interest and Rule 43 sets out how that should be achieved.

It is apparent from the national practice addressing the purpose for which *amicus* submissions may be admitted – that is, in the public interest – that the *amicus* will not become a party to the proceedings. In effect, the position of the *amicus* is traditionally (at least in Europe) closer to that of an expert witness than to that of a party to the proceedings. It follows that the *amicus* should be disinterested and therefore not be in a position to claim any remedy or otherwise derive direct monetary benefit as a result of the proceedings. He is, in particular, in a completely different position *vis-à-vis* the court than a 'qualified entity' acting for a group of claimants under the collective redress proceeding chapter in the ERCP.

Nor will an *amicus* be in the same category as an intervenor in support of a party. Interventions in support are (at least primarily) intended to allow persons who are not litigating to support a party where the outcome of the case may have an impact on the intervenor's legal rights. The relative impartiality required in an *amicus* position (at least in the European concept of the term) puts the *amicus* in a different position from an intervenor in support, even though there may be a significant overlap in the substantive content of contributions to the proceedings.

---

[60] Murray and Sturner (n 54), 205; Jeuland (n 26), 416; for the United Kingdom, see, for example, *In re Northern Ireland Human Rights Commission* [2002] UKHL 25.

[61] National competition authorities now have the right to intervene in civil cases on competition matters under Regulation 1/2003, [2003] OJEU L1/1, Article 15(3).

4.2 Intervenors in support of a party

ECPR Rule 40 on intervention in support of a party provides as follows:

(1) Anyone who has a legitimate interest in one or more parties succeeding in proceedings may intervene in support of their claim or defence. They may intervene at any time before the final hearing is concluded.
(2) The intervenor in support of a party may not object to any procedural step already taken in the proceeding. They may, however, take any procedural step that the party they support may take in so far as doing so is not in conflict with any procedural step taken by that party.

Intervention in support of a party in a proceeding is a feature of many, but not all (eg, the English) national civil procedure rules. There is again a wide variation in the detail of rules on intervention in support, not least in the names used – in France, it is '*accessoire*' (accessory); in Germany, '*Neben*' (subsidiary). Such forms of intervention are, however, always voluntary.

The diversity of approach in national rules means that the drafters of the ERCP have had to take a relatively 'light-touch' approach, although the framework of the ERCP follows most closely the German civil procedure code. The main issues where divergence in national practice may be important are: (1) the nature of the interest that the prospective intervenor in support must show for his or her application to be admitted; (2) whether the subsidiary intervenor himself becomes a party to the proceedings; (3) the degree of procedural freedom allowed to the subsidiary intervenor (given that he is supporting a party in the proceedings); and (4) the effect of judgment in the proceedings on the intervenor in support.

4.2.1 The intervenor's interest in the proceedings

ERCP Rule 40 (following German practice)[62] allows an intervention in support of a party where the proposed intervenor can show a legitimate interest. The kind of interest must, however – and in contrast to an *amicus* – be in a party succeeding in the proceedings: a general 'interest' is not sufficient to ground an intervention in support. As well as allowing the court to exclude vexatious intervention applications, 'legitimacy' would appear to indicate that the outcome of the litigation should have an impact on the legal situation of the intervenor.[63] For example, where there is a dispute between A and B over the ownership of a house, a tenant of the house who has a lease with A (but not B) will be able to intervene in support of A.

---

62 German ZPO, Section 66(1).
63 Murray and Sturner (n 54), 206.

The French civil procedure code is a little more precise on the nature of the connection between the 'accessory' intervenor and the claims of the parties to the proceedings. Not only must the intervenor support a party to the existing proceeding, but he must show that he has an interest in intervening to conserve his own legal rights.[64]

It therefore appears that there must in practice be a twofold connection between the intervenor and the proceedings: he must support a party and his legal interests must be affected (short of giving him a claim) by the outcome of the proceedings.

4.2.2 The intervenor in support as a party to the principal proceedings

Rule 40 leaves open the question of whether an intervenor in support of a party becomes party to the proceedings himself. Since the ERCP also contains express provision for persons to join the proceedings as a party, the intention might be that those who choose to engage with the proceedings as intervenors in support do not become parties to those proceedings.[65] However, the commentary to Rule 40 explains that the assumption is that the intervenor will become a party.

This conclusion is inconsistent with the position in the German civil procedure code, where the intervenor does not become a party in his or her own right.[66] However, even the German approach does not mean that the intervenor is a 'dumb mute', condemned to slavishly follow the procedural steps of the principal party. The German code expressly provides that the intervenor is entitled to take all kinds of procedural steps in the proceedings in support of the principal party.[67]

The ERCP position does follow the position in France, however. A common method of asserting a civil law claim is for the claimant(s) to intervene in support of the public prosecutor in a criminal case in order to claim compensation – the civil law claimant will become a '*partie civile*' to the principal criminal action.[68] The intervenor therefore appears to be a 'party' to the underlying

---

[64] French Civil Procedure Code, Article 330.

[65] The explanatory note to ERCP Rule 40 notes the difference in treatment between France and Germany, in France, intervenors are considered as parties – in Germany they are not. However, the case law of the Court of Justice of the European Union has found that intervenors are not parties for the purpose of the European small claims procedure; C-627/17 *ZSE Energia v RG* ECLI:EU:C:2018:941, paras 27–30.

[66] Murray and Sturner (n 54), 207.

[67] German ZPO, Section 67.

[68] Jeuland (n 26), para 417. Criminal proceedings are outside the scope of the ELI/UNIDROIT project.

action, but he or she clearly cannot be a party in the fullest sense of the term, since the underlying proceedings are not civil law in nature. The intervenor (*partie civile*) would appear to be able to play only a relatively passive role in the underlying criminal action and his or her civil law claims will depend on the outcome of that proceeding.

4.2.3 Procedural freedom of the intervenor in support

Since 'subsidiary' intervenors are permitted to participate in the main proceedings only to support one of the principal parties, their freedom of procedural manoeuvre is necessarily more limited than that of a full party. Rule 40 – following German practice[69] – makes this explicit in two ways: the intervenor must take the proceedings as he finds them at the time of intervention, and may not do anything which would conflict with the procedural steps taken by the principal party he or she supports.

In addition, German law is also clear that the intervenor in support may not appeal the final judgment in the proceedings unless the party supported does so.[70]

The French '*partie civile*' intervenor may have more freedom to act. Since the public prosecutor should not have an interest in the civil law claims, the intervenor cannot be limited to following the procedural steps of the party supported – the prosecutor – some of which may be irrelevant for the civil claim. However, it would clearly be contrary to the public interest for the intervenor to make submissions which contradicted the case of the public prosecutor.

From this, we conclude that the intervenor 'in support' of a party is not required to *actively* support the principal party: 'support' in this context means no more than not undermining the supported party's case. Otherwise, the subsidiary intervenor should be able, under the ERCP, to take all of the procedural steps that a party of the kind he or she is supporting (ie, either claimant or defendant) could take in the proceedings.

4.2.4 Effect of judgment on intervenor in support

The ERCP does not indicate what the effect of the final judgment in the proceedings will be on the legal position of any subsidiary intervenors. Clearly, if the mechanism of subsidiary intervention is to have any utility, there must be some effect, but its extent and impact are left open.

In cases where there has been no intervention, the effect on third persons of a judgment in a case which may have an impact on the legal rights of those third persons varies significantly from country to country. However, the

---

69 German ZPO, Section 67.

70 Murray and Sturner (n 54), 207.

majority of countries start from the position that a judgment has no effect on persons who are not parties to the proceedings leading up to it. This position may be changed by legislation or practice. For example, in England, a conviction for a crime may be presented in evidence in a civil case without the need to further prove the guilt of the defendant.[71]

How far should this basic position be modified for subsidiary intervenors? As a first observation, if the intervenor has later become a full party to the proceedings (eg, by joinder), it should follow that the judgment binds him or her (unless it says otherwise) as it will other parties. But what of subsidiary intervenors who remain at the periphery of the circle of parties?

The German code – under which the intervenor does not become a party – does not allow parties to enforce the judgment against the intervenor.[72] However, with limited exceptions, the (relevant) findings in the judgment will bind the intervenor in later litigation, at least between him and one of the parties to the original proceeding. The intervenor cannot challenge the factual and legal findings simply on the basis of inadequate reasoning or incompetent conduct of the proceedings by the party he supported.[73] Rather, he must show that this party actually hindered his ability to bring forward argument or evidence.[74] Nevertheless, where the judgment has altered his legal rights in relation to one or more of the opponents of the party supported, the intervenor will be deemed to have become a (joint) party with the party supported.[75] In this case, if there are grounds to do so, he will be able to appeal the judgment independently of the supported party.[76]

Although the detail of the German code is probably superfluous in the context of ERCP rules intended to apply within diverse national legal systems, the code does give a good indication of the legal effect which a judgment should have on any subsidiary intervenors. We believe that two conclusions can be drawn. First, the judgment should not be enforceable against the subsidiary intervenor, even in the very unlikely event that it actually contains a finding directly 'against' him.

Second, however, the findings in the judgment should be at least highly persuasive in any later proceedings between the intervenor in support and other parties to the proceedings. Unless the intervenor can show some serious

---

[71] England and Wales Civil Evidence Act 1968, s 11.

[72] Murray and Sturner (n 54), 207.

[73] German ZPO, Section 68.

[74] German ZPO, Section 68; Murray and Sturner (n 54), 208.

[75] German ZPO, Section 69.

[76] In case of a third-party notice (German ZPO, Section 72) under German law, this effect (German ZPO, Section 68) takes place regardless of whether the third party intervened in the pending action (German ZPO, Section 74(3)).

irregularity in the proceedings which he could not have dealt with himself at the time it arose, he should be held bound to the conclusions in the judgment.

We have thus far discussed multi-party proceedings in which the parties or intervenors all conduct their own affairs independently (or at least autonomously). However, where the number of persons engaging with the proceedings exceeds the level beyond which the court can manage the proceedings effectively, specialist case management regimes will need to be used. In the next section, we will consider the use of group claims developed to manage multi-party cases *without* the use of an intermediary 'representative' or 'qualified entity'.

5. GROUP CLAIMS

The ERCP does not contain group proceeding provisions, preferring instead to rely on the opt-in or opt-out collective redress proceeding mediated through a 'qualified entity' as set out in Chapter XI. Our discussion will therefore contrast this collective redress proceeding mechanism with group proceedings – using the English GLO and the German capital markets group proceeding as Europe's leading examples.

This lack of a mechanism designed to complement traditional joinder techniques while allowing a 'multi-party' group to maintain their individual claims follows from the conditions for allowing a collective redress proceeding under the ERCP. The 'numerosity' threshold for the use of a collective redress proceeding is precisely that the number of parties exceeds the number which can be efficiently joined to or consolidated in a single proceeding.[77] At that point, the collective redress chapter in the ERCP becomes available to the court. In contrast, both England and Germany have fairly long-standing group litigation mechanisms designed to allow multi-party claims to proceed as such, but also to ensure that the proceedings do not degenerate into an unmanageable mess.

In this section, we will first attempt to define 'group claim' or 'group proceeding', and contrast it with a 'collective redress proceeding' as set out in the ERCP. We will then examine the idea of an 'opt-in' collective proceeding and how it differs in practice (if at all) from a group proceeding. And finally, we will address some of the main case management effects of group claims and compare them to the position under an (opt-in) collective proceeding.

[77] ERCP Rule 212(1)(a).

5.1 Distinction between group claim and collective proceedings

There are two main distinguishing features which separate a group claim from any form of collective proceeding. The first is that each group member in a group claim is (and remains) party to the action until it is concluded. The group proceeding is therefore still – at least formally – a bundle of the individual claims of the (claimant) group members. In contrast, a collective proceeding is a bilateral claim by the qualified entity against the defendant: the group members are not parties to the claim. This has significant consequences for the management of the case – and in particular the procedural freedom of individual group members – as well as for the availability of remedies (which we deal with in Section 6) and the allocation of the costs of the proceedings if the group is unsuccessful.

The second difference is that there is no intermediary 'qualified entity' acting for the group in a group claim. The management of the group is therefore mainly in the hands of the judge. This feature of the group proceeding allows the group members not only to assert their claims against the defendant which fall within the scope of the 'common' proceedings, but also to ensure that any individual issues they may have arising from the same event of mass harm can be appropriately dealt with.[78] In contrast, in a collective proceeding, individual issues cannot normally be dealt with as part of the collective claim and may need to be asserted in separate proceedings (if at all).

A collective redress proceeding – as discussed in Chapters 4 to 10 – is likely to be of most use where the losses caused to the group members arising from the mass harm event form a set of fairly homogenous economic loss claims. This is the main reason why, in the United States, the class action under Rule 23 of the Federal Rules of Civil Procedure is most commonly used for losses either caused by antitrust infringements or caused by fraud connected with the sale of financial securities, which both lead to a money remedy. In contrast, where a single event causes non-economic loss to a group – for example, physical injury from an environmental accident or a pharmaceutical mistake – the individual issues for claimant group members, who may be differently affected by the same event, may be more easily and efficiently dealt with using a group proceeding mechanism. So, for example, liability for the consequences of the event could be established in a group claim, whereas the amount of compensation to each group member could be dealt with individually.

---

[78] For example, England and Wales CPR PD 19B, para 14.1.

5.2 Types of group claims: test cases, common issues

We have now defined a group claim by what it is not: a proceeding by numerous claimants without a qualified entity as an intermediary between the claimant group and the court. But this does not, of course, explain what it is. In effect, the group proceeding mechanism provides a case management 'wrapper' to draw together a significant number of claims in a single proceeding. But the group 'wrapper' mechanism (eg, the English GLO) does not go so far as to require the group members to proceed only through a qualified entity.

Definition of a group proceeding is hampered by the variety of actual or possible methods used to form the 'wrapper' and the diversity of the situations in which national civil procedure rules allow group proceedings to be used. Rather than attempt a – necessarily vague – definition here, we will instead describe common features of an advanced group proceeding 'wrapper' by reference to two main jurisdictions' group proceeding rules: the English GLO[79] and the German *Kapitalanlegermusterverfahren* (KapMuG).[80] Both of these group 'wrappers' have been in use for more than a decade and are both now complemented by more advanced collective proceeding rules (in both cases of considerably younger vintage).[81] They are also rather different in their approach and therefore provide a good insight into the variety of group proceeding techniques available.

Before contrasting the two group proceeding mechanisms, it is first worth highlighting the common features:

- They both require the court where the group proceedings will take place to make an order allowing a group of claims already commenced to continue within the group proceeding 'wrapper'. Even if it is requested to do so, the court has some discretion in both systems as to whether to make the order.
- A public (or semi-public) register of the claims to which the order relates must be set up under both systems. Any settlements or judgments in the group proceeding will apply only to claims (and claimants) on the group register.
- If claims which are put on the register are already pending in other courts in the relevant country, they are suspended at the point that the order is made.
- The group proceeding order should include details of the 'common issues' (*Feststellungsziele*) which are to be included in the group proceeding and in respect of which any judgment or settlement will be binding.

---

79 England and Wales CPR 19.10-19.15 and PD 19B.

80 25 October 2012; BGBl I S2182.

81 12 July 2018; BGBl I 1151; England and Wales, Consumer Rights Act 2015, sch 8.

The ERCP *collective* redress proceedings chapter – whose default is that collective redress proceedings should be 'opt-in' – also contains provisions reflecting these common *group* proceeding requirement. There is significant overlap in the grouping techniques used under both types of proceedings:

- Rule 212 empowers the court to make an order admitting a collective redress proceeding if the conditions in that rule are met. However, there is no right to a collective redress proceeding order – the court always has a discretion.
- Rules 211 and 220 require the establishment of a public and accessible register for collective redress proceedings.
- No further collective redress proceeding against the defendants can be admitted once a claim is entered on the register (Rule 211(2)).
- The collective proceeding order must contain a description of the 'event of mass harm' which gives rise to the collective redress proceeding (Rule 213(1)(b)).

Beyond these common features, however, the further procedural elements included in a group proceeding 'wrapper' may vary substantially. There are (significant) differences between the English GLO and the German KapMuG, which are (for our purposes) best discussed in two areas. The first is the use of lead or test claims to decide the common issues: the GLO permits, but does not require this; while the KapMuG makes the use of lead claimants mandatory. Second (and connected to the first issue), the position of those group members who are not actively involved in the proceedings differs significantly as between the two regimes. We consider each of these in turn.

The GLO rules in the English Civil Procedure Rules (Rules 19.10–19.15) are fairly broad brush and designed to give the court discretion to manage the case according to its needs within the GLO 'wrapper'. Rule 19.13(b) permits (but does not require) the court to direct that one or more of the claims on the group register should proceed as a test claim (a term which is undefined). The solicitors (lawyers) representing one or more of the group *may* be appointed to represent the whole group for the purposes of the group proceeding.[82] However, the court *will* also appoint a 'managing judge' for the group proceeding, and he assumes overall responsibility for the management of the claims on the group register rather than the group solicitor.[83]

In contrast, the German KapMuG mechanism *requires* the court to designate a lead claimant (*Musterklager*) from among those whose claims have been

---

[82] England and Wales CPR 19.13(c).

[83] England and Wales CPR PD 19.13 §8.

entered on the group proceeding register.[84] The selection is made on a general 'equity' test and cannot be appealed, although other claimants may request his or her removal. However, the legislation is clear that the non-selected group members whose claims appear on the group register remain associated closely to the proceedings, although they are not full parties.[85] The KapMuG legislation does not specify the rights and obligations of the *Musterklager*, although it can be assumed that the general procedural rights of all claimants under the German civil procedure code are available to him, and that he is bound by equivalent obligations to the court.[86]

In addition to the differences in the use of lead or test claimants, the English and German group proceeding rules also treat the position of group members who are not lead claimants rather differently. Perhaps unsurprisingly, in view of both the general scope of the GLO mechanism and the discretion given to the managing judge not to appoint a lead claimant, the GLO rules do not differentiate between lead and other group members. In particular, any procedural order or final judgment binds all of the claimants whose claims are on the register at the time the decision is made, unless the court orders otherwise.[87] With some (fairly limited) exceptions,[88] each group member – being a separate party to the group proceeding – has the individual right to appeal against a final judgment which adversely affects him or her.[89] Similarly, each group member is entitled to access to documentary evidence filed in the group proceeding not only by the defendants, but also by other group members.[90]

The German KapMuG mechanism takes a noticeably different approach to the non-lead group members. This is likely to be due to the requirement that there is a lead claimant – who can then be expected to pursue the claim in all group members' interests – and also by the specialist nature of the KapMuG procedure. It can be used only in claims of mass mis-selling of certain kinds of securities: it is therefore highly likely that the potential claimants will be identifiable by inspecting the relevant share or securities registers.

---

84 German KapMuG, Section 9(2).

85 *Ibid*, § 9(1). The legislation uses the term '*Beigeladene*', which has its roots in administrative proceedings and is not otherwise used in civil proceedings. The '*Beigeladene*' have a number of rights, but not all rights that a party to the litigation would have. In Section 14 of the KapMuG, there are similar restrictions as for subsidiary intervenors: the '*Beigeladene*' may not act in any way which is in conflict with the procedural acts of the '*Musterklager*'.

86 German KapMuG, Section 11, which refers to the Civil Procedure Code and its general rules.

87 England and Wales CPR 19.12(1)(a).

88 *Ibid*, 19.12 (3).

89 *Ibid*, 19.12(2).

90 *Ibid*, 19.12(4).

There is, though, no possibility in the German legislation for claims which are covered by the group proceeding to be continued individually: they must all be stayed, regardless of whether they were brought before or after the order establishing the group proceeding.[91] The non-lead claimants (*Beigeladenen*) remain as 'quasi-parties' to the group proceeding.[92] Although they can take available steps in the proceedings as a whole (presumably on an individual basis), this freedom is restricted in two ways. First, if they join the group proceeding after it has begun, they must take the proceedings in the state in which they find them. Second, their procedural steps must not run counter to the procedural steps which are taken by the lead claimant.[93]

The position of the non-lead claimants in a KapMuG group proceeding is almost identical to that of intervenors in support of a party under both the German code and the ERCP (discussed in Section 4.2). The ERCP can therefore form the basis of a near equivalent to a 'German-style' group proceeding, where a claimant brings a claim as a test case and other members of the affected group join as intervenors in his or her support. However, unlike the German and English group proceeding mechanisms, this *ad hoc* 'group-style' proceeding would have significant drawbacks. In particular, there would be no group register and therefore no possibility of preventing parallel group claims from springing up.

How then does the ERCP address the possible need for a mechanism allowing both common and individual claims to be dealt with at the same time, as represented by the English GLO? Is the proposed 'opt-in' collective redress proceeding capable of covering this gap left by not having a group proceeding mechanism in the ERCP?

5.3 The 'opt-in' principle and group claims

The two distinguishing features of an ERCP collective proceeding are that the proceeding is conducted by a qualified entity on behalf of the group, and that the group members are not parties to the collective proceeding. However, despite not being parties, there must of course be some methods for group members to be identified and to adhere to the collective proceeding – the relevant ERCP rules are considered in more detail in Chapters 6 and 7.

In brief, there are broadly two methods for defining the group which is litigating: the 'opt-in' method and the 'opt-out' method. The ERCP collective redress proceeding rules permit both kinds of techniques, but with a preference

[91] German KapMuG, Section 8(1).
[92] *Ibid*, Section 9(1).3.
[93] *Ibid*, Section 14.

for 'opt-in' collective redress proceedings.[94] This follows current EU practice, both in the European Commission Recommendation on collective redress and in the more recent consumer redress draft Directive.[95]

So what is an 'opt-in' proceeding (and how does it differ from a group proceeding)? There are a number of possible definitions. The Commission Recommendation notes that the group 'should be formed on the basis of express consent of the natural or legal persons claiming to have been harmed ("opt-in" principle)'.[96]

The UK Competition Act – which also provides for the use of either opt-in or opt-out collective redress – says:

> 'Opt-in collective proceedings' are collective proceedings which are brought on behalf of each class member who opts in by notifying the representative, in a manner and by a time specified, that the claim should be included in the collective proceedings.[97]

The Belgian collective redress statute similarly permits the court to make an order on either an 'opt-in' or 'opt-out' basis:[98]

> 'opt-in system': a system in which the only members of the group are those consumers affected by the collective harm and who have made known their consent to form part of the group.

From these examples, 'opt-in' therefore requires an indication of consent from each group member to form part of the collective proceeding. It would appear that the indication must be an express one – so implied consent to join an 'opt-in' collective proceeding is not sufficient. An opt-in collective proceeding therefore shares with a group proceeding the requirement that each group member has actively decided to join the proceedings. Can the opt-in collective redress proceeding model therefore carry out the same functions as a group

---

94 ERCP Rule 215(1).

95 Commission Recommendation, 11 June 2013, common principles for injunctive and compensatory collective redress mechanisms [2013] OJEU L201/60, para 21; proposal for a Directive on representative actions for the protection of the collective interests of consumers, 11 April 2018, COM/2018/0814 final, Article 6.

96 Recommendation, *ibid.*

97 Competition Act 1998, Section 47B(10) (as amended by the Consumer Rights Act 2015).

98 Law of 28 March 2014: Collective redress actions. *Moniteur belge*, 29 April 2014, 2014 011217, Article 2, 5° (our translation). Original reads: '*système d'option d'inclusion : système dans lequel sont seuls membres du groupe les consommateurs lésés par le préjudice collectif qui ont manifesté leur volonté de faire partie de ce groupe.*'

proceeding mechanism, as used (for example) in Germany and the United Kingdom?

The German group proceeding mechanism was designed specifically for claims of mis-selling of securities in financial services markets – a relatively specialized use of the group mechanism. In particular, it is quite likely to be fairly easy to identify both the actual and the potential members of the group (there will usually be a register of the holders of the affected securities). The model proceedings claimant (*Müsterklager*) and the 'quasi-parties' (*Beigeladene*) must all have commenced proceedings individually against the defendant – either before or after the court makes the model proceedings order. The consent to group proceedings is therefore the commencement of a claim within the scope of the model proceedings order. This variant of the 'opt-in' principle is perhaps some way from what is envisaged in more general European procedural practice noted above.

In contrast, the English GLO is a generally useable mechanism and affords the managing judge more procedural freedom. In practice, GLOs are most commonly used in cases of mass harm causing non-monetary injury (eg, through defective pharmaceutical products or environmental accidents).[99] This means that identifying the group members individually at the point the GLO order is made may be much more difficult than under the German system. Furthermore, because of the nature of the harm caused, individual issues as well as common issues will often need to be decided before a group member's claim can be finally dealt with and he or she is compensated. However, group members whose claims fall within the scope of a GLO's 'common issues' can decide not to continue within the group litigation by applying to be removed from the register. Although perhaps also not fully 'opt-in' in the sense contemplated in the European Commission's collective redress recommendation, a positive (express) decision to commence proceedings and whether to continue within or outside the GLO 'wrapper' is available under the English rules.

The 'gap' in procedural protection which the group proceeding fills is, therefore, in those cases where there is a single cause of harm to a substantial number of (usually) identified persons, but where their claims may also have significant individual elements outside the common aims of the group proceeding. These types of claims may not be well addressed by collective proceedings mediated through a single qualified entity.

Typically, these cases will also be characterized by requiring specialized (and therefore expensive to obtain) technical or other opinion evidence, so that avoiding duplication in evidence requirements is a major aim for the group (as

---

99 See www.gov.uk/guidance/group-litigation-orders (last accessed 27 July 2020).

well as for the court itself). In the following sub-section, we consider the case management tools available in the ERCP to address these issues.

5.4 Case management: contrasting collective and group claims

How well then does the model collective redress proceeding proposed in Part XI of the ERCP address the two issues (evidence and individual 'sub-claims') identified above?

First, on streamlining evidence requirements, a collective proceeding – as a bilateral claim between the qualified entity and the defendant – will almost always be less 'evidence heavy' than a 'traditional' multi-party mechanism (eg, joinder) where the proceedings are otherwise of comparable size. The qualified entity – which is required by the ERCP to act in the best interests of the whole group[100] – will be responsible for the collection or commissioning of evidence to support the collective claim of the group. There will be only one set of evidence from the group's side in relation to the common issues or aims of the proceedings. This will be the case whether the collective proceeding is marshalled on an opt-in or opt-out basis. Collective proceedings therefore have potential significant advantages over joinder or even using most group proceeding 'wrappers', as far as the organization and presentation of the evidence on behalf of the group are concerned.

On the second issue identified above – the treatment of group members' individual claims outside the common issues – the picture is perhaps more nuanced. Collective (class) proceedings have usually been used, in those jurisdictions which permit them, where the members of the claimant group have a homogenous set of claims with relatively few individual issues requiring resolution by group members separately.[101] However, the ERCP collective redress proceeding rules do contain two provisions which should assist courts in managing collective redress proceedings, even where there may be noticeable individual issues related to the collective proceedings, which cannot be taken up as part of the collective claim.

The court is empowered under the rules to divide a group in a collective redress proceeding into sub-groups.[102] This is likely to be particularly useful where the disclosure of evidence shows that, in addition to the issues common to the whole group, there is a sub-set of issues which affects a specific number of group members and can therefore be dealt with on a sub-collective basis. Where necessary – for example, where the group is litigating against several

---

[100] ERCP Rule 214.
[101] ERCP Rule 217.
[102] ERCP Rule 218(d).

defendants, only some of whom are affected by the sub-group's parallel claims – the court is also permitted under the rules to give separate or partial judgment against some only of the defendants.[103]

Nevertheless, the ERCP rules do not expressly permit a group member to assert a wholly individual element of a claim which is connected to the collective redress proceeding in the same proceedings.[104] This is a potential area of disadvantage for collective redress (even on an opt-in basis), as compared with a group proceeding.

Of course, the ERCP collective redress proceeding chapter sits within the framework of the ERCP in general. In particular the 'Principles' given at the beginning of the ERCP give the court a general case management duty to pursue the effective management of the case.[105] This could include the use of case management powers to order a separate hearing of an individual group member's discrete issue, for example. This possibility may, however, be hampered by the fact that the group member (in a collective proceeding) will not be a party to the main proceeding: it is difficult to see how the court can have procedural jurisdiction over him or her individually.

6. REMEDIES AND SETTLEMENTS IN GROUP CLAIMS

The normal reason for bringing a group proceeding – and indeed a collective proceeding – is to claim compensation for the consequences of a 'mass harm situation' (to use the terminology in the European Commission's collective redress recommendation).[106] There will usually be little point in deploying the relatively more complex group proceeding 'wrapper' or collective proceedings in applications for an injunction, since the unsuccessful defendant will normally be bound to comply with the injunction even as against non-parties. The effect of the injunction (if granted) on the defendant's behaviour should be the same for all.

The sole nuance will be that an injunction will be enforceable only by the original applicant, so group members who have an interest will need to persuade (or, where possible, require) the applicant in the injunction proceedings to seek an enforcement order. Perhaps for this reason, the Commission Recommendation also makes recommendations for collective injunctive relief

---

[103] ERCP Rule 130(1).
[104] ERCP Rule 217.
[105] ERCP Rule 4.
[106] Recommendation (n 95), para 3(b).

so that group members can enforce any injunction directly.[107] It is doubtful, however, whether an individual small claimant would wish to do so.

Many national regimes treat the issue of applying for an injunction in what is a collective interest as an issue of standing. For example, in some EU countries,[108] either public bodies or recognized consumer or similar associations have standing to apply for injunctions against traders who may be breaching consumer laws – indeed, EU Member States must implement the Injunctions Directive, which requires public consumer enforcers to be able to seek an injunction in the public interest.[109] Enforcement of the injunction will therefore be in the hands of either a recognized representative entity or a public body – which can be expected to act in the general interest – rather than the private interests of a group member.

This use of public bodies as principal parties in public interest claims (addressed in ERCP Rule 205) may also extend to money actions which are not intended to compensate the group of victims.[110] Actions intended to deprive wrongdoers of the profits they have made from their unlawful activities, without necessarily aiming exactly to compensate group members, exist in some countries.[111] In many cases, however, they will not be claims in civil proceedings, but will be brought as an adjunct to criminal proceedings.[112] Even where civil 'confiscation' or 'disgorgement' claims are permitted, the circle of bodies with standing to bring them is usually fairly small and the destination for the funds seized can be used is usually defined in legislation – often the state's general 'consolidated' account.[113]

Confiscation orders of this kind should be distinguished from collective redress judgments (eg, under the ERCP); they are not intended to compensate the group. In principle, therefore, the group should be able to claim compensation whether or not a confiscation order has been made. And although the methods of calculating the amount of 'ill-gotten gain' may be similar to some

---

[107] *Ibid*, paras 1920.

[108] For example, Netherlands Civil Code, Article 6:240 – representative consumer organizations' claims against unfair trading practices.

[109] Directive 2009/22/EC, currently the subject of a proposal for repeal and replacement (see n 95).

[110] ERCP Rule 205(2).

[111] For example, unjust enrichment claims in England: see *Lipkin Gorman v Karpnale Ltd* [1988] UKHL 12, [1991] 2AC 548.

[112] For example, UK confiscation orders under Part II of the Proceeds of Crime Act 2002 (PoCA).

[113] In the United Kingdom, confiscated assets are paid into the government's general consolidated fund: PoCA 2002, Section 55(6); Courts Act 2003, Section 38(4).

methods used to calculate the total compensation payable to the group,[114] civil law damages and confiscation (usually under criminal law) are not the same. In particular, it is not a condition for an award of *damages* that the defendant has made a profit from his or her unlawful activity.[115]

The ERCP collective redress proceeding rules require that the total amount of damages as well as the criteria for distribution be included in any final judgment.[116] The total compensation received forms a 'common fund'.[117] This fund is first used to pay the (reasonable) costs of conducting the litigation, if it exceeds the amount of costs paid to the qualified claimant by losing defendants; the remainder is then divided among the group members.

Using an overall damages calculation is a common feature of collective proceeding (including class action) regimes worldwide.[118] It has at least two distinct advantages. First, it reduces the amount of evidence needed for the collective proceeding to reach a successful conclusion. There is no need for evidence relating to each group member to be available before a compensation award can be made. Many national civil procedure rules permit the court to use estimating techniques to calculate damages in a wide variety of contexts.[119] This power is useful in assessing the total compensation payable to the group as a whole in a collective proceeding. Second, it is likely to be far easier for a collective proceeding to be settled before trial if the qualified claimant and the settling defendant can agree on a total sum representing the compensation and legal costs payable by the defendant to the group, without having to undertake in-depth examination of each group member's individual loss.

In contrast, group proceedings may raise difficult issues of quantification. Since group members each remain a party to the group proceeding, the starting point must be that each must show his loss individually. Indeed, the German KapMuG does not envisage a 'group award' of damages at all: rather, judgment is given on liability to the group and the *Beigeladene* claimants' (stayed) individual actions will then be resumed, so that their compensation can be

---

[114] See Chapter 8 for the methods of calculating the damages available to collective claimants. Confiscation orders normally proceed on the basis of the calculation of the defendant's benefit ('top down') (PoCA 2002, Section 7), not the collective loss.

[115] Compare with the Competition Damages Directive 2014/104, [2014] OJEU L349/1, Article 2(5).

[116] ERCP Rule 228 The techniques used to calculate the 'common fund' – whether by aggregation ('bottom-up' method) or a calculation of the overall harm caused to the group as compared with the position if the mass harm event had not taken place ('top-down' method) – are considered in more detail in Chapter 10.

[117] ERCP Rule 238(2).

[118] Rachel Mulheron, *The Class Action in Common Law Legal Systems* (Hart, 2004) 407–09.

[119] *Ibid*, 412–16; ERCP Rule 228 (and notes).

awarded individually. The English GLO rules do not specify how compensation to group members for harm caused as a result of the 'common issues' is to be assessed: there are only specific rules on the costs relating to a GLO judgment. [120] In any event, it is probably unrealistic for a general damage calculation rule to be included in the GLO mechanism, since the managing judge can use a wide variety of techniques to assess damages arising from the common issues.[121]

Nevertheless, the aggregation of damages – as used in a collective proceeding – is not possible in a group proceeding. This in itself will inevitably lead to greater complexity and (as noted above) will therefore make the whole of a group claim more difficult to settle in a single agreement. Defendants will be tempted to 'pick off' the lead claimants in order to destabilize the group proceeding in the hope that it will collapse: the English GLO rules allow the judge to intervene to replace lead claimants precisely so as to try to prevent this tactic and ensure that a GLO proceeding has a lead claimant as long as a willing party can be found to step forward.[122]

Although it is in the area of the remedies available (and therefore ease of settlement) where the differences between group and collective proceedings are perhaps most noticeable, in many areas – as we conclude in the next section – the group proceeding may be superseded by the collective proceeding as representing a more modern and efficient way of managing complex 'mass' litigation.

7. CONCLUSIONS ON MULTI-PARTY PROCEEDINGS

'Traditional' methods of dealing with disputes which have more than two antagonists — joinder, consolidation and intervention — remain the foundation of addressing the procedural challenges caused by multi-party civil litigation. It is only where the number of participants in the dispute resolution process goes beyond what can be sensibly dealt with by these means that the

---

[120] England and Wales CPR 46.6 – in general, each losing party is severally liable for the group costs. Under the German KapMuG proceedings, the group costs are deemed to be part of each individual action filed by the shareholders. Therefore, the *Beigeladene* will have to pay their share of the costs of the group proceedings. However, the shares will not necessarily be equal, because according to Section 24 II 2 of the KapMuG, the share of costs depends on the amount of the claim the individual shareholders advances in his or her individual action.

[121] For a recent example of the complexity of damages calculations (in a competition claim), *BritNed Developments Ltd v ABB AB* [2019] EWCA Civ 1840.

[122] England and Wales CPR 19.15.

judge need even begin to consider the use of group or collective redress procedural mechanisms.

Assuming a choice in the judge's civil procedure rules between more advanced solutions, should he or she always opt for the most modern 'collective' techniques? Or are there circumstances where a group proceeding remains superior?

It is worth bearing in mind the two main differences between a collective redress proceeding and a group proceeding: group proceeding claimants each remain a party to the proceedings, while collective proceeding claimants do not. And there is no qualified entity as an intermediary for the claimant group in a group proceeding.

The types of disputes in which there are too many parties to simply join them all into one proceeding, but where their claims will be too differentiated to be properly put forward by a qualified entity as part of a collective proceeding, may be rather limited. The experience with the English GLO suggests that disputes where a single unlawful act has caused non-economic loss to a wide group of claimants – physical injury from an environmental disaster, for example – are probably of the kind best suited to group proceeding treatment. The questions of liability for the harm caused and to whom an obligation to compensate arises (causation) can be dealt with as 'common issues', and the question of the amount of compensation (quantum) – which may vary significantly from person to person – can be dealt with at a more granular level in the same proceeding. Collective proceedings seem less well suited to this type of dispute.

The choice between group and collective proceedings cannot, however, be based on static criteria. The development of collective proceeding mechanisms in the last decade in European civil procedure has been very substantial, and this continues. Thus, although there may currently be a sub-set of multi-party claims where a group proceeding might be superior to both 'traditional' case management and a collective proceeding, the increase in sophistication of collective proceeding rules may reduce this gap even further.

We do not believe that the current trajectory in the development and use of collective proceedings in Europe will slow soon. The European Commission's 2018 proposals for a collective proceeding for consumers, to replace the current Injunctions Directive,[123] will (if adopted) give even greater impetus to case law and national legislative developments in this area. Group proceedings are likely to become something of a niche for a minority of multi-victim cases where local collective proceeding rules cannot be flexed to ensure effective management of certain issues. It is therefore probable that national judges

[123] See nn 95 and 109.

will increasingly look to collective proceedings – and develop use of them through decisional practice – to manage large-scale litigation in a wide variety of settings.

4. Change of parties: representation, substitution, assignment

Emmanuel Jeuland

Certain civil procedures intended for use by an individual party, which may nevertheless be used to change or assist the parties to a proceeding – assignment, intervention in support, representation and substitution – can also be used to 'group' multiple parties in the circumstances of a mass claim. One may speak of *de facto* collective action. However, since these methods are intended for 'isolated' parties, they are not especially well adapted to mass litigation. Mass actions would generally be more difficult to manage or more limited in scope using these methods. For example, judicial document would still have to be served on all parties individually, even though there may be hundreds or thousands of them.

The main methods used are well known. A group of natural persons who have been victims of mass harm may be represented in court by the same representative – which can be an organization (see Section 1). Legal persons are represented by natural persons entitled to represent them. Since the legal person may have many affected members, it may bring a 'mass claim' in court. Third parties may become intervenors, as noted in Chapter 2. It may also be useful for mass litigation to allow third parties to join a case brought by other victims (discussed at Section 2). Persons who have litigation capacity must bring actions in their own name, unless a rule permits otherwise (see Section 3). Thus, multi-party litigation can take the form of a 'substitutive action'. At any time after commencement of the action, the substitution or succession of one party by another is possible on certain conditions (European Rules of Civil Procedure (ECRP) Rule 16, 'Substitution and Succession'). Claim assignments may also be used to unify all cases under the head of the same assignor when there has been a mass tort (see Section 4). Lastly, whatever the procedural tools used to bring a mass claim, a test case may be envisaged (discussed in Section 5).

1. REPRESENTATION AND MASS CLAIMS

'Representation' in court is when a representative brings an action on behalf of a party who does not have litigation capacity. We do not consider here the representation by lawyers of parties who have litigation capacity. This situation must also be differentiated from collective redress proceedings, in which a qualified entity pursues a claim on behalf of a group of (non-party) claimants who (usually) do have litigation capacity. The representative may bring the action on behalf of a natural person (ERCP Rule 30(3); see Section 1.1) or a legal person (Rule 31; see Section 1.2). There are also common or general rules covering both situations (see Section 1.3).

1.1 Representation of natural persons

Persons who, although a party to the proceedings, do not have full capacity under the applicable substantive law cannot conduct civil actions on their own. ERCP Rule 30 requires that they be represented during the proceedings by their legal representative (not to be confused with the lawyer acting in the litigation based on a power of attorney or retainer).

The applicable law in the sense of Rule 30(3) can be either substantive (eg, where the law requires a person to be 18 years of age to litigate) or procedural (eg, where the person has entered an appearance before the court), but it does not mean applicable law in the sense of conflict of laws rules. This rule is common to all Member States.[1]

[1] For example: Croatia – Civil Procedure Code, Section 79, 80; France – Civil Procedure Code, Article 117; Hungary – Civil Procedure Code, Section 4(2); Italy – Civil Procedure Code, Section 75(2); Latvia – Civil Procedure Code, Sections 72(2)–(4)). Section 75 of the Italian Civil Procedure Code provides: 'Persons who do not have the free exercise of their rights may take legal action only if they are represented, assisted or authorized in accordance with the rules governing their capacity.' Article 117 of the French Civil Procedure Code (1976) provides the same rule from the sanction perspective: 'Substantive irregularities are those affecting the validity of the pleading: Lack of capacity or of power of attorney of a person legally representing a party before a court of law.' Article 80 of the Croatian Civil Procedural Act provides (2003): 'Parties who do not have the litigation capacity shall be represented by their legal representatives.' English law recognizes the right for a litigant in person to have a litigation friend – see A. Zuckerman, *Civil Procedure, Principles of Practice* 3rd edn (Sweet & Maxwell 2013), 145–46. This friend is called a 'McKenzie friend' after the case *McKenzie v McKenzie* (1971) P 33 (1970), 3 All ER 1034 (CA). Outside Europe, in Brazil, Article 71 of the Code of Civil Procedure (2015) provides: 'The incapacitated person will be represented or assisted by his parents, guardian or curator, in accordance with the law.'

Several natural persons may give a mandate to the same person so that there is only one representative for a mass claim. However, the regime permitting this may be limited. An old principle in France and Belgium states that nobody can plead through a representative.[2] There was an exception during the *Ancien Régime*: the king could be represented in court. That is the origin of the modern public prosecutor. This rule was made to avoid 'undisclosed' or ghost parties. Today, the meaning of the adage is rather limited: parties may be represented in court, but their name must appear in the pleadings.[3] This principle has long been an obstacle to class actions in France, since the claimant brings a collective action without knowing the names of some or all group members. This is one of the reasons why class action in France is considered not as a representative action, but as a substitutive action.[4]

In France, the 'action in joint representation'[5] has been created in consumer, financial or environmental law as an alternative to class action. Where several identified consumers have suffered individual damage caused by the same trader that has a common origin, an association (approved and recognized as nationally representative) which has been mandated by at least two of the consumers concerned may initiate proceedings for damages before any court on their behalf. However, this mandate may not be requested by means of a public television or radio call, or by means of posters, leaflets or personalized letters. This explains why this representative action is very rarely used under French consumer law (fewer than ten cases in several decades).

In 1994, the legislature extended the rights of these associations by allowing them to seek compensation before any court for individual losses incurred by identified individual investors whose individual losses were caused by the same person and had a common origin. However, they could act only on behalf of those investors who had given them a written mandate, and only if those investors had not been solicited by 'public call, television or radio, or by means of posters, leaflets or personalized letters'. In addition, these associations had to be approved. Indeed, in practice, investors who complain of false information use ordinary associations under the previous 1901 Act.[6] So this mass claim device has not proved very useful in practice.

---

2 In Belgium: G. de Leval, *Eléments de procédure civile*, 2nd edn (Larcier, 2005), 11.

3 In France: F. Caballero, '*Plaidons par procureur! de l'archaïsme procédural à l'action de groupe*', *RTD civ* 1985, p 247; in Belgium, the '*prête-nom*' is illegal only if it is to the detriment of the other parties or if it is a fraud – De Leval (n 2), 11.

4 See Section 3.1.

5 Article L622-1 of the French Consumer Code.

6 The act which authorizes and organizes associations in France.

1.2 Legal persons and other entities

Legal persons and other entities must be represented in court (ERCP Rule 31). Again, this rule is widespread in Europe.[7]

According to Rule 31, the capacity to sue or to be sued includes legal persons, but also other entities if, under the applicable substantive law, the entity has the capacity to hold a right. These 'other entities' include trusts, partnerships and unincorporated associations, among others. In future, they may also include natural entities (eg, animals, trees) and technical entities (eg, robots), if they have legal capacity under substantive law (see Chapter 2). Substantive law will have to specify who is the representative of such entities or give power to the court to decide who may be such a representative.

This rule is generally found in EU Member States. For example, in Croatia, Section 81 of the Civil Procedure Code 2003 provides:

> The legal representative may undertake all procedural actions on behalf of the party. However, if separate regulations provide that a legal representative must have special authority to file or withdraw a complaint, admit or waive a claim, reach a settlement or undertake other procedural actions, he or she may undertake these actions only if he or she has been given such authority.

The victims of a mass tort may choose to become part of the same association which will represent them in court (this is called 'league of defence' in France). The compensation obtained through the lawsuit will benefit the victims, not the organization. However, a party may revoke a mandate at any time. For example, this form of co-mandate was used in the *AFER* case in France to recover misappropriated sums belonging to more than 55,000 victims.[8] An exclusive individual mandate was given to an association. The French Court of Cassation accepted the legality of this procedure, since the names of all individual principals were listed in the proceedings. This procedure presupposes that the victims are grouped together in an association. The disadvantage is that some victims may decide at any time to revoke the mandate and thus

---

7 For example, Bulgaria – Civil Procedure Code, Section 30(1); France – Civil Procedure Code, Article 117; Germany – Civil Procedure Code, Section 51, which provides: 'the ability of a party to appear before a court, the representation of parties having no capacity to sue or be sued by other persons (legal representatives), and the need for a special authorisation for the pursuit of court proceedings are determined pursuant to the stipulations of civil law'; Italy – Civil Procedure Code, Section 75(3); Latvia – Civil Procedure Code, Section 82(2); Sweden – Civil Procedure Code, Chapter 11, Section 2(2).

8 Cass Crim, 20 May 2015, No 14-81147; and Y.M. Serinet, '*L'affaire Afer et la voie du "co-mandat"*', *JCP* 2019, No 657.

weaken the operation. Furthermore, the association itself must be represented by a natural person in accordance with its statutes.

1.3 General rules on representation

The court may, at any time in the proceedings, order a representative to prove the existence or scope of his or her power to act (ERCP Rule 32). This rule may apply to the representation of a legal or natural person. This rule is common to all EU Member States, but with some nuances. In Austria, Section 4(1) of the Civil Procedure Code specifies: 'unless the power of representation is obvious.' In Croatia, Section 81(2) of the Civil Procedure Code provides:

> The person appearing as a legal representative shall, at the court's request, prove that he or she is a legal representative. When special authority is required for undertaking particular procedural actions, the legal representative shall prove that he or she has been given such authority.[9]

The court may ask for proof of the power of attorney in case of doubt. Rule 32 applies only to representation according to Rule 31, not to representation by a lawyer, and is a supplement to the more general Rule 33, which permits the court to verify compliance with these rules, on its own motion if necessary.

Rule 33 reflects national civil procedure rules – in particular, Section 6(1) of Austria's Civil Procedure Code and Section 83 of Croatia's Civil Procedure Code, which provides as follow:

> When the court establishes that the legal representative of a person who has a legal guardian does not exercise sufficient care in representation, it shall inform the guardianship body about it. If the representative's failure to act may result in damage for that person, the court shall hold the proceedings and propose that another legal representative be designated.

Section 82 further provides:

> In the course of the whole proceedings the court shall, *sua sponte*, pay attention to whether the person appearing as a party may actually be a party in the proceedings, whether he or she has litigation capacity, whether the party who lacks litigation capacity is represented by his or her legal representative.[10]

---

[9] See also Germany – Civil Procedure Code, Section 56(1); Finland – Civil Procedure Code, Chapter 12, Section 5; Sweden – Civil Procedure Code, Chapter 11, Section 4.

[10] Also France – Civil Procedure Code, Article 120: 'The judge may raise *sua sponte* the nullity due to lack of capacity to sue or to be sued'; Germany – Civil Procedure Code, Section 56: '(1) The court is to take account *ex officio* of any lack in

Although explicitly forbidden in some EU Member States (eg, Belgium), an *ex officio* review seems to be the prevailing concept in Europe and modifies to some extent the general principle of party disposition. ERCP Rule 33 also provides a broad discretion for courts to take the necessary steps in order to protect a party who lacks litigation capacity and has no representative as yet (Rule 30(3)). In such a situation, the court may appoint a representative or take other steps to ensure representation and stay the proceedings until a representative has been appointed.

2. INTERVENTION TO HELP A PARTY OR THE JUDGE

Intervention is a widely accepted concept, whether voluntarily or compulsorily (by notice), and the essential principles have been discussed in Chapter 3. Intervention can be used as the basis for a form of mass or 'representative' action – for example, where a group of victims of a mass harm event intervenes in support of an entity which is claiming compensation on behalf of other victims of the same event or, conversely, when an association intervenes in support of a mass claim. The concept of *amicus curiae* is not an intervention in support, again as noted in Chapter 3. It is intended to help the court to adjudicate the case, not to assist a party.

2.1 Intervention in support

Intervention in support (or accessory intervention) may be found in many European states.[11] Accessory intervention permits a party who is originally not a party to the action to intervene in support of one of the parties whose success (or failure) in the pending action affects the interests or the legal position of the intervening party. In practice, intervention in support is used in mass litigation

terms of the capacity to be a party to court proceedings, of the capacity to sue and be sued, of the legitimisation of a legal representative, and of the required authorisation to pursue legal proceedings'; and Hungary – Civil Procedure Code, Section 50.

[11] Austria – Civil Procedure Code, Sections 17, 19; Bulgaria – Civil Procedure Code, Section 218 (the intervenor has an interest in a decision); Croatia – Civil Procedure Code, Section 206: 'A person who has a legal interest that one of the parties succeeds in litigation pending between other persons, may join that party'; France – Civil Procedure Code, Article 330 ('Intervention will be accessory where it supports the claims of a party. It will be admissible where its originator, in order to preserve his rights, has an interest in supporting that party'); Germany – Civil Procedure Code, Section 66; Greece – Civil Procedure Code, Articles 80, 83; Hungary – Civil Procedure Code, Section 54; Italy – Civil Procedure Code, Section 105; Latvia – Civil Procedure Code, Section 80; Switzerland – Federal Civil Procedure Code, Section 74.

by organizations which are not victims, but have an interest in the action. For example, in proceedings before the French civil courts for compensation for damage suffered by one or more consumers for acts which do not constitute a criminal offence, consumer associations may act jointly (intervention in support) to obtain compensation for any event causing direct or indirect damage to the collective interests of consumers.[12] The public prosecutor is often an intervenor in support in mass litigation, as we note in more detail in Section 3.2. These organizations may have been contacted by the victims, but do not want to assume the financial responsibility of a class action. The individual victims bring a joint action and the organization acts in support without claiming compensation.

The consequences of such an intervention differ across Europe (see Chapter 3). In France[13] and Bulgaria,[14] the intervenor becomes a party to the action and the judgment has binding effect on him or her. However, since the intervention in support is accessory to the main claim, the intervenor may participate in an appeal procedure or second appeal procedure (*cassation*) only if the supported party brings an appeal and a second appeal. Nevertheless, the intervenor may bring an appeal alone if the opposite party does not contest it (the judge has no power to dismiss this appeal). In other EU Member States, the intervenor does not become a party to the litigation, but he or she can act in the interest of the supported party or even take over the presentation of the case. The court will not decide on the alleged claim of the supported party against the intervenor. Nevertheless, the final judgment has a particular binding effect on the intervenor.[15] This effect becomes relevant only in a subsequent litigation between the supported party and the intervenor. In order to avoid rather complex rules on the special binding effect of the judgment between the parties on the intervenor, ERCP Rule 42 assumes that the intervenor in support becomes a party to the litigation.

Some national rules permit intervention in support at any time until the end of the trial (eg, Belgium, France, Germany), whereby the intervenors take the case as they find it. This has been adopted as a general principle in ERCP Rule 40(1). As the court must decide on the application to intervene in any event

---

12 French Consumer Code, Section 3: Joint action and court intervention chapter on consumer action.

13 French Civil Procedure Code, Articles 331–33.

14 Bulgarian Civil Procedure Code, Section 223.

15 Austria, Supreme Court JBl 1997, 368; Germany – Civil Procedure Code Sections 72–74, 68; Hungary – Civil Procedure Code, Sections 58–60; Italy – Civil Procedure Code, Sections 106, 167(2), 272; Sweden – Civil Procedure Code, Chapter 14, Section 12; Switzerland – Federal Civil Procedure Code, Sections 80, 77.

(Rule 41), it may weigh the pros and cons of an intervention even at the appellate level of the proceedings.

Furthermore, it is common ground that intervenors in support must accept the procedural situation as it is at the time of intervention. They cannot contradict the position already taken by the supported party and therefore, the intervenor cannot take procedural actions which contradict the acts of the supported party.[16]

It is a common concept that an intervention in support of one of the parties must be admitted by the court.[17] Therefore, a formal application is necessary and the parties must be notified. 'Notice' as used in Rule 41(1) means formal service on the parties. The court should hear the parties before it decides on the application of the intervenor. If the requirements of Rule 40(1) are not met, intervention shall be denied. If there is a dispute over the admissibility of the intervention, the proceedings should not be delayed and the court may continue with the proceedings in order to avoid misuse.

Rules 40 and 41 adopt a system according to which the third party becomes a regular party to the proceedings and can be subject to a *res judicata* decision with respect to the claim against him or her. Therefore, a third-party notice must fulfil the requirements of a document instituting the proceedings and formal service of third-party notice is necessary.

2.2 *Amicus Curiae*: a friend to the court

The ERCP rules authorise a third-party to provide the court with submissions concerning important 'public interest' issues of a case. American Law Institute (ALI)/UNIDROIT Principle 13 is a model rule in this matter. It provides:

> Written submissions concerning important legal in the proceeding and matters of background information may be received from third persons with the consent of the court, upon consultation with the parties. The court may invite such a submission. The parties must have the opportunity to submit written comment addressed to the matters contained in such a submission before it is considered by the court.

This procedural device is widespread in common law and international litigation (there are longstanding traditions in the United States, Canada and the

---

16 For example, Germany – Civil Procedure Code, Section 67; Greece – Civil Procedure Code, Section 82; Switzerland – Federal Civil Procedure Code, Section 76-2.

17 Austria – Civil Procedure Code, Sections 18, 434; France – Civil Procedure Code, Article 330.

United Kingdom, and it is also developing in other countries.[18] A distinction may be drawn between *amicus curiae* (who speak for themselves only, but in the public interest) and US *parens patriae* suits (where the person indeed acts as a 'representative' of the public interest and claims damages for those harmed within his or her state).[19] Attorneys-general often fill both roles, although not in the same case.

An *amicus curiae* may be considered as a kind of intervenor, since it is a third party which participates in the proceedings. However, the *amicus curiae* does not become a party. It is not a kind of expert or witness, since the *amicus curiae* participates in the lawsuit not to establish evidence, but rather to give a statement or advice on the issue.

Rule 43 permits 'entities' to act as *amicus curiae.* These include unincorporated public or private organizations, non-governmental organizations and other interest groups, and public regulators, ombudsmen and so on. Since the concept of 'entities' has been interpreted in Chapter 2 as also able to designate natural entities, it is theoretically possible that a natural entity (or a set of natural entities) may be *amicus curiae.* It is hard to imagine how this would happen in practice, except in the form of an environmental organization on behalf of natural entities. However, in this situation the organization will be considered the *amicus curiae* itself. In time, a natural entity such as a river might – through an appropriate representative – be able to act as *amicus curiae* in a mass claim brought by victims of pollution (eg, worshippers of the Ganges river).

3. SUBSTITUTION OF PARTIES

Two kinds of procedural substitution of parties are provided for in the ERCP rules: when bringing the original action or to change a party during the proceedings. The former may be used in mass litigation, since a substitute may bring a single action instead of many victims.

---

18 For example, France – Statute of 18 November 2016, Article 38; Code of Judicial Organization, Article L431-3-1 (only before the Court of Cassation).

19 *Louisiana v Texas*, 176 US 1 (1900) and in antitrust law in favour of victims, 15 US Code § 15c: 'Actions by state attorneys general: (a) Parens patriae; monetary relief; damages; prejudgment interest (1) Any attorney general of a State may bring a civil action in the name of such State, as parens patriae on behalf of natural persons residing in such State, in any district court of the United States having jurisdiction of the defendant, to secure monetary relief as provided in this section for injury sustained by such natural persons to their property by reason of any violation of sections 1 to 7 of this title.'

3.1 Substitution when commencing an action

The concept of substitutive action (in German: *Prozesstanschaft*) was developed by Joseph Kohler in Germany at the end of the nineteenth century. He defined it as the power of a person to exercise in justice the civil law of another individual on whom the effects of the action fall.[20] In German law, there are specific substitutive actions, but not a general rule which could, for example, allow class action. E. Garbagnati developed the idea in Italian law[21] and this concept was enshrined in Article 81 of the Italian Code of Civil Procedure:[22]

'Procedural substitution. *Apart from the cases provided for by law*, no one may exercise in justice the right of others in his own name.'

The principle is therefore that everyone exercises his or her own rights, and that a law is needed to ensure that this is not the case in exceptional cases.[23] The Italian text refers to the right of others. It does not seem impossible to qualify a natural entity as 'another'; it is even the 'other' of man *par excellence.*

The rule that claimants can bring an action based only on their own substantive rights is a basic principle in many European civil procedure codes – although often without an explicit rule in this respect. Actions for collective redress are an exception to the rule; but there are also other situations in which procedural or substantive law may exceptionally allow an action in one entity's name, but based on the claim of another person. Rule 31 therefore refers to the ERCP rules on collective redress (Part XI, Section 2) as an exception from the principle laid down in this rule.

Furthermore, insurance law, trust law and rules under substantive law permitting derivative actions (which are substitutive actions) can also provide exceptions.[24] Such actions, promoted by the European Commission, are also possible under labour law: a trade union may bring action in the place of employees who are in such a weak situation that they dare not bring action

---

20 J. Kohler, '*Über die Succession in das Processverhältnis*' (1894), in *Gesammelte Beiträge zum Zivilprozess*, (Ahlen 1969 reprint), p 296: '*ein civilistisches Verhältnis der einen Person zum Civilrecht einer anderen Kraft welchen Verhältinisses es der einer Person zusteht einen Prozess zu führen, dessen civilistische Folgen auf die andere Person fallen.*'

21 E. Garbagnati, *La sostituzione processuale*, 1942; Italian Civil Procedure Code, Section 81.

22 Emphasis added. The original reads: '*Sostituzione processuale. Fuori dei casi expressamente previsti dalla legge, nessuno puo fare valere nel processo in nome proprio un diritto altrui.*'

23 '*Action de substitution*/Substitutive action' (bilingual) in: E. Jeuland and S. Lalani, *Lexicographical Research on Civil Procedure* (IRJS, 2017), p 25.

24 Italy – Civil Procedure Code, Section 81 (general rule); France – Civil Code Article 1341-1 '*action oblique*', and Insurance Code, Article L121-12.

themselves (eg, employees who have been harassed or discriminated against).[25] A collective substitutive action is possible where the trade union brings the action in the place of numerous employees. There is no need for an express mandate, but the trade union must keep the employees informed during the course of the proceedings.[26]

Derivative actions are brought by a minority of stockholders against the representatives of a company which commit fault or infringement. They exist in many European states, such as Germany and France;[27] as well as England,[28] where this rule:

> applies to a derivative claim where a company, other body corporate or trade union is alleged to be entitled to claim a remedy, and a claim is made by a member of it for it to be given that remedy.[29]

Where an action brought by someone other than the owner of the claim is based only on an agreement between the two, the requirements under national law vary. Some require that the claimant have either a legal interest or at least a substantial economic interest in bringing an action in the interests of another person. For example, the activities of debt collection agencies are often a controversial issue in some European states. Details of limits on substitution in these circumstances can be left to substantive law. In any case, there must be safeguards in place to prevent the general owner of the claim from authorizing a third party who has insufficient financial resources to meet an adverse costs order.

The basic position under the ERCP is that persons with litigation capacity must bring proceedings in their own name and on the basis of their own substantive rights (Rule 34), unless either Part XI or the substantive law permits otherwise.

The procedural regime of the act of substitution is quite simple. The substitute becomes a party as claimant or defendant. Service of documents is made to him or her personally or at his or her domicile. He or she performs all procedural acts on his or her own behalf.

Where natural entities are collectives (eg, bees, flocks of birds), the technique of collective redress action will be appropriate, since the substitute – the

---

[25] France – Labour Code, Articles L1144-2, L7423-2, L8255-1, L1251-59, L1253-16, L1247-1, L8233-1 and L1134-2 (discrimination).

[26] French Cass soc, 1 February 2000: *Bull civ* 2000, V, Nos 52 and 53; *Procédures* 2000, No 128, Sportouch; *JCP* G 2001, II, 10451, Jeuland.

[27] French Commercial Code, Article L225-120 '*action ut singuli*'.

[28] England and Wales Companies Act 2006, Part 11; Civil Procedure Rules, 19.9.

[29] A. Zuckerman, *Zuckerman on Civil Procedure*, 3rd edn (Sweet & Maxwell, 2013) paras 13.14–13.26.

qualified claimant – will act for an indeterminate group of victims who do not become parties. Remedies must be adapted to these 'victims': restoration and an end to pollution seem to be acceptable solutions. It is logical that reparation should be in kind, rather than in the form of financial compensation.

It is not certain whether legislation will always be necessary to achieve this result, since case law authorizes a trustee to act for a trust.[30] A collective of natural entities could be said to be the beneficiaries of the compensation 'fund' being claimed. A statute would no doubt be needed to facilitate and simplify any development of case law on this point; but – unlike the creation of a 'legal person' – it would not lead to a distortion of categories. The boundaries between natural and human beings would be respected by including the former within the symbolic space of the trial without making them a part of it.

So: is a class action a kind of representation or a kind of substitution?

If it is a kind of representation, group members in a class action will become parties to the (civil) litigation. In contrast, if it is a kind of substitution, they will not become parties. The difficulty stems from a concept of 'representation' which – for the historical reasons noted above – is wider in common law than it is in civil law. Consequently, the category of 'representative action' may encompass class actions in common law systems, but may not necessarily fit the notion of collective redress actions in civil law countries such as Spain, Brazil (see Chapter 14) and France. The expression 'representative action' is used in some European countries (eg, the Netherlands, Belgium and Norway) that are closer to the common law tradition than to southern countries. However, it creates some kind of confusion between a traditional representative action (by substitution) – where the represented person remains a party – and the new ERCP collective redress action.

We therefore avoided writing in the ERCP rules that collective redress actions are 'representative actions'.[31] So, under common law, it is possible to talk about 'representative action' in lieu of 'class action' – in a very wide sense. This is not the meaning used in the ERCP when mentioning 'representation', since in this situation, the owner of the right remains a party to the action. To be consistent and give only one meaning to the notion of 'representative action', we consider that it applies only to the situation where a party is represented in a civil action by another while also remaining a party to the proceedings himself or herself.

[30] Court of Appeal, Aix-en-Provence, 4 February 2004, RG No 98/5533, LPA 12 October 2004, p 11, note Zulian.

[31] In Canada, Quebec: J.C. Gémar and V. Ho-Thuy, *Nouvelles difficultés du langage du droit au Canada* (Thémis, 2016), pp 488–91.

In a collective redress action, the person who brings the action is the party, while group members do *not* become parties. There is no 'representative' party, but rather a 'qualified entity' claimant. This analysis underpins the whole system of collective redress proceedings in the ERCP. This way of thinking also allows us to have a collective redress regime which fits in with all European legal categories and hence is culturally acceptable.

However, there is an ongoing discussion to determine whether collective redress actions are substitutive actions in Italy[32] and in France;[33] and the point could also be debated in Germany.[34] The European Commission used the expression 'representative action' in its proposal for a Directive 'on *representative* actions for the protection for the collective interests of consumers' (11 April 2018), but stuck to the idea of a 'qualified entity' to bring the action, rather than the idea of a representative.[35] In the French version, '*action representative*' means an action in which the qualified claimant is an organization 'politically' representative in its field.

3.2 Substitution during the proceedings

ERCP Rule 44 deals with voluntary substitution (eg, where a claimant discovers that he has sued the wrong defendant) or where a claimant is not the proper party (eg, where the director of a company brings the company's action in her own name).

In many EU Member States (eg, France and Belgium), the substitution of a person who is not a proper party is not possible (or traditionally was not

---

[32] R. Caponi, '*Litisconsorzio "aggregato" L'azione risarcitoria in forma collettiva dei consumatori*', *Rivista trimestrale di diritto e procedura civile*, 2008, p 819, No 14. R. Caponi's idea is that a qualified association to bring the class action is a formal party, not the real party, so it has no extraordinary standing to bring the action. Other Italian scholars analyse the Italian class action (Article 140) as a substitutive action (Briguglio, '*L'azione collective resarcitoriia, risposta n 1. Più cauta sul punto la posizione di Consolio*', in Consoliao, Bona and Buzzelli, *Obiettivo class action: l'azione resarcitoria collettiva* (Ipsoa, 2008), VI, 4).

[33] See E. Jeuland, '*Substitution ou représentation? À propos du projet d'action de groupe*', *JCP Générale* No 37, 9 September 2013, 927; E. Jeuland, '*Retour sur la qualification de l'action de groupe à la lumière de la loi "justice du XXI° siècle"*', *JCP* 2017, 354.

[34] German Civil Procedure Code, Sections 51 to 54 on *Processstandschaft* could be understood as a mechanism of substitution (the idea of the German scholar Kohler – see Section 3.1 and n 17).

[35] Proposal for a directive of the European Parliament and of the Council on representative actions for the protection of the collective interests of consumers, and repealing Directive 2009/22/EC, COM(2018) 184, 11 April 2018.

possible)[36] before the final judgment. The final judgment will usually find that the claim was wrongly addressed. In other states (eg, the United Kingdom and Germany), it is possible to substitute the wrong party by the proper party as soon as the mistake is discovered. In many cases the substitution may be subject to the other party's consent or the permission of the court. This solution avoids delay and, for this reason, was proposed in a recent report in France to simplify and accelerate proceedings (January 2018) and eventually included in the Decree of 11 December 2019.[37]

Where substantive law or other procedural rules *require* a substitution (eg, insolvency law), the court may not normally deny the substitution (as set out in ERCP Rule 44(1)). In all other cases, the court must decide on the substitution in accordance with Rule 44(2). Normally, the proceedings are not suspended; but it may be necessary for the new substitute parties to be given some time to properly prepare their case. The court may grant a delay before resuming the proceedings.

ALI/UNIDROIT Principle 12.3 provides that: 'When appropriate, the court should grant permission for a person to be substituted for, or to be admitted in succession to a party.' This voluntary substitution exists, for example, in Sections 61 to 65 the Hungarian Civil Procedure Code and in English Civil Procedure Rule 19.2. Professor Zuckerman specifies that the substitution of parties in the United Kingdom must be 'necessary', in the sense that without it, the claim could not properly be carried on by or against the original party. The substitution may be refused by the court if the new party is deprived of an 'accrued limitation defence'.[38]

4. SUCCESSION AND ASSIGNMENT OF CLAIMS

ERCP Rule 44 deals with succession of parties during the proceedings:

> At any time after proceedings are commenced the Court must permit the substitution or the succession of a party by another person where the law requires it. At any time after proceedings are commenced the Court may permit the substitution or the succession of a party by another person if that is necessary in the interest of the good administration of justice.

---

36 For example, in France before the Decree of 11 December 2019.

37 Decree 2019-1333 of 11 December 2019 reforming the civil procedure, OJRF No 0288, 12 December 2019.

38 A. Zuckerman, *Civil Procedure* (LexisNexis, 2002), para 12.9.

This rule deals with the succession of parties due to the assignment of claims and transfer of a debt during the proceedings, the death of a party, the loss of capacity to litigate or insolvency.

The route of assignment may be used for mass claims before the commencement of proceedings, rather than during the course of proceedings. It is more flexible than a subrogation, which would presuppose a fixed sum (eg, an insurance company is subrogated in the rights of the victim after indemnification).

The Court of Justice of the European Union's (CJEU) *Courage v Crehan* judgment[39] made it clear that the full effectiveness of Article 101 of the Treaty on European Union and the effectiveness of the prohibition of cartels would be called into question if any person could not claim compensation for damage caused to him or her by a contract or by conduct liable to restrict or distort competition.

C. Evrard and F. Gordon write to this effect:[40]

> actions for compensation of victims of anti-competitive practices are becoming a reality in Europe, a reality that cartel participants can no longer ignore in the analysis of their risks, but also as a new legal issue, revisiting certain traditional notions of substance and procedure, in a context of competition between the legal systems of the Member States ... We must first observe the quantitative development of these liability disputes, marked by the preponderance of follow-on actions (follow-on actions, which follow the sanction by a competition authority of the practice presented by the plaintiff as causing the alleged damage), over stand-alone actions (stand-alone actions, which are not based on a prior decision by a competition authority, making it more complex for the plaintiff to prove fault in the action). Qualitatively, a few cases appear to be emblematic of the rise of these indemnity actions.

Thus, the European Commission – having sanctioned an elevator cartel – itself brought an action before the Belgian courts for compensation for the damage that this cartel would have caused to the European institutions.[41]

However, this type of action presents the difficulty of access to the judge for individual victims, for reasons of proof or the small amount of their claims. It is therefore important to recognize the possibility of group actions in this area. Several companies and investment funds (eg, Cartel Damages Claim (CDC)) offer these alleged victims various options to pursue their right to compensation. These can go as far as taking assignment of the claim for compensation, whereby a special purpose vehicle (SPV) takes assignments of the individual

---

39 CJEU, 20 September 2001, Case C-453/9 [2001] ECR I-6297.

40 *Revue Lamy de la concurrence*, No 41, 1 October 2014.

41 CJEU, 6 November 2012, Case C-199/11, *Europese Gemeenschap v Otis* ECLI: EU:C:2012:684.

claims from several companies in order to exercise them itself by bringing an action in its own name.

This type of assignment of claims has caused difficulties in Germany, where a court of appeal required that the SPV obtain a licence to provide legal advice (requiring registration in the Legal Services Register) and have sufficient funds to comply, if necessary, with an adverse costs order.[42] The judgment has not been appealed, so this may be considered as a landmark case. The requirement to register is usually fulfilled by SPVs in Germany. The assignment of claims for debt collection (in contrast to factoring – the sale of a claim) is subject to a number of restrictions. For example, it is allowed only if the assignee bears the full financial risk of recovering the claims and has sufficient funds to cover the defendant's costs if necessary. The assignment of claims thus seems to be common in consumer law to pool small and medium-sized claims.

In France, the assignment of a claim appears theoretically lawful, even though it remains to be seen how it could be used to obtain compensation for anti-competitive practices.[43] However, if the claim which is subject to assignment is already in litigation (ie, the proceedings have started), the debtor may obtain a release from the assignee by reimbursing the actual price paid for the assignment (under a rule called '*retrait litigieux*'). This rule aims to avoid speculative assignments.

In common law, the assignment of tort actions is traditionally prohibited, since these actions involve personal interests of the victims. In England, the rule against maintenance and champerty probably still applies (although with some modifications to allow commercial litigation funding).[44] In the United States, the assignment of contractual debts, but not tort claims, is lawful; but courts in some states have taken the contrary view and held that tort claims are assignable.[45] There is thus competition between legal systems, and actions

---

[42] Dusseldorf Court of Appeal, 18 February 2015, IV-U Kart 3/14, BeckRS 2015, 5317, confirming Dusseldorf Regional Court, 17 December 2013 CDC Case, 37 O 200/09 (Kart) U, NZKart 2014, 75.

[43] R. Amaro, *Le contentieux privé des pratiques anticoncurrentielles*, PhD, 2012, Nos 210 *et seq.*

[44] N. Andrews, *Contracts and English Dispute Resolution* (Jigakusha Japan, 2010), *Nagoya University Comparative Study of Civil Justice*, vol 5, No 5.25: 'certain rights of action are not assignable. There are four categories: (1) most tort actions' (which means not all tort actions – in particular, if there is no personal aspect in the tort action).

[45] Assignment of Claims Act, 1940, 31 USC § 3727, 41 USC § 15). Also *Comunale v Traders & General Ins Co* 328 P2d 198 (Cal 1958); *Optimal Strategic US Equity Ltd v SPV OSUS Ltd*, 2017 NY Slip Op 50284(U): Justice Scarpulla: 'The Assignment at issue in this case, like the assignment in the Banque Arabe case, does much more than assign to SPV all of OSUS's "rights, title and interest in and to the" Allowed Claim Section 1 (b) of the Assignment also transferred to SPV "all rights and benefits of

(also called private enforcement) are currently concentrated in the United Kingdom, using the group litigation tool (see Chapter 3); or in Germany and the Netherlands, using simple joinder.

Since Directive 2014/104/EU[46] aims to offer equivalent protection in all Member States by harmonizing the rules governing such actions, it is important that the technique of the SPV – a vehicle that redeems victims' compensation claims – be available in all Member States. It also guarantees access to the courts. In France, Article L481-2 of the Commercial Code allows liability actions to be based on the decision of the Competition Authority.

Vasil Savov, executive director of CDC, has asked the following question:

> Will we see an increase in the number of actions for damages before the French courts or will we continue to see the attractiveness of courts in other European Union Member States also for companies that have suffered damages in France? ... Clearly, companies can no longer ignore the existence of a right to compensation and will henceforth have to take into account, as part of their legal strategies, the recovery of potentially significant indemnity claims. In the case of injured companies in particular, certain difficulties inherent in litigation can be overcome, for example by opting to assign the claims to a specialised entity. This mechanism, whose effectiveness has been tested in several national courts, has also been recognised by the Damages Directive.[47]

The CJEU has handed down several decisions aimed at determining which judge was competent under the Brussels I Regulation in cases where a group assignment of compensation claims took place.[48] The issue was to determine which court had jurisdiction under the Brussels 1 Regulation. The CJEU did not challenge these SPVs in principle, however. Apparently, in the *CDC* case, the transfer was made without fixing a prior amount, but only a percentage of the future results.

Assignor *related to* the Purchased Claim, including . . . (ii) any action or claim . . . *of any nature whatsoever*, whether against the Debtor or any other party, arising out of or in connection with the Purchased Claim" (emphasis added). This language plainly includes third party tort claims, so long as the claims arise out of, or are in connection with, the Allowed Claim.'

[46] Directive 2014/104/EU of the European Parliament and of the Council of 26 November 2014 on certain rules governing actions for damages under national law for infringements of the competition law provisions of the Member States and of the European Union, OJ L 349, 5 December 2014, pp 1–19.

[47] *Contrats Concurrence Consommation* 7, July 2019, *alerte* 24, *Actions indemnitaires des pratiques anticoncurrentielle*.

[48] CJEU 25 January 2018, Case 498/16, *Schrems v Facebook* ECLI:EU:C:2018:37; 21 May 2015, Case 352/13, *Cartel Damage Claims (CDC) Hydrogen Peroxide SA v Akzo Nobel NV* ECLI:EU:C:2015:33; 29 July 2019, Case C-451/18, *Tibor-Trans Fuvarozó és Kereskedelmi Kft v DAF Trucks NV* ECLI:EU:C:2019:635.

In France, the cost of the assignment must be determined or determinable, which means in particular that the price may be determinable partly at the time of the assignment and partly at the time of collection.[49] A future receivable may, moreover, be assigned if it is determinable at the time it arises. Thus, if a claim for compensation has disappeared at the time of the assignment, assignment is not possible which, *e contrario*, implies that the assignment of a claim for compensation is possible if it exists at the time of the assignment and can be determined.

Finally, the assignment of a claim for compensation can be used in the absence of a group action for the victims of anti-competitive practices (for example) who cannot be qualified as consumers. It may also favour the proper administration of justice by scoping the procedure accurately for the court. In addition, this technique can help to avoid litigation by facilitating the conclusion of a global settlement agreement. Since the principle of the assignability of claims for compensation is accepted in the case of anti-competitive practices in most EU Member States, it is necessary to specify arrangements for its implementation.

The price of an indemnity claim cannot be known with certainty at the time of the assignment, even if, following a decision of the competition authority, the existence of the claim seems quite certain.

Several options may be considered in this regard. The first is an approximate price calculated on the basis of the competition authority's decision minus the assignee's commission and costs. This price is attractive, but risky for the assignee. And if the price is too low, there is a risk of an action for nullity for an illusory consideration.

The second is no price, just a percentage of the future result at the time of assessment of the loss. This percentage is itself calculated taking into account the assignee's costs and commission. This solution – which appears to have been adopted in Germany – is low-risk for the assignee, but low incentive for the assignor and may not create sufficient confidence to ensure the subsequent cooperation between the assignee and his or her assignors.

The third is a minimum price of (for example) €0.50 or €1 per claim, plus a percentage of the future result. This solution has the advantage of providing a greater incentive to the assignors without being too risky for the assignee. It corresponds to the practice of debt collection agencies.

The assignment of a claim presupposes formal requirements (in France at least) between the assignor and the assignee. The effectiveness of the assignment against the original debtor of the obligation being assigned derives from the fact that he or she has been notified of it or has taken note of it. If the debtor

---

49 French Court of Cassation, 7 April 2009, 07-18907.

has been notified of the assignment, or has taken note of it or accepted it, he or she validly discharges the debt by paying the assignee.

The debtor may raise the defences against the assignee which it could have raised against the assignor: set-off of related debts, defences inherent in the debt (whatever their date of origin) and defences arising from its relationship with the assignor prior to notification of the assignment. Some cooperation from the assignors might therefore be necessary during the subsequent litigation proceedings in the context of the deal in question.

5. OTHER PROCEDURAL TOOLS

Mass litigation cases linked to collective risks are now emerging and it is important to identify procedural forms to deal with them: filtering of claims, single judges, co-mandate, pilot judgment, class action or claim assignment. However, these developments must not be to the detriment of the search for truth and justice in each individual case. Mass litigation expresses a trend towards the industrialization of justice and the introduction of competition between judicial systems, to which other efficiency initiatives also respond. Current public sector management policy now requires judiciaries in Europe to deal with cases in reasonable time, with efficiency and proportionality.[50] The digitalization of proceedings has contributed to this streamlining. There are specific approaches of court management for mass claims litigation (in terms of courtroom process, communication and media). The new international business sections created in the courts of Paris, Amsterdam and Frankfurt are now dealing with international cases, which may include mass litigation.[51]

Test cases may be useful to bring a *de facto* class action (see Chapter 3). Where there are many victims, a first case may help to predict the outcome of future litigation. In common law, test cases establish legal rights or principles and may thereby serve as precedent for future similar cases. Test cases save the judicial system the time and expense of hearing each and every case that involves the same issue or issues. However, in civil law, where the rule of precedent does not apply, a test case may be only an 'authoritative precedent' (ie, a model which is not binding on other judges; even in England, a test case is usually not formally binding, although in practice it will be followed in similar cases).

---

[50] E. Jeuland (ed), *Court Management, Gestion du tribunal* (bilingual) (IRJS, 2019), including reports from England and Wales, the Netherlands, Spain, Chile, India and Argentina.

[51] X. Kramer and J. Sorabji (eds), *International Business Courts: A European and Global Perspective* (Eleven International Publishing, 2019).

In France, the development of the pilot judgment mechanism in the administrative tribunals has also made it possible to deal with a series of cases by judging only one of them (a French report on civil procedure in January 2018 suggested that this mechanism also be developed in the civil courts).[52] However, there is a risk that this technique will marginalize contentious litigation and focus on flow management, thus missing the mission of justice. The latter implies, for each individual claim, the use of techniques which require a minimum of procedural time face to face and in-depth evidence-based litigation.

In administrative litigation, the pilot judgment is a procedural means of dealing with mass litigation – that is, identical cases brought in large numbers before the same court.[53] A typical case is selected and treated as a priority by the rapporteur (not the parties). The court makes a decision and issues a pilot judgment. That judgment is then handed down in all other cases according to a rapid procedure, without debate and before a single judge, who merely reproduces the same reasoned assessment of the facts. An appeal is always possible and the judgment will not apply to other situations in the future; although it will apply to similar current situations and those which arose in the past. Moreover, the pilot judgment is not binding; it is rather a model that the single judge takes over if the circumstances are identical. The limitation of this procedure is that it applies only to cases already brought before the same court.

This pilot judgment procedure was also introduced before the European Court of Human Right (ECtHR) to relieve congestion in the docket.[54] It has made it possible to freeze almost 700 cases concerning excessive length of proceedings pending before the ECtHR. It is similar in effect to a group action when it comes to dealing with mass litigation. Many of the approximately 60,000 cases (2019) pending before the ECtHR are so-called 'repetitive cases', which derive from a common dysfunction at the national level.

The pilot judgment procedure was developed in the ECtHR as a technique for identifying the structural problems underlying repetitive cases against many countries and obliging those states to address those problems. A key feature of the pilot procedure is the possibility to adjourn, or 'freeze', related cases for a certain period, on condition that the government acts promptly to adopt the national measures required to satisfy the judgment. The ECtHR can resume examining adjourned cases whenever the interests of justice so require. Rule 61 of the ECtHR Rules of Court (February 2011) codifies the ECtHR's

---

52 N. Molfessis and F. Agostini, Ministry of Justice Report, January 2018.

53 Article R222-1 of the French Judicial Administrative Code.

54 ECtHR, 22 June 2004, *Broniowski v Poland*, 31443/96; ECtHR, 10 May 2011, 48059/06 and 2708/09, *Dimitrov and Hamanov v Bulgaria*; and ECtHR, 10 May 2011, 37346/05, *Finger v Bulgaria*, JCP G 2011, 660.

existing 'pilot judgment procedure', introduced for cases where there is a systemic or structural dysfunction in the country concerned which has given or could give rise to similar applications.[55]

Strong procedural safeguards are needed to ensure that these other cases are studied in their particular circumstances. A distinction must be drawn between mass litigation and serial litigation. Group actions are more likely to concern mass litigation than serial litigation. In the former case, a large group of victims has suffered similar damage (same cause of action) which may be of little individual importance. This procedure is more suited to situations where the victims are not in a position to act personally. Serial litigation involves victims who act before the court, but where the facts are similar rather than identical (eg, where the victims suffered the same kind of hospital-acquired condition, but not at the same time). It is therefore not a question of creating a group, but rather of organizing the work of the courts as well as possible in order to have a quality trial with a panel of judges.

A distinction should also be drawn between mass litigation which may give rise to a group action, serial litigation specific to the pilot judgment and what is also known as 'mass litigation' in the sense of specific litigation giving rise to numerous linked trials. In the latter case – for example, in the field of construction – one could imagine a system of collective mediation, such as exists in relation to traffic accidents in France.

Several procedural devices may be combined and new technologies may assist in dealing with 'serial' cases.[56] A platform may gather individual claims and then help victims to bring an action (eg, Weclaim and Myright in the *Dieselgate* litigation in Germany, the Netherlands and France). An SPV may be the assignee of claims in mass litigation. This SPV may choose to bring only one case in court to obtain a test or pilot judgment. This is procedurally lighter and may put pressure on the defendant to settle (since there may be individual actions for years or by groups). This is ultimately a matter of litigation strategy.

An organization that sets up an electronic platform may bring a class action. In the *Dieselgate* litigation, the foundation (*Stichting*) *Diesel Emission* gathered together, through an online platform, victims in France, Belgium and the Netherlands to bring a class action against Volkswagen in the Netherlands

---

[55] www.echr.coe.int/Documents/FS_Pilot_judgments_ENG.pdf (last accessed 10 October 2020).

[56] Christopher Hodges, 'Collective Redress: The Need for New Technologies', *Journal of Consumer Policy*, March 2019, Vol 42, Issue 1, pp 59–90.

(since the French class action is not available in such a situation).[57] Christopher Hodges adds:

> There are several other mechanisms that deliver collective redress—new technologies. The first is the *partie civile* mechanism in which a civil claim "piggy backs" onto a criminal conviction. The most important mechanisms are "regulatory redress"—where a regulatory authority intervenes and agrees or orders redress to be paid—especially if coupled with an ombudsman scheme (not arbitration-based alternative dispute resolution (ADR) schemes).[58]

At any rate, it seems that we need an effective collective redress mechanism in Europe.

---

[57] On 23 January 2020 the Foundation Diesel Emissions Justice initiated a class action in the Netherlands against Volkswagen. Affected car owners can register in France on the foundation's website www.emissionsjustice.com/en_fr/ (last accessed 23 January 2020). See S. Mandard, '"*Dieselgate": première action collective en France contre Volkswagen' Le Monde* (Paris, 23 January 2020), www.lemonde.fr/planete/article/2020/01/23/dieselgate-une-action-collective-europeenne-lancee-contre-volkswagen_6026899_3244.html (last accessed 23 January 2020).

[58] See n 54.

5. Introduction: collective redress

Astrid Stadler, Emmanuel Jeuland and Vincent Smith

1. ERCP COLLECTIVE REDRESS IN CONTEXT

Part XI of the European Rules on Civil Procedure (ERCP) provides more than 30 rules on collective proceedings, including some rudimentary provisions on costs and common cross-border issues. In contrast to many other parts of the European Law Institute (ELI)/UNIDROIT project, there is no equivalent to Part XI in the American Law Institute/UNIDROIT principles, which did not touch on the subject of collective redress. Nevertheless, we did not have to start from scratch. On the contrary, since the 2000s, there has been an intense academic and practitioner debate on the subject, and an increasing number of Member States have decided to enact new procedural instruments and rules for mass harm situations. We took into account the existing proposals at the European level, but above all the newly implemented instruments in the Member States and proposed legislation act in Switzerland. At a later stage, the EU draft directive on a representative action in the interests of consumers was also considered, but it did not lead to substantial changes to Part XI as then drafted.

Between 2002 and 2010, some of the smaller EU Member States (Italy, Poland and Bulgaria) – following the example of the Nordic countries (Sweden, Denmark, Finland and Norway) – introduced representative actions or group actions for the recovery of damages, but with a broad range of different features. In 2013, after years of discussions, the European Commission – in an effort to harmonize the legal landscape of group or class actions – published a Recommendation that suggested that the Member States should implement instruments of collective redress into their national systems.[1] Its non-binding character was the result of a highly controversial political debate at the European level which was characterized by strong lobbying from the business sector against anything that looked like a US class action.

[1] European Commission Recommendation 2013/396.

Five years later, in 2018, the situation in Europe was far from a harmonization of collective redress. The European Commission kept a note of the ongoing reforms in the Member States:[2] none had fully 'implemented' the 2013 Recommendation, but several had cut their own path.[3] In particular, the United Kingdom, France and Belgium had implemented new instruments of collective redress – mainly in the areas of consumer protection and competition law. Lithuania, Hungary and Slovenia followed suit; and in March 2019, a draft for a new collective redress action with a broad scope of application was adopted by the Dutch Parliament.[4] In April 2018, the European Commission presented its current initiative, called 'New Deal for Consumers', and issued a bundle of new proposals to improve the situation of consumers and the enforcement of consumer rights. The proposal for a directive on representative actions in the collective interests of consumers[5] takes the Injunctions Directive of 2009

---

2 Study on the State of Collective Redress in the EU in the context of the implementation of the Commission Recommendation, https://ec.europa.eu/newsroom/just/item-detail.cfm?item_id=612847 (last accessed 10 August 2020).

3 Belgium: 2014: '*L'action en réparation collective*' [*Livre* XVII, *Titre* 2 *Code de droit économique*]; Bulgaria: Code of Civil Procedure, Chapter 33, Articles 379–88); Denmark: Law 181 of 28 February 2007, Sections 254a–k, Administration of Justice Act); England and Wales: Consumer Act 2015, Schedule 8 and Competition Act 1998), Section 47B; France: Law 2014–344 of 17 March 2014 and Decree 2014–1081 of 24 September 2014, which inserted Articles L423–1 to L423–32 and R623–1 to R623–33 into the Consumer Code [*Titre* II, *Chapitre* III]; Law 2016-41 of 26 January 2016; and Decree 2016-1249 of 28 September 2016 (which inserted Articles L1143–1 to L1143–22, R1143–1 to R1143–11 and R1526–1 of the Public Health Code); Finland: Class Action Act (444/2007); Germany: Sections 606–14 of the Civil Procedure Code as of 1 November 2018; Hungary: Civil Procedure Code 2 December 2016, MK 2016 190 p 7878, Part 8, Chapter XLII; Italy:'*Azione di Classe*', introduced by Article 140*bis* of the Consumer Code by Law 244 of 24 December 2007, and subsequently amended by Law 99 of 23 July 2009, and Law 27 of 24 March 2012); Lithuania: Articles 441–1 to 441–17 of the Code of Civil Procedure; Norway: Chapter 35 of the Act relating to Mediation and Procedure in Civil Disputes 2008 ('Disputes Act')); Poland: 2010 – Law of 17 December 2009 (*Diziennik Ustaw* no 7 pos 4); Portugal: Law 83/95; Law 24/96); Spain: Article 11 [2] of the Civil Procedure Code 2001); Slovenia: Law on Collective Actions, *Official Journal of the Rep of Slovenia* 51/2017 (*Zakon o kolektivnih tožbah* (ZkolT)), in force since March 2018; Sweden: 2003: Group Proceedings Act, SFS 2002:599; Switzerland: Tentative Draft (March 2018), Article 89a of the Swiss Code of Civil Procedure.

4 An English translation of the new Dutch Bill is available at www.houthoff.com/doc/English_translation-Bill_on_Redress_of_Mass_Damages_in_a_collective_action.pdf (last accessed 10 August 2020).

5 Proposal for a directive of the European Parliament and the of the Council on representative actions for the protection of the collective interests of consumers, and repealing Directive 2009/22/EC, available at: https://eur-lex.europa.eu/legal-content/EN/TXT/?uri=COM:2018:184:FIN (last accessed 10 August 2020).

as a starting point and further specifies that representative entities such as consumer associations should be in a position to sue traders on behalf of consumers not only for injunctive relief, but also for any other redress – including damages. The proposal met with criticism in the European Parliament. In March 2019, a revised version was published with a number of major changes and the European Council adopted a 'general approach' in November 2019, proposing some modifications to the Parliament and Commission's proposal. The proposal is now in the 'trilogue' phase and is expected to be voted on by the European Parliament in December 2020.[6]

The European Commission's proposal of April 2018 deviates to some extent from the Recommendation of 2013. The scope of application is much narrower and covers only consumer law (most likely so as not to provoke a challenge of the European legislature's competence). For consumer law, it is clear that the Commission has the power to propose EU legislation; but that is far from being clear for general civil procedure law – particularly for domestic cases without a cross-border element. The narrow scope of application also appears to be a strategic move for the European Commission. In order to improve the chances of acceptance, the proposal for a representative action is presented as an amendment of the Injunctions Directive of 2009,[7] which was well accepted and implemented in the Member States. As a consequence, the scope of application, the question of legal standing and the main structure of the new EU collective redress instrument build on the Injunctions Directive.

The following chapters in this book will not only deal with the ELI/UNIDROIT rules on collective redress, but also compare them to the final proposal at the European level and to national law in the Member States and beyond.

---

[6] As of 10 March 2020; www.europarl.europa.eu/legislative-train/theme-area-of-justice-and-fundamental-rights/file-representative-actions-for-consumers (last accessed 10 August 2020). The latest version of 30 June 2020 is available at www.consilium.europa.eu/media/44766/st09223-en20.pdf (last accessed 10 August 2020); a four-column document comparing the different draft versions is available at https://data.consilium.europa.eu/doc/document/ST-6759-2020-INIT/en/pdf (last accessed 10 August 2020).

[7] Directive 2009/22 EC [2009] OJEU L 110.

2. THE COLLECTIVE REDRESS RULES WITHIN THE ELI/UNIDROIT PROJECT

2.1 Structure and terminology

The chapter on collective redress in the ELI/UNIDROIT project (Part XI, 'Collective Proceedings') includes 35 rules and is divided into four sections. Section I contains only two rules (Rules 204 and 205), and deals with injunctions in the collective interest. As injunctive relief was not considered an instrument of collective redress in a narrow sense,[8] a separate section was established for these rules. The following Sections II–IV (Rules 207–38) have an introductory part (Part A), which includes a definition of 'collective redress proceedings' (Rule 207), requirements to be fulfilled by claimants (Rules 208–09) and requirements for the collective redress claim to be filed with the court (Rules 210–11).

Part B deals with the certification stage of the proceedings (Rules 212–13). It defines the conditions for the admissibility of collective redress actions, the types of actions available and the relation between collective claims and individual claims (Rules 215–17). Part C concerns the case management powers of the court and the establishment of an electronic platform for communication between the court and parties, group members and the public (Rules 218–20). Part D includes rules on settlements in collective redress actions already commenced, with a focus on how to obtain court approval of the proposed settlement (Rules 221–26).

Part E is a short chapter on judgments which supplements the general rules on judgments of the Model Rules[9] (Rules 227–28). Part F deals with standalone proceedings for obtaining court approval of a collective settlement negotiated outside pending collective actions (Rules 229–32). Last, but not least, there are some rudimentary rules on cross-border situations (Section III, Rules 233–36) and on costs (Section IV, Rules 237–38), which supplement the general chapter on costs in Part XII of the ERCP.

Some terminology points. Part XI deviates to some extent from common English language legal terms and needs some explanation. First, all participants in the project tried to avoid using English legal terminology where it is closely linked to particular procedural instruments or has particular connotations. In the collective redress part, therefore, the term 'class action' has been avoided throughout the text. Moreover, the text does not use the term 'representative' to describe the lead plaintiff or the representative of the group, to avoid causing

---

8 For details, see Chapter 6.

9 Part VII, 'Judgment, *res judicata* and *lis pendens*'.

confusion in the French civil procedure system. Instead, the ERCP collective redress rules refer to the 'qualified claimant' to describe the entity or person that is entitled to bring a collective action. Although US-style terminology has been avoided in the black-letter rules and comments, the following chapters of this book will compare the ERCP with US class action provisions and court practice. European courts can especially benefit from experience of judges in traditional class action countries such as the United States, but also Australia and Canada, when scrutinizing and approving mass settlements

2.2 Three pillars of collective redress

The mainstream in collective redress, as it emerged from a comparative European approach, led us to identify three main developments and to draft three 'pillars' of collective redress. First, a great number of EU Member States have put in place a collective instrument for the consumer recovery of damages or for other redress, such as reimbursement or reduction of the sales price, repair and so on. An important exception to this approach is provided under German law, where the legislature was forced to react to the Volkswagen *Dieselgate* scandal and provide at least 'something' in order to help diesel car owners and lessees to enforce their claims against Volkswagen. Eventually, due to very successful lobbying of the German business sector, a representative action for declaratory relief was enacted in November 2018.[10] According to the new rules, consumer associations can apply for a court declaration confirming that a trader or service provider is liable in principle to pay compensation, or for a binding declaration of certain factual or legal issues relating to the defendant's liability. Then, in a second step, it is up to consumers or victims of a mass tort to sue the defendant individually for the recovery of damages based on the declaratory judgment. The concept of ERCP collective redress includes, as a main remedy, a collective redress action for the recovery of damages (compensation) or for a declaratory judgment (Rules 207–20; 228).

Furthermore, it includes as a second and third pillar a mechanism of declaring a mass settlement entered into by the parties to a *pending* collective redress action binding (Rules 221–26) and a parallel 'standalone' mechanism for a collective settlement entered into outside a collective action (Rules 229–32). National legislatures across Europe have emphasized that a collective settlement is often the best way to handle mass harm events, to provide a quick solution for group of victims or consumers and spare the judicial system complex and lengthy proceedings. In particular, the calculation of damages in a mass claim situation can overburden courts if they need to go into the details

---

[10] Sections 606–14 of the German Civil Procedure Code.

of each individual claim. Settlements are therefore a preferred instrument once the defendant's liability has become undisputed, as they allow the consolidation into a lump sum for the whole group or for sub-groups of the aggrieved persons. Even where no mass settlement can be reached, collective redress instruments must provide courts with more flexibility regarding the calculation of damages. Details are discussed in Chapter 10.

Dutch law was the first in Europe to offer the possibility of a court decision which declares binding a collective settlement (without an action pending) negotiated between an organization representing the victims of a mass harm event and the undertaking allegedly responsible for the harm. Since 2005, a number of very big international securities cases have been resolved through this Dutch mechanism.[11] The Dutch legislature has thus set a precedent for other Member States. The United Kingdom,[12] France[13] and Slovenia[14] have more or less copied the instrument since 2014;[15] and so did we for the ELI/UNIDROIT project. Declaring a settlement binding before needing to initiate contentious court proceedings may become an important tool in practice in cases where potential defendants admit that they are liable in principle and want to get the mass harm 'off their books' as soon as possible.[16]

However, experience in the Netherlands since the entry into force of the Collective Settlement Act in 2005[17] teaches us that 'standalone' mechanisms to declare settlements binding are not sufficient to establish an effective system of private enforcement. Only if representative entities or victims of a mass harm event are also in a position to start court proceedings will those who are

---

[11] *Stichting Vie d'Or* (2009) LJN BI2717; *Shell Petroleum v Dexia Nederland* (2009) LJN BI5744; *Stichting uitvoering Vedior schikking* (2009) LJN BJ269; *Stichting Converium Securities Compensation v Liechtensteinsche Landesbank*, 12 November 2010 LJN BO3908 and 17. 1.2012, LJN BV1026; Fortis case ECLI:NL:GHAMS:2018:2422. Some of these were big international securities cases and settled for hundreds of millions of US dollars. In some of them, investors domiciled in Europe had not been admitted by US courts to US securities class actions and therefore needed a mechanism in Europe to settle the dispute on a global scale.

[12] England/Wales Consumer Rights Act 2015, Section 49B, Competition Act 1998 and Competition Act 1998, Section 49C (approval of redress schemes by the Competition and Markets Authority).

[13] Articles 75–76 of Law 2016–1547 of 18 November 2016 on the modernization of justice in the twenty-first century.

[14] Articles 12–25 of the ZkolT.

[15] Also Switzerland, Tentative Draft March 2018, Articles 352a–352k of the Swiss Civil Procedure Code.

[16] For details, see Chapter 11.

[17] *Wet om collective afwikkeling van massaschade* (as amended on 26 June 2013 in *Burgerlijk Wetboek*, 7, Articles 907–10; *Wetboek van Burgerlijk Rechtsvordering*, Articles 1013–18a).

allegedly liable for the mass harm be inclined to enter into settlement negotiations. Together, the three pillars of the ERCP are meant to provide a consistent concept for the private enforcement of mass claims; but due to the nature of 'model rules', they may also be regarded as a toolbox for legislatures that prefer to implement only parts of it into national law.

2.3 How the commentary is arranged

The following section of this book follows the schema of the ERCP Part XI collective redress rules. We deal first with the types of claims and how they can be 'certified' to form a collective redress action (Chapter 6), and then with who may be a 'qualified entity' to pursue the group's claim (Chapter 7). We move on to some case management issues specific to collective redress and dealt with in Part XI (Chapter 8), and a separate chapter on the gathering and use of evidence in collective redress cases (Chapter 9). In Chapter 10, we look at how compensation is calculated for the group in collective redress claims (with a focus on competition claims); while in Chapter 11 we consider the settlement regimes mentioned earlier and in Chapter 12 we look at costs and funding for collective redress cases.

Chapter 13 considers some cross-border issues; and our final Chapter 14 (as noted in Chapter 1) looks to cast the net wider than Europe and see what lessons might be learned from further afield.

6. Types of claim, structure and certification of collective proceedings

Astrid Stadler

1. TYPES OF CLAIM AVAILABLE IN COLLECTIVE REDRESS PROCEEDINGS

1.1 General principles

This chapter will provide an overview of the remedies available and the structure of collective redress proceedings as designed in the European Rules of Civil Procedure (ERCP). In the third section, it considers in particular the certification of collective redress actions.

With regard to the available remedies in collective redress actions, the ERCP takes a broad approach. Rule 210(1)(e) simply requires that the collective redress claim specify whether the qualified claimant seeks compensation or any other redress remedy. This includes actions for the reimbursement of a price paid, the repair of goods purchased or the replacement of defective products. Thus, collective actions for any kind of performance on the defendant's side are admissible. Collective redress remedies may also be in the form of a declaratory judgment or a cease-and-desist order. Any combination of those remedies is also possible. The ERCP thus follows the example of several Member States that have implemented collective redress mechanisms and provides a wide range of remedies.[1] It is also in line with the Draft Directive on representative actions of the European Commission, which has a focus on the combination of injunctive relief and compensatory remedies.

---

[1] For example, France – Articles L623–1 *et seq Code de consommation* and the general rules (health sector, discrimination, environmental law and data protection); Article 62 of Law 2016–1547; England/Wales, Competition Act 1998, Section 47D. Other national rules on collective actions do not restrict the remedies available – for example, Finland – Class Action Act, 444/2007 para 1; Norway – Disputes Act, Section 35–1; and Sweden – Group Proceedings Act, Section 1. In Belgium, collective actions can be filed only for the recovery of damages: Book XVII, Title 2 'collective damages actions', *Code de droit économique*.

The court is also provided with as much flexibility as possible with respect to interim or final decisions. In cases in which the courts and the qualified claimant assume that settlement negotiations would be easier once the court has decided on the liability of some or all of the defendants, the court may do so in a final (partial) judgment (Rule 130(1)(d)). If settlement negotiations fail nevertheless, the court may, in a subsequent judgment, decide on the redress sought – in particular, on the amount of compensation payable. In any case, it is not necessary that the court adjudicate on each individual claim of the group members. The court may fix only the total amount of compensation payable and provide general criteria for its distribution among the group members.[2]

1.2 Skimming off illegally gained profit

Particularly in consumer protection law and cartel law, mass harm events are often characterized by small or even trivial individual losses. Those individuals have no rational incentive to sue the liable trader or companies separately, because they cannot afford to litigate these 'negative value' claims: 'they cost more to assert individually than the claimant would recover, even if victory were certain.'[3] Due to this rational inaction or 'apathy', one of the aims of liability rules – to influence the market behaviour of companies – is not met. In order to maintain or establish a deterrent effect on market participants, court proceedings are important, but they need not necessarily aim at the recovery of damages. What is more important against the background of the amount of deadweight loss in these cases and the detriment caused to the 'rule of law' is that policy makers intervene and provide instruments which allow claimants to exercise their rights effectively so as to prevent the wrongdoer from keeping the profits gained.

1.3 Damages actions

Cases which involve negative value claims often arise in competition law or other situations in which the victims are a large group of unidentified persons. With regard to collective actions, only the opt-out mechanism can reasonably be used, because persons with trivial loss will not care to opt in to those proceedings. Whenever national systems have put in place opt-out group actions for negative value claims, the distribution of compensation funds becomes difficult and often disproportionate. Even though an opt-out mechanism

---

2 For details on the calculation and distribution of damages, see Chapter 10.

3 Definition of 'negative value claim' given by John Coffee, *Entrepreneurial Litigation* (HUP 2015) 3.

applies during the litigation, it often becomes an opt-in system when it comes to the distribution of funds.[4] All group members must be informed and invited to claim their share of a compensation fund. They must step forward and claim their part of the fund actively. For many reasons, this does not happen to a significant extent in practice. Consumers may simply avoid the hassle of applying for a small amount of compensation, or may consider themselves not to be in a position to prove that they are indeed entitled to compensation.

Imagine the case of a price-fixing cartel. Consumers at the end of the distribution chain will often not have kept receipts or other documents that provide evidence that they bought overpriced products during the time the price cartel was operating on the market. In the United States and England, unclaimed funds are often subject to so-called '*cy-près*' solutions,[5] and a residue of the funds goes to charity, public institutions or consumer associations. In any case, one should avoid giving the money back to the defendants, because the defendant should not be the one to benefit from the reluctance of consumers to claim their share of the funds.

1.4 Disgorgement proceedings

It is worth considering whether small and trivial damages caused to a large number of consumers really call for an instrument for the recovery of damages.

---

[4] In consumer law, there will sometimes be cases in which all consumers who are entitled to compensation are clearly identifiable – at least by the defendant – and a settlement may provide that the defendant simply sends them a cheque or pays back a certain amount to them (eg, where the defendant has overcharged its customers based on illegal general contract terms). In this situation, it is not necessary that the victims step forward and actively claim compensation.

[5] '*Cy près*' is old French and means 'as close as possible'. In the legal context, *cy près* was historically used in English charity trust law. Today it describes the use of compensation funds in mass litigation in a way that does not compensate the loss of consumers (because it is too small to justify costly distribution processes), but directs the money to charity, public regulators and research, or not-for-profit organizations in order to use it for the benefit of consumers more generally. For a possible transfer into European law, Rachael Mulheron, *The Modern Cy Près Doctrine: Application and Implications* (Cavendish Publishing 2006); Rachael Mulheron, 'Cy Près Damages Distribution in England: A New Era for Consumer Redress' (2009) 2 *European Business Law Review* 307; Jay Tidmarsh, 'Cy Près and the Optimal Class Action' (2014) 82 *Geo Wash L Rev* 767, 773. The US Supreme Court was expected to decide whether *cy près* solutions were adequate in mass settlements in *Frank v Gaos*, 139 SCt 1041, 203 LEd 2d 404. On 20 March 2019, however, after an oral hearing in December 2018, the US Supreme Court issued a *per curiam* decision vacating the Ninth Circuit's decision based on a question of legal standing as decided in the *Spokeo* case (*Spokeo, Inc v Robins*, 136 SCt 1540, 194 LEd 2d 635 (2016)), and did not express its view on *cy près*.

Given that deterrence can be more important in these cases than compensation, an alternative solution to opt-out collective actions could be a representative action for skimming off the illegally gained profit from traders that have violated consumer or antitrust law. Such an instrument – known in the United States as 'disgorgement' – does not aim to compensate consumers, but is primarily implemented for its deterrent effect. It may be used where it seems more important that the wrongdoer cannot keep the money gained by a violation of the law than that individual consumers are compensated with small amounts of money.

In Switzerland, the proposal for a representative action (Article 89a of the Civil Procedure Code) suggests that the representative entity can sue either for damages or for skimming off illegal profits. In Germany, Section 10 of the Unfair Competition Act and Section 34a of the Antitrust Act have provided such a mechanism since 2005. Designated entities have legal standing to bring such an action. The amount to be paid by the defendant goes to the federal budget. In practice, very few actions have been filed, because consumer associations will not take the high procedural risk involved in the proceedings where they have no financial incentive to do so.[6] Although German consumer associations are relatively well equipped compared to similar associations in other Member States, they do not have a great budget for litigation and can afford only a few actions per year. Disgorgement proceedings seem to be an adequate mechanism to fight against violations of consumer law in principle, but they require a different approach compared to what the German rules currently provide.[7]

---

[6] Case studies on the Unfair Competition Act, Section 10 are available from Astrid Stadler, in Christopher Hodges and Stefaan Voet (eds), *Delivering Collective Redress: New Technologies* (Hart Publishing, 2018) 76 *et seq.*

[7] In Germany, academics have suggested lowering the substantive law threshold for skimming-off illegally gained profit (currently the violation by the defendant must be intentional) and for allowing at least part of the amount to be paid by the defendant to go to the claimant or to a kind of access-to-justice fund. For a critical review of the instrument, see Caroline Meller-Hannich and Armin Höland, '*Gutachten Evaluierung der Effektivität kollektiver Rechtsschutzinstrumente*' in Bundesministerium für Ernährung, Landwirtschaft und Verbraucherschutz (eds), (2011) 141 *et seq*; Caroline Meller-Hannich,'*Gutachten 72. Deutscher Juristentag (DJT)* 2018' (Report for the bi-annual conference of the German Association of Lawyers, 2018) [2018] 42 *et seq*; Christian Alexander, '*Marktsteuerung durch Abschöpfungsansprüche*' [2006] JZ 890; Olaf Gärtner, *Der Gewinnabschöpfungsanspruch nach § 10 UWG* (Herbert Utz Verlag 2006) 146 *et seq*; Stefan Sieme, *Der Gewinnabschöpfungsanspruch nach § 10 UWG und die Vorteilsabschöpfung gem. §§ 34, 34a GBW* (Duncker & Humblot 2009) 50 *et seq*.

In 2018, the instrument suffered another setback when the German Federal High Court[8] decided that consumer associations must not use the support of commercial third-party funders to finance actions under Section 10 of the Unfair Competition Act. Without funding agreements, which regularly offer the third-party funder a success fee, German consumer associations will not be in a position to finance skimming-off actions in the future.

The European Commission's 2018 proposal for a Directive[9] on a collective action included a particular rule on collective actions for cases of small individual loss in Article 6, paragraph 3(b). Where 'consumers have suffered a small amount of loss and it would be disproportionate to distribute the redress to them', no opt-in collective actions for the recovery of damages or actions for a declaratory judgment were intended to apply: 'In such cases, Member States shall ensure that the mandate of the individual consumers concerned is not required. The redress shall be directed to a public purpose serving the collective interests of consumers.'

For the first time, the European Commission acted on the suggestion to distinguish between small individual loss and mass harm cases with considerable individual damages.[10] In contrast to its 2013 Recommendation,[11] the approach also no longer gives absolute priority to the principle of compensation. The idea that the money should be directed to a public purpose was in line with the *cy près* solutions practised in the United States and the United Kingdom. Nevertheless, the proposal did not survive the subsequent legislative proceedings at the European level and has been modified considerably. The European Parliament's legislative resolution of 26 March 2019 deleted Article 6, paragraph 2 and suggests returning to the principle of full compensation of consumers without any differentiation among trivial, small or large loss. The

---

[8] *Bundesgerichtshof* (BGH), 13 September 2018, I ZR 26/17, BeckRS 2018, 24788. The court's decision was heavily criticized by the Schleswig Court of Appeals (14 February 2019, 2 U 4/18- juris), but the *Bundesgerichtshof* overruled that decision and confirmed its earlier holdings, 9 May 2019 (I ZR 205/17); for a detailed analysis, see also Astrid Stadler, '*Anmerkung*' (2019) 4 *Juristenzeitung* 203 *et seq*; and Michael Loschelder, '*Prozessfinanzierung bei Gewinnabschöpfungsansprüchen unzulässig*', [2018] GRUR-Prax 534.

[9] Proposal for a Directive on representative actions for the protection of the collective interests of consumers, and repealing Directive 2009/22/EC COM/2018/0184 final.

[10] For details, see Astrid Stadler, '*Der Gewinnabschöpfungsanspruch: eine Variante des "private enforcement"?*' in Susanne Augenhofer (ed), *Die Europäisierung des Kartell- und Lauterkeitsrechts* (Mohr Siebeck, 2009) 17 *et seq*; Astrid Stadler, 'Group Actions as a Remedy to Enforce Consumer Interests' in Fabrizio Cafaggi and Hans-Wolfgang Micklitz (eds), *New Frontiers of Consumer Protection: The Interplay Between Private and Public Enforcement* (Intersentia, 2009) 305 *et seq*.

[11] Recommendation 2013/396 No 21.

European Parliament's amendments also avoid mentioning *cy près* explicitly or allowing to direct payments of the defendant to charity or another public institution. Instead, the proposed new Article 6, paragraph 4a[12] reads as follows:

> The redress measures aim to grant consumers concerned full compensation for their loss. In case of unclaimed amount left from the compensation, a court shall decide on the beneficiary of the remaining unclaimed amount. This unclaimed amount shall not go to the qualified representative entity nor to the trader.[13]

In particular, the second sentence again reflects a general fear that qualified entities might abuse collective actions as a source of making profit. Notwithstanding the fact that legislatures must avoid an incentive structure that would allow misuse of legal standing, one should not rule out from the outset the idea that ideological plaintiffs could at least get a percentage of the amount to be paid by the defendant. Where such direct payments to the qualified plaintiff are politically unacceptable, one should at least consider directing the money to an 'access-to-justice' fund[14] and permit qualified entities to apply for financial support from the fund in the future.

2. APPROACH IN THE ERCP COLLECTIVE REDRESS RULES

The ERCP has opted for collective redress actions for the recovery of damages for which an opt-out mechanism may be applied in order to cope with 'negative value claims'. The working group dropped the idea of a particular instrument for skimming off illegally gained profit.

One reason for this decision was that offering a completely different set of instruments for minor loss and for other cases would have required a clear definition of 'minor loss'. This is a tricky question with no obvious answer, but with numerous legal – even constitutional – implications. Giving up completely the principle of compensation for minor loss might be considered

---

12 EP 2014-2019, P8_TA-Prov(2019)0222 (Ordinary legislative procedure: first reading), Amendment 66.

13 The latest draft of 30 June 2020 (www.consilium.europa.eu/media/44766/st09223-en20.pdf, last accessed 10 August 2020) is even more general. Article 5b(6) simply says: 'Member States may lay down rules on the destination of any outstanding redress funds that were not recovered within the established time limits.'

14 For such a proposal, see Astrid Stadler, 'Third party funding of mass litigation in Germany. Entrepreneurial Parties – Curse or blessing?', *Privatizing Dispute Resolution and its Limits: 3rd IAPL-MPI Summer School at Max-Planck Institute for International* (Nomos, 2019), 209–32.

to violate constitutional rights of the group members in some Member States. It may be accepted, however, if only trivial amounts of individual loss are at stake and if a balancing of interests speaks in favour of a deterrent effect – particularly against the realistic assumption that individual actions would not be filed anyhow. If consumers are not expected to enforce a claim for the compensation of trivial loss, disgorgement proceedings or *cy près* solutions are less likely to violate their rights. Nevertheless, what amounts to 'trivial loss' is difficult to define in national law, but almost impossible to circumscribe adequately at the European level; and there is not a single piece of national legislation that defines 'minor' or 'trivial' loss.

For the ERCP, it therefore seemed more appropriate to adhere to the instrument of a collective redress action. Rule 215(2) leaves it within the court's discretion to decide on a case-by-case basis whether the use of an opt-in or opt-out mechanism would be favourable by taking into consideration whether the individual loss of group members is likely to give them sufficient incentive to opt in. This provides the necessary flexibility to define the group in the most efficient way and offers at least the chance for consumers to obtain compensation. The working group was aware of the problems which can arise when it comes to the distribution of compensation funds subsequent to an opt-out group action. The comments of Rule 215 therefore explicitly explain that *cy près* solutions should be accepted in settlements (which are subject to court approval).[15]

As commercial third-party funding has met with considerable scepticism in some Member States,[16] one should also support the idea that the residues of compensation funds are to be directed to an 'access-to-justice fund' in order to be available for the funding of future mass litigation. Courts, however, should be reluctant to allow back-payment of the unclaimed amount to the defendant.[17] Details of how to use the unclaimed part of a compensation fund and to whom the money might go or not go were beyond the scope of the project, and are probably better left to be decided by the parties of the settlement contract and to court approval.

---

[15] In a court judgment, *cy près* solutions would require a basis in the applicable substantive law, which was beyond the ELI/UNIDROIT project.

[16] For the position of the ERCP, see Rules 237, 245.

[17] In the United States, this is called 'reversion' and it is also increasingly disfavoured.

3. STANDALONE ACTIONS FOR INJUNCTIONS TO STOP ILLEGAL PRACTICES

Unlike the EU Proposal of April 2018, the chapter on collective redress in the European Law Institute/UNIDROIT project does not consider injunctions in case of mass harm events to be a collective instrument in a strict sense. The reason for this approach is that injunctive relief is different in its effect from collective redress remedies and therefore less difficult in terms of procedural safeguards. Collective redress instruments for damages or any other kind of payment or performance by the defendant require a number of safeguards for the absent group members, because the outcome of the proceedings is formally binding on them with respect to their individual claims, although they did not actively participate in the action. In proceedings for injunctive relief, the situation is different and easier to handle. It is not necessary to bundle individual claims for injunctive relief in a collective action; instead, it is sufficient to give legal standing to representative entities, which can act in the public or general interest of consumers in order to stop the violation of consumer or competition law.[18] However, this should not prevent qualified entities from applying for a combination of injunctive relief and other remedies which must be dealt with under the rules of collective redress.

The idea that applications for a cease-and-desist-order do not require the participation of consumers was also the driving force behind the original EU Injunctions Directive 2002. It is not necessary that the court order obtained by a representative entity becomes formally binding on consumers or other victims of a mass harm event. If the defendant complies with the court order and stops the violation, or if the claimant enforces the injunction against the defendant, everybody will automatically benefit from it without extending the *res judicata* effect of the court order.[19] This follows from the nature of injunctive relief and its *de facto erga omnes* effect. Moreover, it is not necessary that consumers participate directly or indirectly (opt-in/opt-out) in the proceedings;

---

[18] The latest draft of the EU Directive (30 June 2020) reflects the same idea. Article 5a (2) reads as follows: 'In order to seek an injunction measure, individual consumers concerned shall not be required to express their will to be represented by the qualified entity. The qualified entity shall not have to prove the actual loss or damage on the part of individual consumers affected by an infringement nor the intention or negligence on the part of the trader.'

[19] If a defendant does not comply with the court order, individuals are protected: CJEU case law (Case C-472/10 *Hatóság v Invitel Távközlési Zrt* [2012], ECLI:EU:C: 2012:242 no 43) requires that a court decision that declares standard contract terms illegal be considered *ex officio* in a subsequent individual action against the same defendant.

no safeguards are necessary to protect their interests. Such safeguards must be in place only where a representative entity has legal standing to make individual consumer claims subject to court proceedings with a *res judicata* effect for the individual claimholder. Representative actions for an injunction cannot affect the situation of individuals in a negative way, as long as a dismissal of the action has no binding effect on them.

The ERCP provides a single rule on injunctions in Rule 205 in Section I of the chapter on collective redress. It reads as follows:

> Rule 205 [Entitlement to apply for a Collective Interest Injunction]
> (1) Any entity authorized under national law to bring actions in the collective interest may apply for a collective interest injunction that requires the cessation of any infringement of the law.
> (2) Where appropriate the court may order additional measures such as the publication of its decision with a view to eliminating the continuing effects of the infringement.

Rule 205 does not prevent courts before which a collective action is pending from granting injunctive relief. A combination of both remedies can be necessary in many cases.

4. STRUCTURE OF COLLECTIVE PROCEEDINGS UNDER THE ERCP

Figure 6.1 explains the structure of the collective proceedings under the ERCP.

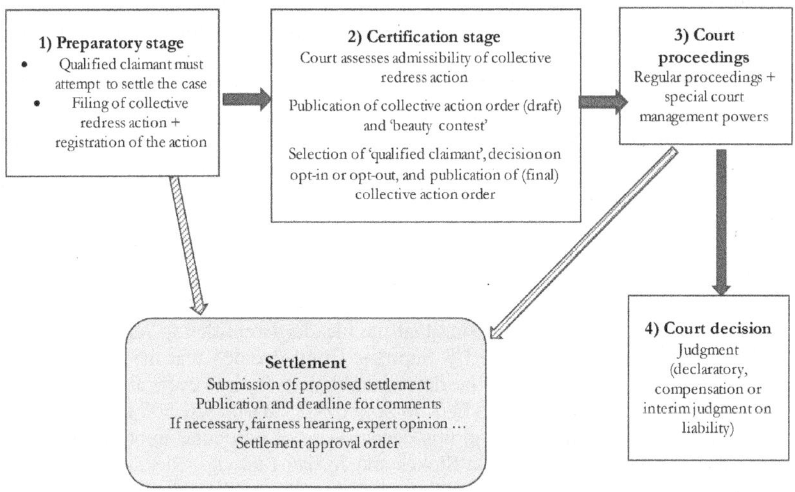

Figure 6.1 Structure of collective redress proceedings

Regular collective redress actions under the ERCP progress through four stages: preparatory stage, certification stage, court proceedings and judgment stage. At any time during the litigation, the parties are free to submit a settlement proposal to the court for approval.

4.1 Preparatory stage – attempt to settle the case

4.1.1 Comparative background

Some Member States oblige a group representative or qualified claimant to contact the defendant early and attempt to enter into settlement negotiations prior to filing of a collective action. Such rules are not only inspired by the hope that contentious litigation may be avoided in the first place, but also implemented as a safeguard against a race to the courthouse. Experience with US class actions tells us that without such an obligation, and in combination with only minimal requirements to be met by the claim, lawyers tend to file class actions very early.

In the Volkswagen *Dieselgate* case, it took just a few hours after the US Environmental Protection Agency had published its notification about the use of illegal software in Volkswagen and Audi diesel cars on 18 September 2015 before the first class action was filed in the United States.[20] Within less than four days, 25 additional class actions had been filed.[21] It is in particular the principle of notice pleading in US procedural law that allows for the quick filing of an action, since statements of claim need not specify in detail the background of the claim[22] and no evidence must be listed in the claim because the identification of evidence is left to the subsequent pre-trial discovery phase. The US rule of cost also allows for an early filing of claims because claimants

---

20 It was a consumer rights class action firm that filed the action in the District Court of the Northern District of California; Jenny Gesley, 'The Volkswagen Litigation' (*In Custodia Legis*, 27 October 2016), https://blogs.loc.gov/law/2016/10/the-volkswagen-litigations (last accessed 10 August 2020).

21 See Alison Frankel, 'How U.S. lawyers were so quick off the mark to sue Volkswagen' (*Reuters*, 23 September 2015), www.reuters.com/article/us-usa-volkswagen-lawyers-idUSKCN0RM2QZ20150922 (last accessed 10 August 2020).

22 Rule 8(a)(2) of the Federal Rules of Civil Procedure requires only a 'short and plain statement of the claim showing that the pleader is entitled to relief'. In *Conley v Gibson,* 355 US 41 (1957) the US Supreme Court decided that the plaintiff needs to provide only 'fair notice' to the defendant. This was, however, abrogated in the 2007 US Supreme Court decision *Bell Atlantic Corp. v Twombly,* 550 US 544 (2007). The stricter standards described in this decision are of particular importance in antitrust cases; for details, see Joshua Stokes and Jordan Ludwig, 'Pleading an antitrust conspiracy in a post-Twombly world', www.crowell.com/files/Pleading-an-Antitrust-Conspiracy-in-a-Post-Twombly-Wolrd.pdf (last accessed 10 August 2020). Stricter standards also apply in securities class actions according to 15 US Code § 78u-4 (b)(1).

do not have to consider the procedural risk exactly at the outset. Although in this respect the procedural framework in Europe and in the ERCP is different, there is a general concern to avoid the filing of ill-prepared actions. In the case of a mass harm event in which several qualified claimants might have legal standing to sue, it is particularly important to avoid overhasty actions that burden the court system and defendants.

Some Member States have also put in place national rules that require pre-action attempts to settle a mass dispute or that allow the court to require such efforts at a very early stage of the proceedings. The new Dutch Act on redress of mass damages in a collective action adopted in March 2019 requires that the foundation or association planning to bring a legal action on behalf of the similar interests of other persons conduct consultations with the defendant beforehand.[23] This is set out in Article 305a(3) lit c of the Dutch Civil Code as a precondition of legal standing and a period of two weeks following receipt by the defendant is deemed sufficient.

According to Article 64 of the French Act on Group Actions,[24] a four-month period is granted to the defendant to stop the infringement and/or pay damages before claimants can file a group action. In Belgium, the judge may oblige the parties to enter into settlement negotiations for a period of between three and six months (which starts to run at the end of the period fixed for the opt-in or opt-out of the group members).[25] Similar rules apply for collective actions before the English Competition Appeal Tribunal (CAT).[26] The Lithuanian Class Action Act 2015 also requires the group plaintiff to send a draft of the complaint to the defendant and specify a period for fulfilling the group claims.[27] At the European level, the latest version of a proposal for a representative action leaves it to the Member States to decide whether a prior consultation is necessary.[28]

4.1.2 Position under the ERCP

In order to prevent a race to the courthouse in the event of a mass harm situation, the ERCP requires the qualified claimant to attempt to settle the case

---

23 For details on the Dutch Act, see Chapter 7.

24 Law 2016–1547.

25 Belgium, Article XVII43 para 2 no 8 and Article XVII45 of the *Code de droit économique*.

26 Competition Appeal Tribunal Rules 2015 (SI No 1648/2015) ('CAT Rules'), Rule 76(10)(e).

27 Article 441[2] of the Lithuania Code of Civil Procedure.

28 Council of the EU, Interinstitutional File 2018/0089 (COD), 30 June 2020, Article 5a(3). This rule applies only to injunction measures and there is no equivalent in Article 5b for redress measures.

before filing an action. According to Rule 212(1)(d), the defendant must be given at least three months to respond to the qualified claimant's settlement proposal or the offer to negotiate. If the defendant does not respond or if the parties did not achieve a settlement, the qualified claimant can file the action and the court will enter the claim in a publicly accessible electronic register (Rule 211). A timeframe of three months was deemed an adequate period for the defendant to decide whether and on what basis to start settlement negotiations, even in complex mass harm events. It is also an acceptable period for the group to wait before the qualified claimant can take court action because the same rule applies for all potentially qualified claimants. If the defendant(s) fails to respond or settlement negotiations fail, information on such an attempt must be included in the collective action statement.

However, asking the claimant to contact the defendant before filing an action involves another potential risk that had to be considered when drafting the rules. Particularly in cross-border cases, defendants might be tempted to avoid a collective action by bringing a so-called 'torpedo action' under the Brussels I *bis* Regulation. Although the Brussels I *bis* Regulation rightly aims to avoid parallel proceedings, the principle of priority as expressed in Articles 29 and 30 of the Regulation favours 'torpedo actions'. The broad definition of *lis pendens* applied by the Court of Justice of the European Union (CJEU)[29] (which was adopted in Rule 142 of the ERCP) also gives priority to an action for a negative declaratory judgment filed in one Member State by the party that is potentially liable for damages. As a consequence, all subsequent actions against that party brought in another Member State for redress or damages are barred if they are based on the same event and if the same 'core questions' appear in the second litigation. If the first action was filed in a Member State in which courts tend to be very slow and it is likely that it will take years, for example, to dismiss the action for lack of international jurisdiction, a collective redress action under Part XI would be barred for a long time. The drafters of the ERCP were not in a position to ignore the Brussels I *bis* Regulation and CJEU case law, or to assume that the CJEU would change its position soon. Therefore, Rule 210(2) provides a solution of its own by granting courts the power to issue an anti-suit injunction. Such a rule can be considered to be in conflict with the Brussels I *bis* Regulation because the CJEU has banned anti-suit injunctions in the context of this jurisdictional regime.[30] Nevertheless, the CJEU has not considered the situation of collective redress in this regard.

[29] CJEU Case C-406/92 *Tatry v Maciej Rataj* [1994] ECLI:EU:C:1994:400; CJEU Case C-144/86 *Gubisch Maschinenfabrik KG v Palumbo* [1987] ECLI:EU:C:1987:528.

[30] CJEU C-185-/07, ECLI:EU:C:2009:69 – *West Tankers*; CJEU C-159/02, ECLI:EU:C:2004:228 – *Turner/Grovit*.

Mass litigation requires a different approach and the proposed rule should be understood to contribute to a further development of the Brussels regime. In some situations, a consolidation of actions[31] according to ERCP Rule 146 may also prevent a 'torpedo effect'.[32]

4.2 Registration of the claim

ERCP Rule 211 requires early registration of the collective action in the publicly available part of an electronic register. Collective action registers are available in some Member States – such as Germany,[33] the Netherlands,[34] Norway[35] and Slovenia[36] – but they serve various purposes, and the responsibility to register the claim can lie with either the court (as in the ERCP) or the claimant (which reflects a more English approach). Electronic registers are often established to provide a quick and easy means of communication with a great number of participants in litigation, including group members. This has also been the basic idea of establishing an electronic register in the first place for collective actions in Part XI of the ERCP.

Rule 211, however, does not only have an information objective; the rule was also put in place as a safeguard for the defendant against multiple collective actions.[37] Traditional *lis pendens* rules cannot preclude a second collective redress action filed against the same defendant(s) by another qualified claim-

---

[31] For collective redress actions pending in different Member States, see Chapter 12.

[32] 'Rule 146 "Consolidation of Proceedings" (1) Where the jurisdiction of the Court first seised is established, it may, upon application of one of the parties, order the consolidation of several sets of proceedings under Rules 142 and 144. (2) The Court first seised may only consolidate proceedings when it has jurisdiction to hear them and when such parallel proceedings are pending at the first instance. (3)…(6).'

[33] In Germany, an electronic register for claims was established for securities cases under the so-called *Kapitalanlegermusterverfahrensgesetz* (KapMuG) (Section 4 of the KapMuG). Such a register is now also in use in the context of the representative action for declaratory relief in consumer cases, in order to publish the filing of the action, to inform the public and to provide a platform for the registration of individual consumers who want to benefit from the outcome of the proceedings (Section 609 of the German Civil Procedure Code).

[34] In the Netherlands, Article 305a (7) of the Civil Code establishes a central register for collective actions. Claimants must enter the writ in the central register within two days of submitting the writ in order not to lose legal standing.

[35] Norway Disputes Act, Section 35–6.

[36] Slovenia, Article 10 of the ZkolT, *Official Journal* 51/2017.

[37] For rules on parallel collective actions or subsequent proceedings, see, for example, Belgium – Article XVII54 para 5 and Article XVII69 *et seq* of the *Code de droit économique*; France – Article 80 of Law 2016–1547; Germany – Section 610 of the Civil Procedure Code.

ant, because the parties to the actions will be different. The general rules on *lis pendens* in ERCP Rules 142–46 are not intended to apply to collective actions; therefore, a specific rule was necessary in the collective redress chapter. The effect of registration of a collective action is to bar any other collective redress action against the same defendant(s) with respect to the same mass harm event, as long as the first collective action is still pending and the second action will be filed in the interests of the same group. Parallel proceedings are possible, however, if the qualified claimant in the second action acts on behalf of a class of group members with different interests. The admissibility of a subsequent collective action based on the same mass harm event against the same defendant depends on the outcome of the first action (settlement or judgment), and on whether the opt-in or opt-out mechanism has been used (see Rules 225, 226, 227, 232(4), 235(2)).

4.3 Proceedings connected with certification

The next important step in the proceedings is the certification of the collective redress action by the court. For details of that part, see Section 4.4 below.

4.3.1 Case management powers of the court

Once the court has admitted the action by issuing a collective proceeding order (Rules 212, 213), the rules of regular court proceedings will apply with respect to pleadings, the taking of evidence and so on. The ERCP, however, gives the court some additional case management powers – in particular, to supervise the qualified claimant with respect to his or her duty to act in the best interests of the group (Rule 214) – which are discussed further in Chapter 8. If the claimant no longer satisfies the conditions set out in Rules 208 and 209, or does not act in the interests of the group members, the court can remove him or her and authorize a new qualified claimant. The rule again has its roots in the national law of some Member States.[38] The court is also free to give interim or declaratory judgments if it considers this appropriate and helpful to promote the settlement of the dispute. The parties to the collective redress action may at any time during the proceedings jointly propose a settlement and ask the court to approve it (Rule 222).

[38] Belgium – Article XVII40 of the *Code de droit économique*; Denmark – Administration of Justice Act, para 254e(3); France – Article 81 of Law 2016–1547; Lithuania – Article $441^4(6)$ of the Civil Procedure Code; Norway – Disputes Act, Section 35–9; Poland – Article 18 of the *Diziennik Ustaw* 2010; Sweden – Group Proceedings Act, Sections 21–22.

4.3.2 Settlement

If the case is settled and the settlement agreement is approved by the court, enforcement of the settlement will follow the terms of the settlement contract. The extent to which group members are bound by a court-approved settlement depends on whether the proceedings were based on an opt-in or opt-out scheme (Rules 225, 226). Where an opt-in mechanism is applied, the settlement will be negotiated only on behalf of those group members who have opted in. Where the proceedings used an opt-out scheme, a settlement will have binding effect on all group members who have not opted out.

The ERCP does not provide the chance for a second opt-out, as is possible, for example, in the context of US class actions. National legislatures in Europe have taken different approaches in this respect. Where group members have decided to mandate the qualified claimant entity by not opting out of the proceedings, they have agreed to accept the decisions to be made by the qualified entity during the proceedings. There are good arguments to modify this 'principle of mandate' when it comes to a settlement that typically involves a cutback or partial waiver of the substantive claims. Nevertheless, any chance to opt out of a settlement negotiated between the qualified entity and the defendant implies uncertainty for the negotiations. A potentially high opt-out rate may be an incentive for the parties to find the best possible bargain for the group members; but a second opt-out chance would not allow the defendant to calculate the risks and financial implications of a settlement with the necessary degree of finality. There is a legitimate need for legal certainty for the defendant with respect to the scope of claims to be finally settled. The best way to protect the interests of the group is not a second opt-out; but court approval of the settlement is needed and a broad range of instruments is available to the court to collect all information necessary to assess the fairness of the settlement.

4.3.3 Judgments

In the case of a judgment, the court must not give a decision on each individual claim of the group members. Where appropriate, the court may set the total amount of compensation to be paid by the defendant to the group or to the sub-groups, and list abstract criteria for the distribution of compensation and the method of administration of a compensation fund (Rule 228). This includes the nomination of one or several persons as administrators of the compensation fund or supervision of the distribution by the court, a public regulator or specially appointed legal and/or economic experts.[39]

---

[39] In Belgium, for example, Article XVII57 of the *Code de droit économique* requires the appointment of a liquidator. Persons eligible as a liquidator are only '*les*

It is primarily up to the qualified claimant to enforce the judgment against the defendant. If the qualified claimant takes no steps to enforce it within reasonable time, any group member request court permission to do so (Rule 227(3)). It will be up to the court to decide whether the applicant is sufficiently qualified and motivated to do so.

Moreover, a final judgment will protect the defendant from other collective redress actions filed by another qualified claimant based on the same mass harm. The only exception applies with respect to claims that are not subject to the collective action. Group members who have not opted in during the litigation or those who have opted out in case of opt-out proceedings may bring individual actions or may participate in another collective action brought on their behalf by a different qualified claimant. These options can be exercised only as long as the limitation period has not expired.

4.4 Certification of the collective redress action

4.4.1 Comparative background

Numerous national collective action rules require a formal certification or admission of the action by the court.[40] In US law, certification of a class action is the most important step for the claimant's side.[41] According to Rule 23(c)(1)(A) of the Federal Rules of Civil Procedure (FRCP), the court must 'at an early practicable time after a person sues or is sued as class representative, determine

avocats, les officiers ministériels ou les mandataires de justice dans l'exercice de leur profession ou de leur fonction, présentant des garanties de compétence en matière de procédures de règlement de préjudice' (Article XVII57 para 2).

[40] Report on the implementation of the Commission Recommendation of 11 June 2013 on common principles for injunctive and compensatory collective redress mechanisms in the Member States concerning violations of rights granted under Union law (2013/396/EU) Nos 8, 9; Commission's Report (COM [2018] 40 final) 5–7; Belgium – Article XVII43 para 1 of the *Code de droit économique*; England/Wales – Competition Act 1998, Section 47B (7); CAT Rules, Rule 80; Hungary – Civil Procedure Code, Section 585; Lithuania – Article 444[1] of the Civil Procedure Code; Netherlands – Article 1018c (5) of the Civil Procedure Code; Slovenia – Articles 28, 29 of the ZkolT; Sweden – Group Litigation Act, Section 13. In Germany, the court seised with a '*Musterfeststellungsklage*' must decide only whether to make a public announcement of the claim in the electronic register (Section 607 of the Civil Procedure Code). This does not include a decision on the admissibility of the claim.

[41] Defendants will often file a motion to dismiss based on Rule 12(b)(6) FRCP or seek a summary judgment before class certification. For details of the pros and cons of pre-certification summary judgments, see Linda S Mullenix, 'Dropping the Spear: The Case for Enhanced Summary Judgment Prior to Class Certification', (2015) *Acron Law Journals* 1198.

by or whether to certify the action as a class action'.[42] Once the class action has been certified, the vast majority of actions will be settled.[43] Therefore, in US class actions, the real 'battle' takes place at the stage of certification. In order to protect defendants against unmeritorious actions, paragraphs 8 and 9 of the EU Recommendation 2013 also proposed a formal decision of the court to admit a collective action. Several national rules follow that example, but they differ with respect to the scope of court review during that early stage of the proceedings. The claimant must often demonstrate only that, generally speaking, the claims of all group or class members derive from the same mass harm event and are similar in law and fact.[44] Furthermore, a demonstration that in the particular case, a collective action is a more appropriate instrument compared to a joinder or individual lawsuits is sometimes necessary.[45]

In the majority of national rules, certification of a group or class action does not require a review (even a summary) on the merits of the case. An exception to this observation is provided by Article 1018c(5)(c) of the Dutch Civil Procedure Code, according to which the action will be certified only if the claim is not 'summarily unfounded, as is apparent at the time of submitting the document instituting the proceedings'. At the European level, the Recommendation 2013 and the 'New Deal' proposal in its version amended by the European Parliament require that the court be in a position to dismiss an action 'at the earliest possible stage of proceedings' if it is 'manifestly unfounded'.[46] In the United States, the question of whether certification of a class action should take into account the merits of the case has been a controversial issue for many years.[47] In the *Amgen* case, the Supreme Court made clear that certification may also require that the court take into consideration to

---

42 Certification includes the definition of the class and the class claims, issues, or defences and the appointment of a class counsel – Rule 23(c)(1)(B), Rule 23(g) FRCP.

43 Richard Marcus, Chapter 14.

44 Recommendation 2013/396 no 23; England/Wales, Competition Act 1998, Section 47B [6] and CAT Rules 79 [1] [b], 73 [2]; Finland – Class Action Act, 444/2007 para 2; France – Article 62, Law 2016–1547; Lithuania – Article 441^7 of the Civil Procedure Code; Sweden – Group Proceedings Act, Section 8.

45 Recommendation 2013/396 recital 21, no 8; Belgium – Article XVII36 [3] of the *Code de droit économique*; Lithuania – Article 441^7 of the Civil Procedure Code; Norway – Disputes Act, Section 35–2(1)(c); Sweden – Group Proceedings Act, Section 8.

46 EP 2014-2019, P8_TA-Prov (2019)0222 (Ordinary legislative procedure: first reading), Amendment 73 Article 7 para 3a. In the draft of 30 June 2020, Article 5(6) says: 'Member States shall ensure that the court or administrative authority may decide to dismiss manifestly unfounded cases at the earliest possible stage of the proceedings in accordance with national law.'

47 For details Richard Marcus, 'Reviving Judicial Gatekeeping of Aggregation: Scrutinizing the Merits on Class Certification', 79 *Geo Wash L Rev 324* (2011).

some extent the merits of the case: 'Merits questions may be considered to the extent – but only to the extent – that they are relevant to determining whether the rule 23 prerequisites for class certification are satisfied.'[48]

Continental civil procedure law does not have a common tradition of formal summary examination of the claim at the beginning of the proceedings. Before the taking of evidence, there is no reliable information available to the court about the merits. Whereas in US class actions, pre-trial discovery can take place for the purpose of certification, no such instrument is available in most continental systems: the court only has the allegations of the parties. ERCP Rule 212 builds on that tradition and demands that the statement of claim include 'all relevant information available'. This is not to be misunderstood as referring to information available from the defendant or third parties. The qualified claimant is expected only to share all information available to him or her with the court and the defendant.[49]

Nevertheless, 'manifestly unfounded' cases will not get far in the litigation. According to the procedural traditions in some Member States, the claim will be dismissed at an early stage if the claimant was unable to present a conclusive and coherent set of facts from which the alleged claim may arise ('*Schlüssigkeitsprüfung*').[50] This seems to be close to the idea of Article 1018c(5)(c) of the Dutch Civil Procedure Code, which also requires a summary evaluation based only on the documents submitted by the claimant. Anything that goes beyond a test of *prima facie* 'conclusiveness' would protract a 'real' examination of the parties' arguments and is not necessary as a safeguard for the defendant.

One must keep in mind that, contrary to the US class action system, the 'loser pays' rule applies in Europe and under the ERCP.[51] Frivolous claims or clearly unmeritorious collective actions should therefore be the exception,

---

[48] *Amgen, Inc v Connecticut Retirement Plans and Trust Funds*, 568 US 455 (2013) 1194; for a stricter standard, however, *Wal-Mart Stores, Incorporated v Dukes*, 564 US 338 (2011) 2551.

[49] Richard Marcus (Chapter 14) has pointed out rightly that from a US perspective, one might misunderstand such a broad requirement.

[50] In Germany, Section 331 of the Civil Procedure Code requires the conclusiveness of the claim as a prerequisite for a judgment by default against the defendant. Section 139 of the German Civil Procedure Code imposes an obligation on the court to invite the plaintiff to further specify his or her claim if it is not sufficiently detailed or specified to provide a basis for the relief sought; Austrian civil procedure law follows the same principles, see Walter Rechberger and Daphne-Ariane Simotta, *Zivilprozessrecht*, (7th ed 2009) 524, 385, 865. In both countries, claims that do not allow subsuming the plaintiff's allegations under a particular legal rule that provides the relief sought will be dismissed.

[51] ERCP Rule 241.

given the adverse costs risk. As mentioned above, there is also no extremely expensive US-style pre-trial discovery stage (against the background of the US rule of costs), and which therefore requires a mechanism such as a dismissal by a summary judgment in clearly unmeritorious cases. Unlike in the United States, claims in Europe (and particularly according to the ERCP)[52] require substantial and detailed allegation of the plaintiff's side ('fact pleading'), and the taking of evidence will take place only with respect to directly relevant facts.[53] Therefore, there is no need to copy safeguards that have merit in the US system, but not in a completely different procedural context in Europe.[54]

4.4.2 Position in the ERCP

The ERCP collective redress rules require a formal collective action order by the court seised in order to certify the collective action at the beginning of the litigation. Before making such an order (ie, during the certification stage of the proceeding), the court will: (1) assess the admissibility of the collective redress action (Rule 212) based on the information in the statement of claim (Rule 210) and the defendant's response; (2) decide on the application of the opt-in or opt-out scheme; and (3) select a 'qualified claimant' (Rule 213(3)).

4.4.2.1 Requirements for the admissibility of a collective action

The collective action must resolve the dispute more efficiently than a simple joinder of the group members' claims or than individual actions. All claims must arise from the same event or series of related events, and the claims must be similar in law and fact. Regulations that can be found in the Member States vary in their wording, but are more or less identical in their objectives.[55]

---

[52] ERCP Rule 53 ('Contents of the Statement of Claim').

[53] ERCP Rule 89 ('Relevance').

[54] In 2007, an evaluation of the Swedish Group Proceedings Act of 2002 concluded that the act had not been abused as a means of extorting settlements. Annina H Persson, 'Collective enforcement: European prospects in light of the Swedish experience' in Stefan Wrbka, Steven Van Uytsel and Mathias Siems, *Collective Actions* (CUP 2012) 341–56.

[55] France – Article 62 of Law 2016-1547: '*Lorsque plusieurs personnes placées dans une situation similaire subissent un dommage causé par une même personne, ayant pour cause commune un manquement de même nature à ses obligations légales ou contractuelles. . .* '; Article L623-1: '*afin d'obtenir la réparation des préjudices individuels subis par des consommateurs placés dans une situation similaire ou identique et ayant pour cause commune un manquement d'un ou des mêmes professionnels à leurs obligations légales, relevant ou non du présent code, ou contractuelles. . .* '. Finland – Class Action Act (444/2007), Section 2: 'several claimants have claims against the same respondent, which are based upon the same or similar issues'. Hungary – Civil Procedure Code, Section 583: claims of at least ten claimants must be in their substance similar and be based on the same facts. Lithuania – Article 441^1 of the Civil

Collective redress actions must, due to the number and similarity of the claims, be a more efficient way of solving the mass dispute.

The action filed must pass a 'superiority test', which is also part of US class action rules,[56] as well as of many national rules in Europe.[57] The court will consider the number of group members and whether individual actions arising from the mass harm event would be manageable. Some Member States have established a minimum number of group or class members to allow the use of a collective instrument;[58] others do not specify the number of group or class members.[59] The ERCP also refrains from defining a minimum threshold.

Procedure Code: 'when an action is grounded on identical or similar factual circumstance and. . . brought a claim, identical or similar substantive rights or interests'; Netherlands – Article 1018d (1) of the Code of Civil Procedure: 'a collective action for the same event or events. . . involving similar factual and legal questions.' Norway – Disputes Act, Section 35–1 (2): 'A class action is an action that is brought by or directed against a class on an identical or substantially similar factual and legal basis.' Poland – Article 1(1) Dz U 2010: 'similar claims, which arise from the identical or same set of facts'. Slovenia – Article 28(4) of the ZkolT: 'the same, similar, or related to similar or connected factual and legal issues'; common legal and factual questions must be predominant. Sweden – Group proceedings Act, Section 8 No 1: 'the action is founded on circumstances that are common or of a similar nature for the claims of the members of the group.'

[56] Rule 23(a)(1) of the FRCP: 'the class is so numerous that joinder of all members is impracticable'; Rule 23(b) (3): 'the court finds that the questions of law or fact common to class members predominate over any questions affecting only individual members, and that a class action is superior to other available methods for fairly and efficiently adjudicating the controversy. The matters pertinent to these findings include:

(A) the class members' interests in individually controlling the prosecution or defense of separate actions;
(B) the extent and nature of any litigation concerning the controversy already begun by or against class members;
(C) the desirability or undesirability of concentrating the litigation of the claims in the particular forum; and
(D) the likely difficulties in managing a class action'.

[57] Recommendation 2013/396 No 23; England/Wales – Competition Act 1998, Section 47B(6); Netherlands – Article 1018c (5) lit b of the Civil Procedure Code; Lithuania – Article 441[7] of the Code of Civil Procedure; Norway – Dispute Act, Section 35–2(1)(c); Sweden – Group Proceedings Act, Section 8.

[58] Hungary – Section 583 of the Civil Procedure Code: ten claimants; Poland – Article 1(1) of the *Dziennik Ustaw* 2010: ten group members; Lithuania – Article 441[3] (2) of the Code of Civil Procedure: group actions require 20 natural or legal persons; Germany – KapMuG: ten investors; Section 606(2) No 2 of the Code of Civil Procedure: ten consumers, and 50 consumers must register their claims in order to allow the representative action to become admissible.

[59] For example, England/Wales – CAT Rules: Rule 79(1)(a) 'identifiable class' – the CAT will consider the size of the group in determining whether the claims are suitable for a collective action; Rule 79(2)(d)); Finland – Class Action Act, para 2: 'several

Giving the court broad discretion provides more flexibility than any rule that requires a particular minimum number of group members. In England, the *MasterCard* competition law case,[60] which involved more than 46 million consumers as group members, demonstrated that courts must also take into account the manageability of the case when the group becomes too large.

With respect to the similarity of claims pooled in the collective action, courts will also have broad discretion and will decide on a case-by-case basis. Similarity of claims may arise from the same facts underlying each claim, but also from the applicable law. In any case, claims need not be 'identical'. In this respect, narrow interpretation of the English representative action[61] by the English Court of Appeals[62] demonstrates clearly that such a strict requirement restricts the scope of application to very few cases. According to the test established by the Court of Appeals in *Emerald*, the group members must have a common grievance and the relief sought must be beneficial to all. This made the bringing of representative actions in competition law extremely difficult, and the 2015 rules for collective actions before the CAT are different: group members must simply have claims arising from a violation of competition law raising 'common issues'.[63] However, more recent Court of Appeal decisions in England – in particular, in *Lloyd v Google*[64] – suggest that the very narrow interpretation of the English rule in *Emerald* may now be more relaxed.

According to the ERCP, the court will also take into account the nature of the claims and the prospects of dealing with them in a single proceeding. This is more likely to be efficient in the case of pecuniary loss of the group members than in the case of personal injury claims (physical harm).[65] Where the calculation and distribution of damages among the group seem to be impossible from the outset, courts will not grant certification or require the

---

claimants'; France – Article L623-1 of the Consumer Code and Article L1143 – 1 of the Public Health Code use the plural: 'consumers' and 'users of the health system'; Article 62 of Law 2016-1547: 'plusieurs personnes'; see also Norway – Disputes Act, Section 35–2: 'several'.

[60] *Walter Merricks v MasterCard* [2017] CAT 16, [2018] CLY 476, collective redress order denied on 21 July 2017. For the decision of the Court of Appeals, see *Walter Merricks v MasterCard* [2018] EWCA Civ 2527 [2019] Bus L R 1287.

[61] Rule 19.6 of the Civil Procedure Rules.

[62] *Emerald Supplies Ltd v British Airways Plc* [2010] EWCA Civ 1284 [2011] 2 WLR 203. Representative actions in England have been extremely rare. Even before the 2010 Emerald decision, only two cases had been reported since its implementation in 2000.

[63] CAT Rules, Rules 79(1)(b) and 73(2).

[64] *Lloyd v Google* LLC [2019] EWCA Civ 1599.

[65] The ERCP Rules do not exclude personal injury claims from a collective redress action.

formation of sub-groups.[66] However, the downside of the court's discretion is that judges may dismiss collective actions based on the 'superiority test' in order to avoid complex and burdensome litigation. Therefore, any court order on the admissibility or non-admissibility of a collective action is subject to appeal (Rule 213(5)).[67]

In cases in which, according to the conflict of laws rules, different sets of substantive law apply to the claims of the group,[68] the collective redress action should be admissible in principle (Rule 236), but the court may divide the group into sub-groups according to the applicable law and appoint a representative for each sub-group.

4.4.2.2 Opt-in or opt-out

Before admitting a collective action, the court must decide whether the proceedings should be based on an opt-in or opt-out mechanism. As a default rule, an opt-in mechanism will apply under the ERCP. Only where the court makes a finding that (in particular, given the small amount of individual loss) the group members will not become active can it decide to apply an opt-out mechanism. The ERCP, in this respect, follows the national rules in Belgium, Denmark, England, Norway and Slovenia.[69] For the sake of efficient enforcement of liability and tort rules, which is a public good, exceptions from the opt-in principle must be available. It is therefore in the interests of justice

---

[66] The English *MasterCard* case again illustrates the difficulties – for details, see Chapter 10.

[67] The necessity of an appeal has also been emphasized from the US perspective – see Richard Marcus, Chapter 14.

[68] For a more detailed analysis, see Astrid Stadler, 'Conflicts of Laws in Multinationals Collective Actions: A Judicial Nightmare?' in Duncan Fairgrieve and Eva Lein (eds) *Extraterritoriality and Collective Redress*, British Institute of International and Comparative Law London, (Oxford University Press, 2012) 191 – 214; Jacqueline Chabrny, *Grenzüberschreitende Sammelklagen* (Verlag Dr Kovač, 2019) 176 *et seq*.

[69] Belgium – Article XVII43 of the *Code de droit économique*; Denmark – Administration of Justice Act, para 254e(8); England/Wales – CAT Rules 79(1), 79.3; Norway – Disputes Act, Section 35–7; Slovenia – Article 29(2) no 4 of the ZkolT. Other Member States have chosen opt-in as a regular mechanism and have defined clear exceptions for the application of an opt-out scheme: Finland – Class Action Act, para 8 (opt-out in proceedings initiated by the Consumer Omudsman); France allows a simplified group action if consumers are identified and have suffered exactly the same loss; the judge may then order the defendant to compensate the consumers directly without the necessity for them to opt in – Articles L623-14 to L623-17 of the *Code de consommation*. For more details, see Stefaan Voet, 'Consumer Collective Redress in Belgium: Class Actions to the Rescue?' (2015) 16 *European Business L Rev* 121–43; Jules Stuyck, 'Class Actions in Europe? To opt in or to opt out, That is the Question' (2009) 20 *European Business L Rev* 483–505.

to enable a collective redress action on an opt-out basis where it is the most efficient way of organizing the group. Any abstract rule on when the opt-in or opt-out mechanism should apply, such as based on the amount of the group members' claims, risks being arbitrary.

The court's decision on whether opt-in or opt-out is adequate does not depend solely on the amount of the claims involved, although this can be a strong indication of whether group members will bother to become active. The court may also take into account the size of the group, whether group members are identified and the chance of notifying all or almost all group members. As the opt-out scheme may be considered a violation of group members' right to be heard, courts must be careful to balance the pros and cons. This includes the availability of personal notification of the group members where their names and addresses can be easily identified, but also cross-border implications. Due to the difficulties of giving adequate notice to group members in other Member States,[70] Rule 235(3) stipulates that group members outside the forum state become part of the group only if they opt in. This has developed as a European standard over the last decade.[71]

Another element to be considered by the court is whether group members have a realistic chance of bringing their own individual actions. Where such an alternative to the collective action does not exist because of the procedural costs arising and/or the unavailability of third-party funding for individuals, an opt-out mechanism may be appropriate.

4.4.2.3 Selection of the qualified claimant

The selection of the qualified claimant is another very important decision to be made by the court during the certification stage. Whereas numerous Member States simply accept the first claimant who files a collective action as the representative of the group if he or she meets the requirements of legal

---

[70] Publications on the Internet are not always an adequate mechanism to give information about a pending collective action. While advertisements in newspapers, on television and so on provide an opportunity for people to come across them by accident, information given on websites often requires active research by group members, which cannot be expected in all cases. In the Netherlands, Articles 1018 *et seq* of the Code of Civil Procedure rely very much on publications on websites, particularly the website of the exclusive representative. The court may, however, decide that publications must be made in one or more languages other than Dutch (No 3).

[71] Belgium – Article XVII38 § 1 [2], opt-in for non-Belgium residents; England/Wales – Competition Act 1998, Section 47A[11][b], non-UK residents; Commission's Report (COM [2018] 40 final) 13–14.

standing,[72] Dutch[73] and English[74] law allow the court to decide who should be the lead plaintiff. The ERCP has adopted the Dutch approach, for the following reasons.

The group needs the best-qualified claimant in order to be represented adequately before the court. In the United States, any certification order by the court must also decide on the appointment of the class counsel. Contrary to the situation in Europe, in the US system it is not so much the plaintiff himself or herself, but the counsel, who is subject to court selection and appointment.[75] If more than one counsel seeks appointment as class counsel, the court must appoint the one who is best able to represent the interests of the class.[76] In Europe, expertise of the qualified claimant's counsel can be an important factor in the selection process. However, it not possible for a court to require representation of the qualified claimant by a particular law firm. The CJEU, the European Free Trade Association Court and the European legislature have emphasized on several occasions that claimants have the right of free

---

72 For example, Germany – Sections 606, 610(1), (2) of the Civil Procedure Code. In other Member States, the acceptance of the lead plaintiff is at least modified by a supervisory function of the court, which allows the court to substitute the lead plaintiff if he or she does not act in the best interests of the group.

73 Netherlands – Article 1018d, 1018e of the Code of Civil Procedure.

74 CAT Rule 78.

75 Rule 23(g) of the FRCP reads as follows:

(1) *Appointing Class Counsel.* Unless a statute provides otherwise, a court that certifies a class must appoint class counsel. In appointing class counsel, the court:
  (A) must consider:
    (i) the work counsel has done in identifying or investigating potential claims in the action;
    (ii) counsel's experience in handling class actions, other complex litigation, and the types of claims asserted in the action;
    (iii) counsel's knowledge of the applicable law; and
    (iv) the resources that counsel will commit to representing the class;
  (B) may consider any other matter pertinent to counsel's ability to fairly and adequately represent the interests of the class;
  (C) may order potential class counsel to provide information on any subject pertinent to the appointment and to propose terms for attorney's fees and nontaxable costs;
  (D) may include in the appointing order provisions about the award of attorney's fees or nontaxable costs under Rule 23(h); and
  (E) may make further orders in connection with the appointment.

76 Rule 23(g)(2) of the FRCP.

choice of a lawyer, which cannot be restricted, for example, in legal insurance contracts.[77]

The ERCP has decided in favour of a court-appointed qualified claimant (and his or her counsel). Once a collective action has been registered, no parallel actions regarding the same mass harm event and the same claimant group are admissible. The group members must therefore rely on the pending action and need the best possible representation during the proceedings. In order to prevent the qualified claimant who is the first to file a collective action from being the qualified claimant in any case, the court must follow a two-step procedure: it must publish the collective action in the electronic register and set a deadline for other potential qualified claimants to apply (Rule 213(2)). In mass harm events, several representative entities may prepare or may have prepared a collective action, and their ability and qualification to act on behalf of the group can vary considerably. In order to find the best-qualified claimant, the court should be able to select from among several applicants (Rule 213(3)). If there is more than one applicant who seeks appointment to act as the qualified claimant, no matter whether the applicant is an individual group member or a representative entity, the court must select the most suitable qualified claimant. It is also an option for the court to appoint several qualified claimants who must act jointly; but courts should do so only in exceptional situations, where they expect that the qualified claimants will cooperate efficiently. When the claimant group has to be divided into sub-groups according to the applicable law or due to other differences within the group, the court will also appoint a qualified claimant for each sub-group (Rules 218(1) and (2), 214).

The ERCP does not specify in detail the standard to be met by the qualified claimant in order to be selected.[78] Rule 213(3) simply refers to the general requirements for qualified claimants in Rule 209. When several individual group members apply to become a qualified claimant, the court will take into account not only their financial backgrounds and the expertise of their counsel, but also the amount involved with respect to the individual's claim. The bigger the amount at stake for the qualified claimant, the more he or she

---

77 CJEU C-199/08, ECLI:EU:C:2009, 538 – *Eschig/UNIDQA*; EFTA Court E-21/16 – *Nobile v DAS Rechtsschutz Versicherungs AG* (27 October 2017); Article 201(1) lit a Solvency II Directive 2014/51 (EU) (based on the former Directive 2009/138/EG) confirms the free choice of a legal representative for insured persons under a legal expenses insurance.

78 English CAT rules also start with a rather general provision: Rule 78(1): 'The Tribunal may authorize an applicant to act as the class representative (a) whether or not the applicant is a class member, but if the Tribunal considers that it is just and reasonable for the applicant to act as a class representative in the collective proceedings.'

can be expected to have a substantial interest in the outcome of the litigation.[79] As one may also assume that, as a matter of principle, his or her personal interest is not in conflict with the interest of the group, but is rather a parallel one, that claimant will also act in the best interests of the whole group.[80] Rule 209(a) will in any case prevent the appointment of a qualified claimant who has a conflict of interest with any group member as far as is obvious at the beginning of the litigation.

If several entities fulfil the requirements of Rule 209, some of them may do so in a better way than others. The more financial and human resources, the better the qualification of an applicant – at least in principle. Moreover, the court may take into account criteria of transparency and internal governance of the entity when they indicate to what extent the entity respects the interest of the group members and the public. The new Dutch collective action, for example, specifies in Article 305a of the Dutch Civil Code a number of factors that are important for legal standing and the qualification as a lead plaintiff.[81] They have been adopted from the so-called 'Claim Code'[82] and include, for example: (1) the existence of a supervisory board; (2) the existence of an appropriate and effective mechanism for the participation of group members in the decision-making processes; (3) sufficient resources to bear the costs; and (4) a generally accessible website with information on the articles of association, the management structure of the entity, the remuneration of directors

---

[79] This is also a decisive criterion in the German KapMuG proceedings for the selection of a test case plaintiff (Section 9(2) no 3 of the KapMuG).

[80] For similar criteria in US securities class action law, see 15 US Code para 78u-4 (3) (B) (iii):

Rebuttable presumption

(I) In general. Subject to subclause (II), for purposes of clause (i), the court shall adopt a presumption that the most adequate plaintiff in any private action arising under this chapter is the person or group of persons that—

(aa) has either filed the complaint or made a motion in response to a notice under subparagraph (A)(i);

(bb) in the determination of the court, has the largest financial interest in the relief sought by the class; and

(cc) otherwise satisfies the requirements of Rule 23 of the Federal Rules of Civil Procedure'.

This provision of the Private Securities Litigation Reform Act 1995 was designed to prevent the use of professional plaintiffs (hired by the lead counsel) and to shift control over the action to institutional investors; John Coffee (n 3), 73. See also Rule 23(g) of the FRCP (courts shall focus on 'the work counsel has done in identifying or investigating potential claims in the action').

[81] For details, see Chapter 7.

[82] The claim code is available at https://stichtingservice.nl/wp-content/uploads/2014/07/claimcode-voor-claimstichtingen.pdf (last accessed 10 August 2020).

and members of the supervisory board, and outlines of annual reports of the supervisory board and management reports.[83]

Apart from these more general requirements, the court should also take into account the efforts of an entity to prepare a collective action in the particular mass harm event.[84] This may include the number of victims or consumers who may have joined a foundation, regardless of whether it is a long-standing or *ad hoc* founded entity;[85] the efforts to identify common facts and legal issues; and the collection of evidence.

5. STRUCTURE OF STANDALONE PROCEEDINGS FOR DECLARING A SETTLEMENT BINDING

Figure 6.2 provides an overview of the proceedings. Details of the proceedings to declare such a settlement binding will be discussed in Chapter 11.

5.1 Comparative background

Section II(F) of the chapter on collective redress provides rules for situations in which no collective action is pending, but a qualified entity has negotiated an out-of-court settlement with a potential defendant. Such standalone proceedings, with the sole purpose of obtaining a court decision that declares a collective settlement binding on the group members, follow the role model of the Dutch Collective Settlement Act 2005. The mechanism has been used successfully in the Netherlands in a number of big international cases.[86] Today, some

---

[83] For a general analysis, see Heiko Dürr-Auster, *Die Qualifikation als Gruppen- oder Verbandskläger im kollektiven Rechtsschutz* (Mohr Siebeck, 2017).

[84] See also the English CAT Rules, Rule 78(3)(c).

[85] In some cases, this will raise the question of whether those who have registered with the qualified claimant can be entitled to so-called incentive awards (so that they will receive higher payments from the compensation fund than 'normal' group members). In the Netherlands, the Amsterdam Court of Appeals rejected such an approach in the *Fortis/Ageas* case and allowed incentive awards only if they have a clear link to costs and expenses, 16 June 2017, JOR 2018/10, 5 February 2018, ECLI:NL:GHAMS:2018:368 and 13 July 2018, ECLI:NL:GHAMS:2018:2422 (Ageas). In the United States, the issue of incentive awards was supposed to be subject to court review in *Bowes v Melito*, but on 16 December 2019 the Supreme Court denied the petition for writ of certiorari; 140 S Ct 677 (2019).

[86] *Stichting Vie d'Or* (2009) LJN BI2717; *Shell Petroleum v Dexia Nederland* (2009) LJN BI5744; *Stichting uitvoering Vedior schikking* (2009) LJN BJ269; *Stichting Converium Securities Compensation v Liechtensteinsche Landesbank*, 12 November 2010 LJN BO3908 and 17 January 2012, LJN BV1026; *Fortis* case ECLI:NL:GHAMS:2018:2422 (short English summary available www.stibbeblog.nl/all-blog-posts/commercial-litigation/amsterdam-court-of-appeal-declared-e1-3-billion-fortis

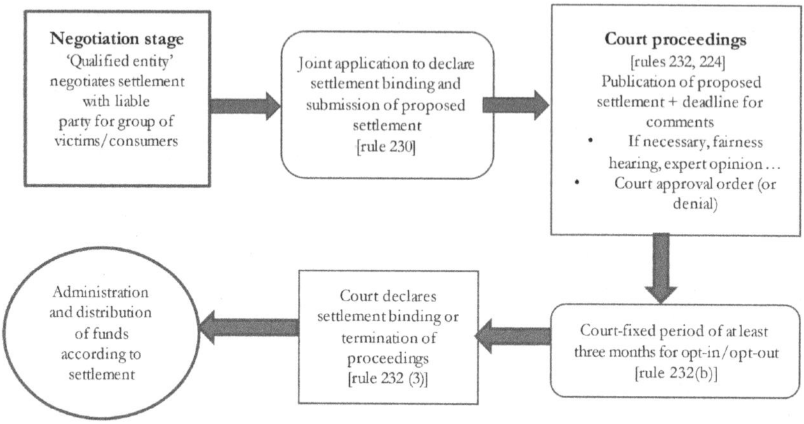

Figure 6.2 Structure of standalone proceedings for declaring a settlement

Member States[87] have already implemented similar rules, while others plan to do so.[88] A standalone settlement mechanism is also part of the European Commission's proposal for a Directive on collective actions in Article 8:

> (1) Member States may provide that a qualified entity and a trader who have reached a settlement regarding redress for consumers affected by an allegedly illegal practice of that trader can jointly request a court or administrative authority to approve it. Such a request should be admitted by the court or administrative authority only if there is no other ongoing representative action in front of the court or administrative authority of the same Member State regarding the same trader and regarding the same practice. . .
>
> (4) The settlements referred to in paragraphs 1, 2 and 3 shall be subject to the scrutiny of the court or administrative authority. The court or administrative authority shall assess the legality and fairness of the settlement, taking into

-collective-settlement-binding-will-the-critical-observations-of-the-court-have-an -impact-on-future-use-of-the-wcam (last accessed 10 August 2020). In some of them, investors domiciled in Europe had not been admitted as class members by US courts to US securities class actions and therefore needed a mechanism in Europe to settle the dispute on a global scale. For case studies on the Dutch cases, see Christopher Hodges, *The Reform of Class and Representative Actions in the European Legal System* (Hart Publishing, 2008) 70 *et seq.*

87 England/Wales, Competition Act 1998, Sections 49B and 49C (approval of redress schemes by the Competition Market Authority); France, Articles 75–76 of Law 2016-1547; Slovenia – Articles 12–25 of the Zkolt.

88 Swiss Tentative Draft Collective Redress (March 2018), Articles 352a–352k of the Swiss Civil Procedure Code. For details, see Matthis Peter, '*Kollektiver Rechtsschutz im Vorentwurf zur Änderung der ZPO*', ZZZ 2019, 108.

consideration the rights and interests of all parties, including the consumers concerned. . .

(6) Individual consumers concerned shall be given the possibility to accept or to refuse to be bound by settlements referred to in paragraphs 1, 2 and 3. . .[89]

The proposal does not specify the proceedings for obtaining court approval, and paragraph 6 leaves it to the Member States to decide whether an opt-in or opt-out mechanism should apply. The basic idea behind that mechanism, however, is simple: where a potential defendant admits its liability in principle, it should not be necessary to initiate collective redress court proceedings with the mere objective of settling the case with a binding effect for the group members.

Nevertheless, a special procedure is necessary that provides safeguards for the interests of the group members, who are typically not involved in the negotiation of the settlement. Courts must be in a position to carefully scrutinize the terms of the settlement and to identify conflicts of interests that might have led to a settlement that is not completely fair and adequate to all or to some of the group members. Such an evaluation also requires court instruments to get access to the necessary information, because the parties to the proceedings have a common interest to receive court approval and cannot be expected to submit arguments against the fairness and adequacy of their settlement contract.

5.2 Standing to negotiate settlements

Although the Dutch Collective Settlement Act 2005 was more or less a role model for this part of the chapter on collective redress in the ERCP, there are some differences. National rules differ, for example, with respect to the question of who has the right to negotiate a settlement on behalf of the group members without a prior mandate. Often longstanding representative entities such as consumer associations or *ad hoc* founded entities have such a right. In the Netherlands, however, it turned out that the rules of the Collective Settlement Act 2005 were too open, and in some mass harm events numerous newly founded entities were mushrooming and competing with each other to negotiate a settlement. This resulted in difficult situations for defendants, as they did not know which entity would be the best to enter into negotiations with. The foundations, for their part, started to compete for the support of victims in the media and on the Internet in order to come up with a large

[89] In the latest document (Council of the EU, Interinstitutional File 2018/0089 (COD), 30 June 2020), there is no explicit rule on settlements negotiated without a representative action pending (Article 8).

number of 'registered victims' to improve their chance of negotiating a settlement with the potentially liable party. Victims and consumers did not know which entity they should join or trust to represent their interests. Finally, due to the missing specifications under Dutch law, a so-called 'Claim Code' – a soft law instrument – was developed to provide guidance for the representative entities. The new Dutch class action rules of 2019 have implemented the most important guidelines of the 'Claim Code' into Article 305a of the Dutch Civil Code.

Rule 229 of the ERCP grants the right to negotiate a settlement to all entities that have legal standing to bring a collective action under Rules 208 and 209. This includes entities authorized by national law that have a direct relationship with the event giving rise to the harm, but also entities that were established solely for the purpose of obtaining redress for a particular group. Both must have sufficient capability to conduct such proceedings with regard to their financial, human and other resources. Although individual group members have legal standing to bring a collective action, they are not in the position to negotiate a settlement out of court (Rule 229(1)). The reason is simply a practical one. Liable parties will not normally be interested in negotiating a settlement with a single person who does not have any mandate by the group members. Qualified entities can be expected to act in the group interests according to their statutory aims, regulations and governance rule. They may also come up with a list of 'supporters' and are thus the likelier candidates to be selected for settlement negotiations.[90]

5.3 Structure of settlement proceedings

If we take a closer look at the structure of the proceedings, the first step (without any court involvement) is the 'negotiation stage', during which a settlement is entered into between the representative entity and the allegedly liable party. Second, the parties to the settlement agreement must file a joint application to the court for approval of the settlement and submit the proposed settlement to the court (Rule 230). The court will then follow the procedure described in Rules 223 and 224. It will publish the settlement, set a deadline for comments and interventions, and, if necessary, hold a fairness hearing, to which all group members can be invited.

When deciding on whether the proposed settlement should be approved, the court will take into consideration the following criteria (Rules 232, 224):

---

[90] According to the Swiss Draft of 2018, legal standing to negotiate a settlement is given to all representative entities that can bring a representative action for damages or skimming-off illegal profits; Articles 352a, 89 of the Swiss Civil Procedure Code.

(1) whether the amount of compensation agreed for the group or sub-groups is manifestly unfair; (2) whether the terms of any other undertaking by a defendant are fair or whether the settlement is, all in all, manifestly contrary to public policy; and (3) whether the payment of costs is manifestly unreasonable.[91] From the wording of Rule 224, it is clear that, when assessing the fairness and appropriateness of the settlement, the court should not consider the legal situation in detail and should not implicitly conduct complete contentious proceedings. Rule 224 leaves room for trade-offs negotiated by the parties, but the court must be aware of possible conflicts of interest behind the scenes and prevent collusive agreements from which only lawyers benefit at the end of the day. The wording also makes clear that approval of the settlement should be the rule and a denial the exception.

If the settlement meets the requirements for approval, the court will publish the collective settlement via the electronic platform and give information on whether the settlement shall become binding based on an opt-in or opt-out procedure. The Dutch Collective Settlement Act and other national rules that have copied the Dutch model generally apply an opt-out mechanism.[92] In cases in which the group members are a large group of unidentified individuals – as in securities, product liability or cartel cases – there is no guarantee that information on the settlement and the necessity to opt out within a fixed timeframe will be obtained by all group members. Notification can be affected only by public announcements in the media or on certain websites. The full consent of group members to the settlement can therefore be fictitious. A settlement based on an opt-out mechanism may therefore face problems in terms of recognition[93] in some states, due to a public policy argument (violation of the right to be heard). This is why the ERCP leaves it to the parties of the settlement to assess that

---

[91] For details, see Chapter 11.

[92] England/Wales – Competition Act 1998, Section 49B(10) (Consumer Rights Act 2015): opt-out as a general rule (a); opt-in for group members domiciled outside the United Kingdom (b); Germany – Section 19 of the KapMuG. The opt-out mechanism is not an issue in the KapMuG proceedings with respect to the investors' right to be heard. As the KapMuG proceedings require individual actions by all investors, the proposed settlement must be formally served on each investor. Therefore, all of them can make an informed choice and notification does not depend on public announcements.

[93] Cross-border enforcement of the settlement will often not be an issue because the defendant will voluntarily comply with the settlement contract. The preclusive effect of the settlement on individual group members, however, may require recognition of the settlement respectively of the court decision approving the settlement. Recognition is pivotal, for example, if one of the group members who did not opt out of the settlement during the period set by the court ignores the binding effect of the settlement and sues the defendant individually for the whole amount of his or her damages in another Member State. For details, see Chapter 14.

risk and decide whether they prefer an opt-in or opt-out mechanism; but their choice is also subject to court approval. Whenever the group is small and the group members can be easily identified, the court must send personal notifications to the group members. In any case, the group members must be given a timeframe of at least three months to opt in or opt out (Rule 232).

Once this timeframe has expired, the court will declare the settlement binding, taking into account whether – if provided for in the settlement – a necessary percentage of group members have given their consent to the settlement by opting in or not opting out. The ERCP does not require a minimum number of group members to accept the settlement, in contrast, for example, to the German KapMuG regulations.[94] The reason is that any particular percentage may be arbitrary and the parties to the settlement contract are in a better position to decide whether and, if so, what threshold should apply.

The ERCP does not provide in detail any regulations on the administration and distribution of the settlement funds. It is up to the settlement agreement to provide rules in this regard – which are, of course, subject to court approval.

[94] Germany – Section 17(1) of the KapMuG: the settlement becomes binding only if less than 30% per cent of the persons involved opt out.

7. Legal standing in collective redress

Ianika Tzankova[1]

1. COLLECTIVE REDRESS DESIGN

1.1 Introduction to design basics

When legislatures design collective redress schemes, they can choose from a number of options. Depending on their choices, the scheme will be more or less frequently invoked. The key features[2] tend to relate to the scope of the legislation; who should have standing to act; how the group is formed; the (legal) costs and fee infrastructure; how binding the scope of the decision is; and the kinds of remedies that are available. In terms of its scope, a collective redress mechanism can, for example, have a horizontal approach and be applicable on a trans-substantive basis – meaning in all areas of law, as opposed to a sectoral approach. The scope is then restricted to certain areas of law – for example, consumer matters[3] or antitrust litigation.[4] It is evident that a horizontal approach potentially facilitates the use of the collective redress device more than a vertical approach.

With respect to who should have standing to act, the choice can be between a member of the group or be restricted to certain pre-approved or designated entities. If only certain designated entities are allowed to file collective actions, this can potentially have a restrictive effect on the use of the collective redress device as compared to the situation in which any member of the defined group can act as the qualified claimant. The overall 'score' on the various key features must be taken into account when evaluating the design of a particular scheme.

1 The author thanks Marijne Mevius for her assistance and Rick Marcus for his helpful comments on an earlier draft.

2 Deborah Hensler, 'The Global Expansion of Class Actions: Power, Politics and Procedural Evolution' in R Thomas and B Fitzpatrick (eds), *The Cambridge Handbook of Class Actions* (Cambridge University Press, 2020) (forthcoming).

3 Belgium, Japan and France.

4 The UK Competition Act 1998, sch 8.

This chapter focuses on the key design feature of legal standing.

1.2 Basic models of legal standing in collective redress

When it comes to determining who should have standing to act as a claimant in collective redress, there are two basic models: the *individual* qualified claimant and the *institutional* qualified claimant.[5] The latter is, by design, a non-profit entity and can be further divided into three sub-categories: (1) (semi)public entities; (2) (statutory) pre-approved or designated non-profit organizations (foundations and associations) – so-called 'designated entities'; and (3) *ad hoc* certified or ad hoc court-approved entities (eg, Dutch claim foundations – so-called '*Stichtingen*').[6] This model is predominantly found in civil law jurisdictions, such as the Netherlands,[7] Brazil,[8] Belgium, France, Germany and Chile.

In the first model, an individual member of the group who has suffered damage acts as a qualified claimant. That could be a private person or a legal entity whose claim meets certain criteria set out in a statute; but the qualified claimant in this model is always someone who has suffered damage or has been negatively affected in some other way by the wrongdoing that the action seeks to address. The individual qualified claimant model is to be found predominantly in common law jurisdictions such as the United States, Israel, Canada, the United Kingdom and Australia; whereas Bulgaria, Poland and Denmark are examples of jurisdictions outside of the common law family that have also introduced this model.

European Rules of Civil Procedure (ERCP) Rule 208 allows for either model at the discretion of the court or legislature.

---

[5] Byron Stier and Ianika Tzankova, 'The Culture of Collective Litigation: A Comparative Analysis' in Deborah R. Hensler, Christopher Hodges and Ianika Tzankova (eds), *Class Actions in Context: How Culture, Economics and Politics Shape Collective Litigation* (Edward Elgar Publishing, 2016).

[6] See also: European Law Institute, *Statement of the European Law Institute on Collective Redress and Competition Damages Claims* (ISBN: 978-3-9503458-4-1, ELI 2014) 18–60; John C. Coffee Jr., 'The Globalization of Entrepreneurial Litigation: Law, Culture, and Incentives' (2017) 165(7) *University of Pennsylvania Law Rev* 1895.

[7] Ianika Tzankova, 'Everything You Wanted to Know About Dutch Foundations but Never Dared to Ask: A Check List for Investors' (2015) 05 VbR 149 (part 1), 06 VbR 178 (part 2).

[8] See Chapter 6 on certification.

1.3 Overview of discussion in this chapter

This chapter is organized as follows. Section 2 addresses potential agency issues with respect to the two basic approaches of legal standing design. It also considers whether differing rules on legal standing in collective actions versus collective settlements are appropriate. Section 3 assesses the topic of legal standing under the ERPC and Section 4 assesses the topic of legal standing in collective redress at the EU level: two EU initiatives to guide discussions on collective redress design within the Member States will be briefly discussed. Finally, Section 5 deals with parallel actions, both in the national context and in the cross-border EU setting: the design of legal standing rules in collective redress has an immediate effect on the frequency with which potential parallel, competing or overlapping collective actions occur, and therefore impacts on how effective the mechanisms are in the cross-border context.

2. AGENCY ISSUES UNDER THE BASIC APPROACHES

A characteristic feature of collective redress schemes is their representative or substitutive nature. This implies a principal-agent relationship on multiple levels. Conceptually speaking, there are three different types of agency issues in collective redress on the claimant side. First, there is the conflict of interest between the representative claimant and the group; then there is the potential internal conflict of interest between the different sub-categories of group members;[9] and finally there is the conflict between the group as a collective and the group's lawyer.[10]

Academic literature and European policy discussions on agency issues in class actions and collective redress seem to be dominated by concerns about the latter – and more specifically, about the US contingency fee regime, where the class action lawyer runs no adverse cost risk and is paid on a percentage of outcome basis (in case of success) from a common (settlement) fund,

---

[9] Victims of the same type of wrongdoing might have diverging interests with respect to the outcome of the action, especially in view of their differing factual or legal positions. Forming subgroups is viewed as an appropriate remedy for that.

[10] See, for example, John Coffee, 'Understanding the Plaintiff's Attorney: The Implications of Economic Theory for Private Enforcement of Law through Class and Derivative Actions' (1986) 86 *Colum L Rev* 669; and Michael Dorf, 'The Indictment of the Milberg Weiss Law Firm and America's Love/Hate Relationship with Class Action Litigation' (*FindLaw*, 22 May 2006), https://supreme.findlaw.com/legal-commentary/the-indictment-of-the-milberg-weiss-law-firm-and-americas-lovehate-relationship-with-class-action-litigation.html (last accessed 18 February 2020).

constructed via an opt-out device. The underlying assumption of these discussions seems to be that the US contingency fee regime is the only procedural design setting where agency issues in representative or collective litigation on the claimant side emerge. However, such an assumption is inaccurate.[11] As Professor Kritzer has observed: 'all fee arrangements [= principal-agent relationship] create actual and potential conflicts; only the nature of the conflicts differ. Awareness of the conflicts may be lacking, but that does not mean they do not exist.'[12]

This section will focus on one specific type of potential agency issues in collective redress: that between the qualified claimant (or class representative) and the group. Kritzer's observation is equally relevant here: any principal-agent relationship creates actual and potential conflicts of interest; only the nature of the conflicts differs. Awareness of what these conflicts might entail might be lacking, but this does not mean that they do not exist. In Section 2.1 we briefly outline potential agency issues under the individual claimant model as they have been identified in academic literature; while Section 2.2 focuses on potential agency issues under the institutional claimant model, as they emerge from the case law and practice in a number of civil law jurisdictions.

2.1 The individual claimant model

The major agency issue between the representative individual claimant and the group in this model is caused by asymmetry in the stakes held in the litigation by the group members and the individual representative claimant on the one hand, and the group's lawyer on the other. This asymmetry between the lawyer and the group also affects the relationship between the individual representative claimant and the group, because the representative claimant is viewed as a mere extension of the lawyer. This can result in the lack of a proper incentive on the part of the individual representative claimant to monitor the conduct of the lawyer. It can also lead to collusion between the two to both benefit from the outcome of the action, to the detriment of the group. This is why, in many jurisdictions that make use of this model, considerable emphasis is put on judicial oversight in appointing 'adequate' (United States) or 'genuine' (Canada) individuals to act as a representative plaintiff.

Scrutiny is given to their personal motives for initiating or supporting the action. So-called 'incentive awards' for the representative plaintiffs – intended

---

11 For a brief discussion of potential (agency) issues in funding models of collective redress outside contingency fees, including legal expense insurance and legal aid, see: Ianika Tzankova, 'Funding of Mass Disputes: Lessons from the Netherlands' (2012) 8(3) *Journal of Law, Economics & Policy* 549.

12 Herbert Kritzer, 'Fee Regimes and the Cost of Civil Justice' (2009) 28 *CJQ* 36.0.

to reimburse them for the time and effort put into their role – are considered controversial[13] in these jurisdictions and have a limited scope, to avoid inappropriate financial incentives for the representative plaintiff. Critics of the model in the United States suggest that the individual representative plaintiff should be seen as nothing more than a 'figurehead',[14] put in place only to facilitate entrepreneurial lawyering and playing no meaningful role whatsoever in the process. They advocate that the representative plaintiff as such be abolished.[15]

Another disadvantage, which is not necessarily an agency issue, concerns the vulnerability of a model (in fact, of any model) which is dependent on one individual and his or her personal circumstances, especially if the litigation could go on for many years. A different example of this disadvantage was illustrated by a case reported in the media in which the suitability of the suggested individual representative plaintiff in US proceedings was disputed on the basis that he had refused an earlier monetary settlement proposal from the defendant. The candidate representative plaintiff was not interested in monetary relief, since that was not what the class was aiming for. However, the defendant alleged that the refusal of the monetary settlement disqualified him as a suitable representative plaintiff.[16]

As mentioned above, discussion of agency issues in relation to the individual plaintiff model in US academic literature and policy initiatives often

---

13 C.T. Micheletti and H.T. Rankie, 'Incentive Awards Guidance from Recent Class Actions' (Competition Law 360, 6 September 2013), www.zelle.com/news-publications-238 (last accessed 18 February 2020); and A. Frankel, 'The Misguided Attack on Incentive Awards in Class Actions' (*Reuters Blog*, 13 May 2014), http://blogs.reuters.com/alison-frankel/2014/05/13/the-misguided-attack-on-incentive-awards-in-class-actions/ (last accessed 18 February 2020); Elisabeth Sperle, 'Here Today, Possibly Gone Tomorrow: An Examination of Incentive Awards and Conflicts of Interest in Class Action Litigation' (2010) 23(3) *Geo J Legal Ethics* 873.

For Canada, see: Jasminka Kalajdzic, *Class Actions in Canada: The Promise and Reality of Access to Justice* (UBC Press 2018).

14 Jean Wegman Burns, 'Decorative Figureheads: Eliminating Class Representatives in Class Actions' (1990) 42(165) *Hastings LJ* 165; Jonathan R. Macey and Geoffrey P. Miller, 'The Plaintiffs' Attorney's Role in Class Action and Derivative Litigation: Economic Analysis and Recommendations for Reform' (1991) 58(1) 93–94.

15 *Ibid.*

16 Alison Frankel, 'A New Way for Defendants to Kill Class Actions by Picking Off Plaintiffs?' (*Reuters Blog*, 24 July 2018), www.reuters.com/article/legal-us-otc-campbellewald/a-new-way-for-defendants-to-kill-class-actions-by-picking-off-plaintiffs-idUSKBN1KE2TY (last accessed 18 February 2020): 'The plaintiff's refusal to accept Allied's offer made him an unsuitable candidate to lead the class action because he's not a typical class member. His "unique circumstances as the only member of the putative class to have been compensated for his claim have irreparably compromised his role as lead plaintiff in this litigation," according to the defendant's counsel opposing class certification.'

relates to entrepreneurial lawyering. Indeed, class actions under this model tend to promote lawyer-driven litigation.[17] However, experiences with the Canadian regime of individual representative plaintiff demonstrate that this is not necessarily a bad thing and does not generate 'abusive litigation' or 'meritless litigation'.[18] In fact, what seems to be underappreciated in policy discussions is that none of the real or potential agency problems signalled in US academic research suggests the existence of abusive litigation or blackmail settlements resulting from class actions applying this model.[19] The reality in US class actions is that there is a regular and continuous process of evaluation, as a result of which the US Federal Rules of Civil Procedure have been modified a number of times, and case law has been established to deal with potential agency and other related issues.[20] Put bluntly: the agency issues in this model do not give rise to abusive or meritless litigation, but rather issues of potential

---

[17] According to Jasminka Kalajdzic, who conducted an empirical study on class actions initiated in Ontario between 2009–14, only 25 per cent of the cases were 'client-initiated'. In the majority of the studied cases, class actions were the result of publicly announced regulatory investigations, referrals by third parties or the firm's own research and investigations: all considered to be variations of entrepreneurial lawyering: Jasminka Kalajdzic, *Class Actions in Canada: The Promise and Reality of Access to Justice* (UBC Press 2018) 16, 72–75.

[18] *Ibid* 75–80.

[19] John C. Coffee Jr, 'Accountability and Competition in Securities Class Actions: Why "Exit" Works Better Than "Voice".' (2008) 30 *Cardozo L Rev* 407: 'As a result of the PSLRA, recent Supreme Court decisions, and recently tightened class certification standards, the truly "frivolous" securities class action is today relatively rare – possibly even a mythic creature of folklore, like the unicorn, in that it is much discussed, but seldom objectively observed.' See also: Deborah R. Hensler, 'Third-Party Financing of Class Action Litigation in the United States: Will the Sky Fall?' (2014) 63 *DePaul L Rev* 499: 'This assertion is based on three assumptions about U.S. class actions: first, that the current class action regime produces a host of frivolous class actions that defendants are forced to settle because of their in terrorem effect; second, that class action jurisprudence enables easy access to courts for frivolous class claims; and third, that litigation investors' business models will favor frivolous claims. The available empirical data do not support the first assumption about the current regime, and recent U.S. Supreme Court jurisprudence as well as the economics of third-party litigation financing militate against a flood of frivolous class actions going forward.' Indeed, one must be cautious not to mix lobby rhetoric with empirical reality. For information on the far-reaching lobby activities of the US Chamber of Commerce, see: Jason Rathod and Sandeep Vaheesan, 'The Arc and the Architecture of Private Enforcement Regimes in the United States and Europe: A View Across the Atlantic' (2015) 14 *University of New Hampshire L Rev* 303. See also Hensler (n 19).

[20] Class Action Fairness Act of 2005, 28 USC §1712 (b(2)). For a discussion of the 2003 and 2018 amendments of Rule 23, which expanded the parties' reporting obligations regarding settlements and also focused on the court's judicial oversight, see R. Marcus, 'Revolution v. Evolution in Class Action Reform' (2018) 96(3) *NCL Rev* 903.

'sell-out' or 'sweetheart' settlements between the class lawyer and the defendant, to the detriment of the class.

2.2 The institutional claimant model

Unlike the model mentioned above, little attention is paid in academic writing to the real and potential agency issues with the institutional claimant model. It is anything but self-evident that this model is immune from such problems, and this is borne out by several empirical case studies.[21] The following paragraphs briefly discuss some of the real or potential issues that can arise under this model. They will do so by reference to case studies and experiences in a number of civil law jurisdictions, both inside and outside Europe.

2.2.1 Governmental and other public bodies

In some civil law jurisdictions, there is a general tendency to rely on governmental and semi-governmental entities to file collective actions. Brazil and Chile are examples of such jurisdictions. In Chile, *Servicio Nacional del Consumidor* (SERNAC), the national consumer protection agency, has standing to bring class actions and to intervene in class actions brought by private lawyers.[22] That said, a number of concrete examples show that even an agency which is well respected and which has taken on numerous cases against big corporate opponents[23] can also suffer from severe agency issues. Although there is little doubt as to the good intentions of such agencies, good intentions are not enough.

As some commentators have observed – and many will find these observations applicable cross-culturally – SERNAC's faithful advocates of consumer rights are also structurally understaffed and have not developed expertise in collective actions.[24] Also, the leadership of such agencies has little incentive to bring complex collective actions, since these often continue for years, which means that those who take the initiative will often be unable to take the credit for potential successes. And even if they do bring such cases and

---

[21] For a brief overview of relevant case studies illustrating some of the issues that arise in this model, see Byron Stier and Ianika Tzankova, 'The Culture of Collective Litigation: A Comparative Analysis' in Deborah R. Hensler, Christopher Hodges and Ianika Tzankova (eds) (n 5), 36–40; and Agustin Barroilhet, 'Self-interested Gatekeeping? Clashes Between Public and Private Enforcers in Two Chilean Class Actions' in Deborah R. Hensler, Christopher Hodges and Ianika Tzankova (eds) (n 5), 362–84.

[22] Similar to the powers of the public prosecutor in Brazil: see the comments of Hermes Zaneti in Chapter 14.

[23] Barroilhet (n 21) 362–84.

[24] *Ibid* 381.

eventually achieve success, 'compensation for small-value claims and the imposition of ridiculous fines is hardly an attractive announcement to make years after the complaint'.[25] Therefore, the natural attitude of such agencies is not to proactively engage in private law enforcement and, whenever they are approached by a corporation that has decided for whatever reason to provide some form of redress, to engage in collective mediation and secure a quick result. Unsurprisingly, that result is often favourable for the corporation in comparison to its potential exposure in private litigation. Nevertheless, that outcome helps such agencies to preserve their most important asset: their public image.[26] In the words of one commentator:

> On the institutional side, SERNAC competes with other agencies for influence and relevance within the administration, and with private enforcers for its public image. Its advantages in this competition are its constant presence in the media and its undisputed position as an uncompromising consumer defender that can provide the best possible compensation within a period when it still matters, politically speaking. If private enforcers surpass SERNAC in the media. . . , or if courts and class actions start to be perceived as the institutions where the consumers can find substantive and timely relief. . . SERNAC would become largely irrelevant within the administration and more likely to be sidelined by other agencies.[27]

An additional concern emerges when the action is not against a private entity, but rather against the state or (another) state-related agency.[28] Such institutional claimants could develop their own institutional agenda, which does not necessarily result in the best outcome for the group in a given case. Also, there could be abrupt governmental reversals on enforcing regulatory limits, which is an additional reason why legislatures may not want to be dependent on action by an executive branch of government.[29]

Although these agency issues are of a different nature from those discussed in the previous paragraphs, they are no less concerning. They matter, because they seem to be less transparent and camouflaged by the veil of public interest and non-profit motives. As the Chilean experiences show,[30] absent enforcement by private lawyers, the institutional agency issues could also easily result in sell-out or sweetheart settlements. The only difference with the model

---

[25] *Ibid* 380.

[26] *Ibid* 381.

[27] *Ibid* 381–82.

[28] See comments of Richard Marcus in Chapter 14. An issue that seems to be of less concern in Brazil: see Hermes Zaneti's comment in Chapter 14.

[29] As examples under the President Trump administration demonstrate. After the 2016 election, some agencies (eg, the Environmental Protection Agency) reversed their position in pending litigation.

[30] Barroilhet (n 21) 379–82.

discussed in the previous paragraphs seems to be that the agencies do not receive an immediate monetary gain, but are 'rewarded' in a different way: by maintaining strategic institutional power and relevance, politically justifying their existence.

The SERNAC example also shows that lawyers and staff members frequently change jobs between agencies, law firms and corporate clients, and move swiftly and seamlessly between roles and parties, which is not immediately known by or visible to the outside world, adding an extra layer of opacity.[31] In the literature, this phenomenon is also known as 'agency or regulatory capture' or the 'revolving door'.[32] While the specific Chilean examples might look like 'folklore local', the underlying theme of agency capture and 'institutional power wars' in high-profile collective actions is universal and arguably recognizable for those who deal with (semi)governmental organizations. The (collective actions) context might be different, but the institutional behaviour pattern and related institutional agency issues remain more or less the same. At least three noteworthy lessons can be drawn from the Chilean experiences:[33]

1. non-coordinated public enforcement has a lower chance of success than sophisticated private enforcement;
2. special attention should be paid to the independence and status of the public agency in charge of controlling class actions' private enforcement; and
3. ideally, class actions should be fully integrated into the toolkit of the agency and fully aligned with the agency's institutional mission.[34]

This also shows that institutional monopolies are a bad idea, and that a balanced system of checks and balances between private and public enforcers contributes to effective collective redress.[35] More generally, the long-term adverse effects for the collective redress claimants of uneven competition and

---

31 *Ibid* 366: 'they had a former SERNAC official on their team who had been hired amidst the class action debate precisely to defend corporate clients. Using him as a liaison, they contacted SERNAC, which until then, had been silent and likely unaware of the case. The defense and SERNAC met at least once before the class actions complaint was served and apparently reached an informal agreement that has never been disclosed to the public.'

32 This means that the people who get control of enforcement agencies may be allies of the industries they oversee – hence, 'agency capture'; and that they may rotate between government and high positions in industry ('revolving door').

33 Barroilhet (n 21) 382.

34 Brazil seems to offer an example of where that is the case: see the comments of Hermes Zaneti in Chapter 14.

35 See also S. Farhang, *The Litigation State: Public Regulation and Private Law Suits* (Princeton University Press, 2010).

power games between public and private enforcers, leaving wrongdoers as the proverbially 'laughing' third party, should not be underestimated:

> in a country where class actions are a cumbersome procedure offering little chance of success unless some loophole is exploited, a politically-bound agency with few other powers which lives in competition with other agencies, cannot risk being displaced by aggressive private class action enforcers who threaten to supplant it in the fulfilment of its perceived institutional mission.[36]

The above shows that reliance on this type of institutional representative claimant is not a panacea, and reveals how little we know about the adverse consequences and long-term effects of this model of standing in collective redress.

2.2.2 Pre-existing non-profit organizations

Another popular practice in civil law jurisdictions is to grant standing to act in class actions to pre-existing non-profit organizations. These are typically structured as independent private associations, but some are still publicly funded. The Taiwanese Securities and Fortunes Investors Protection Center (SFIPC) is an example of the latter.[37] The Dutch *Consumentenbond* and the Dutch Investors Association (VEB) are examples of pre-existing organizations that are privately funded via donations and membership fees.

Examples from these jurisdictions confirm similar *institutional* agency issues to those identified in the previous paragraph; the Dutch experiences are especially relevant in the European context, since the Netherlands has had more than 25 years of experience with these types of institutional representative claimants. One might expect that other European jurisdictions that have just introduced these types of institutional representative claimants will experience a similar development and similar agency issues. In the *Dexia* case, which concerned consumer financial products, the Dutch *Consumentenbond* endorsed a collective mediation process with Dexia Bank, resulting in a collective settlement that was considered by a group of consumers to be a sell-out or sweetheart settlement.[38] In fact, it was considered unfavourable by a specific sub-group of consumers, but not by others. This reveals a structural internal conflict of interest that institutional representative claimants must deal with

---

[36] Barroilhet (n 21) 383.

[37] Experiences with the Taiwanese SFIPC offer another example of how the institutional agenda of the organization, rather than the strength of the case, determines choices in (collective) action. Kuo-Chang Huang, 'Using Associations as a Vehicle for Class Action: The Case of Taiwan' in Deborah R. Hensler, Christopher Hodges and Ianika Tzankova (eds) (n 5), 88–90.

[38] Tzankova (n 11).

when the interests within the group are not sufficiently homogenous. Such concerns become more apparent when monetary relief is involved.

The *Vie d'Or* case reveals a similar internal conflict of interest: the *Consumentenbond* did not act for small business owners who suffered substantial damages on their pension plans as result of the bankruptcy of a life insurer, because it considered the cause of action (liability of a financial supervisor and the state) too complex and the business consumers' background not sufficiently representative of the average consumer.[39] In that case, the *Consumentenbond* did not have the institutional will, resources and expertise to achieve tangible results for the consumers, and was continuously battling financial and other constraints in pursuing consumer matters.

By comparison, the VEB has taken a different approach and has managed to develop expertise, build an impressive war chest and secure significant successes for its members.[40] However, in relation to the *World Online* and *Fortis* settlements, it faced heavy criticism of a similar nature to that which *Consumentenbond* had to contend with in *Dexia*: that it does not properly represent the interests of its entire constituency, which is 'the universe of investors', and in settlement negotiations achieves results only for its members and for itself.[41] This again generated the perception of a sweetheart settlement culture.

In addition, in the *Fortis* case, new concerns have been raised by the court with respect to the 'business model' of a non-profit organization that negotiates settlements with additional contributions to the war chest of the organization for its future activities.[42] Although such an approach might be inspired

---

[39] Ianika Tzankova, 'Collective Redress in Vie d'Or: A Reflection on a European Cultural Phenomenon' in Deborah R. Hensler, Christopher Hodges and Ianika Tzankova (eds) (n 5) 117.

[40] Some of the examples concern the *Shell* settlement, *World Online*, the *Unilever* settlement and the *Landis* settlement. For more information, see: *Vereniging van Effectenbezitters, 'Juridische Acties voor Beleggers'* (*VEB,* 2020), www.veb.net/acties-menu/actieoverzichtspagina (last accessed 20 February 2020).

[41] For a description of the Fortis settlement, see Jonathan Richman and Ianika Tzankova, 'Fortis Case Confirms Viability of Dutch Settlement Law' (*Law360*, 27 July 2018), www.law360.com/articles/1067106/fortis-case-confirms-viability-of-dutch-settlement-law (last accessed 18 February 2020); and Kevin Lacroix, 'Dutch Court Declares Largest Ever European Investor Claims Settlement Binding' (*the D&O Diary,* 30 July 2018), www.dandodiary.com/2018/07/articles/international-d-o/dutch-court-declares-largest-ever-european-investor-claims-settlement-binding (last accessed 18 February 2020); Christoph Van der Elst and Wim Weterings, 'The Solid Dutch Mechanisms for Collective Settlement' in R Thomas and B Fitzpatrick (eds), *The Cambridge Handbook of Class Actions* (Cambridge University Press 2020) (forthcoming).

[42] Richman and Tzankova, *ibid.*

by the doctrine behind *cy près* distribution, one may wonder whether this is an acceptable practice for a number of reasons. What makes this practice problematic from a conflict of interest perspective is that these types of institutional plaintiffs could combine a number of roles at the same time. First, they could be a 'case originator' because they signal wrongdoings that might give rise to an action. Second, they could be a party to the proceedings. Third, they could act as a litigation funder. Finally (as the Dutch example shows), they could even be the lawyers instructed on the case, taking autonomous decisions. The agent becomes the principal, with very little clarity as to how the potential (new) agency issues are addressed.

It is unclear what the impact of the *Fortis* ruling that questioned the business model of the VEB will be on future securities litigation activities of the association, and whether it will be able to reinvent itself and find an acceptable new business model. This might lead to the separation of roles.[43] In 2018[44] the *Consumentenbond* – inspired by the 'commercial successes' of its non-profit colleague – took a similar path, but it structured its commercial activities differently. It established a separate, yet related joint venture with a commercial partner to finance and run collective damages actions. The commercial partner would lend its capital and expertise to new actions, while the *Consumentenbond* would lend its name and reputation. The *Consumentenbond*, as a partner and shareholder in the joint venture, would profit from the successes of the joint venture and invest proceeds in other activities. It remains to be seen whether this structure will sufficiently address potential agency problems.

The Dutch experiences in the past 25 years show in any event that the choice that these types of institutional plaintiffs have is either to find ways to become more business minded to be effective or to remain non-profit, understaffed and ineffective. Those that choose the former may struggle to reconcile that which seems irreconcilable: the need to somehow make a profit and be accountable for it on the one hand, and the need to comply with restrictive statutory requirements on their non-profit making nature on the other. Depending on the choices that such organizations make, they will go in either the direction of (and with the related agency issues discussed in) the previous paragraph, or the direction discussed in the following paragraph. Meanwhile, real and potential agency issues within this type of institutional claimant seem to be overlooked by policy makers and legislatures.

---

[43] See also R. Simon, 'Fee Sharing Between Lawyers and Public Interest Groups', 98 *Yale LJ* 1069 (1989).

[44] Martijn Klerks and Edwin van der Schoot, '*Consumentenbond in Zee met Claimclub*', *De Telegraaf* (Amsterdam 11 July 2018), www.telegraaf.nl/financieel/2285373/consumentenbond-in-zee-met-claimclub (last accessed 20 February 2020).

2.2.3 *Ad hoc* non-profit organizations

A last category concerns non-profit organizations: foundations or associations that are established for a particular collective action. Some jurisdictions allow for *ad hoc* organizations to act in collective actions if they meet certain criteria. The Netherlands once again offers a relevant point of reference in the European context. Over the past 25 years, *ad hoc* organizations have proved to be a useful addition to the collective redress toolkit, since there might not always be a pre-existing organization that is willing or able to address certain mass harms. And even if there were one, monopolies need to be avoided for the necessary checks and balances. If the Netherlands had not had this option, the 13 000 Dutch consumers in the *Vie d'Or* case mentioned above would have been unable to obtain redress.

The criteria that such *ad hoc* organizations must meet can vary. The criteria could be formal, requiring merely a non-profit making character, a certain legal structure and adequate articles of association to be able to run the collective action in question. However, this relatively low threshold is insufficient to adequately protect the legitimate interests of group members and defendants, as was demonstrated in a few cases where (in themselves meritorious) consumer collective actions were initiated either by a large number of *ad hoc* foundations with differing governance structures (*DSB* case) or by a single *ad hoc* foundation backed by a commercial initiative (*Dutch State Lottery* case).[45] In the *DSB* case, the consumers were unclear as to which foundation to support and the defendant was unclear as to whom to address with respect to the potential resolution of the matter. In the *Dutch State Lottery* case, the foundation – which initially did a good job in obtaining favourable court rulings – seemed to have been overtaken by the commercial interests of its founder and single board member.[46]

In order to address issues such as those illustrated above, a self-regulatory initiative from 2011 resulted in a Claim Code providing (comply or explain) rules for the governance of *ad hoc* foundations acting in collective actions.[47] For example, the Claim Code provides guidelines for the composition and remuneration of board and supervisory board members, conflicts of interest and communications by the foundation with the public and its constituency. Although the idea behind the Claim Code (improved governance and accountability) was generally endorsed, there were also criticisms. The Claim Code

---

[45] Ilja Tillema, 'Entrepreneurial Mass Litigation; Balancing the Building Blocks' (Doctoral Thesis, Erasmus University Rotterdam 2019) 274–76.

[46] *Ibid.*

[47] *Ibid* 272.

increased further the financial burden on non-profit organizations in collective actions without recognizing the (commercial) litigation funding reality.

In 2019 the Claim Code was revised and a new version was published, recognizing that commercial litigation funding plays a meaningful role in collective redress, but also needs to be scrutinized. The revised Claim Code[48] attempts to strike a balance between accountability and burden by stipulating that board members must be independent and have no personal interest in the outcome of the action; but at the same time allowing the appointment of a representative of the funder to sit on the supervisory board. The new Dutch act on collective damages actions[49] codifies some of the principles laid down in the Claim Code 2011. The existence of *ad hoc* claim organizations has not led (in the Netherlands) to more collective actions in comparison to those brought by other types of institutional representative claimants[50] and do not support claims of increased meritless litigation – in fact, they suggest the opposite: 'The findings did support the claim that there is an increased detection of mass wrongdoings, although the number of collective actions appears to have remained modest.'[51]

It remains to be seen how the structural entrance of commercial litigation funding will influence collective redress practice in jurisdictions where contingency fees are not allowed and lawyers and board members of the foundations are remunerated on a continuous basis, similar to the lawyers of defendants in collective redress, so there are little economic incentives on both sides to litigate swiftly and efficiently. Judicial case management will become even more essential.

2.2.4 Collective action or collective settlement

One last question that deserves attention in the context of real or potential agency issues, irrespective of the type of claimant, and which is also closely related to the topic of certification, is whether differing legal standing (and certification) rules should apply depending on the context: a collective action or a collective settlement. The prevailing view is a strict one: the same rules on

---

[48] A.H. van Delden and others, *Claimcode 2019* (Boom Juridisch, 2019) https://warehouse.budh.nl/system/assets/uploads/001/111/662/23f4d501a23fc1e779865e822c7cc0c5a1b30345/Claim Code_2019_9789462906082_original.pdf (last accessed 20 February 2020).

[49] *Wet Afwikkeling Massaschade in Collectieve Actie*, *Stb* 2019, 130.

[50] Tillema (n 45) 273: 'The number of cases brought by entrepreneurial representative organizations starts to gradually climb from 2008 onwards, but remains (well) under the level of the number of cases brought by the other representative organisations.'

[51] *Ibid* 274.

legal standing (and certification) should be applicable in collective actions and collective settlements to reduce sell-out or sweetheart settlement concerns.[52] However, there are also more nuanced views to be found both in academia[53] and in practice.[54] The common theme there seems to be that legal formalities should not stand in the way of a critical substantive evaluation of a settlement result. Indeed, the fact that a settlement agreement has been concluded by a non-profit organization does not make a collective settlement by definition a good one, and a settlement co-negotiated by a profit organization does not necessarily disqualify an otherwise adequate settlement. Courts should evaluate both scenarios with equal scrutiny, as the analyses above demonstrate.

2.3 Concluding remarks on agency and incentives

The above analysis reveals that any model of standing in collective redress comes with its own agency issues; one approach is not, by definition, better than the other. As problematic as the model of the individual plaintiff or claimant may look at first sight, the jurisdictions that are applying it seem to be aware of what the real and potential agency issues are and have taken various measures to address them. With respect to the institutional claimant model, however, the situation seems different. Very little is known about how the three subcategories of non-profit entities discussed above act in collective actions, what drives them, how they are monitored and held accountable on a case level, how they finance their actions and how all of this influences their long-term performance and short-term behaviour when protecting the interests of the group members they claim to represent in collective redress. There seems to be very little awareness among academics and policy makers that non-profit entities acting in collective redress are also exposed to agency issues, and increasingly experience pressure to develop profit-making activities to be able to play a meaningful role in collective redress in general and in competition with private actors.

---

52 See comments of Richard Marcus in Chapter 14.

53 Francis McGovern and William Rubenstein, 'The Negotiation Class: A Cooperative Approach to Class Actions Involving Large Stakeholders', Duke Law School Public Law & Legal Theory Series (2019) 41.

54 In the *Fortis* settlement, one of the settling and petitioning parties was a profit organization and admitted by the Amsterdam Court of Appeal in the collective action proceedings.

3. LEGAL STANDING UNDER THE ERCP COLLECTIVE REDRESS RULES

One conclusion after applying the above analysis to the ERCP is that it follows a 'liberal neutral' approach with respect to the topic of legal standing in collective redress, by allowing both the individual claimant model and the institutional claimant model in its various appearances: public entity; longstanding or pre-existing associations; *ad hoc* established special purpose vehicles; and individual group members.[55] In this way, the ERCP implicitly recognizes that each model of standing of collective redress has limitations and real and potential agency issues, and prioritizes substance over form. The ERCP therefore provides that, irrespective of the chosen agent model, the persons or entities acting in collective redress actions must demonstrate that they meet additional criteria such as no conflict of interest with the group; comply with governance and accountability requirements; or demonstrate sufficient financial and other capability to run the action.[56] They might be required to substantiate such capabilities. The only exception is with respect to public entities: Member States should be in charge of appointing these if that is under consideration and it would go too far to lay down more specific rules for these entities also.

The reasoning behind this 'liberal neutral' approach with respect to legal standing is straightforward and follows from the discussions in the previous paragraphs. One model is not, by definition, better than the other: there may not always be a pre-existing organization willing or capable to run a specific action; while generally, monopolies of organizations with respect to standing in collective redress must be avoided. Moreover, establishing *ad hoc* organizations might be disproportionately burdensome – hence the option for a group member to act as the class representative. A noteworthy restriction with respect to individual group members is that they cannot be a lawyer or exercise any legal profession. This is to prevent entirely lawyer-driven litigation, even if that might be meritorious. Another restriction is that individuals cannot negotiate a collective settlement. Apart from that, there is no difference between standing rules in collective action or collective settlement; nor is there a ranking in the ERCP among the different types of claimants in collective redress. It is up to the courts to determine in a given case which type of candidate claimant is the most appropriate.

---

[55] ERCP Rule 208.

[56] ERCP Rule 208. See also Chapter 6 on certification.

4. LEGAL STANDING IN COLLECTIVE REDRESS AT EU LEVEL

For non-European readers who have lost track of the status and nature of the various European initiatives in the field of collective redress, a brief overview is helpful. The closest the European Commission has come to designing its own preferred system of collective redress[57] was in 2008, when – under the watch of Neelie Kroes, the former commissioner for competition – a White Paper on private damages actions for breaches of competition law was introduced, including a proposal on collective damages actions.[58] The strong opposition from the business lobby[59] and the wish of the European Parliament to have a say in any legislative proposal concerning collective actions[60] delayed the decision-making process and the Commission did not manage to pass the antitrust package it had prepared (of which the White Paper formed part) before the end of its term. The three new commissioners from the Directorate General (DG) of Justice, DG Competition and DG Sanco in charge of the collective redress file[61] underlined in their Joint Information Note of 5 October 2010 the need for a coherent European approach to collective redress.

The result of this joint effort was a new round of consultations in early 2011,[62] which was followed by negotiations between the three DGs and a resulting compromise: a Directive on competition follow-on actions for

---

[57] This term was invented to underline the European nature of the proposal and to avoid any negative connotation with 'US style class actions'.

[58] Commission, 'White Paper on Damages Actions for Breach of the EC Antitrust Rules' COM (2008)165.

[59] 'EU Antitrust Abuse Action in Doubt' (*Financial Times*, 2 October 2009), www.ft.com/content/0fca38e8-af52-11de-ba1c-00144feabdc0 (last accessed 18 February 2020); Commission (n 58).

[60] Slaughter and May, 'Private Enforcement of Competition Law – Commission's Proposals on Hold' (*EU Competition & Regulatory Newsletter*, 2009/3), www.slaughterandmay.com/media/875420/eu_competition_newsletter_30_oct_-_05_nov_2009.pdf (last accessed 18 February 2020).

[61] Vice-President Reding (responsible for Justice, Fundamental Rights and Citizenship); Vice-President Almunia (responsible for Competition); and Commissioner Dalli (responsible for Health and Consumer Policy).

[62] Consultations, impact assessments, evidence of need studies and the like are part of a better or smarter regulation policy of the European Union to improve the quality of regulation: COM(2012)0746 (EU Regulatory Fitness); COM (2013)0686 (Improving evaluation), COM(2012)0746 (EU Regulatory Fitness), COM(2013)0686 (Improving evaluation). From: '*Commissie wil Adviezen over Toekomst Collectieve Rechtsgang in Europa (en)*' (*Europa Nu*, 4 February 2011), www.europa-nu.nl/id/vimkhnyu06vg/nieuws/commissie_wil_adviezen_over_toekomst?ctx=vg8xdjeo1zoj&v=1&start_tab0=260 (last accessed 18 February 2020).

damages only and a (legally non-binding) Recommendation on collective redress of June 2013. Whereas private enforcement via collective redress was part of the earlier draft directive on competition follow-on actions proposed in the 2008 White Paper, that was taken out of the Directive and laid down in a Recommendation with horizontal reach, not limited to competition law. The legal standing rules under the Recommendation are discussed in Section 4.1.

An evaluation of the implementation of the Recommendation was conducted in 2017[63] and found that Member States, to the extent they have introduced any mechanism of collective redress, have done so in different ways, which not only jeopardizes the uniform enforcement of legal rights across the European Union, but also presents a whole new set of issues in the context of cross-border recognition and enforcement of collective proceedings judgments (discussed further in Chapters 13 and 14). That has led to follow-up measures in a new draft directive on representative actions for the protection of the collective interests of consumers, which should replace the current Injunctions Directive. The legal standing rules under the Injunctions Directive and under the draft Directive are discussed in Section 4.2.

4.1 Legal standing for collective redress in the 2013 Recommendation

The Recommendation makes a clear choice for the model of the institutional representative claimant as the European way of dealing with collective redress, and rejects the individual representative claimant model as a facilitator of unwelcome US-style abusive litigation. No distinction or reservation is made in the Recommendation in relation to different types of remedies, such as injunctive and declaratory relief as opposed to compensatory damages, to *actio popularis* or group actions; or in relation to the three sub-categories of institutional representative claimants discussed in Section 2 above.

Moreover, the Recommendation seems to acknowledge that initiating collective actions creates a significant financial burden and risks that the representative claimant should be able to bear, by stipulating that the non-profit representative claimant and its funder should demonstrate sufficient financial means to litigate the action. However, in most European jurisdictions, sufficient financial sources to adequately finance collective actions are lacking. In the European context, one could generally think of 'traditional' funding

---

[63] British Institute of International and Comparative Law, *State of Collective Redress in the EU in the Context of the Implementation of the Commission Recommendation JUST/2016/JCOO/FW/CIVI/009* (BIICL 2017), www.biicl.org/documents/1881_StudyontheStateofCollectiveRedress.pdf (last accessed 20 February 2020).

sources such as legal aid, legal expenses insurance and individual contributions or donations of group members. However, each of these has significant shortcomings in the context of collective redress: full contingency fees are generally unavailable, while legal aid is not available for representative organizations and is generally restricted in its scope.

To the extent that legal expense insurers have not excluded mass claims in their polices,[64] they offer only limited coverage, which generally makes that funding source most of the time inadequate for the funding of many types of mass claims. Furthermore, special funds designated specifically for the funding of collective redress actions are lacking in Europe and collecting individual contributions from group members tends to be problematic for a variety of reasons. The experiences in the Netherlands, which has one of the oldest collective actions regimes in Europe, reveal why claimants increasingly rely on external commercial funding in relation to collective redress:[65] the traditional funding options provide only a very limited solution in the context of collective redress, if at all. The topic of funding in collective redress is dealt with more extensively in Chapter 12. It is, however, closely related to the topic of legal standing, because insufficient funding will have a negative effect on the legal standing and certification of the potential representative organization.[66]

4.2 Legal standing in the 2018 draft Directive

On 11 April 2018 the European Commission announced, in its 'New Deal for Consumers', a proposal that would replace the existing Injunctions Directive[67] and would allow consumers to collectively claim damages if certain consumer laws are infringed. Under the Directive, which applies only to a number of EU Directives and Regulations aimed at enhancing consumer protection, certain 'qualified entities' can initiate a number of proceedings, including injunction proceedings. They can file for an injunction in their Member State or before competent courts or administrative authorities in another Member State (if an

---

64 Axel Halfmeier, 'Litigation Without End? The *Deutsche Telekom* case and the German Approach to Private Enforcement of Securities Law' in Deborah R. Hensler, Christopher Hodges and Ianika Tzankova (eds) (n 5) 88–90.

65 Tzankova (n 11).

66 For a critical discussion of the Recommendation (including legal standing and the interaction with funding), see also: ELI, *Statement of the European Law Institute on Collective Redress and Competition Damages Claims* (ISBN: 978-3-9503458-4-1, European Law Institute 2014).

67 Directive 2009/22/EC of the European Parliament and of the Council of 23 April 2009 on Injunctions for the Protection of Consumers' Interests [2009] OJ L110/30.

infringement originates there). The latter must accept the legal standing of the qualified entity, but still have the right to examine whether the purpose of the qualified entity justifies it to take legal action in a specific case. The European Commission must publish an official list of all qualified entities in the European Union in the *Official Journal of the European Union* every six months.

4.2.1 Starting point for the Commission's 'New Deal for Consumers'

The draft Directive builds on the starting point of 'qualified entities', but also requires EU Member States to ensure that 'in particular consumer organizations and independent public bodies' are eligible for such status. However, Member States would still be able to appoint qualified entities on an *ad hoc* basis and would be required to place the designated qualified entities on a public list. They would need to assess regularly whether the entities on the list still meet the necessary criteria, one of which is having a non-profit-making character.

In return, any recognized qualified entity from the European Union would be allowed to bring action in any other EU Member State and national entities could also combine efforts to that end.

4.2.2 Current status of the 'New Deal' proposal

The next step in the EU legislative process after the European Commission's announcement was for the European Parliament to take a view on the draft. That resulted in a legislative resolution adopted by the Parliament on 26 March 2019, which proposed that Member States or their courts be required to name at least one qualified representative entity that can bring representative actions. The criteria for entities aspiring to acquire such status would be further specified to require from them, among other things, not to have financial agreements with claimant law firms beyond a normal service contract and to disclose publicly how they are financed, organized and managed. Member States would be required to maintain a public list of qualified representative entities and to communicate it to the Commission, which would publish the list of qualified entities from all Member States on a publicly accessible online portal.

An important change in the proposal is that Member States would not be allowed to designate qualified entities for cross-border cases on an *ad hoc* basis. Another major change in the proposal is to distinguish between domestic and cross-border representative actions. Member States would decide on the criteria for designation of qualified entities for domestic representative actions by themselves, while the criteria for the designation of qualified entities for cross-border actions would be decided at EU level. *Ad hoc* designation would be possible only for 'domestic' actions. This would mean that ad hoc established associations could bring international or cross-border actions only in the jurisdiction that recognized their legal standing. Only designated or qualified entities would be able to bring international or cross-border cases outside the jurisdiction in which they were established.

The criteria for designation of qualified entities in cross-border actions can be summarized as follows. Qualified entities would have to prove that they had been in existence at least 18 months prior to the designation request and would have to demonstrate 12 months of actual public activity in the protection of consumers' interest. They would have to have a non-profit character and the knowledge and skills necessary to bring cross-border representative actions. They would also need to show that, in bringing 'any representative action', they are not influenced by companies having an economic interest, including those offering third-party funding. They would be required to publicly disclose information on the source of their funding in general.

In June 2020, the European Council reached agreement with the European Parliament (in a 'trilogue' procedure) on the basis of the Parliament's 2019 resolution; the Directive is therefore expected to be adopted by the end of 2020.[68]

4.3 Concluding remarks

The EU approach to standing in collective redress is 'restrictive' under the Recommendation and 'conservative restrictive' under the draft Directive in the cross-border context, where standing to act is further limited to public and pre-existing designated entities. There seems to be little awareness of the real and potential agency issues under the institutional representative claimant model as discussed above. At the same time, a clear evidence-based and reasoned choice for the ban of *ad hoc* entities is lacking.

5. PARALLEL ACTIONS

As was briefly mentioned in the context of the draft Directive discussed above, parallel actions[69] for collective redress can take place within a national system and in the cross-border context. Section 5.1 addresses the national issues, while 5.2 discusses some recent developments with respect to cross-border issues, both outside of the context of the consumer matters that fall within the scope of the draft Directive. As more EU Member States are introducing collective redress mechanisms of differing design and reach, while markets

---

68 Council of the European Union, File 2018/0089(COD), Doc 9223/20.

69 Another term that is often used is 'competing actions'.

globalize, questions about the effects of parallel actions under different collective redress schemes in relation to the same facts and against (partly) the same defendant(s) should be expected to arise more frequently in the future. Absent any coordination mechanism at EU level, this will raise questions with respect to the scope and reach of Articles 29 and 30 of the Brussels I *bis* Regulation.[70]

This topic was addressed for the first time by a court of an EU Member State on 26 September 2018. The Amsterdam District Court had to rule on a *lis pendens* defence raised by the defendant in a securities collective action initiated by the VEB against Steinhoff International Holding NV. Section 5.2 outlines the relevant facts in the *Steinhoff* case, summarizes the decision of the Amsterdam District Court and provides a brief reflection.

5.1 Parallel actions at national level

In the national context, parallel actions are most likely to arise in collective redress regimes that apply the individual claimant model or an institutional claimant model with a liberal approach to legal standing, where not only designated entities but also *ad hoc* entities are allowed to initiate collective actions. While avoiding 'standing monopolies' of entities entrusted with the capacity to initiate collective actions should be viewed as something positive, this also creates challenges. Two scenarios can emerge. In the first scenario, the national collective redress design requires that an exclusive lead (individual or institutional) claimant be appointed. Ideally, in a case in which there are multiple entities aspiring to act as a lead plaintiff, these manage to find a way to coordinate their actions and to collaborate and seek for a joint appointment. If multiple candidates remain, a choice must be made.[71] Chapter 6, which deals with certification, addresses that scenario and surrounding issues.

However, in the second scenario, the national collective redress design does not require the appointment of a single or joint lead claimant and the various collective actions proceed in parallel. In that case the *res judicata*

---

[70] Article 29(1) of the Brussels I bis (Regulation (EU) No 1215/2012 of the European Parliament and of the Council of 12 December 2012 on Jurisdiction and the Recognition and Enforcement of Judgements in Civil and Commercial Matters [2012] OJ L351/1) stipulates that where proceedings involving the same cause of action and between the same parties are brought in the courts of different Member States, any court other than the court first seised shall of its own motion stay its proceedings until such time as the jurisdiction of the court first seised is established. It follows from Article 30(1) of Brussels I bis that where related actions are pending in the courts of different Member States, any court other than the court first seised may stay its proceedings.

[71] Some speak of 'beauty contests' (in US context); others of 'carriage fights' (Canadian context).

effect of a potential judgment is limited.[72] However, jurisdictions that allow for parallel collective actions have introduced or are considering introducing mechanisms to bring such practices of overlapping classes to an end, since they are viewed as confusing for class members and burdensome for the judiciary and defendants.[73]

5.2 Cross-border issues: the *Steinhoff* example[74]

Steinhoff was domiciled in Amsterdam; hence, the Amsterdam District Court had jurisdiction to hear the case.[75] The VEB issued the writ of summons in a collective action on 2 February 2018, which implicated that the Dutch proceedings were pending from that date.[76] Since Steinhoff was listed on the German stock exchange, proceedings including a petition to the German court of first instance to start a model case under the German *Kapitalanlegermusterverfahren* (KapMuG) group mechanism were initiated on 19 December 2017.[77] The question was raised whether the Dutch collec-

---

[72] The Dutch 305a collective action 'old style' and the Australian class action are examples of parallel actions.

[73] The Netherlands has introduced a new collective action regime that requires certification and the appointment of a lead plaintiff, including its selection if there are multiple candidates, while one of the proposals of the Australian Law Reform Commission to deal with parallel actions included a similar concentration mechanism.

[74] Rb Amsterdam 26 September 2018, ECLI:NL:RBAMS:2018:6840.

The ruling can be found on the website of the Dutch Judiciary, https://uitspraken.rechtspraak.nl/inziendocument?id=ECLI:NL:RBAMS:2018:6840&showbutton=true&keyword=29+Brussel+I (last accessed 18 February 2020). On 5 February 2020 the Amsterdam District Court ruled for the second time in an action initiated by 84 institutional investors against Steinhoff and concluded that although Article 29 Brussels I bis is not applicable, the procedure should be stayed on the basis of Article 30, paragraph 1 Brussels I bis until 7 April 2021, when it will be evaluated again – based on the progress made in the German KapMug-procedure – whether the stay should be lifted. This decision will be discussed in more detail in a forthcoming publication of the author in the *International Journal of Procedural Law*.

[75] Pursuant to Regulation (EU) No 1215/2012 of the European Parliament and of the Council of 12 December 2012 on Jurisdiction and the Recognition and Enforcement of Judgements in Civil and Commercial Matters [2012] OJ L351/1 Article 4 jo. Article 99 para 1 of the *Wetboek van Burgerlijke Rechtsvordering* (Dutch Code of Civil Procedure).

[76] Regulation (EU) No 1215/2012 of the European Parliament and of the Council of 12 December 2012 on Jurisdiction and the Recognition and Enforcement of Judgements in Civil and Commercial Matters [2012] OJ L351/1 Article 32 jo. Article 125 para 1 of the *Wetboek van Burgerlijke Rechtsvordering* (Dutch Code of Civil Procedure).

[77] Rb Amsterdam 26 September 2018, ECLI:NL:RBAMS:2018:6840.

tive proceedings should be suspended pursuant to Articles 29 and 30 of the Brussels I *bis* Regulation.

The Amsterdam District Court was of the opinion that the condition in the Brussels Regulation that the parallel proceedings must be between the same parties had not been met. The court took a formalistic approach: the VEB was a foundation, while the parties in the KapMuG proceedings were individuals. Moreover, the VEB did not represent the individuals in the KapMuG proceedings and would not do so in relation to the action at hand in Amsterdam. Concerning Article 30 of the Brussels I *bis* Regulation, the Amsterdam District Court considered that proceedings are regarded as related actions only in the event that adequate resolution demands simultaneous adjudication. Against this background, the Amsterdam District Court ruled that the *res judicata* effect of a decision in the KapMuG proceedings was limited to German proceedings that were stayed or registered at the time of the model decision, and that they had no binding effect elsewhere, other than that (part of) those affected could not sue Steinhoff in Germany for lack of jurisdiction. Moreover, the progress of the KapMuG proceedings was still unclear and conditional on the approval of the German court.

Following the formalistic logic of the district court here, a 305a action could never be suspended by a KapMuG procedure or by any other opt-in, non-representative joinder of parties mechanism,[78] as the 'same parties' criterion will never be met. Moreover, its considerations on the limited effects of a model decision in the KapMuG remain valid, as they follow from the limited *res judicata* nature of the KapMuG system itself.

The ruling of the Amsterdam District Court has been criticized. Some authors[79] have pointed to Court of Justice of the European Union (CJEU) case law to criticize the interpretation by the district court of the 'same parties' condition. Although the starting point is that the 'same parties' means literally the 'same parties', there are also exceptions where the parties are not identical, but their procedural stance is the same and they aim for the same outcome.[80] This follows from the autonomous interpretation of EU legislation by the

---

[78] Another similar example is the UK group litigation order (GLO) procedure or procedures on the basis of assignments of claims.

[79] C.F. Kroes, '*Noot bij Rechtbank Amsterdam 26-09-2018*' [2019] 121/5 JOR 1445.

[80] For example, Case C-351/96 *Drouot Assurances SA v CMI Industrial Sites, Protea Assurance and GIE Réunion Européenne* [1998] ECR I-03075; Case C-133/11 *Folien Fischer AG, Fofitec AG v Ritrama SpA* [2012] OJ C204/12; Case C-452/12 *Nipponkoa Insurance Co. (Europe) Ltd v Inter-Zuid Transport BV.* [2013] OJ C52/19.

CJEU.[81] However, even critics of the district court ruling point out that the end conclusion was correct, and it would be hard to accept that the filing of an individual case in a Member State would result in a stay of collective proceedings in another Member State with respect to the same or a similar matter by a qualified claimant (different from that in the first action) against (partly) the same defendants. According to some, the exceptions on the interpretation of 'same parties' as formulated in the case law of the CJEU are applicable to the case at hand. Nevertheless, the condition of 'same cause of action' should be the critical test here and considered problematic, since the scope of a collective action[82] is much more comprehensive than the (bundled individual claims in) KapMuG actions. However, this line of reasoning has the same implications as the ruling of the Amsterdam District Court: a KapMuG individual action could never suspend a 305a collective action, because its scope remains as a (bundle of) individual actions, contrasted with a single collective representative action.

One may wonder whether the limited scope of an individual KapMuG proceedings changes once a sufficient number of individual claimants have come forward to participate in the action and the test case has been approved by the German first-instance *Landgericht* as the model case. This might change the nature of the KapMuG procedure from individual to collective. It is arguable, however, that this would not be the case because the KapMuG, by its nature, is not a collective action, but is arguably (similarly to the UK group litigation order (GLO)) only a sophisticated procedural joinder of parties device or a 'test' case that is more or less comparable to preliminary or pre-action proceedings, as discussed in Chapter 3. This point is also supported by the limited *res judicata* effect of a model decision in the KapMuG proceedings (even for German claimants only), which is relevant from the perspective of Article 30(1) of the Brussels I *bis* Regulation.

In summary, the current view (of courts and commentators) seems to be that a collective action probably could not be suspended in the European Union pursuant to Article 29 or 30 of the Regulation by a collective redress mechanism that is designed as a test case, only some aspects of which are binding on a collection of individual cases[83] – either because the requirement of 'same parties' is not met or because the requirement of 'same cause of action' becomes problematic. However, the discussions have only just started and it will ultimately be for the CJEU and the highest national courts to shed light on *lis pendens* in collective redress. The *Steinhoff* example gives us a flavour

---

[81] Case C-406/92 *The Owners of the Cargo Lately Laden on Board the Ship "Tatry" v the Owners of the Ship "Maciej Rataj"* [1994] ECR I-05439, para 30; and Case C-617/15 *Hummel Holding A/S v Nike Inc. and Nike Retail BV.* [2017], para 22.

[82] In this particular case: Article 3:305a of the Dutch law on collective action.

[83] Such as the German KapMuG procedure or the UK GLO procedure.

of the discussions that are yet to come and shows that differing approaches to legal standing in collective redress have unforeseen, far-reaching consequences in cross-border disputes.

6. CONCLUDING REMARKS

In view of the fragmented landscape for collective redress within the European Union and the potential approval of the draft Directive in its current status discussed above, claimants in a collective redress action might in future be faced with at least three different collective redress regimes, depending on whether the action is domestic or cross-border and whether it falls within the substantive scope of the draft Directive. One might reasonably expect that there will be grey areas in any one of these scenarios that will raise lengthy legal discussions, a final answer to which can be provided only by the CJEU. For this, however, in addition to patience, substantial financial resources are required. Ironically, the unintended consequence of the envisioned increase in consumer protection might just produce the opposite effect.

8. Case management and the role of the judge

Magne Strandberg and Vincent Smith

1. ERCP AND ACTIVE CASE MANAGEMENT: BACKGROUND AND SOURCES OF INSPIRATION

'Case management' is one of the most fashionable expressions in modern European civil procedural law and doctrine. While no one used this phrase in the 1980s, it is commonly used today. It is fair to say that the expression had its breakthrough after the English Woolf reform in the second half of the 1990s, which resulted in the entry into force of the Civil Procedure Rules in 1998.[1] This reform introduced a new concept of the role of a judge under English law,[2] which Rolf Stürner – one of the founding fathers of the American Law Institute (ALI)/UNIDROIT principles – described as necessary for the inclusion of rules on active case management: 'Without the major change in modern English procedure, international harmonization on the basis of active court management would have been inconceivable and impossible.'[3]

That reform brought English civil procedure closer to continental law.[4] Most importantly, there seems to have been greater congruence between English law and German law, which the English reform was partly inspired by and which already entailed a long-established duty for courts to manage cases actively. At least some aspects of active case management had also long been acknowl-

---

1 Lord Woolf MR, *Access to Justice*, Final Report to the Lord Chancellor (1996).

2 John Sorabji, *English Civil Justice after the Woolf and Jackson Reforms* (CUP, 2014) pp 184–87.

3 Rolf Stürner, 'The Principles of Transnational Civil Procedure. An Introduction to Their Basic Conceptions', *Rabels Zeitschrift für ausländisches und internationales Privatrecht*, (vol 69) 2005 pp 201–54 at p 227.

4 Rolf Stürner, 'Anglo-American and Continental Civil Procedure', in: Andenæs, Andrews and Nazzini, *The Future of Transnational Civil Litigation. English Responses to the ALI/UNIDROIT Draft Principles and Rules of Transnational Civil Procedure* (London, 2004) pp 9–12 at p 11.

edged in French law, Spanish law and Scandinavian law.[5] The Woolf reform also gave momentum to further reforms in other countries – for instance, the Scandinavian countries included several new clauses on the judges' duty to manage cases actively in their codes of civil procedure.[6]

These lines of recent development provided a sound basis for active case management to become an important ingredient of the European Law Institute (ELI)/UNIDROIT European Rules of Civil Procedure (ERCP). One of the first working groups established under the project, it had a mandate to suggest rules on the roles and obligations of judges and parties. While the structure of the ERCP final rules on case management deviates somewhat from the rules suggested by that working group, the basic content of the rules remains and case management has as prominent a role in the ERCP as was suggested by the working group.

The court's duty to manage cases actively is found throughout the rules. First, Rule 4 establishes case management as a basic principle and takes active management as the only aspect mentioned under the heading 'The Role of the Court'. Second, an entire chapter of the rules is devoted to general rules on case management. Third, numerous special rules on case management are found in other chapters of the ERCP.[7]

There were several sources of inspiration for the rules on case management.[8] An important starting point was Article 14 of the ALI/UNIDROIT principles:[9]

---

5 For example, Danish Code of Procedure (*Retsplejeloven*) § 339; Norwegian Code of Civil Procedure of 1915 § 87 (*tvistemålsloven*, now longer in force); Swedish Code of Procedure (*Rättegångsbalken*) 17:3.

6 For example, the Norwegian Dispute Act (which, despite its misleading English name, is a full-blown code of civil procedure law) §§ 9–4, 9–13 and 11–6. The trend of including new clauses on case management is especially important for the preparatory stage of proceedings, see: Laura Ervo, 'Swedish-Finnish Preparatory Proceedings: Filtering and Process Techniques', in: Ervo and Nylund (eds) *Current Trends in Preparatory Proceedings. A Comparative Study of Nordic and Former Communist Countries* (Springer, 2016), pp 19–56; Anna Nylund, 'Preparatory Proceedings in Norway: Efficiency by Flexibility and Case Management', in: Ervo and Nylund (eds), pp 57–80, Jakob Juul-Sandberg, 'Reform and Development of Preparatory Proceedings in the Danish Civil Justice System: Toward (Even) More Efficient Courts', in Ervo and Nylund (eds), pp 81–107.

7 See, in particular, ERCP Part III (Case Management) and Part VII (Access to Information and Evidence).

8 See R.H. van Rhee, 'Case Management in Europe: A Modern Approach to Civil Litigation', *International Journal of Procedural Law* (vol 8) 2018 pp 65–84 at p 83.

9 See in general, on the use of ALI/UNIDROIT for the new European project: Rolf Stürner, 'Principles of European civil procedure or a European model code? Some considerations on the joint ELI-UNIDROIT project', *Uniform Law Review* (vol 19) 2014 pp 322–28 at p 322–23; and John Sorabji, 'The ELI-UNIDROIT project. An

14. Court Responsibility for Direction of the Proceeding

14.1 Commencing as early as practicable, the court should actively manage the proceeding, exercising discretion to achieve disposition of the dispute fairly, efficiently, and with reasonable speed. Consideration should be given to the transnational character of the dispute.

14.2 To the extent reasonably practicable, the court should manage the proceeding in consultation with the parties.

14.3 The court should determine the order in which issues are to be resolved, and fix a timetable for all stages of the proceeding, including dates and deadlines. The court may revise such directions.

However, while that article offers only a brief and broad principle, an ambition for the new ERCP was to further develop active case management. Several national laws were used as sources of inspiration for that development. The working group which prepared the rules on case management included scholars from all across Europe and a survey of country reports on all Member States' national laws was provided.[10] While no genuine core of case management rules was found in all jurisdictions, a tendency towards more explicit and frequent inclusion of rules on case management was discovered in national codes. This tendency towards more duties of active management was found even though the types of activities and the actual use of such powers may vary.[11]

Most of the ERCP rules on active case management are general, which means that they are applicable to all cases within the scope of the rules (thus excluding, for example, family or administrative law matters).[12] Nevertheless, certain special types of cases may give rise to special case management issues that can be dealt with either under the general rules or under a special rule applicable to that type of case. Cases in which the court's duty of active management may become particularly challenging include those in which numerous persons' interests are at stake or are directly affected by the judgment.

Cases in which many persons have an interest may take several procedural forms: multi-party cases with many joined parties; a test case with just one formal party; a representative declaratory action (eg, where a public body

---

Introduction and an English Perspective', in: Nylund and Strandberg, *Civil Procedure and Harmonisation of Law* (Intersentia, 2019) pp 35–59 at pp 39–41.

[10] The group comprised C.H. van Rhee (Netherlands), A. Uzelac (Croatia), E. Jeuland (France), B. Karolczyk (Poland), W. Rechberger (Austria), E. Silvestri (Italy), J. Sorabji (England) and M. Strandberg (Norway). The questions are listed in Sorabji (n 9) p 49 fn 63.

[11] van Rhee (n 8) p 77.

[12] The scope is defined in ERCP Rule 1 and is 'domestic and cross-border disputes in civil and commercial matters', except for cases on capacity, family disputes and insolvency.

stands as the formal party in the interest of clarifying the law); or a class action where a judgment will have *res judicata* effect even for non-parties. In all these types of cases, the court's case management duties will be affected by the high number of interested persons. The court will face additional challenges to organize the case and ensure that the interests of affected non-parties are properly taken care of.[13] Therefore, an important question concerning the new model ERCP is: are these rules fit for purpose when many persons are directly or indirectly affected by a judgment?

This chapter considers case management in a specific type of case: cases covered by collective proceedings under Part XI of the ERCP.[14] There are many reasons to exclude other sorts of collective redress from this chapter – not only the need to narrow the subject in itself, but also because the role of the judge is normally more active (and difficult) in a class action than under other forms of collective redress.

However, a main element that is crucial for the remaining parts of this book – the certification of a group and definition of a group – is also addressed in detail in Chapter 6.

As the approach taken by the working group that prepared the rules on case management was based more on best practice than on comparisons or a search for common European ground, our approach in this chapter follows that line of methodology. Our approach is to critically examine whether the ERCP rules on case management actually create workable solutions for the difficulties arising in class actions, and to suggest the solution that would be most coherent with the aim and structure of the rules in general.

Before considering questions concerning the application of the specific ERCP rules on case management in collective proceedings in Part XI of the ERCP, we must introduce the model rules on case management generally and discuss why they were chosen.

---

13 See, for instance, Per Henrik Lindblom, *Grupptalan. Det Anglo-Amerikanska Class Actioninstitutet ur Svenskt Perspektiv* (Iustus, 1989) pp 254–64; Rolf Stürner, 'The Role of Judges and Lawyers in Collective Redress', *ZZPInt* 2012 pp 259–91 at p 274.

14 Chapter 3 also covers other types of collective redress and multi-party cases.

2. THE NATURE, JUSTIFICATION AND PRINCIPLES OF RULES ON CASE MANAGEMENT

2.1 What is case management?

The ERCP does not provide an explicit definition of 'case management' and such a definition is not easily provided in a European context. While the term 'case management' obviously refers to one or several kinds of court activity or court decisions in ongoing litigation, it is not entirely clear what forms of activity or decisions are covered by the term. There is a risk that some of the activities that a court has a power or duty to take under the civil procedure law of one jurisdiction, and which could be translated (perhaps due to a lack of better expressions) to the English language as 'case management', differ quite significantly from other activities in other countries which would also be translated as 'case management'.

One example of this potential linguistic problem may be taken from Scandinavian law. For many decades, all of the Scandinavian countries have had rules allowing a judge to give suggestions and feedback to parties on both substantive and procedural matters.[15] While these unstructured rules have been maintained and have had growing importance over the years, newer rules on other sorts of court activity have emerged in Scandinavian civil procedure law in the last 20 years or so. These new rules concern the organization of proceedings, the setting of calendars, the duty to concentrate proceedings, the duty to decide on the number and length of court hearings and so on.[16] These new rules have been influenced by English law after the Woolf reform.

Today, after the influence of German-Austrian law from the early 1900s and the English influences from before or just after the millennium have both been incorporated, a distinction has developed whereby '*prosessledelse*' (German: '*prozessleitung*') covers the old rules on German-style judicial activity, while '*aktiv saksstyring*' (active case management) covers English-style judicial activity. As these rules exist side by side, there is now a more nuanced terminology in order to distinguish between these different kinds of judicial activity – all of which could be called 'case management' in the English context.

However, these distinctions from Scandinavian law may not be readily applicable as clarifications of what 'case management' means under the

---

[15] Danish Code of Procedure § 339; Swedish Code of Procedure § 42:8 (2) and § 43:4(2); Norwegian Dispute Act § 11–5, previously found in the Code of Civil Procedure of 1915 § 87.

[16] Norwegian Dispute Act §§ 9–4, 9–13 and 11–6.

ERCP. The ERCP is not based on concepts taken from a single jurisdiction or legal culture. Arguably, the concept of case management under the ERCP must be autonomous and understood within the framework of the ERCP itself. Within the ERCP, case management should be understood as having its core identified by the general principle in Rule 4 and the more specific rules set out in Parts III, IV and V.

At the core of the term 'case management', then, are a court's duties and powers to decide on organizational matters of a case, such as providing timetables, choosing procedural tracks, deciding whether a case should be split, deciding whether a case should consist of several parties on each side and deciding whether a party must have legal representation.[17] Furthermore, within the ERCP, 'case management' also covers the court's duty or power to monitor the parties' procedural behaviour, and to sanction parties if they do not comply with procedural norms set by the law or by the court under its case management powers.[18]

While the factors mentioned above are at the core of case management, Rule 61(4) includes a rule that conceptually may seem to be on the border of what 'case management' (in the English sense) covers:

> Whenever appropriate, the Court may provide parties with advice relevant to their preparation for the final hearing and judgment.

A power for the court to provide advice is similar to one of the elements contained in the German and Scandinavian rules on procedural or substantive '*prozessleitung*' or '*prosessledelse*' – namely, the court's power or duty to encourage a party to produce or introduce additional evidence or to address certain substantive issues. Even though the German and Scandinavian traditions would distinguish such judge activity from other sorts of judge activity, within the context of the ERCP it seems more plausible to regard this as a sort of 'case management'. In accordance with this view, it seems plausible to regard also Rule 92(2) on suggestions on the taking of new evidence as being 'case management' under the rules:

> The Court, while affording the parties an opportunity to respond, may suggest evidence not previously proposed by a party that it considers may be relevant to an issue in dispute. If a party accepts that suggestion, the Court will order the taking of that evidence so that it may be offered in support of that party's contentions of law and fact.

---

[17] Especially ERCP Rules 49 and 61.

[18] Especially ERCP Rules 4, 48; Adrian Zuckerman, *Civil Procedure. Principles of Practice*, 3 ed (Sweet & Maxwell, 2013) p 566.

While suggestions of new evidence or facts would be regarded as suggestions and feedback under the German and Scandinavian traditions, and would therefore fall under the label of '*prozessleitung*' or '*prosessledelse*', there does not seem be any option under the ERCP other than to consider even this power as a 'case management' power. Even the court's *ex officio* taking of evidence, in situations where none of the parties – even after the judge has made a suggestion – has taken an active step to offer the evidence should be regarded as a kind of case management activity. Rule 92(3) provides the court with such an *ex officio* power to take evidence and that rule is put under the heading of 'management'.

Even though the concept of case management within the ERCP seems to be rather broad, there are reasons to distinguish between 'court management' and 'case management'. Court management relates to internal matters in a court, such as the division of the court's manpower, the use of clerks and assistants, the use of court buildings and the allocation of cases to judges.[19] Case management relates to relationships between the court and the parties (and to some degree, the relationship between the parties). Such 'case management' primarily relates to a specific case, while court management is typically an administrative activity for the organization of a court's overall caseload. However, rational use of the court's resources and fair apportionment of resources to each case are key reasons for a duty of active *case* management. Decisions on court management may be of special importance in relation to collective proceedings – especially because such proceedings frequently present a need for specialized judges and are heavy users of court resources. We will nevertheless stick to the distinction between case management and court management, and thus will not deal with court management matters – especially concerning the choice or appointment of judges in collective redress proceedings.

2.2 Justification for rules on case management

While enhancing duties on judges for active case management is a general tendency in European civil procedural law, there is no inherent value in active case management as such. Therefore, establishing rules on such activities and choosing between several possible guiding principles for such rules call for justification. As any other part of civil procedure law, rules on case management must find their justification in the basic goals and purposes of a civil justice system. While active case management may contribute to the realiza-

[19] Emmanuel Jeuland, 'Towards a New Court Management?', *General Report*, Université Paris 1 – Panthéon Sorbonne, 2018 p 1: 'Court management may be defined as the administration inside the court and outside the case.'

tion of several of these goals, the most direct goal of rules on case management is simply *to save time and money*.

Reducing court costs and time is important for the state economy: one should not waste taxpayers' money. Active case management should also contribute to a fairer distribution of the court's resources – case management will impact on court management. The court's resources are limited and should be apportioned fairly between cases.[20] Time and money wasted in one case will not only affect that case, but also affect the time and money available for other cases. In practice, it may be hard to prove that active case management actually has a cost-saving effect, but at least general rules and principles will ensure that the court's resources are spent on the basis of a uniform set of criteria that should be applied in a similar fashion in all cases.

The guiding general criterion chosen by the ERCP is one of *proportionality*.[21] Fair allocation of the court's resources between cases does not mean that the court will spend the same time and effort on all cases. As different cases need different procedural direction, different evidence and a different number of days spent in court, the overarching principle should be that the time and money spent on a case are reasonable on the basis of the importance of the issues in that case and the complexity of those issues.

Active case management and the principle of proportionality may also be justified by arguments relating to the parties in a particular case. In most cases, both parties have an interest in spending an amount of time and money that corresponds to the complexity and importance of the case. Active case management steps taken by a judge may help the parties to find such a balance. If the rules on active case management work as suggested, they will also reduce the effect of economic and other inequalities between parties. Active management based on a principle of proportionality should prevent a wealthy party from misusing his or her economic power – for instance, by taking procedural steps that are too frequent or too complicated compared to the value of the case.

If the level of money spent on a case is proportional to the value of that case, it may also enhance a party's willingness to go to court in the first place. If the economic risk of going to court is more easily assessed beforehand and more proportionate to the importance of the case, it may enhance the parties' access to justice in practice. Active case management should hinder one party from causing procedural obstacles for the other party, and the principle of proportionality will also hinder a party from unnecessary delay in procedural steps.

---

20 Sorabji (n 2) pp 135–99.

21 ERCP Rule 5(6).

2.3 Principles of active case management

Let us now describe the main features of the content of the ERCP rules on active case management. As has already been mentioned, the court's duty of active case management is a general principle of the rules and the characteristic features of that duty are dealt with here.

First, the court has a duty of active case management *throughout the proceeding* in all its stages, from when the application arrives at court until a final judgment is given.[22] However, active case management shall be *proactive*, which means that the court's management is more important in the early stages of the proceedings than in the later stages. A basic feature of proper case management is to plan the later parts of proceedings to decide on the number of case management hearings and other aspects of the 'calendar', how evidence shall be taken (by document disclosure or appointment of legal experts) and so on. Hence, the very idea of case management points in the direction of early intervention by the judge. In jurisdictions following a 'main hearing' model of proceedings – a system in which one hearing is regarded as the vital event where (all) evidence is presented to the court, and all other meetings are regarded as a preparation for that main event – the court's case management duty is of special importance during the preparatory stage of the proceedings. The very function of case management during the preparatory stage is to plan for the later main hearing.[23]

In line with this, the court's active management under the ERCP is supposed to be of special importance in the preparatory stages of the proceedings and its main function is to plan for the final hearing.[24] Nevertheless, the very purpose of rules on case management – to save time and money through active and early intervention and planning by the court – should also be relevant for proceedings structured as (for instance) many inter-related stages, where no specific 'meeting' is regarded as a main hearing. The ERCP rules on case management could arguably be applied even in jurisdictions that do not apply a main hearing model.

Second, a main characteristic in the ERCP case management rules is that *the court is afforded a relatively wide degree of discretion* on how to manage a case. However, the rules are a deliberate mix of rather detailed rules on case management and rather open rules. The idea behind this structure is to provide judges with both detailed lists of matters which they must take into consider-

---

[22] Also ALI/UNIDROIT Article 18(1): 'The court should assume active management of the proceeding in all stages of the litigation'.

[23] Ervoand Nylund, *Current Trends in Preparatory Proceedings. A Comparative Study of Nordic and Former Communist Countries* (Springer, 2016) p 7.

[24] Especially ERCP Rule 61.

ation when managing a case, and general case management principles which may both fill in the gaps and work as a relevant context for the interpretation of the detailed rules. Perhaps the most important of the detailed rules on case management, Rule 49, lists many aspects that the court 'must' decide on whenever necessary for proper management:

(1) encourage the parties to take active steps to settle their dispute or parts of their dispute and, where appropriate, to use alternative dispute resolution processes or practices;
(2) set a timetable or procedural calendar with deadlines for the parties' procedural steps;
(3) determine form and structure of procedure;
(4) limit the number and length of future submissions;
(5) determine the order in which issues should be tried and whether proceedings should be consolidated or split;
(6) determine the separation of questions of jurisdiction, provisional measures and statutes of limitation for early decision upon special hearings;
(7) address necessary amendments regarding the parties' proper representation, the consequences of changes related to the parties to litigation and the participation of third parties or other persons;
(8) address amendments of the pleadings for the addition, deletion, or revision of claims, defences, factual allegations or offers of evidence in the light of the parties' contentions at that stage;
(9) require a party's appearance in person or require a party's representative, who should be fully-informed of all matters relevant to the proceedings, to be present at a court hearing;
(10) address the availability, admissibility, form, disclosure and exchange of evidence and, if adequate to the state of proceedings;

    (a) determine the admissibility or exclusion of evidence; and
    (b) order the taking of evidence by the production of documents, the appointment of an expert, make requests for witness statements, order the examination of parties, order judicial inspection, or the production of information by public authorities.

On the other hand, Rule 49 does not in detail prescribe *how* the judge shall cope with this duty of active management. Most often, whether the judge has a discretion in his or her case management decision depends on other rules. For instance, Rule 49(10) provides that the judge shall take a decision on several aspects concerning evidence, but the degree of discretion for the judge is not really governed by Rule 49 – it relies on the rules on evidence found in Part VII. For many other case management decisions – such as the setting of calendars – the judge's discretion is rather wide, as long as decisions are within the principle of proportionality.

Third, as the rules on case management put duties of activity on the judges, they affect *the role of the court and the role of the parties*. Basically, proceedings under the ERCP are still party driven and with a high degree of party autonomy. It is for the parties to decide whether proceedings shall be initiated;[25] they may at any point end proceedings by settlement, admission or withdrawal;[26] they determine the scope and content of proceedings;[27] and they are responsible for the introduction of facts and evidence.[28]

However, the ERCP modifies these classical party autonomy principles. Both parties and their lawyers have a general duty to 'co-operate to promote the fair, efficient and speedy resolution',[29] which includes both cooperation *vis-à-vis* the opposite party and cooperation *vis-à-vis* the court. The parties are explicitly required to cooperate in the proper management of proceedings,[30] and to present their claims, defences and so on as early and completely as possible.[31] The court, on the other hand, has an ongoing duty to monitor the parties' cooperation and to consider sanctioning parties who do not comply with the duties imposed on them.[32] While the initiative to take a management order or decision may very well come from one of the parties or several of (or all of) them together, it is characteristic of the court's duty to manage cases actively that it may take any necessary case management order on its own motion.[33] The parties still have a basic right to be heard,[34] of course, and that right also applies to case management orders. If the court has to take a management order or decision without consulting all parties, parties not previously heard may apply for reconsideration, either through written application or in a court hearing.[35]

---

25 ERCP Rule 21(1).
26 ERCP Rule 21(2).
27 ERCP Rule 23.
28 ERCP Rules 22 and 24(1)–(2) and 25 (1).
29 ERCP Rule 2.
30 ERCP Rule 3(b).
31 ERCP Rule 47.
32 ERCP Rules 4 and 48.
33 ERCP Rule 50(1).
34 ERCP Rule 11.
35 ERCP Rule 50(1).

3. SPECIAL CHALLENGES FOR THE APPLICATION OF RULES ON CASE MANAGEMENT IN COLLECTIVE PROCEEDINGS

3.1 Interplay between general and special rules

As most of the ERCP case management rules are general in scope, there may be a risk that the rules cannot be straightforwardly applied in collective proceedings. While no features of the ERCP case management rules exclude their application in collective proceedings, such proceedings may obviously present the judge with greater challenges in the application of these rules. These challenges arise not only from the complexity of collective proceedings and the (often high) economic values at stake in those proceedings, but also from the special need to protect the interests of non-present (and non-party) claimants. These challenges involved in collective proceedings will occur both at the preparatory stage and during the final hearing.

It is far from obvious that all the general rules on case management are suitable for handling the special challenges of collective proceedings. But the rules are flexible and are supposed to provide the judge with the necessary tools, at least when combined with the special rules on collective proceedings. Therefore, it is important to highlight the interplay between the general rules on case management and the special rules on collective proceedings. We will illustrate this interplay by analysing the case management issues related to two particular issues: whether to allow a case to proceed on track as a collective proceeding, and whether the rules on case management can give particular procedural rights to group members.

3.2 Choice of procedural track

At the very earliest stages of proceedings, the judge must decide on *the choice of form of proceeding* – that is, whether the case should proceed as a multi-party case under the ordinary rules of joinder of parties; under the special track for collective proceedings; as a pilot case; or under another available form of collective redress. In practice, one of the most important issues is whether a case involving many claimants shall be opened as a collective proceeding.

Let us start with the role of parties and the judge – or, more precisely, the division of procedural competence between them. In general, under the ERCP, the choice of procedural form is an aspect of the judge's active case management power and duty. Under Rule 49(3), it is for the judge to 'determine the type and form of the procedure'. However, a judge cannot decide that a case shall proceed as a collective proceeding unless a party has applied for this.[36] It is for a person who wishes to become a qualified claimant to apply for a collective proceeding order by delivering a statement of claim that provides the court with information on most of the matters necessary for the opening of such proceeding.[37] In addition, the proposed qualified claimant has a duty to cooperate with the court to enable it to reach a decision on whether to accept the application for a collective proceeding.[38] The defendant is also under a duty to cooperate. The defendant must take a stance on the application for a collective proceeding. Even though the special ERCP rules on collective proceedings (in Part XI) impose no specific requirements on the defendant, the defendant must deliver a statement of defence according to Rule 54 and must protest as soon as possible if it disagrees with the application for a collective proceeding.

Most often, the defendant will not agree to the application for a collective proceeding; but if it does so, one may ask whether the parties' agreement binds the court. Under Rule 58, a procedural agreement between the parties binds the court if the procedural rules in question are 'subject to party disposition'. This clause presupposes the existence of procedural issues that parties may agree on, but does not say which issues are dispositive, other than matters of jurisdiction, provisional measures and publicity. Whether other procedural issues are subject to parties' disposition depends on which interests are involved in that issue. Arguably, the parties may decide on an issue if interests between them are the only ones involved in that issue; and they may not themselves decide if general public interest is involved or if the interests of third parties are involved.

It is perhaps debatable whether the rules on collective proceedings are open for parties' disposition, but the structure of the rules in Part XI on collective proceedings does not immediately suggest such an interpretation. Several of those rules seem to protect not only *inter partes* interests, such as finding the most economically effective method of proceeding, but also the interests of (non-party) group members. Furthermore, the effect of agreements between the parties on case management issues is regulated in Rule 50(2), which provides that the court cannot disregard the application unless it has 'good reason' for doing so. This rule clearly assumes that the judge has the final word on matters of case management and the choice of procedural type and form is

---

36 A court may encourage or advise a party or a group of claimants to organize a collective proceeding instead of proceeding with a case with very many joined parties, or if a party has fronted a test case or a pilot case. ERCP Rule 212(2) provides for such a shift of a classic proceeding to become a collective proceeding, but only upon application and only if the criteria for opening a collective proceeding are met.

37 ERCP Rule 210.

38 ERCP Rule 6.

regarded as a case management power.[39] Hence, the judge has the final word on choice of procedural form, even if an agreement between the parties points to one specific type or form. This assumes that the certification of a collective proceeding is not subject to parties' disposition – which (since it affects third-party legal rights) appears to be the correct approach.

Moreover, the court must base its decision on whether to admit or deny the application for a collective proceeding on the criteria found in Rules 207–10 or Rule 212. If any of these criteria is not met, the court shall deny the application. The agreement between the parties has a role to play only if the criteria in question are met, which in practice is the case if the criteria leave the judge with a degree of discretion so that the agreement of the parties may be relevant. Arguably, such discretion is left to the judge by Rule 212(1)(a) by the important criterion that a collective redress proceeding 'will resolve the dispute more efficiently than a joinder of the group members'. While the decision on whether a collective proceeding will be more efficient than a joinder of group members cannot in itself be regulated in a contract, the agreed opinions of the parties may be a factor for the judge to consider if he or she is in doubt as to whether a collective proceeding will be more efficient than the alternative.

The judge shall take the decision on procedural form at the preparatory stage of proceedings and as soon as possible after commencement. The decision on the admissibility of the collective proceeding action shall be taken as a separate decision following the criteria set out in Rule 212(1).[40] The decision can be appealed.[41]

3.3 Case management decisions and the role of group members

Whilst the case management difficulties characteristic of a bilateral case concern the relationship between a plaintiff and a defendant, relationships between individuals on the same side of the dispute may present additional difficulties in a class actions. These additional difficulties are most often caused by the potential tensions between a party (the qualified claimant) and a group of non-parties (group members), or the relationship between several group members.[42] Since a future judgment or a group settlement will be binding for all group members (or at least all of those who opt in or do not opt out), there

---

39 ERCP Rule 49(3).

40 ERCP Rule 212.

41 ERCP Rules 178 and 179.

42 As was noted by Lindblom (1989) p 256, two key issues require judge activity in a class-action: (1) fast and cheap handling of a complex case; and (2) protection of non-active class-members, and of broader societal interests if that is a part of the justification for a class action.

are no reasons why group members should have a lower degree of protection under the case management rules than is the case for parties. Therefore, there are reasons to expect that a judge will monitor these relationships during all stages of the proceedings. That leaves judges with several additional problems, because it means they must monitor relationships with persons who are absent for most of the proceedings.

The general ERCP case management rules are not particularly developed for use in collective proceedings: the language chosen for most of the rules establishes rights and powers only for judges, parties and their lawyers; and it is not straightforward to see how the interests of non-present persons or affected non-parties could be protected under the general rules. There are reasons to ask, therefore, how the general model rules on case management are to be applied during a collective proceeding; how these rules interplay with the special rules on collective proceedings; and whether these sets of rules, taken together, may fit for such cases.

A particular problem arises if group members have conflicting interests on a procedural issue or if there are conflicting interests between group members and the qualified claimant. If the qualified claimant refuses to take a procedural step or to ask for a case management order, can one or several group members initiate such a step or ask for such an order? Or if the judge has taken a case management order and the qualified claimant refuses to appeal it, can one or several group members appeal?

The general principles of case management under the ERCP exclusively concern the relationship between the judge, the parties and their lawyers.[43] Since group members are not regarded as parties, they are neither bound by those rules nor entitled to any direct rights thereunder. One might also say that the direction of procedural rights through the qualified claimant, and not the group member, is in line with the general functioning of a collective action. The simplification of proceedings which is gained by channelling the procedural rights to the qualified claimant more or less exclusively would be lost if any group member, at any stage, could take any procedural action or protest against any case management order. Seen from the group members' perspective, one might say that such a direction of procedural competence to the qualified claimant alone is a part of the very concept of a collective proceeding – it is to go forward as a group represented by one entity *vis-à-vis* the court and the defendant.

The potential clash of interests between the qualified claimant and group members, or between several group members, must be dealt with by an interplay of general case management rules and the special rules on collective

[43] ERCP Rules 2 to 6 and 47 to 50.

proceedings. One of the additional case management powers that the judge disposes of in collective proceedings is the removal of a qualified claimant if he or she does not act in the interests of all group members.[44] Another such special competence is to order the construction of sub-groups within the group.[45] Most importantly, part of the judge's duty of active case management is to ensure that group members receive proper information from the qualified claimant or from the court. Under Rule 219, the judge must advertise or require advertisement in a number of situations, such as 'when an order or judgment is made' (sub-paragraph (d)), which will cover quite a lot of those situations in which a case management decision has been taken. Whenever a case management decision affects a group member, the court may hear that member before a decision is taken, under Rule 218(2):

> The Court may hear any person it considers has an interest in the management of the case before making any case management order under this Rule.

Explicitly, this rule applies only to special collective proceedings case management under Rule 218, which basically has to do with removal of qualified claimants and (re)construction of sub-groups; but the judge arguably also has such a power under the general case management rules.

Based on the information provided, the judge has the power to take most case management decisions on his or her own motion, and has the final word on case management decisions. In making decisions, the judge will take any relevant interests into account, including the interests of group members.

Hence, the main rule is that the power to take procedural steps, request case management orders or appeal such orders is exclusively left to the qualified claimant. There are certain exceptions to this rule, which apply when a case management order is directed against a group member – for instance, if the defendant asks for access to evidence that is under the possession of one group member.[46] In such a situation, the group member – as any other third party – has a right to be heard before a decision is taken and has a right to appeal the decision.[47]

---

44 ERCP Rule 218(1)a; see Section 4.1.
45 ERCP Rule 218(1)d.
46 ERCP Rule 100 b on access to evidence orders against third parties.
47 ERCP Rules 107(3) and 180.

4. ADDITIONAL CASE MANAGEMENT FOR COLLECTIVE ACTIONS

The collective proceedings mechanism put forward in Part XI of the ERCP is, as we have noted above, subject to the case management rules applying generally to proceedings under the rules.[48] However, the relatively more complex nature of a collective proceeding requires additional case management powers for the court.

In addition to the rules relating to the appointment of a qualified entity to lead the group members' claim (dealt with in Chapter 6), additional case management rules are needed, in particular, to ensure that:

(1) the qualified entity continues to conduct the proceedings properly in the interests of all group members;
(2) a failing entity can be sanctioned or removed and, if necessary, replaced;
(3) the group members are kept properly informed of what is being done in their name; and
(4) any damages awarded to the group in aggregate are fairly distributed to group members.

Although perhaps not traditionally seen as 'case management' in Europe – since there may technically no longer be an active case to manage on the court register – these issues have sometimes assumed considerable importance in class action jurisdictions outside Europe. The court therefore must retain the power to intervene to ensure fairness and proportionality, if needed.

This section looks in a little more detail at each of the areas where special case management rules have been provided.

4.1 Acting in the interests of group members

Rule 2014 of the ERCP provides as follows:

> Rule 214. Obligation of Qualified Claimant
> A qualified claimant must at all times act in the best interests of the whole group or sub-group, if a qualified claimant for a sub-group.

The requirements to be appointed as a qualified entity are set out in detail in Rule 209. In particular, an entity cannot qualify to act for group members in collective proceedings if it has a conflict of interest with some of them or if it

---

48 Section 2 and ERCP Rule 46.

does not have sufficient resources to properly maintain the group members' action.

Rather than set out in extensive detail the duties of the appointed qualified entity during the case, the ERCP takes a general approach. The qualified entity must always act in the best interests of the group members – in essence, it is in an analogous position to an agent acting for the group members. As noted above, this will enable the court to use its case management powers (both general and specific to collective proceedings) in a wide range of circumstances where the appointed qualified entity has not properly conducted the proceedings.

So when might conflicts of interest arise?

First, conflicts may arise between different members of a single group: usually, these can be fairly easily dealt with either by excluding some members of the group (if the proceedings have only just commenced and they can maintain their own separate actions) or by the use of sub-classes within the overall collective proceeding. This raises the question of whether the same qualified entity can act for different sub-groups within the same overall collective proceeding without a conflict of interest arising.

The answer to this question should depend on the reason for the creation of the sub-groups and the type of entity in question – specifically, whether it has an interest which unduly favours one of the proposed sub-groups.

If the sub-groups have been created in a situation where there is a strong degree of commonality between all of the group members in the collective proceedings and the areas of conflict are relatively contained, there should be no reason for the same qualified entity not to act for both sub-groups. An example of this type of situation might be where a large group has been affected by the operation of a cartel raising the price of an input to a consumer good. The group might include both distributors of the good and end consumers. Although they both have a common interest in claiming compensation collectively from the manufacturer cartel members, they will be in a different position as regards the calculation of the amount of compensation. The distributors will wish to demonstrate that the increased price was absorbed by them and that relatively little was passed thorough to the consumers, while the consumers will wish to show the contrary. But both will have a common interest in showing that the overall amount of the cartel overcharge is as high as can be sensibly evidenced.

Even if the entity cannot act for all sub-groups in relation to some issues, it may be able to do so for others. For example, in our hypothetical cartel above, the same entity may be able to act for all sub-groups on the issue of liability so that the collective proceedings will only need more than one entity to represent the overall group at the point of quantification of compensation.

The model rules envisage three types of qualified entities:[49] (1) entities authorized by the forum state to bring collective proceedings on behalf of groups of victims of mass harm; (2) entities set up or appointed *ad hoc* for the purposes of a particular collective proceedings; and (3) a group member who meets the qualifying criteria. In determining whether the same entity can act for a number of sub-classes, the principal question must be whether the entity has any interest in the outcome of the proceeding. The 2013 Commission Recommendation proposes that state-authorized entities and also (it appears) *ad hoc* entities should not have an interest in the outcome of claims in which they act, but rather be not-for-profit bodies.[50] Clearly, in the case of such 'ideological' entities, which are not themselves substantively affected by the outcome of the collective proceedings, the possibility of conflicts of interest will be very small.

Provided that the qualified entity does not itself have an interest in the claim (by belonging to one or other sub-group), it should be able to represent both sub-groups. Nevertheless, it would be prudent for the entity to use separate legal counsel to advise each group – the sub-groups must both have legal representation[51] – and probably also different experts to advise on quantification issues. The requirement for the different sub-groups to take separate legal and other expert advice may need to be considered at the 'certification' stage – not least to ensure that the costs involved are not disproportionate.

However, where the entity or person is (or could become) a group member, the possibility of a conflict of interest becomes real. It would appear impossible as a matter of principle for a group member of a sub-group of direct purchasers (eg, retailers) from our cartel also to be the entity acting for a sub-group of indirect purchasers (eg, consumers). Although the indirect purchasers from the cartel (the consumers) would be within the scope of the overall claimant group, they will have a less tight relationship with the defendant manufacturers than members of the direct purchaser group (eg, retailers), who have purchased the goods in question from the cartel members and will inevitably have different – and partly conflicting – interests in the outcome of the overall collective proceeding.

Second, a conflict of interest may arise between the entity and the groups for which it acts.

Although this situation might most often occur where the qualified entity has a substantive interest in the outcome of the proceedings, there are other

---

[49] ERCP Rule 208.

[50] Commission Recommendation, 14 June 2013, 2013/396/EU, [2013] OJEU L201/60, para 4(a).

[51] ERPC Rule 209(c).

circumstances in which the interests of the entity could conflict with those of group members – often referred to as the 'agency' issue.

Particular concern has arisen in non-European 'class action' jurisdictions over the incentives of representatives when looking to settle claims on behalf of the class prior to trial. There is said to be a strong commercial need for the class representative and his or her counsel to ensure that the case is disposed of efficiently and cost effectively (and therefore, in practice, often quickly), so that counsel can maximize their 'investment' return on the costs they have incurred on behalf of the class in pursuing the class claim. This driver is in turn said to lead to a risk that class actions will be settled at an undervalue – to the detriment of class members.[52] In some cases, it appears that class counsel have received substantial fees, while class members receive only a 'coupon' for future purchases from the defendant.[53]

These concerns can be reduced in a European context: first, by reducing or removing lawyers' (and others') incentives to 'short settle' group claims through the use of case management rules; and second, by ensuring thorough court 'fairness' scrutiny of the terms of any settlement of collective proceedings. The ERCP rules on collective settlements – which deal with 'fairness' scrutiny – are discussed in more detail in Chapter 11. Here we look at the specific case management rules designed to moderate the incentives of the qualified entity (and those employed by it) to pursue the collective claim in ways contrary to the group members' interests.

One of the principal drivers of incentives to act unfairly towards class members is the use of contingency fees (*pars quota litis*) to remunerate lawyers in a number of class action jurisdictions outside Europe. In many situations, counsel may be motivated to seek an early settlement (on the basis that money now is better than money later), rather than hold out for the highest possible deal or proceed to (expensive) trial.

The model rules on collective proceedings deal with this issue in two ways. The first is that lawyers and others exercising a legal profession cannot be qualified entities and the entity must always be legally represented.[54] Maintaining the usual professional relationship and responsibilities between lawyer and (independent) client should go at least some way towards ensuring that the advice given to the entity is to a professional standard of impartiality. Breach of the lawyer's code of professional conduct may lead to sanctions on the lawyer, either by the court in appropriate cases or by his or her bar.

---

52 Rachel Mulheron, *The Class Action in Common Law Legal Systems* (Hart, 2004), pp 397–407.

53 *Ibid*, 406–07.

54 ERCP Rules 209(c) and (d).

Second, although the ERCP generally allows success fee arrangements for litigation,[55] this general rule does not apply to collective proceedings.[56] Lawyers will therefore need to be remunerated on a fixed or time-based fee, calculated without reference to the outcome of the collective proceedings. The funds necessary for these fees (and the other costs of sustaining the collective proceedings) are unlikely to be available to group members from their own resources – and nor will 'not-for profit' qualified entities be in a position to sustain them – so the ERCP permits the use of third-party litigation funding.[57] These rules are discussed in detail in Chapter 12 of this book; it is sufficient here to note that as litigation funding in damages claims universally operates on the basis of a 'success' arrangement, the court is entitled in collective proceedings to require the full disclosure to it of the terms of the litigation funding agreement, precisely so that it can consider whether that agreement may give rise to an 'agency' issue of the kind noted above.[58]

We now turn to the sanctions on qualified claimants (or those working with them) if they breach the requirement to act in the group's best interests.

4.2 Enforcement of rules against qualified entities

Rule 218 of the ERCP provides as follows:

> Rule 218. Case Management Powers
> (1) In collective redress proceedings, the Court has additional case management powers, including the power
> (a) to remove a qualified claimant of a group or any sub-group if they no longer satisfy the conditions in Rule 208 and Rule 209 or fails to act in the interests of all group members,
> (b) to authorise, with their consent, a new qualified claimant,
> (c) [. . .]
> (2) The Court may hear any person it considers has an interest in the management of the case before making any case management order under this Rule.

The ERCP provides for a specific enforcement power – removal – for courts to use against 'misbehaving' qualified entities. This can be used in conjunction with the general case management rules available to supervise the parties' conduct in bilateral litigation, which will also be available to the court in collective proceedings.[59] For example, an adverse costs order could be made by

55 ERCP Rule 245(2).
56 ERCP Rule 245(5).
57 ERCP Rules 237(1) and 245(1) and (2).
58 ERCP Rule 237(2).
59 ERCP Rules 4, 27, 48.

the court where a qualified claimant has made manifestly unfounded interim applications.[60] We do not discuss these general sanctions here, but rather consider the 'collective redress-specific' removal power in a little more detail.

As a first observation, the use of the removal power by the court is something of a 'nuclear' sanction. The removal of the qualified entity will mean that, unless a replacement is appointed, the collective proceeding will not advance and will likely collapse. This will have an immediate effect on group members – many of whom may not be in a position to pursue their claims individually – and also on others engaged to support the action (eg, litigation funders and expert witnesses). Since the court also has other case management powers suitable for most infringements of procedure, the removal power should be exercised sparingly.[61]

Rule 218 therefore limits the use of the removal power to two areas where there may be concern about the entity's ability to continue with the action: first, that it has not acted in the interests of all group members and second, that it no longer qualifies as an entity to conduct collective proceedings.

Since the effects of removal for not acting fairly to group members could terminate the collective proceeding entirely, the court should exercise this power only rarely, even in case of unfairness towards the whole group. The unfairness must, we suggest, be a flagrant one. However, where the unfairness affects only a sub-group of claimants, the rule should allow the court to remove the entity from its position acting for that sub-group and appoint a new entity for those claimants. Although not expressly provided for in the rule, we believe that this power follows inevitably from the purpose of Rule 218, and it is in these circumstances of discrimination by an entity against a minority of claimants in the group that the removal power is most likely to be used.

Removal on the second set of grounds – no longer being 'qualified' – raises a wider range of issues, not least as the circumstances surrounding the loss of 'qualified' status may be varied. Three criteria in ERCP Rules 208 and 209 could in theory change during the course of the collective proceedings: (1) losing (state) authorization to be a qualified entity for that kind of claim (Rule 208(a)); (2) no longer having the material or human capability to continue to act for the group (Rule 209(b)); or (3) no longer having legal representation (Rule 209(c)) – in practice, the last two are likely to be closely linked.

Where the entity has been disqualified by its authorizing authority, it is highly likely that the authority will either have authorized a new body with

---

60 ERCP Rule 241(2). Compare England and Wales Civil Procedure Rules, Rule 44(2)4, for example.

61 The general rule on proportionality (Rule 7) and sanctions for procedural non-compliance (Rule 27) may also apply.

comparable purposes to take its place or have made transitional provisions addressing how the affairs of the entity should be dealt with after disqualification. The court will then be in a position either to remove the first entity and (assuming it consents to act) appoint the new body to continue the collective proceeding or otherwise to follow the transitional provisions set out by the authorizing authority.

If the entity ceases to be qualified for 'capability' reasons, the response of the court will depend heavily on the cause of the lack of capability. If the entity's lawyers or funders have concerns about the progress of the collective claim to the extent that they have withdrawn their support for it, it may well be that the reasons for their view should be made known to the court so that it can consider whether broader case management steps (eg, a stay of the collective proceeding) are required. Indeed, the entity's lawyers may well be under a duty to make at least some disclosure of the circumstances to the court – either under a professional code of conduct or under their general duty to assist the court in resolving the dispute.[62]

If an entity is removed (for either unfairness or incapability), the court has the power to appoint a new entity and, in the interests of resolving the whole dispute efficiently, will probably wish to do so.[63] However, the new entity must consent to act for the group(s) which it is being asked to take over.[64] This in itself implies at least some due diligence by the new entity and the court should allow reasonable time for this, while being sensitive to the case management issues caused by this delay. The court will also need to satisfy itself that the new entity is indeed qualified to act for the group(s).

Finally, the court is permitted to hear anyone with an interest – including the defendant – before making any order under Rule 218. Clearly, the defendant can be expected to take a relatively robust line and test the credentials of any entity wishing to enter the collective proceeding – particularly as regards the ability to cover any adverse costs order which might eventually be imposed. We have already noted that the court may require production of those details in collective proceedings.

4.3 Keeping the group and others informed

The principal method of ensuring that the qualified entity acts fairly towards the group is transparency. The general rule to act in the best interests of the group necessarily implies a high degree of transparency towards group

---

62 ERCP Rules 3(b) and (e). There is a general duty of cooperation.

63 ERCP Rule 218(1)(b).

64 ERCP Rule 218(2).

members, but the ERCP collective proceedings chapter adds some important further detail.

Rule 219 of the ERCP provides as follows:

> Rule 219. Advertisements
>
> (1) In collective redress proceedings the Court shall advertise or shall require advertisement
>   (a) when a qualified claimant is removed or authorised,
>   (b) when the description of the group is modified or the group is divided into sub-groups,
>   (c) when a collective redress settlement is offered,
>   (d) when any order or judgment is made,
>   (e) [. . .]
>   (f) if the collective redress action is dismissed or withdrawn.
>
> (2) The advertisement shall be made in a manner which the Court considers will best attract the attention of any person likely to be affected by the event causing mass harm and in sufficient time to allow affected persons a reasonable opportunity to participate as they see fit in the proceedings.

The use of a qualified entity to conduct proceedings on behalf of others implies that the court should itself have a 'reserve' power to ensure that those others (the group members) are informed of the court's main decision during the proceedings and before any settlement is finalized. Rule 219 requires the court to ensure that these main events in the collective proceedings, which are likely to require some form of decision from the group members, are advertised as widely as needed.

Advertising is needed so that not only those group members with whom the qualified entity is already in communication, but also those who may need to decide whether to opt in or opt out but have not yet actively engaged with the collective proceedings, continue to have an opportunity to do so. The steps which are required to be advertised – presumably, by the qualified entity on the court's order – are based broadly on the notification requirements in the German and UK specialist collective redress statutes.[65]

The importance of Rule 219(2) lies in the discretion it gives to the court as to how the advertisement should be presented, but also as to how long group members might be given to respond to it if necessary. This last point is likely to be particularly relevant to offers of settlement of the collective action: some national collective redress laws – notably the Dutch collective settlement regime of 2005 – imposed a deadline in the legislation (in that case, of three months).[66] However, given the wide variety of collective proceedings – some

---

[65] For example, UK Competition Appeal Tribunal Guide to Proceedings, at www.catribunal.org.uk (last accessed 27 July 2020), para 6.55.

[66] Dutch Civil Code, Book 7:908(2).

of which may, for example, have relatively limited reach – it would not seem appropriate to be prescriptive in model rules of this kind.

Although the form of advertisement is left to the discretion of the court, the court (or the qualified entity) must inform group members of the existence[67] of an online platform which must be set up for each collective proceeding.

Rule 220 of the ERCP provides as follows:

> Rule 220. Communication – Secure Electronic Platform
> The Court must create or authorise the creation of a secure electronic platform for the efficient management of the collective redress proceeding.

The platform for the proceeding will normally be administered by the qualified entity or by the court – practice differs in national rules. Many current national rules require only that the platform records the details of collective proceedings, which are visible only to the courts to prevent duplication of collective proceedings in relation to the same group of claimants or the same event of mass harm. However, the ERCP also encourages the use of the platform to advertise the main steps in the proceeding – there will thus be both a public and a 'restricted' section of the platform.

Although the ERCP has more detailed generally applicable provisions on the service of documents, which state that documents cannot be served electronically unless a means of receipt can be guaranteed,[68] the collective redress platform could be useful to generate information for (and interest by) actual or potential victims of the mass harm event which lies at the root of the collective proceeding. They should be encouraged to contact the qualified entity acting for the group so that they can be properly involved with the case and notified as necessary.

The use of a platform will be particularly helpful where the actual or potential group members are located in several states. The court must keep group members informed even where they are not in its forum state[69] and use of electronic communications, as far as possible, will be the most efficient way of doing this.

As well as keeping non-resident group members informed, the electronic platform will be the means of keeping courts in other European states informed of which collective proceedings have been brought and in which courts. The ERCP requires judicial cooperation both generally in cross-border situations

---

[67] ERCP Rule 219(1).
[68] ERCP Rule 74.
[69] ERCP Rule 235(1).

and specifically in relation to collective proceedings.[70] Judges must exercise their collective redress power with a view to avoiding irreconcilable judgments.[71] In order to do this and ensure adequate information to foreign judges, details of the collective proceeding must be entered on the European e-justice platform (or similar).[72] It should be possible to link the e-justice entry to the national collective redress platform entry as appropriate.

4.4 Distribution of compensation

The final issue on which the model collective redress chapter contains special rules is the method of distributing damages awards.

Rule 228 of the ERCP provides as follows:

> Rule 228. Amount of Compensation
> A final judgment that sets the amount of compensation in a collective redress proceeding shall include
> (a) the total amount of compensation payable in respect of the group or any sub-group. If an exact calculation of this amount is impossible or excessively difficult, the Court may estimate the amount;
> (b) the criteria for distributing the compensation to each group member, and the method of administration of the compensation fund.

The issue of calculating the compensation payable to the group (and indeed to individual group members) is not strictly one of case management – despite being treated together with distribution in Rule 228. Measuring the quantum of compensation is considered in greater depth in Chapter 10 of this book; we confine ourselves here to comments of a procedural and case management nature which may arise during the distribution of the total compensation – that is, issues falling under Rule 228(b).

Any approved settlement or judgment awarding compensation must include both the total to be paid by the defendant(s) and the way in which that amount should be distributed among the group members. As a first point, it is not necessary under the ERCP for the court to set the amount payable to each group member in its judgment. This may not be possible on the information available to the court at the time the judgment is made, and the administrative burden associated with calculating and administering payments is likely to be considerable – particularly for a large group.

---

70 ERCP Rule 234(1).
71 ERCP Rule 234(2).
72 https://e-justice.europa.eu (last accessed 27 July 2020).

The court must, however, establish the criteria for distribution to the group members. These criteria should deal with the way in which the amount payable to each group member is calculated (see Chapter 10), but also the evidence that the group member will need to produce to show eligibility for payment and the way in which the distribution process will be managed.[73]

Although administration of the fund is often delegated to specialist administrators in non-European class action jurisdictions, the court will need to continue to exercise some supervisory role even after the collective proceeding has closed. If (as is likely) the formal responsibility for ensuring accurate distribution of the compensation fund will devolve to the qualified entity acting for the group, that entity will need to have some ruling on the criteria against which payment should be made. And, of course, it will continue (when distributing the funds) to be bound by the obligation in Rule 214 always to act in the best interests of the group as a whole.

The criteria the court should set will vary considerably from case to case. But, consistent with the general principle of effective case management in the ERCP,[74] the evidence bar for compensation applications should not be set too high – although clearly, some evidence of both membership of the group and at least some loss caused by the event of mass harm which was the subject of the collective proceedings will be needed. But using retailer or credit card records rather than evidence directly sourced from the group member himself or herself should be allowed where appropriate.

The related question of how the court can supervise the conduct of the qualified entity is also likely to give rise to interesting case management issues. In principle, in usual (bilateral) litigation, once the court has given final judgment, it no longer has the power to make case management orders – or indeed any other order binding the parties in that (collective) claim. However, in some jurisdictions – for example, England and Wales – this difficulty is overcome (at least in the context of a settlement) by expressly making the judgment not fully final. The parties can then apply to the court for a further order enforcing the judgment.

How does the ERCP deal with a situation where a group member is dissatisfied with the way in which the distribution process is being managed? Two rules may come into play: a general rule (Rule 180) and a collective proceeding rule (Rule 227).

Rule 227, specific to collective proceedings, gives the qualified entity the power to apply to enforce the judgment of the court awarding compensation.

---

[73] See French Law 2014-344, 17 March 2014, inserting new Article L-423-3 into the Consumer Code.

[74] ERCP Rule 4.

However, if it does not do so within reasonable time, any group member (who, of course, was not a party to the original collective proceeding) may apply to enforce the judgment, but will need the court's permission to act in this way before doing so.[75]

However, Rule 227 does not give complete post-judgment protection to the objecting group member(s). If the qualified entity does act to enforce the judgment (including, therefore, the distribution of the compensation to individual group members), but in a way in which the group believes is outside the scope of the judgment, Rule 227 does not on its face apply.

However, Rule, 180 (not specific to collective proceedings) permits a non-party who is 'directly affected' by a procedural ruling of the court to appeal that ruling. This may be of use where the court has indeed made a ruling (eg, in its substantive judgment) as to how the compensation awarded should be distributed, but the qualified entity has ignored or misused it. Although not a direct appeal against a court order, the entity will be acting under the direction of the court: the appeal is therefore indirectly against the court order and, we suggest, should be admissible on that basis.

If neither of these rules appears appropriate (or applicable), it would still be open to dissatisfied group members to bring a new claim against the qualified entity for breach of the duty always to act in the best interests of the whole class (Rule 214) – although starting fresh proceedings is unlikely to be attractive except in the most flagrant of abuse cases.

5. CONCLUSIONS

The ERCP rules on case management are a good example of how the ELI/UNIDROIT's ambition of developing transnational principles into more operationally useful rules for a European context has materialized in practice.[76]

The most basic principles supporting general case management, discussed in Section 1 of this chapter, are valid both for traditional (bilateral) actions and for collective actions, but may need to be adapted according to circumstances. Indeed, the fact that the rules in questions – Rules 2 to 13 – are drafted in a general way makes them very appropriate for use not only in standard litigation, but also in multi-party and collective proceedings.

However, judges will need to exercise their powers under the general parts of the rules – particularly those rules which give the court a wide discretion – with greater care in collective action cases. There are a number of reasons for this. Case management errors have greater 'multiplier' effects in collective

---

[75] ERCP Rule 227(3).

[76] Stürner (n 9).

proceedings given the generally larger overall size of claims and number of persons with an interest in collective proceedings. The consequences of these effects may be fairly unpredictable. Second, the fact that, in a collective proceeding, the qualified entity acts for the injured persons (who are not parties) means that the judge must take care to ensure that the qualified entity is acting properly at all times during the case. The related issue of managing the publicity surrounding the collective proceedings is also significantly more difficult than in a 'standard' litigation action. And the judge's role may not be over even after final substantive judgment has been handed down: the distribution of compensation to the individual group members (by the qualified entity or by a court-appointed trustee) may also require court supervision.

Some additional case management powers are therefore inevitably needed for collective proceedings and we have considered how the collective proceedings chapter in the ERCP has addressed the main issues.

What, however, are the wider consequences – in particular, for court management – of the need for special rules for collective proceedings? States looking to adopt the ERCP on collective actions will, we believe, need to consider at least whether more training and support in case management are needed for judges likely to hear collective actions. But wider questions should also be addressed. Although the rules on collective proceedings are designed to be of application to all kinds of collective disputes, states may wish to consider whether collective actions should be available only in specialist or designated courts (as in the United Kingdom and the Netherlands). An alternative, particularly in smaller states, might be to establish a list of judges in the general civil court system who are authorized and specially trained to deal with multi-party and collective cases.

More practical 'infrastructure' issues will also need to be addressed – for example, providing adequate IT support for the judge to ensure that records are properly kept and notifications are made promptly and accurately. On an even more basic level, are the rooms in the courthouse big enough to hear what is likely to be a case with very many 'players'?

Wide adoption of the collective proceedings rules would undoubtedly bring better access to justice in a wide variety of dispute resolution situations; but the need to adapt both case management and the management of the civil courts dealing with them should not be underestimated.

9. Evidence in collective redress proceedings under the ERCP

Fernando Gascón Inchausti[1]

1. INTERPLAY BETWEEN GENERAL PROVISIONS ON EVIDENCE AND SPECIFIC RULES ON COLLECTIVE REDRESS

1.1 Rules on collective redress and general provisions on evidence

Part XI of the European Rules of Civil Procedure (ERCP) does not include a specific section on evidence. This should not come as a surprise, as collective proceedings are, all in all, civil proceedings to which the general rules of the projected European system apply, albeit with the specialties established in Part XI.

In cases where settlements are envisaged as the most probable outcome – including both types of settlement foreseen in Part XI; that is, once collective redress actions have commenced or outside any judicial action – the evidentiary issue on the merits of the case loses most of its relevance and the discussion shifts to the fairness of the proposed settlement – an issue to be assessed in light of the evidence, if necessary. Where settlement does not (or does not yet) seem a viable option, collective redress proceedings may involve disputes in which the evidentiary issues are of the utmost importance. And in any case, many procedural decisions of the court – especially in the early stages of the proceedings – will rely on the evidence available to the court for each purpose: namely, to decide whether a person or entity may be considered a qualified claimant under Rule 209, or to determine which of several potential qualified claimants shall become the qualified claimant in the proceedings under Rule 213(2).

[1] This chapter was made possible through the support of the Spanish Ministry of Science, Innovation and Universities, within the framework of the project entitled 'Towards a Civil Procedure convergent with Europe. Current Milestones and Future Challenges' (PGC2018-094693-B-I00).

Part XI of the ERCP thus contains some fragmentary provisions that are directly or indirectly related to evidentiary problems that may arise in this type of litigation. The following are good examples of these.

First, Rule 210(1)(g) on the statement of claim in collective redress provides that this must include, among other things, 'evidence on the qualified claimant's attempt to settle the group member's claim' – a provision that must be read together with the privileged nature of negotiations aimed at reaching a settlement, according to Rule 91(2)(d).

Second, Rule 218(2) also impacts on the field of evidence, insofar as it empowers the court to hear 'any person it considers has an interest in the management of the case before making any case management order under this Rule'. Here again, the specific provision should be aligned with the general rules on the management of evidence by the court (see Rules 25, 47 to 50, 61 to 62 and 92 to 99).

Third, Rule 223(1) adds an additional example to the list of *ex officio* powers of the court, this time in order to take a proper decision on the approval of a proposed settlement: the court may then 'make any order necessary to obtain further information in order to assess the fairness of the proposed settlement' and 'appoint an expert to assist the Court'.

Finally, Rule 228 on the content of a final judgment in a collective redress proceeding where compensation is sought establishes that '[i]f an exact calculation of this amount is impossible or excessively difficult, the Court may estimate the amount' – a provision halfway between burden and standard of proof.

However, apart from these special rules, the evidence system of collective proceedings under the ERCP should rest on the general rules on evidence established therein. Therefore, this chapter first presents the general system of the rules on evidence; and then analyses in more detail their potential application within the framework of collective proceedings that conform to the design set out in Part XI of the ERCP.

1.2 The ERCP rules on access to information and evidence

It is clear that different European countries adopt divergent approaches to evidence and, in particular, to the practical problem of gaining access to information. Apart from the classic distinction in this field between civil law and common law jurisdictions, comparative research[2] shows how the current *status*

[2] See, for instance, Oscar G. Chase, Helen Hershkoff, Linda Silberman, John Sorabji, Rolf Stürner, Yasuhei Taniguchi and Vincenzo Varano, *Civil Litigation in Comparative Context*, 2nd ed. (West, 2017) 281–339; Cornelis H. van Rhee and Alan Uzelac (eds), *Evidence in Contemporary Civil Procedure. Fundamental Issues in a Comparative Perspective* (Intersentia, 2015); Remme Verkerk, *Fact-Finding in*

quaestionis in each country is linked to legal (procedural) history, to legal (procedural) culture and to a recurring topic: the distribution of roles among parties and judges in civil proceedings. This entails important differences with regard to issues such as the level of formalism in the taking of evidence; the attachment to orality and, hence, to the principle of immediacy; and the actions taken to overcome difficulties in gaining access to information and/or evidence held by the opponent or third parties. This last issue may have a practical influence on the types and number of claims that eventually come to court, which is clear from the framework of collective litigation.

In the field of evidence – and in accordance with the main aim of the whole European Law Institute (ELI)/UNIDROIT project – the goal pursued[3] was to draft and present a set of rules that would prove acceptable as the most convenient at the European regional level, following an identification of the common core of the law of evidence.[4]

More precisely, the ERCP deals with evidence from three angles: (1) general rules on evidence, which appear partly in Part I ('General Provisions') and, more significantly, in Part VII ('Access to Information and Evidence'), Section I ('General Part', covering 'General Provisions on Evidence', 'Management of Evidence' and 'Presentation and Evaluation of Evidence'; Rules 87–99); (2)

Civil Litigation: A Comparative Perspective (Intersentia, 2010); Heinrich Nagel and Ena-Marlis Bajons (eds), *Beweis-Preuve-Evidence* (Nomos 2003).

[3] The co-reporters of the Working Group were Neil Andrews (England; until September 2016) and Fernando Gascón Inchausti (Spain). The members were Laura Ervo (Sweden and Finland), Frédérique Ferrand (France), Viktória Harsági (Hungary) and Michael Stürner (Germany).

[4] Apart from domestic legislation, the proposed rules on evidence are based on different sources. The American Law Institute (ALI)/UNIDROIT Principles of Transnational Civil Procedure were used as a starting point (for a recent overview, see Michele Taruffo, 'Harmonization in a Global Context: The ALI/UNIDROIT Principles', in Xandra E. Kramer and Cornelis H. van Rhee (eds), *Civil Litigation in a Globalizing World* (Asser Press, 2012), 207–19. The Working Group also looked at the 2010 International Bar Association (IBA) Rules on the Taking of Evidence in International Arbitration, www.ibanet.org/ENews_Archive/IBA_30June_2010_Enews_Taking_of_Evidence_new_rules.aspx (last accessed 30 November 2019). EU law was also considered – namely, the statutes containing specific rules on evidentiary issues, such as the Directives on IP rights, competition damages claims and trade secrets; the Regulation on the European Small Claims Procedure; and the draft Rules of Procedure of the Unified Patent Court, www.unified-patent-court.org/sites/default/files/upc_rules_of_procedure_18th_draft_15_march_2017_final_clear.pdf (last accessed 30 November 2019). Finally, case law of both the European Court of Human Rights (ECtHR) (eg, on the approach to illegally obtained evidence and the right of a party to ask questions directly to a witness hereinafter) and the Court of Justice of the European Union (eg, on the duty to give a reasoned decision and case law pertaining to the Evidence Regulation) was taken into account.

specific rules on access to information and evidence (Section II of Part VII; Rules 100–10); and (3) general provisions on types of evidence (Section III of Part VII, addressing documents, testimony, examination of parties, expert evidence and judicial inspection; Rules 111–27). The final section of Part VII addresses cross-border issues (Rules 128–29).

1.3 Access to evidence: proportionality and efficiency as overriding principles

The ERCP rules on access to information and evidence[5] are based on a pragmatic and realistic approach to the constitutional right to evidence. Access to evidence, proportionality and efficiency are therefore the general principles on which the relevant rules are based.

From a constitutional point of view, any regulation on evidence shall be founded on the fundamental right to evidence, considered as part of the right of access to justice (Article 6 of the European Convention on Human Rights (ECHR)) or the right to an effective remedy before a tribunal (Article 47 of the Charter of Fundamental Rights of the European Union (CFREU)).[6] This idea appears in Rule 11, according to which '[t]he Court must manage proceedings to ensure that parties have a fair opportunity to present their case and evidence;' and also in Rule 25(2), stating that '[e]ach party has, in principle, a right to access all forms of relevant, non-privileged and reasonably identified evidence'.

However, an absolute conception of the right to evidence cannot be sustained – not only from an economic approach, but also if one bears in mind the potential collision with other fundamental rights and/or public interests. The notion of proportionality, therefore, is also applicable in this field as an underlying principle that can be used to justify judicial decisions in controversial situations and, more commonly, to decide on motions submitted by the parties. Proportionality, for instance, can be invoked under certain circumstances to refuse the taking of evidence if this would be too costly or would cause excessive delay to the proceedings. In the current situation of economic challenges and austerity, it is hence necessary to link proportionality to the notion of efficiency: among the relevant criteria in assessing the proportionality of a decision, the time and costs implications cannot be overlooked.

---

[5] On this, see Fernando Gascón Inchausti and Michael Stürner, 'Access to Information and Evidence in the ELI/UNIDROIT European Rules on Civil Procedure: Some Fundamental Aspects' [2019] 24 *Uniform Law Review* 1, 14–41.

[6] The enshrinement of the right to evidence in Article 47 of CFREU was clearly highlighted by the CJEU in the *Peter Puškár* case (Case C-73/16 Peter Puškár EU:C: 2017:725).

In this vein, Rules 5 and 6 develop the main features of the principle of proportionality, taking into account the nature, importance and complexity of the particular case. Limitations on the right to evidence also arise from other provisions of the ERCP, such as the abovementioned Rule 25(2), which clarifies that each party has the right to access evidence *in principle*; in a similar vein to Rule 100(a), pursuant to which '*as a general rule*, each party should have access to all forms of relevant and non-privileged evidence'.

A similar balanced approach to the right to evidence can also be found in the Proposal for a Directive on common minimum standards of civil procedure, included in the recommendation to the Commission on this topic adopted by the European Parliament on 4 July 2017.[7]

On the one hand, Article 7.1 of the Directive Proposal, under the heading of 'Procedural Efficiency', establishes the following:

> Member States' courts or tribunals shall respect the right to an effective remedy and a fair trial which ensures effective access to justice and the principle of an adversarial process, in particular when deciding on the necessity of an oral hearing *and on the means of taking evidence and the extent to which evidence is to be taken.*

On the other hand, Article 10 of the Directive Proposal, devoted to 'Evidence Taking', also reflects this need to reconcile the access to justice and fair trial requirements with the notions of proportionality and efficiency:

> 1. Member States shall ensure that *effective means* of presenting, obtaining and preserving evidence are available having regard to the rights of defence and the need to protection of confidential information.
> 2. In the context of the taking of evidence, Member States shall encourage the use of modern communication technology. *The court or tribunal seized shall use the simplest and least-costly method of taking evidence.*

Both the ERPC and the Directive Proposal confirm that a sustained and proportionate balance between access to court (or access to evidence) and efficiency should be on the basis of any modern procedural regulation. This tension between access and efficiency inspires in parallel ways the rules on evidence and on collective litigation, as will be seen later.

---

[7] Doc 2015/2084(INL), www.europarl.europa.eu/oeil/popups/ficheprocedure.do?lang=en&reference=2015/2084(INL)) (last accessed 30 November 2019).

2. IMPACT OF THE GENERAL RULES ON EVIDENCE ON COLLECTIVE PROCEEDINGS

Although it is impossible to deal in this chapter with all potential implications of the general rules on evidence in collective proceedings, as regulated in Part XI of the ERCP, it is worth analysing the impact of some of the general principles and provisions on the presentation and taking of evidence.

2.1 General provisions

Among the general principles and provisions on evidence set out in the ERCP, at least three may be expected to have specific relevance in collective litigation: burden of proof, standard of proof and illegally obtained evidence.

This choice is not intended to undermine the value of other general principles or rules, of course; they should usually have normal application in collective litigation cases. For example, this is the case for the uncontested principle of free evaluation of evidence, established in Rule 98; and for Rule 88, according to which admitted, uncontested and notorious facts do not require positive evidence.

2.1.1 Burden of proof

Rules 25(1) deals with the burden of proof in a classic manner. First, it establishes that each party must prove all relevant facts supporting its case and offer evidence supporting its factual contentions. More generally, it confirms that '[s]ubstantive law determines the burden of proof'. This reference to substantive law enables the easy application of specific EU rules on burden of proof in cases where collective litigation may be expected to play a significant role. This occurs, of course, in consumer law cases: for instance, the Court of Justice of the European Union (CJEU) has already held in product liability litigation that rules on burden of proof admit a certain degree of flexibility.[8] And it could also arise in collective proceedings in other fields, such as environmental harm[9] or discrimination and infringement of the principle of equality,[10] where a certain level of harmonization has been developed at the European level[11]

[8] Case C-621/15 *N. W. and Others v Sanofi Pasteur MSD SNC and Others* EU:C:2017:484.

[9] Joanne Blennerhassett, *A Comparative Examination of Multi-Party Actions. The Case of Environmental Mass Harm* (Hart, 2016) 110–12.

[10] In the US literature, see Ellen M Athas, 'Defendant's burden of proof in Title VII Class Action Disparate Treatment Suits' [1982] 31 *Am U L Rev* 755.

[11] We can recall, in this vein, Article 8 of Council Directive 2000/43/EC of 29 June 2000 implementing the principle of equal treatment between persons irrespec-

and where national legislatures must provide at least some sort of reversal of the burden of proof, so that where litigants affirming an infringement of the principle of equal treatment establish acts from which it may be presumed that there has been direct or indirect discrimination, it shall be for the respondent to prove that there has been no breach of the principle of equal treatment.

2.1.2 Standard of proof

Standard of proof is a notion that belongs more to academic discussion than to legislation. The ERCP, however, addresses it explicitly, being aware of its increasing influence in the practice and case law of many European countries,[12] affecting the court's fact finding and the parties' strategies. In legal theory, it is common to refer to different possible standards of proof, requiring different levels of conviction from the judge, the minimum acceptable of which would be the balance of probabilities (ie, the judge considering the existence of a fact more probable than the non-existence thereof – the so-called '51 per cent' standard). ERCP Rule 87 provides, however, that a qualified high level of conviction would be more suitable for civil proceedings in Europe:[13] 'A contested issue of fact is proven when the court is reasonably convinced of its truth.'

This high standard sets a demanding threshold for claimants – or for defendants sustaining affirmative defences – which could be difficult to overcome in situations that might commonly arise in collective proceedings.[14] Let us imagine a situation where collective redress proceedings are brought by a qualified claimant on behalf of a group of persons affected by a defective product.

---

tive of racial or ethnic origin, OJ L180 (19 July 2000); Article 10 of Council Directive 2000/78/EC of 27 November 2000 establishing a general framework for equal treatment in employment and occupation, OJ L303 (2 December 2000); Article 9 of Council Directive 2004/113/EC of 13 December 2004 implementing the principle of equal treatment between men and women in the access to and supply of goods and services, OJ L373 (21 December 2004); or Article 19 of Directive 2006/54/EC of the European Parliament and of the Council of 5 July 2006 on the implementation of the principle of equal opportunities and equal treatment of men and women in matters of employment and occupation (recast), OJ L204 (26 July 2006).

[12] See Michele Taruffo, 'Rethinking the Standard of Proof', [2003] 51 *American Journal of Comparative Law* 675; Luboš Tichý (ed), *Standard of Proof in Europe* (Mohr Siebeck, 2019).

[13] See, on this issue, Michael Stürner, 'Evaluation of Evidence and Standard of Proof in the ELI/UNIDROIT European Rules of Civil Procedure', in Luboš Tichý (ed), *Standard of Proof* in Europe (supra note 12).

[14] On this issue, see Diane B. Bratvold and Daniel J. Supalla, 'Standard of Proof to Establish Amount in Controversy When Defending Removal under the Class Action Fairness Act' (2010) 36 *WM Mitchell L Rev* 1397; Stuart Rossman and Charles Delbaum, *Consumer Class Actions*, 9th ed. (National Consumer Law Center, 2016) 338–39.

Let us imagine also that the case is appropriate to be dealt with on an opt-out basis under Rule 215(2). In this example, it may be possible to establish the harmful event using evidence available to the claimant party; but determining the exact monetary value of the harm suffered by the class members may prove almost impossible. In order to prevent potential inconveniences stemming from a strict application of the standard of proof set out in Rule 87, there is a more lenient provision in Rule 228 on the content of a final judgment in a collective redress proceeding where compensation is sought for a group or sub-group: 'If an exact calculation of this amount is impossible or excessively difficult, the Court may estimate the amount.' This calculation by estimation is also envisaged by Article 17(1) of the Directive on competition damages claims[15] – a field very much suitable for collective proceedings – which establishes a clear link between quantification of harm by estimation and the rules on the burden and standard of proof:

> Member States shall ensure that *neither the burden nor the standard of proof required for the quantification of harm renders the exercise of the right to damages practically impossible or excessively difficult.* Member States shall ensure that the national courts are empowered, in accordance with national procedures, to estimate the amount of harm if it is established that a claimant suffered harm but it is practically impossible or excessively difficult precisely to quantify the harm suffered on the basis of the evidence available.

The European legislature explicitly assumes here that national standards of proof tend to be high (as also recognized in Rule 89), and offers a tool to allow for a reasonable degree of flexibility where material and substantial reasons would merit this – a solution once again acknowledged by the ERCP.[16]

---

[15] Directive 2014/104/EU of the European Parliament and of the Council of 26 November 2014 on certain rules governing actions for damages under national law for infringements of the competition law provisions of the Member States and of the European Union, OJ L349 (5 December 2014).

[16] These issues are dealt with in a much more detailed manner in a different chapter of this book. It is worth noting, nevertheless, that some mechanisms to estimate damages have been considered 'dangerous' in legal literature. On this issue, see, for instance, Jonah B. Gelbach, 'The Triangle of Law and the Role of Evidence in Class Action Litigation' [2017] 165 *U Pa L Rev* 1807; Craig Jones, 'Reasoning through Probabilistic Causation in Individual and Aggregate Claims: The Struggle Continues' [2011] 39 *Advoc Q* 18; Robert H. Klonoff, *Class Actions and Other Multi-Party Litigation in a Nutshell*, 4th ed. (Thomson-West, 2012) 34–45; Robert H. Klonoff, *Class Actions and Other Multi-Party Litigation. Cases and Materials*, 4th ed. (Thomson-West, 2017) 359–69; Stuart Rossman and Charles Delbaum, *Consumer Class Actions* (supra note 14) 339.

2.1.3 Illegally obtained evidence

The problems raised by illegally obtained evidence may have an impact on civil proceedings and, more specifically, on collective proceedings. Apart from the general examples imaginable in any civil case,[17] one might also consider the implications in this specific litigation field of the infringement of privacy and data protection rights. This would be the case, for instance, if a party submitted a list of consumers or persons affected by unlawful professional or commercial practices held under confidentiality protective measures by the opponent.

The first challenge regarding this issue consists in defining what is illegal, since not all legal infringements will entail the severe consequences established by the rule. Illegality must refer to the way in which the evidence was obtained – not to its contents or to the way in which it was taken in court; and, more precisely, to the infringement of fundamental rights or other equivalent constitutional values when the evidence was gathered. This is of paramount importance in the context of collective litigation, where it is easy to obtain large amounts of evidence from many different potential sources (eg, each member of the group affected by the mass harm).

The second challenge, of course, is determining the consequences (ie, the sanctions) where evidence has been illegally obtained, bearing in mind that this does not receive the same treatment in all jurisdictions.[18] ERCP Rule 90 follows a strict approach:

> (1) Except where Rule 90(2) applies, illegally obtained evidence should be excluded from the proceedings.
> (2) Exceptionally, the Court may admit illegally obtained evidence if it is the only way to establish the facts. In exercising its discretion to admit such evidence the Court must take into account the behaviour of the other party or of non-parties and the gravity of the infringement.

The general rule is therefore exclusion – that is, the evidence may not be the basis of any decision, whether principal or ancillary. This highlights the prom-

---

[17] Different possible examples can be imagined, such as producing as documentary evidence a letter addressed to somebody that was opened without his or her consent; producing a recording of a conversation that was obtained without the speakers' knowledge; or producing the contents of personal files gathered by an employer by accessing an employee's computer, taking account of ECtHR case law in *Bărbulescu v Romania* App 61496/08 (ECHR, 5 September 2017); or producing images recorded by a surveillance camera focused into a private home.

[18] Nicolò Trocker, 'From ALI-UNIDROIT Principles to common European rules on access to information and evidence? A preliminary outlook and some suggestions' [2014] 19 *Uniform Law Review* 239, 264–65.

inent role of fundamental rights and is consistent with a strict interpretation of 'illegality'.

The rule is nevertheless softened by exceptions for critical cases: the court may admit such evidence if it is the only way to establish the facts, taking into account the behaviour of the other party or of non-parties, and the seriousness of the infringement. This provision reflects the principle of proportionality and may thus be regarded as a concession to the fundamental 'right to evidence'. Therefore, in considering whether to apply an exception to the general rule of exclusion, a balance should be struck between the rules of access to evidence, the protection of fundamental rights – namely, those connected to privacy – and the principles of good faith and fair play. For instance, if one of the parties does not disclose a document required by the opponent, should it be entitled to claim its exclusion if the document is eventually produced after having been (presumably) obtained through illegal methods? On the other hand, it seems important to stress that the admission of exceptions should not be understood as facilitating the illegal gathering of evidence as a sort of 'precautionary' strategy; on the contrary, the aim is to deter this and similar practices. The general rule should be read in conjunction with the system of orders for accessing information and evidence (see Section 3), which should be the tool used to obtain information in difficult situations.

This balanced approach reflects the view taken on occasion by the European Court of Human Rights – namely in *LL v France*,[19] *NN and TA v Belgium*[20] and *Surikov v Ukraine*[21] – and more recently by the CJEU in *Peter Puškár*. The latter was a claim for data protection infringement brought by a citizen

---

[19] In *L.L. v France* App 7508/02 (ECHR, 10 October 2006) the decision concerned a case of infringement of a specific rule of the French Civil Code in divorce proceedings, pursuant to which 'a spouse may not produce in the proceedings any evidence that he or she may have obtained by duress or fraud'. The ECtHR considered that the infringement of this provision in the case (the spouse had produced medical documents that showed her husband's alcoholism) also entailed an infringement of Article 8 of the ECHR, since this was not the only available way to prove that fact in the proceeding.

[20] *N.N. and T.A. v Belgium* App 65097/01 (ECHR, 13 May 2008) was also a divorce proceeding, in which the spouse bringing the claim produced private letters of her husband to prove the existence of a durable relationship he allegedly had with another person: once again, compliance with Article 8 of the ECHR was at stake, and the ECtHR considered that no infringement had taken place because that fact had never been denied by the defendant during the proceedings.

[21] *Surikov v Ukraine* App 42788/06 (ECHR, 26 January 2017) was a labour dispute, in which the employee claimed a promotion; in order to justify its refusal, the defendant company produced old medical-military records of the plaintiff which stated that he had been exempted from mandatory military service due to psychiatric illness. The production of this evidence in the proceedings, along with other factors, was considered to constitute an unjustified infringement of Article 8 of the ECHR. However, the impact

included on a confidential list of persons considered by the Slovak tax authority to be 'front-men' and which, according to the defendants, could have only been accessed illegally by the plaintiff, since it was protected against unauthorized disclosure or access. In its judgment, the CJEU considered that a proportionality test should be carried out in order to decide whether the confidential document should be excluded. This latter case is especially interesting for the purposes of this chapter: although it was an individual case, it is not hard to imagine it as leading to collective litigation, since hundreds of names were included on the contested list.

2.2 Issues concerning the management of evidence

The rules on the management of evidence should be read within the broader framework of the ERCP system on case management and on the development of proceedings. The procedural model of the ERCP is one in which the notions of order and preclusion play a significant role, in order to enhance the general principle of cooperation between parties, lawyers and the court. The fundamentals that underpin the notion of preclusion need not be explained here. The importance of permitting the court to get as close to the truth as possible is equally relevant, although the fairness of proceedings and the right of defence of the opposing party should not be forgotten. At a certain point, all the cards (including evidence) should be on the table.

Among the provisions on the management of evidence, it makes sense now to examine two different issues which may have significant relevance in collective litigation.

2.2.1 Early identification and presentation of evidence

Ordinary declaratory proceedings under the ERCP commence when the claimant submits a written statement of claim (Rule 52) which, among other things, must 'describe with sufficient specification the available means of evidence to be given in support of factual allegations' (Rule 53(2)(b)); in addition, '[w]henever possible, means of evidence on which a claimant relies, must be attached to the statement of claim, if feasible with a copy for the defendant and other parties' (Rule 53(4)). The defendant, in turn, must respond to the claimant's statement of claim within 30 days, submitting a written statement of defence with equivalent requirements as to the identification and presentation of evidence (Rule 54).

---

that the illegally obtained evidence could have had on the decision of the Ukrainian judicial authorities was not subject to discussion or analysis by the ECtHR.

These provisions establishing a duty of early identification of evidence are reiterated in Part VII: pursuant to Rule 94, '[p]arties must identify evidence which they propose to produce to support their respective factual allegations in their pleadings'.

One might wonder, however, whether these general provisions apply as such to collective proceedings. Rule 210(1) establishes the contents of the statement of claim in collective redress proceedings in a very different manner from the general provision of Rule 53. The statement must include all available relevant information concerning the harmful event; the group; the causal connection; the similarity of the claims; the remedies sought; the resources available to pursue the action; and evidence of the claimant's attempt to settle the group members' claims. This information is obviously necessary to justify the admissibility of the claim as a claim for collective redress; but of course, it is insufficient for the claim to be admissible as such by any court. Rule 53 should therefore apply subsidiarily; or, if preferred, Rule 210(1) should be read as complementing Rule 53 in collective redress proceedings. The specific rules on collective proceedings do not envisage any other point at which the general contents of a statement of claim should be set out; which means that within this peculiar procedural framework, there is a duty for the parties to ensure the early identification and presentation of evidence.

This requirement accords with the principles of loyalty – to the court and to the due administration of justice – cooperation and good faith, which have heightened relevance in collective litigation. As a complement to this – and also in accordance with the principles of loyalty, cooperation and good faith – evidence must be notified to the opposing party.[22]

In the context of potential collective litigation, these provisions on early identification and presentation of evidence facilitate the parties' engagement in negotiations and potential settlement. The ERCP system of collective redress requires an attempt at settlement before proceedings are formally commenced. Nevertheless, an agreement is always a desirable outcome, and it should come as no surprise that in practice, a real incentive to negotiate is triggered only when the defendant finds itself facing actual proceedings, where the claimant has revealed clearly 'dangerous weapons' (ie, serious and solid evidence).

---

[22] Under Rule 95 – which has equivalent content to Rule 64(6) – parties must make documentary or tangible evidence available to the other parties; and must give notice to all other parties of the identity of witnesses and the subject matter of the proposed evidence.

2.2.2 Powers of the court

The ERCP makes a clear effort to deal with case management issues in a rational and efficient manner, combining the powers of the court with the duties of the parties in light of the overriding principle of cooperation.[23] Rule 49 is the crux of the system, including a wide set of powers attributed to the court for the proper management of proceedings. These managerial powers are of the essence in collective litigation, for obvious reasons – including the complexity of the case and the need to monitor the qualified claimant of a group or subgroup. Therefore, Rule 218 sets out additional managerial powers for the court in collective redress proceedings, which are considered complementary to those foreseen in Rule 49.

In the specific field of evidence, the managerial powers of the court may also play a significant role in mass litigation, due to the interplay of two factors. On the one hand, as previously mentioned, there is a need to supervise the qualified claimant in order to prevent the negligent conduct of proceedings with a negative impact on the group members (Rule 214); this would be the case if the qualified claimant did not manage the evidentiary dimension of the case appropriately (eg, if he or she did not identify and/or produce evidence in time; make proper use of the power to obtain evidence from the opposing party; or contradict the evidence proposed by the opposing party).[24]

On the other hand, it is worth recalling how many collective cases – in particular, those based on consumers' rights – involve the application of mandatory substantive law. And some of those provisions, according to the case law of the CJEU,[25] demand a positive action from the court, which has a clear connection to the general duty of more in-depth monitoring of the case.

---

[23] Rolf Stürner, 'Principles of European civil procedure or a European model code? Some considerations on the joint ELI-UNIDROIT project' [2014] 19 *Uniform Law Review* 322; Cornelis H. van Rhee, 'Obligations of the parties and their lawyers in civil litigation: The ALI/UNIDROIT Principles of Transnational Civil Procedure', in Jens Adolphsen *et al* (eds), *Festschrift für Peter Gottwald zum 70. Geburtstag* (C.H. Beck, Munich, 2014) 669–79; *id*, 'The development of civil procedural law in twentieth-century Europe: from party autonomy to judicial case management and efficiency' [2011] *Russian Yearbook on Civil Procedure & Arbitration* 7–8, 82–95; Alan Uzelac, 'Towards European Rules of Civil Procedure: Rethinking Procedural Obligations' [2017] 58 *Hungarian Journal of Legal Studies* 1, 3–18.

[24] Addressing the role of the judge as protector of the absent group members, see Élodie Falla, *The Role of the Court in Collective Redress Litigation. Comparative Report* (Larcier, 2014) 152–57.

[25] See, among many others, Case C-473/00 *Cofidis* EU:C:2002:705, [2002] ECR I-10875; Case C-168/05 *Mostaza Claro* EU:C:2006:675, [2006] ECR I-10421; Case C-243/08 *Pannon GSM* EU:C:2009:350, [2009] ECR I-04713; Case C-137/08 *VB Pénzügyi Lízing* EU:C:2010:659, [2010] ERC I-10847; Case C-472/11 *Banif Plus Bank*

The managerial powers of the court as regards evidence are scattered throughout different provisions of the ERCP. The starting point is clear: the burden falls on the parties to find and produce evidence; whereas it is the court's main mission to decide on the admissibility of evidence and arrange for the proper taking of evidence. In this regard, Rules 25(1) and 49(11), 62(2), 63(1), 64(3)–(6) and 92(1) establish the general framework for the efficient management of evidence.

The relevant question, in light of the converging factors described above, concerns the extent of the managerial powers of the court; and more specifically, whether the court has the power to order *ex officio* the taking of evidence not proposed by the parties. A situation may arise where the court, after an initial assessment of the case and of the evidence proposed by the parties, considers that additional evidence would be useful or necessary in order to ascertain the truth of relevant facts as asserted by the parties.

This is a very controversial issue which does not receive a uniform response in national procedural laws: some consider it normal, especially regarding expertise; others, however, are very reluctant – usually because of a strict notion of the principles of disposition and of judicial impartiality.[26]

The ERCP tries to achieve a compromise between the two positions. Article 25(3), addressing evidence among the general rules on proceedings, concisely provides as follows: 'In so far as appropriate the Court may invite the parties to supplement their offers of evidence. Exceptionally, it may take evidence on its own motion.'

This provision is reiterated and developed in Part VII, in Rules 92(2) and (3), in relation to the management and presentation of evidence:

> (2) The Court, while affording the parties an opportunity to respond, may suggest evidence not previously proposed by a party that it considers may be relevant to an issue in dispute. If a party accepts that suggestion, the Court will order the taking of that evidence so that it may be offered in support of that party's contentions of fact and law.
> (3) Exceptionally, the Court may, while affording the parties opportunity to respond, order the taking of evidence not previously proposed by a party.

EU:C:2013:88; Case C-147/16 *Karel de Grote – Hogeschool Katholieke Hogeschool Antwerpen* EU:C:2018:320.

26 Cornelis H. van Rhee, 'Obligations of the parties and their lawyers in Civil Litigation: The ALI/UNIDROIT Principles of Transnational Civil Procedure' (supra note 23); *id*, 'The development of civil procedural law in twentieth-century Europe: from party autonomy to judicial case management and efficiency' (supra note 23); Élodie Falla, *The Role of the Court in Collective Redress Litigation. Comparative Report* (supra note 24) 129–30.

There is therefore a sort of 'escalation' regarding the powers of the court: first, suggesting additional evidence; and *exceptionally*, ordering the *ex officio* taking of evidence. This second step, according to the rule itself, should be envisaged only in exceptional cases – for example, where the court apprehends that the transaction or dealings between the parties are illegal, or that a contract term is null and void (as follows from recurring CJEU case law). In this vein, these powers could be considered as more acceptable in areas of litigation where the principle of party autonomy does not apply in full. As mentioned above – and for the reasons mentioned above – this threshold of exceptionality will be easier to overcome in mass harm cases, where the *ex officio* powers of the court may be exercised not only regarding evidence on the relevant facts to decide on the merits, but also regarding the necessary evidentiary support to take ancillary and managerial decisions for the proper conduct of collective redress proceedings – for instance, assessing whether the claimant meets the requirements to be considered as a qualified claimant (Rule 209). Rule 219(2) implies a clear concretion of this exceptional power in the field of collective litigation, as it enables the court to 'hear any person it considers has an interest in the management of the case before making any case management order'.[27] Ultimately, the need for active involvement of the court increases within the framework of the procedure to approve collective settlements, given the lack of adversarial proceedings and, more significantly, the court's duty to safeguard the legal interests of group members.

An empowered court must fulfil this role in a proper manner. Therefore, pursuant to Rule 223(1), before approving a settlement, the court may: (1) make any order necessary to obtain further information in order to assess the fairness of the proposed settlement; and/or (2) appoint an expert to assist it. The appointment of an expert under (2) may be regarded as a specific example of the general power conferred to the court under (1). All in all, the rule reflects the possibility for the court to take *ex officio* evidence on any issue considered relevant for the purpose of assessing the fairness of a settlement.[28]

---

[27] On evidence to certify a class action and proof of certification criteria, see Catherine Piché, 'Evidence and provisional measures in complex litigation and class actions in Canada', in *Procesos colectivos. Class actions (I International Conference & XXIII Iberoamerican Procedural Law Convention)* (IIDP-IAPL, 2012) 159–91, at 166–80.

[28] On this, see again Catherine Piché, 'Evidence and provisional measures in complex litigation and class actions in Canada' (supra note 27) 188–90.

3. ACCESS TO INFORMATION AND EVIDENCE HELD BY THE OPPONENT OR A THIRD PARTY: DISCLOSURE SYSTEM IN COLLECTIVE PROCEEDINGS?

Both as a general rule and in mass litigation, the parties bear the burden of procuring access to the relevant information and sources of evidence, as this falls under the most elementary procedural strategy to found claims or affirmative defences only on facts that the parties can reasonably expect to establish as true. Difficulties arise in practice, however, when relevant sources of evidence are in the possession of the counterparty or a third party, as a refusal to provide information or sources of evidence could amount to a limitation of the right to an effective remedy before a court. Such situations of evidentiary deficiency[29] or asymmetry are clearly typical of the harmful events that are the subject of collective proceedings.[30] Day-to-day experience – as well as famous films and television series – show how potential defendants in collective litigation that hold relevant evidence in their possession are often reluctant to hand it over to a prospective claimant.[31]

One of the most innovative aspects of the ERCP in the field of evidence was the development of a 'European way to discovery', aimed at surmounting the difficulties in accessing sources of evidence in the possession of the counterparty or of third parties, while avoiding the risks of 'fishing expeditions' and US-style discovery. Due to significant divergences in the rules and practices of national laws,[32] the solution was to create a specific and autonomous set of

---

[29] W. Vandenbussche, 'Dealing with Evidentiary Deficiency in Tort Law', [2019] 9 *International Journal of Procedural Law* 50.

[30] It is significant, in this vein, to note how the only provision of the newly approved 2020 Directive on representative actions for the protection of the collective interests of consumers that deals with evidence is devoted to this problem. Under the heading of 'Disclosure of evidence', Article 18 states the following: 'Member States shall ensure that, where a qualified entity has provided reasonably available evidence sufficient to support a representative action, and has indicated that additional evidence lies in the control of the defendant or a third party, if requested by the qualified entity, the court or administrative authority may order that such evidence be disclosed by the defendant or the third party in accordance with national procedural law, subject to the applicable Union and national rules on confidentiality and proportionality. Member States shall ensure that, if requested by the defendant, the court or administrative authority is also able to equally order the qualified entity or a third party to disclose relevant evidence, in accordance with national procedural rules.'

[31] On the relevance of disclosure for the purpose of efficient collective litigation, see Christopher Hodges, *Multi-Party Actions* (OUP, 2006) 95–97.

[32] On divergences in systems for access to evidence previous to collective redress claims, see Omar Shah (ed), *Class Actions. A Global Guide from Practical Law* (Thomson Reuters, 2015).

rules to deal with this issue, taking inspiration from existing European legislation – namely, the rules on access to sources of evidence as provided by the 2014/104 Directive on competition damages claims.[33]

In general terms, the system proposed by the ERCP – developed in Section 2 of Part VII (Rules 100 to 110) – is based on the criteria of judicial control and strict proportionality, which are considered in deciding whether a party or third party should be compelled to produce information, documents or sources of evidence. At the same time, it establishes strict rules on confidentiality, as well as serious sanctions in case of breach of a court order to deliver information or evidence.

The core of the system is the creation of a common institution: the so-called 'access to evidence order' or 'order for securing access to evidence' (Rules 100 and 101). Granted by the court either before or during the proceedings, this will compel another person – whether party or non-party – to produce documents, information or other relevant sources of information. The rules are clearly positioned here on the side of the party who needs information and evidence; as such, they exclude any margin of action to the *nemo tenetur* rule in civil proceedings – despite the contrary tradition existing in some jurisdictions. The general framework for the system of access to evidence orders is established in Rule 25(2), according to which:

> Each party has, in principle, a right to access all forms or relevant, non-privileged and reasonably identified evidence. In so far as appropriate, parties and non-parties must contribute to disclosure and production of evidence. *It is not a basis of objection to such disclosure by a party that disclosure may favour the opponent or other parties.*[34]

The order will give the applicant access to sources of evidence and to information; but this does not mean by itself that the evidence will necessarily be introduced to the proceedings. On the contrary, the requesting party bears the burden of introducing the gathered information or materials into the proceedings as evidence (Rule 101(3)).[35]

---

[33] Directive 2014/104/EU of the European Parliament and of the Council of 26 November 2014 on certain rules governing actions for damages under national law for infringements of the competition law provisions of the Member States and of the European Union, OJ L349 (5 December 2014), especially Articles 5–7.

[34] Rule 100 reiterates these principles and ideas, although with a slightly different wording.

[35] 'Material or information supplied under this rule only becomes evidence when it is formally introduced as such into the proceedings by a party or exceptionally by the Court according to Rules 25 (3), 92 (2) and 107 (2)'.

It should be neither too easy nor too difficult to obtain such an order, as the system establishes reasonable filters to prevent fishing expeditions (Rule 102). And once the order has been granted, it should not be easy to avoid compliance, thanks to a set of potential sanctions. The whole system is therefore based on balance and proportionality, and will be very demanding for the parties and the judges.

3.1 Parties

The system will be available to any claimant or defendant, or any prospective claimant who intends to commence proceedings (Rule 101(1)).

In the context of collective litigation, the availability of the system for prospective claimants will be of the utmost importance. Meeting the conditions of admissibility of collective redress proceedings set out in Rule 212 will depend on the possibility to gather information on the harm or on the series of related events causing mass harm – and, more specifically, on the ability to establish this as a *mass* harm; and on the group – including their names or a description thereof. Some or all of this information may be in the hands of the prospective defendant; but it is required before proceedings can commence, in order to draft the statement of claim in a way that permits the case to develop as a collective redress proceeding (Rule 210).

This in turn could mean that any prospective 'collective' claimant – that is, anyone seeking an order securing access to evidence before commencing collective proceedings – should make it clear that he or she intends to bring collective proceedings. Rule 102(3) requires identification of the future claim; consequently, the prospective claimant should meet the requirements to be a qualified claimant according to Rules 208 and 209. Non-compliance could constitute valid grounds to refuse the issue of an order.

As regards the person against whom an order can be made, the system is flexible: both parties and third parties may be the addressees of an order for access to evidence. In practice, it might not even be possible for the applicant to determine whether the person against whom the order is sought will be the future defendant: sometimes, the order may be necessary to define who will be the defendant and what sort of relief should be sought from the court.

In addition, Rule 105 clarifies that the system is also fit for gathering information and/or evidence held by public authorities, even if in most cases they will be third parties. This provision is especially significant for collective litigation, where many cases deal with harmful events in legal fields under the regulatory supervision of public authorities (competition, consumer protection, banking and financial services); and where situations in which public and private enforcement converge are common. The only limit to the duty of public bodies to cooperate concerns information that is protected on the grounds of public interest. To prevent vague or general attempts to refuse cooperation by public bodies, Rule 105(2) requires them to provide a reasoned explanation of the grounds for claiming special protection, which in turn may be challenged by the initial applicant (Rule 91(5)). An example of legitimate refusal to provide information may be found in collective proceedings to seek compensation for competition damages under Articles 6 and 7 of Directive 104/2014 (and national implementing provisions), establishing strict limits to the disclosure of evidence included in the file of a competition authority.

Moreover, it is important to avoid misunderstandings regarding third parties in proceedings to gain orders for access to evidence. Even if the addressee of an order is a third party to the proceedings on the merits, he or she must be considered as an actual party for the purposes of the procedure to grant the order, entitled to full defence of his or her legal position, but also compelled to comply (Rule 110).

3.2 Time

Opening the gates of the system to prospective claimants also means that it may be used before and/or during the proceedings. According to Rule 106(1), an application for an order for access to evidence may be made prior to the initiation of proceedings, in the statement of claim[36] or in pending proceedings.

In addition:

> If an order has been made prior to the initiation of the proceedings, where appropriate, the successful applicant might also be required to initiate proceedings within a specified, reasonable, period of time. If the applicant fails to comply with this requirement the Court may set aside the order, direct the return of any evidence supplied to the applicant further to the order, impose an appropriate sanction on the party in default, or make any other appropriate order.[37]

If the aim of the application is to gather information for a prospective collective claim, the specified period within which proceedings must be initiated should be proportionate to the complexity of the case and to the burdens that must be overcome by the qualified claimant in order to comply with the specific requirements of the ERCP: some flexibility from the court would thus be convenient in this regard.

---

[36] According to Rule 53(5), 'A claimant may apply, in their statement of claim, for access to evidence under the custody or control of a defendant or third party and which are to be offered in support of the claimant's allegations'.

[37] Rule 106(2).

As regards the consequences of non-compliance, and in addition to those explicitly mentioned in Rule 106(2), the information that is collected by, or made available to, the applicant cannot be used in any other process by that person or any other person to whom such information has been disclosed. In other words, permitting the circulation of such information between potential subsequent qualified claimants will constitute fraud.

From another perspective, the information gathered (or not gathered) under an order may lead the applicant to abandon his or her intention to commence proceedings, including collective proceedings. In such case, no sanction seems necessary; but the return of documents, records, and objects would still be appropriate.

Alternatively, as a result of the implementation of the order, the applicant may abandon his or her initial intention to commence collective proceedings, but instead present an 'ordinary' claim within the specified timeframe. Conversely, the outcome – in terms of the information and evidence gathered – of an 'ordinary' request for information might also lead the applicant to consider commencing collective proceedings, instead of the initially envisaged ordinary proceedings. As long as no fraud or abuse is established, both situations should be considered acceptable.

3.3 Procedure

The procedure to grant an order for access to evidence must follow the general system on case management orders in Rule 50, except for the specific provisions set out in Section 2 of Part VII, especially Rule 107. As a consequence, orders for access to evidence should normally be adopted on the request of a party. The court should make such an order *ex officio* only in very exceptional cases, and only after hearing the parties and affected non-parties (Rule 107(2)). This exceptional possibility may make sense in the context of collective redress proceedings, especially where the court needs to assess the fairness of collective settlements or considers it necessary to check compliance with specific requirements to conduct the proceedings (eg, if the qualified claimant is acting in the best interests of the whole group or subgroup, according to Rule 214).

Orders for access to evidence should normally be adopted on a contradictory basis – that is, only once all parties and those who will be subject to the order have been given the opportunity to oppose the proposed order and to make representations concerning its scope and implementation. This requirement is explicitly established for applications made prior to the commencement of proceedings (Rule 107(3)). Written submissions can suffice in this regard – adversarial hearings should be arranged only if this is deemed strictly necessary. If the order is made *ex parte*, parties not previously heard may apply for the order or decision to be reconsidered at a hearing or on the basis of written submissions (Rule 50(1)).

3.4 Criteria to obtain an order for access to evidence

The need to avoid abuse is routinely cited in discussions on the implementation of collective proceedings: collective actions are sometimes represented as 'unlawful tools to put pressure on businesses and companies', and forcing such entities to disclose internal information is considered a clear indication of this allegedly 'evil' purpose. To prevent this objection from arising, the ERCP establishes a set of requirements and criteria for the court to consider when deciding on applications for access to evidence orders, which attempts to strike a balance between access to justice – by means of access to information and sources of evidence – and legal 'tranquillity' of the opponent and of non-parties.

3.4.1 *Fumus boni iuris*

According to Rule 102(2), before issuing an order, the court must be satisfied of the plausibility of the merits of the applicant's claim or defence. This assessment should be considered similar to that requested before issuing provisional and protective measures, and protects the system from potential frivolous applications. In order to allow for such an assessment where the application is made prior to the commencement of proceedings, 'the applicant must indicate with sufficient precision all elements necessary to enable the Court to identify the claim which the applicant intends to make' (Rule 102(3)). As previously mentioned, this provision forces the prospective claimant to disclose his or her intention to commence collective litigation if this will be the case; which in turn will enable the court to apply the appropriate balances when assessing the other criteria to grant, refine or refuse the order.

3.4.2 Specificity

Two complementary rules serve the purpose of avoiding fishing expeditions.

On the one hand, Rule 102(4) establishes that '[t]he Court may not grant any application under this Rule which involves a vague, speculative, or unjustifiably wide-ranging search for information'.

On the other hand, Rule 102(1) – in line with the general provision of Rule 25(2)[38] – requires the applicant to: (1) identify, as accurately as possible in the light of the circumstances of the case, the specific sources of evidence to

---

[38] 'Each party has, in principle, a right to access all forms of relevant, non-privileged and *reasonably identified* evidence' (emphasis added).

which access is sought; or (2) alternatively, identify closely defined categories of evidence by reference to its nature, content or date.

One might imagine that provision (2) above would be used more frequently than provision (1) in applications aimed at preparing for collective proceedings. Prospective claimants – and their lawyers – should be aware of the subtle distinction that sometimes exists between a 'vague search' and a category of evidence that has not been sufficiently defined, and prepare their applications accordingly.

3.4.3 Proportionality, necessity and subsidiarity

The core provisions on the criteria to obtain an order for access to evidence aim to strike an adequate balance between all competing interests. It is not just a matter of preventing fishing expeditions, but also of costs: if an applicant requires more information than is necessary, implementing the order may turn out to be too burdensome for the opponent – and will cause unlawful pressure in potential parallel negotiations for settlement.

To enable the court to assess whether the application is premature, unnecessarily broad or somehow disproportionate, Rule 102(2) requires the applicant to demonstrate that: (1) the requested evidence is necessary for the proof or proposed proof of issues in dispute in pending proceedings or in proceedings which are contemplated; (2) the applicant could not otherwise gain access to this evidence without the court's assistance; and (3) the nature and amount of evidence subject to the application is reasonable and proportionate. For this purpose, the court will take into account the legitimate interests of all parties and all interested non-parties.

Rule 107(4) also gives the addressee the power to control the subsidiarity – and hence the proportionality – of the order:

> The party or non-party from whom access to evidence is sought may apply for the grant of a different but no less effective form or method of access. Such an application must demonstrate that the proposed alternative will be less burdensome to the party that is to provide access.

3.4.4 The issue of confidentiality

Confidentiality is a major issue when it comes to orders for access to evidence. In collective redress cases, this question is of the utmost importance, due to the highly sensitive nature of the information that may be gathered pursuant to the disclosure system.

In general terms, orders for access to evidence will grant access only to non-privileged information or evidence (Rules 25(2) and 100(a)); this means that privileges also apply within this framework, pursuant to overarching provisions proposed by Rule 91. The basic principle is set out in Rule 91(1), according to which '[e]ffect should be given to privileges, immunities and similar protections for all persons who are heard in order to provide information in a case or concerning the production of evidence or other information'.

The constitutional right to evidence may be limited in specific situations, due to the need to protect other interests that are also considered of paramount importance. Some legal systems use the terms 'privileges' and 'immunities', from the perspective of the right of a person to refuse to give evidence or to produce information. From a different point of view, the term 'confidential information' is also commonly used; although one cannot always say that both elements are merely different sides of the same coin.

The heads of privilege listed in Rule 91(2) are not exhaustive, but rather a collection of those that seem to be common and/or compulsory at EU level. They could all be operative in collective redress litigation and, more specifically, in proceedings to obtain orders for access to evidence. However, it is possible that two of them may play a more common role in such cases: on the one hand, 'legal professional privilege and other professional privilege or of confidence, trade secrets[39] and other similar interests in the terms provided by law'; and on the other, 'confidentiality of communications in settlement negotiations unless the negotiations have occurred in a public hearing or overriding public interests so require'[40] – bearing in mind that an attempt to reach a settlement is a prerequisite for the admissibility of a collective redress claim pursuant to Rule 210(1)(g).

Within this general framework, Rules 103 and 104 offer more specific and detailed rules when the issue of confidentiality arises in proceedings for orders to access evidence. In these situations, privileges cease to have absolute effect and it will be the court's duty to strike the appropriate balance in light of the circumstances of the case; it is possible, therefore, that disclosure of evidence containing confidential information may be ordered. In such cases disclosure must be performed in an appropriate way to keep relevant information con-

---

[39] Concerning trade secrets, special attention must be paid to the EU Directive on the protection of trade secrets (Directive (EU) 2016/943 of the European Parliament and of the Council of 8 June 2016 on the protection of undisclosed know-how and business information (trade secrets) against their unlawful acquisition, use and disclosure, OJ L157 [15 June 2016]), especially to Article 9.

[40] This provision is in line with the requirement set by the EU Mediation Directive (Directive 2008/52/EC of the European Parliament and of the Council of 21 May 2008 on certain aspects of mediation in civil and commercial matters, OJ L136 (24 May 2008)). According to the Directive, mediators or those involved in the mediation process are not obliged to give evidence in judicial proceedings regarding information obtained during that process, unless: (1) it is necessary for overriding considerations of public policy, particularly to protect the physical integrity of a person; or (2) disclosure of the content of the agreement is necessary to implement or enforce that agreement.

fidential, making use of any of the possibilities established in Rule 103(2), including:[41] (1) redacting sensitive passages in documents; (2) conducting hearings *in camera*; (3) restricting the persons who are allowed to access or inspect the proposed evidence; (4) instructing experts to produce a summary of the information in an aggregated or otherwise non-confidential form; (5) preparing a non-confidential version of a judicial decision in which passages containing confidential data are redacted; and (6) limiting access to certain sources of evidence to the representatives and lawyers of the parties, and to experts, who are subject to a duty of confidentiality.

This list, however, cannot be considered exhaustive. In collective litigation cases, for instance, it might be possible to decide that in the initial phase, the information should be given only to the court, and not to the qualified claimant – especially if the information is ancillary to the appropriate management of the case.

In addition, very severe rules are established to punish any breach of confidentiality. Rule 104 contains a wide range of possible consequences, which include: (1) wholly or partially dismissing the claim or defence of a party in breach, where the substantive proceedings are still pending; (2) declaring the party or other person in breach liable for damages and ordering payment of compensation; (3) ordering the party in breach to pay the costs of the substantive proceedings, irrespective of the outcome; and (4) imposing on the party or person in breach and/or on his or her representatives a penalty appropriate to the breach.

These consequences must be administered very carefully – especially in collective redress proceedings where, for example, the qualified claimant's unlawful conduct regarding confidential information could endanger the legal position of the whole group if the claim is wholly or partially dismissed.

3.5 Implementation and sanctions

The implementation of orders is addressed in a very open manner by Rule 109. The court is empowered to ensure the fair and effective implementation of such orders by any appropriate means, such as issuing directions concerning the appropriate place and manner in which the order should be carried out;

---

[41] Which, in turn, is based on the suggestions of Recital 18 of the Competition Damages Directive. In more general terms, under the heading of 'Public proceedings', Rule 17(2) establishes the general duty of courts to protect confidential information: 'Where necessary the Court may make suitable protective orders to maintain the privacy of confidentiality of hearings held or evidence taken in private'.

directing that the applicant be assisted by an expert; or making orders under the rules on provisional and protective measures.[42]

In order to ensure proper implementation and avoid frustration, Rule 110(1) provides for the imposition of sanctions on any party or non-party who is subject to, and aware of, an order for access to evidence and nonetheless destroys or conceals the relevant evidence, or otherwise renders it impossible to implement the order successfully. The sanctions should be proportionate to the seriousness of the infringement and should be imposed only on application of the party benefiting from the order for access to evidence. The sanctions include: (1) declaring as admitted the facts which form the subject matter of the relevant order; (2) treating the defendant or prospective defendant as having impliedly conceded the basis or any relevant part of the claim which has been made or which was proposed by the applicant; and (3) imposing on the relevant respondent to the order (and in accordance with the relevant court's established disciplinary powers) an appropriate penalty per day of delay in implementing the order.

If properly managed by the court, these sanctions should be sufficient to ensure compliance – especially in collective cases, where the consequences for subsequent proceedings could be dramatic for the defendant.

3.6 Costs and security

Sometimes the implementation of an order for access to evidence may entail significant costs, such as where a large amount of information must be collected from different sources – a common situation where the order relates to a potential collective redress claim. Therefore, the main rule here is that the applicant must bear the financial burden of implementation of the order (Rule 108(1)). Two additional provisions ensure that the applicant is clear from the outset on the level of financial investment required to obtain such an order. First, if necessary, the court may require him or her to make an upfront payment of the costs to the party or non-party respondent to the order (Rule 101(1)). Second, and on the request of the respondent to the order, the court may order that the applicant provide security for any predictable expenses to be incurred in implementing the order. If security is ordered by the court, the applicant will need to provide this security before the order is given effect (Rule 108(2)).

---

42 According to Rule 101(2), applications for orders securing access to evidence may include an application for measures to protect or preserve evidence (falling within the scope of Part X of the ERCP).

This may be too burdensome, especially in the field of collective redress, where qualified claimants may not be in a financial position to assume these costs (also bearing in mind Rule 238(1), which establishes that the qualified claimant is solely liable for the costs and expenses of a collective redress proceeding if it is unsuccessful). It is true that, pursuant to Rule 108(3), '[a]t the conclusion of the substantive proceedings the Court may determine the incidence of costs differently from the general rule'. However, the uncertainty as to whether part of the costs would be recovered may not suffice to overcome the deterrent effect of the general rule. Therefore, especially in the field of collective litigation, third-party funding may be essential (Rule 237), including to cover the financial costs of gathering the necessary information to sustain the claim through the system of orders for access to evidence, among other things.

4. TYPES OF EVIDENCE

As mentioned above, the third section of the rules on evidence and access to information deals with types of evidence. The ERCP addresses here the main features of documents (Rules 111–13), testimony (Rules 114–17), examination of parties (Rule 118), expert evidence (Rules 119–25) and judicial inspection (Rules 126–27). These rules do not aim to make revolutionary proposals, but rather reflect the need to adopt a flexible, not overly formalistic approach, and to allow for the use of information and communication technologies where appropriate. Among these choices, two relevant aspects may be considered of specific interest in the field of collective redress, concerning testimony and expert evidence.

4.1 Admissibility of written testimony

Pursuant to Rule 115(1), '[o]rdinarily, witness testimony should be received orally'. This general rule is directly linked to the notions of immediacy and better evaluation of evidence. However, some additional provisions open the field to written testimony – an option which may prove very useful in complex litigation, to facilitate better case management and speedy proceedings (eg, if there is a large number of injured persons, oral taking of evidence might disproportionately complicate the proceedings, especially if the information expected to be provided by the witnesses will also be confirmed by expert reports).

In the first place, pursuant to Rules 18(3) and 115(1), the court is empowered to require that initial testimony of witnesses be given in writing.[43] In such case, Rule 115(1) provides that the written testimony shall be supplied to the parties in advance of the hearing at which oral testimony will be given. Oral testimony may then be limited to supplemental questioning based on the witnesses' principal written testimony.

In addition, Rule 117, under the heading of 'Witness Statement', admits the use of affidavits, which are utilized in many jurisdictions and aim to offer greater flexibility – especially in complex (including cross-border) cases, or where the information to be provided is neutral and its accuracy does not depend on the credibility of the person submitting it (eg, the written report of a public officer concerning information appearing in his or her files).[44] The ERCP nevertheless adopts a cautious approach and establishes judicial control as the basic criterion: only with the court's consent may a party present a written statement of sworn testimony from any person about relevant facts and formulated in his or her own words. The court, again at its discretion, may consider such statements as if they were provided in oral testimony at a hearing before the court. However, a party may apply for an order of the court requiring the personal appearance of the author of such a written statement before the court; in such case, the examination of that witness may begin with supplemental questioning by the court or opposing party. A balance is thus struck between the interest of the court in gathering written testimony and the right of the opponent to adversarial proceedings and to contradict evidence (Article 6(3)(d) of the ECHR).[45]

4.2 Flexible approach to expertise

In collective redress litigation, expert evidence is essential for many purposes[46] – in particular, to determine the causal connection between the event of mass

---

[43] Rule 62(2), addressing the means of case management during the pre-final hearing phase, echoes this power of the court insofar as it includes, among the list of appropriate measures for the taking of evidence 'requests for written witness statements and their exchange'.

[44] On the utility of affidavits in collective litigation, see Catherine Piché, 'Evidence and provisional measures in complex litigation and class actions in Canada' (supra note 27) 182.

[45] Although Article 6.3 of the ECHR envisages criminal proceedings, the ECtHR has established that the right to supplemental questioning of witnesses belongs to the parties and therefore its use may not be interrupted by unnecessary case management (*C.G. v United Kingdom* App 43373/98 (ECHR, 10 December 2001)).

[46] See Catherine Piché, 'Evidence and provisional measures in complex litigation and class actions in Canada' (supra note 27) 184–85; Christopher Hodges, *Multi-Party Actions* (supra note 31) 98–101.

harm and the loss suffered by the group members;[47] to calculate the amount of compensation;[48] or to assess the fairness of a proposed settlement before approving it.[49]

Apart from the possibility for the court to appoint an expert *ex officio* and entrust him or her with drafting and presenting a report – already discussed in this chapter – a relevant issue in the approach of the ERCP towards expert evidence is how it addresses the dualism between 'court-appointed' and 'party-appointed' experts, which is common to most legal systems. The proposed system is flexible, which in turn is convenient within the framework of collective redress proceedings: parties are always entitled to produce a report drafted by an expert appointed by them (Rule 119); but of course, they need not bear the burden of finding an expert themselves and may ask the court to choose and appoint an expert instead (Rule 120).[50]

To prevent any appearance of preference towards court-appointed experts, Rule 122(1) – under the common heading of 'Duties of Experts' – clearly states as follows: '(1) [a]n expert, whether appointed by the Court or by a party, owes a duty to the Court to present a full and objective assessment of the issue addressed.' Accordingly, party-appointed experts should also be – and should be regarded as – impartial; and, of course, the most relevant criteria to assess the probative value of a report should be its content and its quality. As the main rule is free evaluation of expert evidence, the court must explain in its judgment why one report has been found more credible than the other, in cases where the two conflict.

There are, however, a few differences which should be taken into account when deciding on the most suitable way to appoint an expert in a case. The first is limited to a very specific problem, envisaged by Rule 124 (5): 'If a party-appointed expert duly summoned fails to appear to the oral hearing without a valid reason the court may disregard this expert's written report.'

The second concerns the expert's access to information that is necessary for the preparation of his or her report: the provisions in Rule 123 which

---

47 Rule 210(1)(c).

48 Rule 228.

49 Rule 233 (1).

50 In the less formalistic context of international arbitration, this dualism is accepted by the 2010 IBA Rules on the Taking of Evidence in International Arbitration, considering as different means of evidence party-appointed experts (Article 5) and tribunal-appointed experts (Article 6). This duplicity is also visible, for the specific sector of patent litigation, in Article 57 of the Agreement on a Unified Patent Court (OJ C175 [20.06.2013]) and finds a clear development in the last version of the (draft) Rules of Procedure of the Unified Patent Court, www.unified-patent-court.org/sites/default/files/upc_rules_of_procedure_18th_draft_15_march_2017_final_clear.pdf (last accessed 30 November 2019).

grant the expert access to information cover only court-appointed experts, not party-appointed experts.

Finally, according to Rule 125, the provisions on costs are also different. While the fees and expenses of court-appointed experts shall form part of the costs of the proceedings, those of a party-appointed expert will be recoverable from the other party only if the court so orders.

5. CONCLUSIONS

The ERCP has been designed as a systematic and integrated set of procedural rules which may be applied in full to any dispute. In this context, the special rules on collective litigation should be read in connection with the general rules; they do not, therefore, form a kind of autonomous normative subset within the ERCP. The rules on evidence contained in Part VII of the ERCP, as well as those that appear in a more dispersed way in relation to the principles of proceedings and case management, offer an adequate framework for the appropriate implementation of the collective action system designed in Part XI. In fact, in terms of evidence, the ERCP strikes a balance between access to justice and efficiency; between flexibility and the right to defence; between fair process and proportionality – principles which also underpin the collective redress system and the special rules on evidence established in Part XI.

10. Calculating compensation in collective redress claims

Nils von Hinten-Reed

1. EDITORS' NOTE

This chapter, on the specific challenges in the calculation of damages (or other forms of compensation) in European collective redress actions, is based on the current (but still developing) practice in damages claims through competition collective proceedings in the UK Competition Appeal Tribunal (CAT). This is currently the European jurisdiction which has advanced the most in considering the various issues raised in calculating damages in (opt-out) collective proceedings.

Although the issues raised in the CAT are necessarily based only on competition compensation claims, the issues facing claimants, defendants and their legal and economic advisers will be very similar in other contexts where compensation is claimed through a collective redress procedure for economic harm caused by a single event or series of connected events. So, for example, the economic issues addressed in this chapter will also be relevant to collective claims for compensation for environmental or product liability harms and – as the ongoing *MasterCard* collective proceedings in England demonstrate – in many types of consumer law claims in the financial services sector.

Rule 228 of the model European Rules of Civil Procedure (ERCP) is directly relevant to the discussion in this chapter:

> Amount of compensation
> A final judgment that sets the amount of compensation in a collective proceeding shall include
> the total amount of compensation payable in respect of the group or any sub-group. If an exact calculation of this amount is impossible or excessively difficult, the court may estimate the amount
> the criteria for distributing the compensation to each group member and the method of administration of the compensation fund.

Further discussion of certification criteria is found in Chapter 6. The CAT's current jurisprudence arises as a result of applications for certification of opt-out classes under the UK Competition Act 1998.

2. INTRODUCTION

This chapter concerns damages quantification in collective proceedings and the role of economics. Economics input to damages quantification is critical, but it cannot be conducted in isolation; legal context dictates its course. The applicable legal regime determines at each stage of the proceedings what needs to be established; the required legal standard (the extent of detail and proof required); and the extent of evidence disclosure.[1] The legal context affects what the economic expert does and when, and applies to both non-collective and collective damages claims. The main factors, at a high level, which distinguish collective damages claims from non-collective claims are that:

- there is a defined class of consumers for whom a claim is made; and
- there are common issues across the class.[2]

In many collective proceedings regimes, the damages claim is heard in full only after the claim has been certified; the legal requirements for certification, which in turn determine the role of the expert economist, vary by jurisdiction. In Europe, while not explicitly stating that a certification process is required, the European Commission's proposal for a new directive on representative actions for the protection of the collective interests of consumers implies that a certification stage must be established prior to actions commencing.[3]

---

[1] Who can claim (eg, direct versus indirect purchasers) and what may be claimed over what time scale also vary by jurisdiction. In some jurisdictions, such as in the United States at the federal level, indirect purchasers may not claim damages, whereas they may at the US state-level and in Europe.

[2] Individual jurisdictions may apply further specific factors.

[3] The proposal for the directive continues its course through the European Parliament and Council. Recital 18 states that: 'Member States should require qualified representative entities to provide sufficient information to support a representative action for redress, including a description of the group of consumers concerned by an infringement and the questions of fact and law to be resolved within the representative action. The qualified entity should not be required to individually identify all consumers concerned by an infringement in order to initiate the action. In representative actions for redress the court or administrative authority should verify at the earliest possible stage of the proceedings whether the case is suitable for being brought as a representative action, given the nature of the infringement and characteristics of the damages suffered by consumers concerned. In particular, the claims should be ascertainable and uniform and there should be a commonality in the measures sought, third-party funding

The principles underpinning the recently established collective action regime in the United Kingdom, for example, are based on the Canadian regime. At the certification stage under both regimes, the class representative must demonstrate that the case has 'a real prospect of success', that is, that there is both a plausible method available and evidence of data availability (rather than submitting precise details regarding the proposed methods and data sources).[4]

Various provinces and territories have specific requirements; but generally, for class action claims to be certified in Canada, the following criteria must be fulfilled:

- the claim asserts a sustainable cause of action;
- there is an identifiable class comprising two or more persons;
- the claims of class members raise common issues;
- a class proceeding would be the preferable procedure for the resolution of the proposed common issues; and
- there is a class representative who would fairly and adequately represent the interests of the class, has a workable litigation plan and has no conflicts with other class members.

Expert economic inputs will generally be required in relation to the first and third of the above criteria.

In the United Kingdom, collective proceedings in relation to competition law are certified via the issue of a collective proceeding order (CPO) from the CAT.[5] The CPO approves the class representative; identifies the class of persons with claims eligible for inclusion in the proceedings; and determines whether the proceedings are opt-in or opt-out. For a CPO to be issued, the CAT must be satisfied that the claims raise common issues and are suitable to be brought as collective proceedings. As discussed in Section 4, the two principal UK cases thus far have involved expert economists at the certification stage. Economic evidence has been provided in support of both class definition and damages estimation (see Section 4).

---

arrangement of the qualified entity should be transparent and without any conflict of interest. Member States should also ensure that the court or administrative authority has the authority to dismiss manifestly unfounded cases at the earliest possible stage of proceedings'; www.europarl.europa.eu/doceo/document/TA-8-2019-0222_EN.html (last accessed 10 August 2020).

[4] See www.bailii.org/ew/cases/EWCA/Civ/2019/674.html.

[5] In the United Kingdom, non-competition collective claims may be made via group litigation orders (GLOs). These are 'opt-in' claims, that is, each individual must opt in to the process and submit his or her claim. The court makes the GLO to manage the individual claims in a coordinated manner. There is no certification process.

In contrast, in the United States, at the certification stage, experts' economic evidence is subject to rigorous analysis.[6] Class certification at the federal level (Rule 23(a) of the US Federal Rules of Civil Procedure) requires that certain criteria be met:

- Numerosity: the class is so large that it would not be practical to deal separately with each member's claim.
- Commonality: there are questions of law or fact common to the class.
- Typicality: the claims or defences of the representative parties are typical of the claims or defences of the class.
- Adequacy: the representative will fairly and adequately protect the interests of the class.

Another requirement, the 'predominance' criterion, is set out at Rule 23(b), and this is the area in which expert economic evidence is critical. The economist must demonstrate, on the basis of rigorous analysis, that the principal issues of harm are common to most class members and that there is a robust method with which to estimate damages.

The frequently cited *Comcast* case indicates the importance of robust economic evidence at the certification stage.[7] The case concerned the alleged anti-competitive practices of cable provider Comcast. In the claim, four anti-competitive practices were alleged and a damages estimation model was tabled. At the district level, the court accepted the damages approach, but only one of the four anti-competitive allegations. Ultimately, however, the case was thrown out by the Supreme Court. This was because the legal theory of harm was inadequately captured by the economic analysis – the damages model was based on all four alleged harms. Hence, the claimant's proposed damages model did not solely measure the damages commensurate with the theory of harm.

In contrast, in Australia, there is no certification process. Instead, there are threshold criteria that are straightforward to meet and would appear to require little economics input at that stage.[8] Thereafter, proceedings commence and the defendant must prove that the litigation should not continue as a class action. It is at this stage that expert economists will become involved.

---

[6] The class of claimants must face substantially common issues and certification requires meeting numerous criteria.

[7] www.supremecourt.gov/opinions/12pdf/11-864_k537.pdf (last accessed 10 August 2020).

[8] The criteria are that: (1) seven or more people have claims against the same person(s); (2) the claims are in respect of, or arise out of, the same, similar or related circumstances; and (3) the claims give rise to at least one substantial common issue of law or facts.

The remainder of this chapter is structured as follows:

Section 3 provides **an overview of the key elements of damages quantification.** It discusses **the principal approaches and techniques available to calculate damages, together with some of the typical issues faced by economics practitioners.** Section 4 contains a description of two of the UK collective actions case examples. It presents the facts and considers the principal issues arising in *Gibson* and *Merricks*.

Section 5 focuses on pass-on and the particular challenges it presents. It considers direct and indirect pass-on and explores the specific pass-on issues apparent in the *Merricks v MasterCard* case. It also provides, by way of comparison, a hypothetical scenario involving pass-on in the *Gibson* case.

Section 6 discusses some of the issues arising of sub-classes within class actions. It distinguishes the effects of legal and economic context with reference to the *Gibson* and *Merricks* cases, considering clearly defined groups with differences and some general principles.

Section 8 considers distribution issues, that is, once an aggregate award of damages is established and estimated, how the award is distributed among class members. Preliminary UK case law provides some interesting pointers in this respect.

Section 8 concludes and provides some final remarks on certification.

3. DAMAGES QUANTIFICATION

3.1 Introduction

The calculation of aggregate damages (or at the level of a sub-class) is in principle no different from any other damages calculation: it involves a comparison of the factual position, that is, the position in which the alleged or actual infringement occurred with a 'but for' or counterfactual in which the infringement did not occur. Economists have a range of techniques that can be used to estimate damages, ranging from a simple before and after comparison to complex statistical techniques.

However, to establish the counterfactual scenario requires a hypothetical assessment of how market conditions and market participants' interactions would have evolved absent the infringement. This requires making several assumptions and the exercise is almost always subject to complex economic and competition law issues. Any assumptions made in establishing the counterfactual must therefore be both plausible and reasonable. Due to the process involved, damages quantification produces estimates of harm rather than the precise sum.

Economists' input into competition damages estimation is critical, as the European Commission states: 'Establishing an infringement, causality between the infringement and the harm of consumers, and quantifying actual damages of consumers concerned, require a factual and economic analysis.'[9]

How damages are calculated in practice depends on the specifics of the case in hand, data availability and the relevant legal rules of the jurisdiction. An understanding of the industry, the firm that has committed the infringement and the nature of the infringement are critical considerations for compiling damage estimates. While economic theory may provide some broad-brush rules of thumb as a starting point, it cannot be relied on in itself; the facts of the case and a detailed assessment of how the firm and markets function in practice are of paramount importance.

3.2 The Commission's practical guide

To complement the implementation of the antitrust damages directive,[10] the European Commission published a comprehensive and detailed practical guide[11] that provides an overview of the main methods and techniques available to quantify damages due to infringements of competition law.[12]

The practical guide sets out several methods and techniques that may be employed to estimate damages and how these may be applied in practice. Damages both from increased prices (eg, cartels) and from exclusionary practices are covered. Damages may comprise lost revenues or increased costs (and hence a loss of profits) and interest on the damages is permitted under EU legislation.[13]

There are several broad approaches available to estimate damages and, given a specific approach, there are then various techniques that may be

---

9 See https://ec.europa.eu/competition/antitrust/actionsdamages/quantification_guide_en.pdf (last accessed 10 August 2020), at p 16.

10 See https://eur-lex.europa.eu/legal-content/EN/TXT/?uri=uriserv:OJ.L_.2014.349.01.0001.01.ENG (last accessed 10 August 2020).

11 See https://ec.europa.eu/competition/antitrust/actionsdamages/quantification_guide_en.pdf (last accessed10 August 2020).

12 The European Commission also issued, in August 2019, guidelines for national courts on how to estimate the share of overcharge which was passed on to the indirect purchasers. See https://eur-lex.europa.eu/legal-content/EN/TXT/PDF/?uri=CELEX:52019XC0809(01)&from=EN (last accessed 10 August 2020).

13 Claimants are entitled to full compensation for damages caused by violations of competition law and interest on damages is awarded to account for the time cost of money on the losses incurred. As such, it is an essential component of the compensation to put the claimant in the position it would have been, absent the loss, during the relevant period. Based on the Damages Directive and case law of the Court of Justice of the European Union, interest applies during the period from when the harm occurred until compensation is paid.

selected to implement that approach. Approaches discussed in the practical guide include the following:

- Comparator-based: these consider other appropriate products or geographies as the comparator to the infringement market. The comparison is conducted on one or more of the following bases: 'snap-shot' (or cross-sectional) – comparing at a point in time an alternative market unaffected by the infringement; over time (time series) – before, during and/or after the infringement; or the so-called 'differences-in-differences' method, which combines the time series and cross-sectional methods.
- Financial-analysis based: these compare various financial performance indicators (eg, profitability, rates of return and cost bases) of comparator firms/industries to those of the firm subject to the antitrust harm. The financial information may be used to build counterfactual prices and/or other comparator metrics.
- Market-structure based or simulation-based: these establish the counterfactual scenario based on a combination of economic theory (to determine how a specific market structure functions) and empirical testing. Such models require many assumptions to be made and assumptions based on economic theory may not adequately reflect market realities.

The techniques discussed in the guide range from the simple (eg, comparing average prices or volumes over time or across markets) to more complex statistical methods (econometric analysis). Interpolation, broadly between the two techniques, which essentially extends the trend line (eg, in prices) before the infringement to estimate the counterfactual price, is also referenced.

Some of the issues that economics practitioners may face in damages quantification are discussed below.

3.3 Issues in damages quantification

3.3.1 Comparing like for like

Critically, any comparisons between the actual and counterfactual scenarios must be conducted on a like-for-like basis. This implies that any factors beyond the infringement must be controlled for. Hence, if a comparator market has undergone substantial structural change, if there have been major socio-economic changes or if consumer preferences differ markedly, the comparator market may not be a valid choice for the analysis. Subject to data availability, econometric modelling, a sophisticated mathematical and statistical technique, may be used to isolate the effects of the infringement while controlling for any extraneous factors. However, in some courts, this technique is often seen as overly complex and at times may cause a battle between experts as to who has produced the most statistically valid model.

3.3.2 Case-by-case and local law

Notably, while the European Commission's practical guide provides a menu of approaches and techniques, it does not specify whether any are to be preferred. The choice of approaches and techniques will depend on the specific case, data availability and the likely scale of damages (if the scale is small, it will not be cost effective to employ resource-intensive sophisticated techniques to analyse large amounts of data). Moreover, the applicable national law must be considered. Some jurisdictions may welcome the use of sophisticated econometric techniques for damages estimation, whereas others may favour simpler approaches.

3.3.3 Pass-on

Pass-on occurs when a firm increases its prices in response to an increase in costs. In the context of claims for damages for a breach of competition law, defendants can argue that no or reduced damages should be awarded to the claimant because all or part of the overcharge was passed on by the claimant to its customers such that the claimant suffered no or reduced harm. This is known as the pass-on defence or 'shield' and the burden of proof lies with the defendant.[14]

Pass-on presents particular issues in damages estimation and, as stated, the Commission has published practical guidance on obtaining and assessing economic evidence in relation to pass-on in the context of competition law infringements.[15]

As the guidance states, it is not appropriate to form estimates of pass-on rates based simply on economic theory. While economic theory provides some rules of thumb, these are based on highly restrictive assumptions that tend not to hold in real-world situations.

Moreover, for the pass-on defence to succeed (at least in the United Kingdom), there is a requirement to identify increases in prices that are causally and demonstrably connected with the overcharge. As such, it is not a valid approach to rely on the predictions of economic theory or on estimates from broader studies of the pass-on rate of a different cost change, by a different

---

[14] The pass-on defence is available across the European Union, but has been rejected in both the United States and Canadian courts.

[15] See https://eur-lex.europa.eu/legal-content/EN/TXT/PDF/?uri=CELEX:52019XC0809(01)&from=EN (last accessed 10 August 2020).

firm and/or in a different market. A careful examination of the specifics of the case at hand is required.

This entails an examination of the characteristics of the cost change (eg, its scale relative to the total cost base and profit margin), the firm (eg, its pricing policies and budgeting/financial management processes) and the market (eg, the way firms compete), all of which are specific to the case at hand. Clearly, each case has its own unique facts and each commercial situation has its own dynamics: pass-on can occur in some instances, but not in others. Rules of thumb are therefore not applicable; pass-on must be assessed on a case-by-case basis. As stated in the Commission's practical guide:

> It is not possible to establish a typical pass-on rate that would apply in most situations. Rather, careful examination of all the characteristics of the market in question will be necessary to assess pass-on rates. In a specific case, the existence and degree of pass-on is determined by a range of different criteria and can therefore only be assessed having regard to the conditions of the market in question.[16]

In collective actions for damages that depend on pass-on (in the United Kingdom, *Merricks* and the trucks cases), the claimants must make the case that pass-on has occurred to prove their loss (under such circumstances, pass-on is used as a 'sword' rather than as a defence).[17]

3.3.4 Interest

As a final point, it is worth highlighting interest. Interest is an essential component of the compensation to put the claimant in the position it would have been, absent the loss, during the relevant period; the loss could have been used for alternative means. For example, the injured party may have invested those funds and earned a return on them. Interest is hence part of the compensation for the loss, to reflect both the time value of money and its alternative uses.

Interest may be calculated on a simple or compound basis. Simple interest is calculated by applying the interest rate in each period to the original sum; it ignores any interest relating to earlier periods. Compound interest includes

---

16 European Commission Staff Working Document (2013), 'Practical Guide: Quantifying Harm in Actions for Damages Based on Breaches of Article 101 or 102 of the Treaty on the Functioning of the European Union', paragraph 168.

17 In the United Kingdom, this has presented MasterCard with a tricky situation. MasterCard faces both sides of the coin in relation to alleged overcharges of interchange fees. On the one hand, it needs to demonstrate that retailers passed on all of the overcharge in cases brought by direct purchasers (i.e., retailers) (pass-on as a shield); and on the other hand, it would want to demonstrate that retailers did not pass on any of the overcharge in cases brought by indirect purchasers (i.e., final consumers as per the *Merricks* case) (pass-on as a sword).

both interest on the original sum and 'interest on interest', that is, interest on accumulated interest from previous periods.

The award of interest, the applicable rate and how it is calculated depend on the relevant law in each jurisdiction and the specifics of the case.

4. EXAMPLE: UK COLLECTIVE ACTION CASES

4.1 Introduction

In the United Kingdom, Schedule 8 of the Consumer Rights Act 2015 amended certain provisions of the Competition Act 1998. This enabled claims for damages arising from breaches of competition law to be brought collectively by a proposed representative of the claimant group. Claims may be either 'opt-in' or 'opt-out'. The first stage of the process is an application for a CPO. The CAT considers whether the claims raise 'common issues' and whether they are suitable for collective proceedings. Regarding suitability, the CAT considers:[18]

- whether collective proceedings are an appropriate means for the fair and efficient resolution of the common issues;
- the costs and the benefits of continuing the collective proceedings;
- whether any separate proceedings making claims of the same or a similar nature have already been commenced by members of the class;
- the size and the nature of the class;
- whether it is possible to determine in respect of any person whether that person is or is not a member of the class; and
- whether the claims are suitable for an aggregate award of damages.

Eight collective proceedings cases (under Section 47B of the Competition Act 1998) have been submitted to the CAT as follows:[19]

---

[18] Rule 79(2).

[19] As of 30 November 2019. Consumers can also make collective damages claims in non-competition cases. One example relates to the so-called '*Dieselgate*' scandal regarding diesel car emissions; there are several such claims worldwide. In the United Kingdom, a claim was heard in the High Court during Spring 2020 — *Crossley & Ors v Volkswagen Akteingesellscaft & Ors* [2020] EWHC 783 (QB) (6 April 2020). The claimants had to demonstrate that Volkswagen breached its duty of care; that there was a causal link between the cars' defeat device software and the effect on the vehicles; and that as a result, the owners suffered harm – poorer miles per gallon and drivability, and higher carbon dioxide emissions. See www.autocar.co.uk/car-news/industry/dieselgate-damages-civil-case-against-volkswagen-starts-spring (last accessed 10 August 2020).

- *The Consumers Association v JJB Sports PLC*, 2007;[20]
- *Dorothy Gibson v Pride Mobility Products Limited*, 2016;
- *Walter Hugh Merricks CBE v MasterCard Incorporated and Others*, 2016;
- *UK Trucks Claim Limited v Fiat Chrysler Automobiles N.V. and Others*, 2018;[21]
- *Road Haulage Association Limited v Man SE and Others*, 2018;
- *Justin Gutmann v First MTR South Western Trains Limited and Another*, 2019;[22]
- *Justin Gutmann v London & South Eastern Railway Limited*, 2019; and
- *Michael O'Higgins FX Class Representative Limited v Barclays Bank PLC and Others*, 2019.[23]

The cases cover two broad issues:

- Direct overcharging of consumers: *JJB Sports* in relation to the price of replica football shirts; *Pride Mobility Products* in relation to the price of mobility scooters; the *Justin Gutmann* cases in relation to the pricing of train tickets; and the *Michael O'Higgins* case in respect of the price effect on foreign exchange transactions.
- Indirect overcharging of consumers: that is, where the overcharge in passed on to final consumers by the recipient of the overcharge – *Merricks* and the trucks cases.[24]

Due to the status of most of these cases (either withdrawn or as yet to be heard), our focus in this chapter is on *Gibson* and *Merricks*.[25]

---

[20] The parties reached agreement to settle the claim and the CAT granted the claimant permission to withdraw its claim. This claim was heard prior to the enactment of the Consumer Rights Act.

[21] The main hearing of the CPO applications (i.e., together with the Road Haulage Association Limited has been stayed pending the appeal to the Supreme Court in *Merricks v MasterCard Inc*).

[22] The main hearing has been stayed pending the appeal to the Supreme Court in *Merricks v MasterCard Inc* (along with the *London & South Eastern Railway Limited* case).

[23] A case management conference was held on 6 November 2019.

[24] As per other competition litigation cases, collective actions in relation to competition infringements may be classified as either follow-on (i.e., they follow on from a competition breach determined in law), or standalone (i.e., they are based on an alleged breach of competition law).

[25] *Merricks* went to the Court of Appeal following non-certification at the CAT. The Court of Appeal determined that is was wrong for the CAT to have refused certification. The case has been appealed and is due to be heard at the Supreme Court. The

4.2 *Gibson v Pride Mobility Scooters*

Ms Dorothy Gibson, general secretary of the National Pensioners Convention, an umbrella organisation for around 1000 pensioners' groups, brought the claim against Pride Mobility Scooters. Pride is the United Kingdom's largest supplier of battery-powered mobility scooters used by disabled/elderly persons, supplying around one-third of the market.

The class that Gibson represented comprised any person who purchased a new Pride mobility scooter in the United Kingdom between 1 February 2010 and 29 February 2012, amounting to between 27,000 and 32,000 people.

Pride operated a system of selective distribution with generally one dealer per catchment area. It supplied a high proportion of dealers (600 to 700 dealers out of 800 to 1200) and during the relevant period, around 70 to 75 per cent of its sales were made at bricks-and-mortar outlets. Dealers had experienced difficulties in competing due to online advertising of mobility scooter prices. They contacted Pride to express such concerns and entered into agreements with Pride. The agreements contained a prohibition on online advertising of prices below the recommended retail price (RRP) set by Pride. The agreements applied to seven scooter models.

The Office of Fair Trading (OFT), the then first-stage UK competition authority, had conducted a number of investigations into mobility scooters, finding that purchasers, often first-time buyers, relied on the internet for pricing information. In its October 2014 decision, the OFT concluded that Pride and eight dealers had entered into agreements/concerted practices such that the dealers did not advertise online certain scooters below the RRP set by Pride. The OFT determined that there had been an infringement by object; but as the relevant revenue was below the £20 million threshold, no fines were imposed.

The OFT also stated that the practice had been widespread and went beyond those named in the decision: Pride had been operating a market-wide policy that encouraged retailers not to advertise below-RRP prices online.

Gibson's collective proceedings claim was a follow-on claim, subsequent to the OFT decision dated 27 March 2014. The applicant's expert estimated that each purchaser of a Pride mobility scooter had suffered an average loss, depending on the model purchased, of either £195 or £40 (before interest). This yielded a (preliminary) estimate of aggregate damages in the range of £2.7 million to £3.2 million, given the scale of the class. Due to the OFT's

Supreme Court is expected to provide guidance on the legal framework for certification of all future actions.

finding of infringement by object, no effects analysis was required. This meant that Gibson had to submit an assessment of the effects of the infringements, that is, Gibson had to prove the extent of the overcharge.

It is notable that Gibson's expert economist stated that the infringements had broader effects (i.e., beyond the OFT findings of eight restrictive agreements involving seven Pride models), and the claim form submitted to the CAT distinguished four sub-classes as follows:

- consumers who purchased Pride scooter models that were subject to the online price advertising restriction, in physical stores;
- consumers who purchased Pride scooter models that were not subject to the online price advertising restriction, in physical stores;
- consumers who purchased Pride scooter models that were subject to the online price advertising restriction, online; and
- consumers who purchased Pride scooter models that were not subject to the online price advertising restriction, online.[26]

In contrast, Pride contended that the extent and scope of any overcharge would be limited, as individuals tended to negotiate the price they paid for a scooter. This, Pride stated, meant that there was a lack of common issues among consumers. Moreover, Pride's expert held the view that the effects of the infringements would be 'limited to sales of Relevant Models made by Relevant Retailers within the Relevant Period'[27] and that such sales were online only. This yielded a sub-class and a substantially smaller estimated level of damages than those provided in the claim form.

Importantly, Pride's expert contended that there would be no broader effects of the restrictions, that is, there would be no effects on non-relevant retailers or non-relevant models (no 'umbrella' effects). While the OFT had acknowledged that Pride operated a market-wide pricing policy, as stated, it did not assess any effects.

Following its assessment of the evidence submitted, the CAT did not grant Gibson the CPO, for the following reasons.

The expert calculated the overcharge with reference to the prices of the relevant scooters sold during the period of the infringement compared to so-called 'internet rogue' prices (i.e., prices charged by retailers that did not adhere to the policy) and to prices subsequently charged during the following years. The method was rejected because, according to the CAT, causation

---

[26] While the expert distinguished these sub-classes of consumers, he did not distinguish the types of retailers in his analysis; all were treated the same.

[27] CAT judgment, ¶ 101.

had not been proved. It was deemed not sufficient to assume that any differences in prices were due to the infringement; evidence had to be provided.

With regard to the coverage of the claim (which related to the claimant's counterfactual scenario), the claimant included all consumers who had purchased a relevant scooter during the infringement period. However, as stated, only eight retailers had been found to have entered into the restrictive agreements; and as the CAT said: 'Since this is a follow-on claim, the question is what loss flowed from those infringements, not from Pride's policy.'[28]

Regarding the counterfactual ('no infringement') scenario, Gibson's expert stated that this would comprise: no agreements with the eight retailers and no policy that encouraged other retailers not to advertise below-RRP prices online. In contrast, the defendant contended that the counterfactual scenario comprised: no agreements with the eight retailers and a policy that encouraged retailers not to advertise below-RRP prices online.

Clearly, given the OFT's findings, the actual scenario comprised: agreements with eight retailers and a policy that encouraged retailers not to advertise below-RRP prices online. According to the defendant, therefore, the difference between the two scenarios was the eight agreements. This yielded a sub-class within the Gibson total class of consumers.

For the claimant, the difference between the actual and its counterfactual scenario yielded two classes of consumers:

- those who purchased the relevant Pride scooters from the eight retailers; and
- the remainder, who purchased the relevant Pride scooters from all other retailers.

The CAT encouraged Gibson to resubmit an application with a claim covering consumers who had purchased from the eight retailers. However, Gibson determined that, given the smaller class size, the size of the revised claim was not sufficient to proceed, given the costs versus potential benefits for class members.

---

[28] CAT judgment, ¶ 108. It was not possible for the claim to be brought as a hybrid, part follow-on/part standalone claim, as any alleged further allegations would be out of time due to statutes.

4.3 *Merricks v MasterCard*

The class in this opt-out claim, comprising 40 million UK residents, is huge, as is the size of the claim, at more than £14 billion.[29] The duration of the competition infringement underpinning the claim totalled 16 years.

This is an especially interesting case, as it was brought as a follow-on claim to a Directorate-General for Competition decision which determined that MasterCard had set excessive interchange fees in Europe.[30] Interchange fees are charged to merchants each time a customer uses a payment card. Merricks' claim was that all merchants had passed on these excessive fees, in the form of higher prices, to consumers in the United Kingdom who shopped at merchants that accept MasterCard.

The claim stated that the proposed damages calculation involved estimating:

- the volume of commerce affected (i.e., relevant consumers' expenditure using MasterCard payment cards);
- the overcharge percentages (i.e., the amount of excessive interchange fee); and
- pass-on (i.e., the extent to which merchants passed the excessive interchange fee on to consumers in the form of higher prices).

Merricks appointed an expert economist and an expert accountant to compile the damages estimates. Merricks' expert economist stated that the market structure, conditions of supply and demand, and type of pricing regime adopted would affect pass-on. He acknowledged that there would likely be high variations of pass-on within sectors, and that he would need to form a judgement based on the available data.

---

[29] The proposed class comprised all individuals over the age of 16 who had been resident in the United Kingdom for a continuous period of at least three months and who, between 22 May 1992 and 21 June 2008, purchased goods or services from businesses in the United Kingdom which accepted MasterCard.

[30] Interchange fees were found to be a substantial part of the merchant service charge – a charge levied for the provision of payment card services to merchants by its banks. The CAT accepted this as a follow-on claim even though the Directorate-General for Competition (DG Competition) decision concerned interchange fees between European countries ('intra-EEA') rather than UK interchange fees. The class representative stated that the intra-EEA interchange fees had directly raised UK interchange fees. This approach contrasts to the standalone claims against MasterCard and Visa in the United Kingdom by retailers. In these claims, there is no direct read-across from the DG Competition decision to the United Kingdom, and claimants have instead set out in detail how and why there is a breach of competition law (an Article 101(1) infringement) by MasterCard and Visa in the United Kingdom.

Regarding distribution, Merricks stated that dividing the total damages on a per capita basis would be a simple solution and therefore key to ensure extensive participation.[31]

MasterCard stated that the applicant had calculated the damages the wrong way around: conceptually, the applicant should have estimated each claimant's loss and considered how best to aggregate rather than estimate total damages and then divide up in a way that bore no relation to individual loss (i.e., MasterCard argued for a 'bottom-up' rather than a 'top-down' model). It noted three key types of differences that would prevent the compilation of reliable figures: pass-on rates of different merchants; purchasing history of different individuals; and benefits received by individual cardholders.

MasterCard said that of these, pass-on alone would prevent a reliable estimate of the overcharge, citing sectoral differences, differences over time/across regions and the sheer number of merchants: 500,000 MasterCard merchants in 1992, rising to 800,000 by 2008. It also cited from previous court proceedings that had concluded that there were no reasonable estimates of the pass-on rate of interchange fees by merchants.

As subsequently stated by the Court of Appeal, in the proceedings there were:

> significant disputes about the level of pass-on of the merchant service charge to consumers during the infringement period; the method and feasibility of being able to calculate that level even for the purpose of an aggregate award of damages in collective proceedings; and how any aggregate award of damages would be distributed between the members of the class in a way which adequately (or at all) reflects the loss which they have incurred as individuals as a result of the infringement.[32]

The CAT refused the collective proceedings order, due to **a perceived lack of data to implement the proposed method for determining the level of pass-on of the overcharges to consumers**; and the absence of a plausible means to calculate the loss of individual claimants and hence devise an appropriate method of distributing any aggregate award of damages.

Merrick appealed the decision, largely on three grounds:

- Pass-on: the CAT erred in law and adopted the wrong approach to the assessment of the evidence and the strength of the case.

---

[31] The claim form suggested that individual distribution would simply be on a per capita annualized basis. Various methods had been considered based on factors such as disposable income, age and region. It was concluded, however, that there was no method that could produce a fair distribution.

[32] Court of Appeal, ¶ 11.

- Distribution methods: the CAT adopted the wrong test in relation to distribution, as it determined that a distribution method that did not link the distribution of an aggregate award of damages is some way to individual loss was impermissible.
- Common issues: the CAT adopted the wrong legal approach in its assessment of the extent to which the individual claims raised common issues.

The case is now due before the Supreme Court, so the outcome remains to be determined. However, the published Court of Appeal decision raises some interesting issues:

- Pass-on: it was determined that the CAT at the certification stage set the bar too high for both the data requirements and the method to be employed. Rather than conducting what the Court of Appeal described as a 'mini trial', the CAT should have considered whether the claim had a 'real prospect of success'.[33]
- Distribution method: first, the distribution of an aggregate award need not be conducted on a compensatory basis (indeed, it is not necessary within an aggregate award to prove any individual loss), as long as damages are compensatory at the aggregate level to the whole class. Second, at the certification stage, it is not necessary to consider how the potential award may be distributed; that is a matter to be considered at a later stage, once the aggregate damages have been awarded.[34]
- Common issues: the CAT wrongly concluded that pass-on was not a common issue. The Court of Appeal determined that the issue of whether the interchange fee overcharge was passed on to consumers generally, and in what amounts, was an issue common to all the individual claims.

As stated, a further judgment is due from the Supreme Court in 2020, so the ultimate determinations remain unknown. It will be interesting to observe whether the Court of Appeal's conclusions are overturned or stayed.

---

33 The CAT cited from Canadian class action *Pro-Sys Consultants Ltd. v Microsoft Corporation*, 2013: 'the function of the Tribunal at the certification stage is to be satisfied that the proposed methodology is capable of or offers a realistic prospect of establishing loss to the class', ¶ 50, CoA. Previously, the Court of Appeal stated that it is 'right to treat the Canadian jurisprudence on certification as informing the correct approach', ¶ 40, CoA.

34 Section 47C(2) of the Competition Act 1998 states: 'The Tribunal may make an award of damages in collective proceedings without undertaking an assessment of the amount of damages recoverable in respect of the claim of each represented person.'

5. PASS-ON

Pass-on issues more generally are worth further exploration in relation to the two collective actions cases discussed. As stated, the *Merricks* case concerns indirect pass-on. However, to highlight the issues that pass-on presents, it is instructive to consider a direct pass-on example.

In *Sainsbury's v MasterCard*,[35] a direct pass-on case (did Sainsbury's pass-on the overcharge to its customers in the form of higher prices?), a legal test must be satisfied: the defendant (in this case, MasterCard) had to prove that Sainsbury's had passed on the overcharge. If satisfied, the court would then have to determine what proportion of the overcharge had been passed on. This exercise was subject to numerous challenges, even though it involved only one retailer.

In this case the CAT determined that the legal definition of 'pass-on' is an identifiable increase in prices charged by a firm to its customers which 'must be causally connected with the overcharge, and demonstrably so'. The law determines that the burden of proving pass-on falls on the defendant and the CAT concluded that MasterCard had not provided proof to meet the CAT's legal standard. MasterCard submitted several expert reports on this matter (from an economist and an accountant). However, none of the analysis submitted demonstrated that the interchange fee had led to an identifiable increase in Sainsbury's prices that was 'causally connected... and demonstrably so'.

In *Merricks v MasterCard*, if a CPO is granted, the CAT will need to determine, based on the evidence submitted, what proportion of the overcharge was passed on by the hundreds of thousands of merchants that accept MasterCard. Merricks' expert economist will need to compile estimates of the pass-on rates for specific sectors (eg, supermarkets, petrol stations, DIY stores, travel agents and restaurants). Ultimately, a weighted average will be estimated, given the distribution of expenditure using MasterCard payment cards by sector.

The expert will need to examine the economic characteristics of each sector and then determine whether pass-on is relatively 'high' or 'low'. This exercise is not straightforward and, given the limited available empirical evidence on pass-on, at best any estimates will be 'finger in the air'. Interchange fees are a small cost and apply to all goods and services – they are not product specific. Most large companies can manage such costs (unlike large product-specific input costs, such as the costs of a car engine for a car assembler). As stated, in the standalone interchange fee case, the CAT determined

[35] [2016] CAT 11; on appeal [2018] EWCA 1536 Civ.

that MasterCard had failed to prove that one retailer, Sainsbury's, had passed on the interchange fee in the form of increased prices to its customers.

However, whether or not the CAT (or any other court) may be willing to make an award of damages under such circumstances is, of course, a legal and not an economic question.

The challenges of estimating indirect pass-on would be easier in a less complex case. Assume, by way of example and hypothetically, that in the *Gibson* case, the suppliers of scooters had colluded to raise the price that the retailers had to pay. In contrast to interchange fees, any overcharge is likely to be a high proportion of the wholesale price; and the pass-on of the overcharge would cause a significant and observable change in the retail price of mobility scooters.

With a large increase in a product-specific wholesale price, an observable change in retail price, a limited range of products and a limited number of retailers, it is plausible that a reliable pass-on estimate may be made.

6. SUB-CLASSES

The *Merricks* and *Gibson* cases demonstrate that whether there should be sub-classes and what those sub-classes should be depend on the specific legal and factual circumstances of the case. Some of the issues arising from the two cases are highlighted below.

6.1 *Gibson v Pride Mobility*

The legal context, that is, the fact that this was a follow-on case, meant that only one sub-class (consumers who had purchased the relevant models from the relevant retailers) could be considered in the claim as it stood. The CAT advised that the expert:

> would need to consider separate sub-classes for those who purchased Relevant Models from the Relevant Retailers during the Relevant Period; those who purchased other Pride models from the Relevant Retailers; and then sub-classes for those who purchased from other Pride dealers whose prices were affected by the… Prohibition on the Relevant Retailers, which would be the 'umbrella' claims.[36]

Although Gibson's class comprised 'any person who purchased a new Pride mobility scooter', the claim form identified four sub-classes of consumers. However, its expert economist did not distinguish between the different

---

[36] CAT judgment, ¶ 113.

types of retailers in its analysis (i.e., online versus bricks-and-mortar retailers and relevant retailers versus 'umbrella' retailers).

6.2 *Merricks v MasterCard*

In *Merricks*, the class comprised all consumers who had purchased goods and services during the relevant period at the relevant retailers. Merricks did not distinguish sub-classes, although MasterCard suggested that some consumers who held specific payment cards may have received payment card benefits such that overall, they suffered no loss. However, it would be problematic, given the length of the relevant period, to determine which consumers had which payment cards and what the various payment card benefits were.

In principle, sub-classes could comprise consumers of varying income/wealth and/or expenditure patterns. This in turn would lead to varying levels of exposure to the overcharge (at varying retailers, all of which would have different and unknowable rates of pass-on). Clearly, however, such a micro-approach would be almost impossible to conduct. Moreover, the Court of Appeal stated that the distribution of an aggregate award need not be conducted on a compensatory basis, as long as damages are compensatory at the aggregate level to the whole class. This implies that, at least for this case, distribution and sub-class issues may be related.

7. DISTRIBUTION METHODS

Based on the cases reviewed, the following issues may be highlighted.

In the United Kingdom, distribution is not (at present at least) a matter for the certification stage.

While aggregate damages should be compensatory to the class as a whole, individual payments need not be.

Similar challenges occur with distribution (within either an aggregate class or sub-class). In *Gibson*, it would in principle be possible to base each consumer award on the amount the consumer actually paid – although this might be quite costly to administer. An alternative would be to base the individual award on the model purchased.

In *Merricks*, the large number of 'moving parts' might make a fixed per capita award more practical.

8. CERTIFICATION ISSUES AND CONCLUSIONS

As discussed in Section 2 of this chapter, certification is essentially a legal and process issue. Having reviewed the *Merricks* and *Gibson* cases, and given that all UK cases await the outcome of the Supreme Court, it is worth revisiting certification in this context. As stated, in the United Kingdom, although evidence has a role to play at the certification stage, the standard of proof does not require evidence on a balance of probabilities. The certification process should not involve a detailed assessment of the merits of the claim. Notably, regarding the depth of assessment at the certification stage, the CAT stated in *Gibson*: 'it is not the role of the Tribunal at this stage of the proceedings to choose between the approaches of the two expert economists.'[37]

Nor should it focus on the viability or strength of the action. Rather, as discussed, the class representative must demonstrate, at least in Canada and the United Kingdom, that the case has a real prospect of success: 'The representative should not… be required to demonstrate that more than he has a real prospect of success.'[38]

In respect of data requirements, again in the United Kingdom, the class representative must 'satisfy the CAT. . . that there was or likely to be data available to operate the methodology'.[39]

Regarding the *Merricks* case, it is unclear on what basis the Court of Appeal considered that the CAT could have been satisfied that there was likely to be data available to conduct the analysis and why it decided that the claimant had a real chance of success. Evidence submitted to the CAT included a report prepared for the OFT that noted: 'Empirical work on cost pass-through issues in industrial organisation settings is relatively new, and analysis that attempts to quantify pass-through rates in this context is scarce.'[40]

This was not rebutted by the claimant and the Court of Appeal noted that the experts 'acknowledged that the evidence gathering process was at an early stage'.[41]

However, the Court of Appeal subsequently noted that if it transpired that the expert did not in fact have the necessary data, the CAT could terminate

---

37 CAT judgment, ¶ 106.
38 Court of Appeal, ¶ 54.
39 Court of Appeal, ¶ 44.
40 CAT judgment, ¶ 51.
41 CAT judgment, ¶ 51.

the collective proceedings. On this basis, the challenge for the expert would appear to be not at the certification stage, but rather at a later stage.

Given the lessons learned from the *Gibson* and *Merricks* cases, and pending the Supreme Court ruling in 2020, it will be instructive to review the approach and outcomes of the forthcoming trucks, train tickets and foreign exchange transactions claims in the CAT once the CPO applications are heard.

11. Collective settlements

Astrid Stadler

1. INTRODUCTION[1]

The wheels of justice grind slowly – particularly when it comes to the handling of mass harm events before the courts. Lengthy and expensive court proceedings are one reason why settlement is often a silver bullet. Although group members will not receive full compensation, a mass settlement can be the best way to resolve disputes arising from mass harm events. The tendency to settle mass disputes varies, however, with respect to the legal setting in which claims arising from mass harm events can be litigated.

In the United States, very few class actions reach the stage of trial (less than 1 per cent of all cases filed in federal courts); most of them settle after certification.[2] From a European perspective, the 'litigation industry' and the blackmailing effect of the US class action system are often held responsible for this development. In Europe,[3] the Netherlands has established an excellent reputation as a forum for global settlements, but the absolute numbers are low.[4] The *Volkswagen Dieselgate* case also reflects how the attitude of defendants may vary from one jurisdiction to another. Volkswagen settled the claims of US diesel car owners, lessees and Volkswagen shareholders almost immediately before the multi-district litigation court (MDL) in California; but

---

1 All websites last accessed 11 August 2020.

2 Stefaan Voet, '"Where the wild things are" – Reflections on the state and future of European collective redress' in Marco Loos and Anne Keirse (eds), *Waves in Contract and Liability Law in Three Decades of Ius Commune* (Intersentia, 2017); Richard Marcus, Chapter 14.

3 For settlements in the United Kingdom, Christopher Hodges, 'Settlement and its pitfalls in England and Wales' in Christopher Hodges and Astrid Stadler (eds), *Resolving Mass Disputes* (Edward Elgar Publishing, 2013) 106.

4 Since 2005, eight cases have been dealt with under the Dutch Act on Collective Settlement of Mass Claims (WCAM); see Ianika Tzankova and Deborah Hensler, 'Collective Settlements in the Netherlands: Some Empirical Observations' in Christopher Hodges and Astrid Stadler (eds), (n 2) 91.

there is no nationwide, European-wide or global settlement for car owners or shareholders elsewhere.

Nevertheless, settlements generally afford advantages for both sides.[5] Group members have the chance to obtain at least part of their compensation in due time, without the need to commence enforcement against the defendant and – normally – without the risk of the insolvency of the defendant. For defendants, a mass settlement can be the least expensive way of settling the whole dispute at a single blow and closing the book (buying 'global peace' in US litigation). Due to the nature of mass harm, the potentially liable party has an interest in including as many claims as possible – ideally all claims – in a settlement agreement, although it is not possible to negotiate a settlement with each and every group member individually. Consequently, mass settlements require a mechanism of representation of the group of victims and procedural tools that allow the declaration of a mass settlement which is binding on all victims, even though they did not actively participate in its negotiation. The European Law Institute (ELI)/UNIDROIT European Rules of Civil Procedure (ERCP) provide both mechanisms and distinguish between the situation where a collective action against the defendant is already pending[6] and the situation where a mass settlement has been concluded outside a pending action (so-called 'standalone' settlement).[7] The basic structure of these proceedings is described in Chapter 6. This chapter will reflect on some of the problems that arise regardless of whether the settlement is a standalone settlement or one negotiated during a pending action. In both situations, it meets an international standard of collective redress that the proposed settlement requires court approval.[8] The group members' vulnerability requires a number of safeguards

---

[5] Astrid Stadler, 'Cross-border Mass Litigation – A Particular Challenge for European Law' in Jenny Steele and Willem van Boom (eds), *Mass Justice – Challenges of Representation and Distribution* (Edward Elgar Publishing, 2011), 73–100.

[6] In any case, before filing a collective action, the qualified claimant must at least attempt to enter into settlement negotiations with the prospective defendant (Rule 210 [1] [g]).

[7] A standalone settlement is to some extent the same as a settlement class action in the United States. The latter does not necessarily take place without any pending action (pre-certification discovery may have taken place), but it is characterized by the fact that the applicants apply for certification of the class and settlement approval at the same time.

[8] Belgium – Article XVII.45, para 3 *Code de droit économique*; Denmark – Administration of Justice Act, para 254h; England and Wales – Competition Act 1998, Sections 49A(2), (3); Germany – Article 18 of the *Kapitalanlegermusterverfahrensgesetz* (*KapMuG*), Section 611(3) of the Civil Procedure Code; Lithuania – Article 441–6(3) of the Civil Procedure Code; Netherlands – Article 907 of the Civil Code; Norway – Dispute Act, Section 35–11; Poland – Group Litigation Act 2009, Article 19(2); Portugal – Article 300(3) of the Civil Procedure Code; Switzerland – Article 352a of

– in particular, judicial oversight. Court approval of collective settlements is one of the most important of these.[9]

Approving or disapproving a collective settlement presents a new and exceptional challenge for judges in Europe.[10] The role of judges changes completely when it comes to reviewing a proposed settlement. As the group members often lack knowledge, resources and motivation, it is up to the court to protect the group's interest. Yet in contrast to those in traditional class action jurisdictions,[11] most courts in Europe have no experience, judicial training or statutory guidelines or manuals for handling the process of approval. Judges face the challenge of detecting potential conflicts of interest and unfair settlement terms despite the fact that the procedures become *de facto* non-adversarial, and that the principle of party presentation fails to work in such proceedings. Once the defendant and the representative of the victims have agreed to settle the case, their joint and only interest is to obtain court approval. They will not disclose any conflicts of interest or facts which speak against the adequacy and fairness of the settlement. The victims, however – who were at best only absent group members during a collective action and who are not involved in the negotiations – are normally unable to evaluate the fairness of the settlement. Therefore, courts must *ex officio* use all procedural instruments available to gather information to approve or disapprove the settlement. National rules vary in this respect, but generally grant broad discretion to the court.

This chapter will primarily address the following questions: what is the appropriate standard for courts to apply when scrutinizing a proposed settlement? What instruments must be available for the court to obtain the necessary

---

the Civil Procedure Code (draft version); Slovenia – Article 36 and Article 12 *et seq* of the *Zakon o kolektivnih tožbah* (ZkolT); Sweden – Group Litigation Act, Section 26; United States – Rule 23(e) of the Federal Rules of Civil Procedure (FRCP); Australia – Federal Court of Australia Act 1976, Section 33V.

[9] Therefore, it is quite remarkable that in the German *Musterfeststellungsklage* against Volkswagen, the parties to the litigation chose a mechanism to settle the case which avoided court approval and which also did not allow registered consumers (who were not offered compensation) to exercise their right to vote on the 'settlement'. The typical conflict of interest of the claimant's lawyer to obtain higher remuneration through an agreement with the defendant is likely to be responsible for the deal; for details, see Astrid Stadler, '*Pyrrhussieg für den Verbraucherschutz*', *VuR* 2020, 163–65.

[10] In normal civil proceedings where the parties to the litigation negotiate a settlement themselves, no court approval is necessary or required under most civil procedure codes across Europe. Based on the freedom of contract, one can expect parties to act in their own interests without the interference of the court as long as no public interest is involved.

[11] In the United States, federal judges have been authorized to evaluate class action settlements since 1983.

information? Should proceedings to declare a settlement binding be based on an opt-in or opt-out mechanism; and where a collective action is pending, should the absent group members have a (second) chance to opt out of the proceedings? We will try to answer these questions by juxtaposing the ELI/UNIDROIT rules and national rules. As experience with court approval of mass settlement is limited in Europe, it is helpful to look at the broad experience of courts in traditional class action countries such as the United States, Canada[12] and Australia.[13] The chapter will conclude by emphasizing the need for judicial training, and for the preparation and use of practice guides and manuals for judges in Europe.

2. RULES ON SETTLEMENTS IN THE ERCP

The collective redress part of the ERCP offers two separate set of rules with respect to settlements. Part D (Rules 221–28) provides rules on how to obtain court approval for settlements in collective redress proceedings already commenced. Part F (Rules 229–32) deals with collective settlements outside collective proceedings and provides a special 'standalone' mechanism for the parties to the settlement contract to become binding on the group members.

With respect to the proceedings for obtaining court approval and to the requirements for court approval, Part F refers more or less completely to Part D. In both situations, courts will scrutinize settlements only upon application. For settlements entered into when a collective redress proceeding is already pending, one of the parties to the settlement must file an application (Rule 222); in the case of a standalone settlement, a joint application of the parties to the settlement agreement is necessary (Rule 230). The application must include: (1) a description of the group to be bound by the settlement; (2) a copy of the proposed settlement; and (3) if not already part of the settlement agreement itself, details on the administration of the compensation fund and its distribution (Rules 222(2)(b)–(c)). Moreover, the application must always include a 'concise statement of reasons showing why the terms of the settlement agreement are fair and adequate' (Rule 222(2)(d)). In the case of a standalone

[12] In Canada, all provinces except Prince Edward Islands have implemented a class action regime; Jasminka Kalajdzic, *Class Actions in Canada – The Promise and Reality of Access to Justice* (UBC Press) 2018, p 4.

[13] In Australia, since 1992 class action regimes have been established both in the Federal Court system and in the state courts of New South Wales, Victoria, Queensland and Western Australia (bill of June 2019). 76 per cent of these representative actions are filed in the Federal Court; see Vince Morabito, 'An Evidence-Based Approach to Class Action Reform in Australia: Competing Class Actions and Comparative Perspectives on the Volume of Class Action Litigation in Australia' (11 July 2018) p 8.

settlement, the application must also specify whether a binding settlement shall be reached on an opt-in or an opt-out basis for the group members (Rule 230).

In the next step, the court will publish the proposed settlement in a manner 'which the court considers will best attract the attention of any person likely to be affected by the event causing the mass harm' (Rules 223, 219(2)), and fix a period for comments. In doing so, the court must ensure that the group members do not misapprehend the advertising of the proposed settlement to the effect that the court has already approved the settlement, albeit on a preliminary basis (Rule 223(2)(a)).[14] Before approving the settlement, the court may 'make any order necessary to obtain further information in order to assess the fairness of the settlement', including the appointment of an expert to assist the court or a fairness hearing. Moreover, Rules 223(2)(c) and (3) specify that the court may consider all comments received by the group members, the parties to the settlement contract or any other relevant comment received.

Due to the synchronization of the process by which courts assess and approve settlements, the following reflections will not make a fundamental distinction between whether the settlement has been negotiated and proposed while a collective action is pending or not. The only major difference is that the court will be much more familiar with the whole dispute if the settlement is proposed while a collective action is pending – particularly if the parties decide to settle the case at a very late stage of the proceedings, such as after the taking of evidence. Then it is much easier for the court to compare the proposed settlement to the potential outcome of the litigation and decide whether the proposal is fair and adequate. In case of a standalone settlement, the court is in a less comfortable situation and has only the information offered by the parties to start with.

---

[14] In contrast, US courts must make a preliminary assessment of the proposed settlement. The reason is that the costs of giving notice of the settlement to the class and inviting them to submit comments can be very high and should not be incurred in cases where it is not likely that the court will finally approve the proposed settlement; Rule 23(e)(1)(B) of the FRCP. Notice to class members must be justified by the parties' showing that the court will likely be able to approve the settlement and certify the class. In the context of the ERCP, group members can be given notice in many cases by using the electronic register and the process is thus not expensive. In the case of standalone settlements, however, the situation can be similar to that in the United States, because the group members can be completely unaware of the proceedings and publication in the electronic register will not be sufficient to give them adequate notice.

3. STANDARD TO BE APPLIED WHEN APPROVING SETTLEMENTS

3.1 National standards

Where collective settlements and procedures for court approval are already available, national rules vary with respect to the standards that settlements must fulfil.[15] In essence, they more or less often simply circumscribe a standard of fairness and reasonableness, as is common in US class action settlements according to Rule 23(e)(2) of the Federal Rules of Civil Procedure (FRCP), which provides: 'If the proposal would bind class members, the court may approve it only after a hearing and only finding that it is fair, reasonable, and adequate after considering whether. . .'[16]

Since the latest reform of the FRCP, which took effect on 1 December 2018, sub-paragraphs (e)(2)(A)–(D) provide a list of criteria to be taken into account by courts when approving a settlement. In Australia, Section 33V of the Federal Court of Australia Act 1976 does not specify the standard for approval or the criteria to be applied; but the court has developed its own criteria. Practice Note CM 17 No 11 sets out that the proposed settlement must be 'fair and adequate having regard to the claims made on behalf of the group members', and lists ten factors to be addressed by the parties and the court.[17]

In England and Wales, Sections 49A(5) and 49B(8) of the Competition Act require that the settlement be 'just and reasonable'. In the Netherlands, mass settlements cannot obtain court approval if 'the compensation is not reasonable' and if 'the interests of the group members are insufficiently guaranteed'.[18] The Swedish Group Litigation Act allows approval of a collective settlement if the settlement is 'not discriminatory against particular members of the group and in another way manifestly unfair'.

---

15 A comprehensive comparative study on mass settlement proceedings is provided by Matthis Peter, *Zivilprozessuale Gruppenvergleichsverfahren, Einvernehmliche Streitbeilegung im kollektiven Rechtsschutz* (Mohr Siebeck, 2018).

16 For details, see, for example, Richard Marcus, 'America's experience with collective litigation' in Christopher Hodges and Astrid Stadler (eds) (n 2) p 148, 154 with further references.

17 Practice Note CM 17 – Representative Proceedings Commenced under Part IVA of the Federal Court of Australia Act 1976 (Cth), No 11 ('Court approval of settlement').

18 Articles 7:907(3b and 3e) of the Dutch Cvil Code. These provisions also apply accordingly for settlements concluded during a newly implemented action on the collective redress of mass damages; Article 1018h (2) of the Dutch Code of Civil Procedure.

In German law, there are two separate rules on court approval of mass settlements: Section 18 of the *Kapitalanleger-Musterverfahrensgesetz* (KapMuG)[19] and Section 611 of the Civil Procedure Code. The former applies in test case proceedings in securities law; the latter when a settlement is achieved in proceedings for declaratory relief initiated by a consumer association in the interests of consumers (so-called *Musterfeststellungklage* (MFK) proceedings).[20] Since the 2013 reform of the KapMuG, Section 18 allows the approval of a settlement negotiated by the test case plaintiff on behalf of all group members[21] if the terms of the settlement are 'adequate' considering the factual and legal situation of the test case proceedings.[22] Section 611 of the Civil Procedure Code also requires that a settlement in the MFK proceedings be an 'adequate solution', taking into account the factual and legal situation of the proceedings for declaratory relief or the uncertainty with respect to the claims of the group members.

Although the German legislature seemed to apply an internationally accepted standard, the basis for court approval in Germany is completely different from that in proceedings in the United States, the United Kingdom and the Netherlands. In KapMuG proceedings, only a limited number of factual and/or legal issues that are common to all actions pending against the model case defendant are the subject of the model case proceedings ('*Feststellungsziele*'). Nevertheless, settlements are expected to settle not only the *Feststellungsziele*, but also all actions pending. However, the Court of Appeals, which has exclusive jurisdiction to hear the model case, is familiar only with the model case itself. It has no access to the court files of the other actions against the defendant that are pending before lower courts, which are suspended during the model case proceedings. Before approving a settlement, the court will consider only the status of the model case proceedings and will not get the full picture of the other disputes. Thus, the basis for assessing the adequacy of the settlement

---

19 The procedure is described by Astrid Stadler and Christopher Hodges, 'Introduction' in Christopher Hodges and Astrid Stadler (eds) (n 2) 19, 20.

20 The so-called '*Musterfeststellungsklage*' (Sections 606–14 of the German Civil Procedure Code) came into force 1 November 2018. For details on the possible subject of KapMuG settlements, see Erika Ditler, *Streitgegenstand und Prozessvergleich des KapMuG* (Nomos, 2019).

21 'Group members' in the sense of the KapMuG are claimants who have filed an action for the recovery of damages in a securities case against the defendant. These proceedings are suspended until the Court of Appeals issues a test case decision that is binding for all proceedings pending.

22 The mechanism has been used only once since 2013.

is very limited. The court is not in a position to assess the potential outcome of the suspended damages actions, but only the outcome of the model case.[23]

With respect to settlements under Section 611 of the Civil Procedure Code, the court is also *a priori* not in a position to assess all claims of the group members fully on the merits. Only selected – albeit important – elements of the defendant's liability are the subject of the representative action for declaratory relief. The court will have no information on the amount of loss suffered by the group members, because the quantum of the claims will be subject to individual actions that can be filed by the group members subsequently to a successful MKF proceeding. Thus, the court cannot assess the adequacy of the amount of compensation offered in the settlement proposal.

In conclusion, policy makers are often satisfied to provide a universally accepted rule of thumb which simply requires that the proposed settlement be 'adequate' and sometimes also 'fair'; and it is not even clear whether 'fairness' implies a different perspective from 'adequacy'. It will be necessary to look into court practice for details of the reviewing process.

3.2 How to assess 'fairness' and 'reasonableness'

3.2.1 Insight from class and group action regimes in the United States and Australia

Court approval is necessary in order to protect the interests of the absent group members. The settlement may impair their interests for a number of reasons. Practical knowledge from US class action settlements suggests that collective settlements are vulnerable to collusion and involve a certain risk of rather 'cheap' settlements. Courts must therefore be aware of typical risks arising from collective settlements. The conditions under which settlement negotiations take place are, however, not exactly the same in the United States and in Europe. One must therefore be careful in applying insight from the US class action system to collective actions in Europe.

Two important differences should be mentioned. First, in the United States, individual class members act as a self-appointed representative of the class;[24] while in Europe, this role is more often fulfilled by an 'ideological

---

[23] The model case will have a number of essential facts and legal issues in common with the suspended actions of other claimants (this is a requirement for commencing model case proceedings in the first place). Nevertheless, some cases may have important particularities (eg, contributory negligence, causation, limitation period).

[24] Representatives may therefore give priority to their own interest – a phenomen know as a 'sweetheart settlement' in the United States; see John Coffee, 'Understanding the Plaintiff's Attorney: The Implications of Economic Theorey for Private Enforcement of Law through Class and Derivative Actions' (1986) 86 *Columbia L Rev* 669, 714 and

plaintiff' – a representative entity such as a consumer association, a non-profit interest grouping or even a public authority or ombudsperson. Particularly for standalone settlements, individual group members do not have standing to negotiate such a settlement. This is mostly an exclusive right of representative entitles.[25] They are bound by their statutory goals and are ideally subject to internal and external control of their activities.[26] Accordingly, principal-agent conflicts among those 'ideological plaintiffs' and group members can be less serious than in the typical US class action constellations[27] with a lead plaintiff, who is part of the class and profit-oriented class counsel.[28] The ERCP adds another safeguard by requiring the court to select and appoint the best 'qualified claimant' to represent the group.[29]

Second, a prevailing concern in US class action settlements relates to attorney's fees. Application of the 'common fund' theory entails that class counsel[30] and class members compete for the distribution of the money paid

---

'The Regulation of Entrepreneurial Litigation: Balancing Fairness and Efficiency in large Class Actions' (1987) 54 *Chicago L Rev* 877, 883.

25 ERCP Rule 229; England and Wales – Competition Act 1998, Section 49B(5)(a); Netherlands – Article 7:907(1) of the Dutch Civil Code; Slovenia – Articles 12–25 of the ZkolT; Switzerland – Article 352a of the Federal Civil Procedure Code Tentative Draft (March 2018).

26 For details of legal standing, see Chapter 7.

27 The risk of collusion between class counsel and defendants is analysed by, among others, Robert Bone, *Civil Procedure: The Economics of Civil Procedure* (Foundation Press 2003) 272 *et seq*; Deborah Hensler and others, *Class Action Dilemmas: Pursuing Public Goals for Private Gain (RAND 2000)* 79; John Coffee, 'Rescuing the Private Attorney General: Why the Model of the Lawyer as Bounty Hunter is not Working' (1987) 42 *Maryland L Rev* 215.

28 In the same sense, Rolf Stürner, 'The Role of Judges and Lawyers in Collective Actions. Equality among parties. Conflicts of interest.', I International Conference and XXIII Iberoamerican Procedural Law Convention (Buenos Aires, 6–9 June 2012) 67, 84.

29 ERCP Rule 213(3). As a matter of fact, the court can make a selection only where several entities apply to be nominated as qualified claimant. For details, see Chapter 6.

30 Remuneration of class counsel cannot be based on a contingency fee arrangement with the lead plaintiff. Instead, it is up to the court to decide on counsel's costs (FRCP Rule 23(h)). Notwithstanding the method that courts apply to calculate fees, the results are more or less the same as contingency fees. For a discussion on a common fund approach in Australian class actions, see *Blairgowrie Trading Ltd v. Allco Finance Groupt Ltd* [2015] FCA 811 (Wigeny J); Vicki Wayne/Vince Morabito, in: Willem van Boom, *Litigation, Costs, Funding and Behaviour*, 155 *et seq*; Fabian Stitz, *Class Actions in Australia* (Peter Lang, 2019) 182 *et seq*.

by the defendant.[31, 32] In Europe, there are also good arguments to apply the 'common fund' theory;[33] but contingency fee agreements are subject to restrictions, if national law permits them at all, and the ways in which counsel in group proceedings are paid vary considerably across Europe.[34] The ERCP, for example, takes a very cautious stance with respect to contingency fee arrangements, without excluding them completely (Rule 245(3)). Details are left to national law and therefore court approval of settlements will be done on a case-by-case basis, taking into account the applicable cost rules.

Emphasizing these differences between US law and the situation in Europe does not mean that the task of courts in Europe is less complicated when it comes to the scrutiny of collective settlements. The questions that must be asked before approving a settlement are more or less the same as in the United States, but the answers can differ.

Although courts may be tempted simply to rubber-stamp any settlement in order to close the files of a complex case or to prevent a collective action from being initiated in the first place,[35] there seems to be an international consensus that an attitude according to which 'any settlement is a good settlement' is not acceptable.[36] On the other hand, there are seldom clear cases in which the

---

31 David F. Herr, *Annotated Manual for Complex Litigation* (4th edn, Thomson West, 2019), para 14.231.

32 Where parallel class actions are possible in the United States or reverse auction take place, the risk of a 'cheap' settlement increases. Defendants will attempt to reach an early settlement (with a binding effect of the consent decree on other class actions) and class counsel of the various class actions will compete for the first settlement, because only those attorneys who settle the case will receive contingency fees. For details, see Alexander Eggers, *Gerichtliche Kontrolle von Vergleichen im kollektiven Rechtsschutz* (Mohr Siebeck, 2019) 142 *et seq*; David F. Herr, (n 30), para 21.61; Samuel Issacharoff and Richard Nagareda, 'Class Action Settlement under Attack' (2008) 156 *U Pennsylvania L Rev* 1649, 1667.

33 It applies, for example, in the Dutch WCAM settlement proceedings, but it is also part of the ERCP: Rule 238(2).

34 In the Netherlands, WCAM settlements are often negotiated by foundations established by law firms which operate on the basis of contingency fee arrangements. Approval of WCAM settlements thus always involves a scrutiny of the lawyers' fees.

35 Insights from social sciences may suggest that complex mass claims might have an impact on judicial attitudes and decision making; Michael Faure, 'CADR and Settlement of Claims, A few Economic Observations' in Christopher Hodges and Astrid Stadler (eds) (n 2) 38 *et seq*. For a detailed study, see Alexandre Biard, *Judges and Mass Litigation – A (Behavioural) Law & Economics Perspective* (Erasmus Universiteit Rotterdam 2004) http://amsdottorato.unibo.it/6742/1/Biard_Alexandre_tesi.pdf (last accessed 12 August 2020).

36 However, in the 2012 *Converium* securities case, the Amsterdam Court of Appeal approved a settlement concluded on behalf of non-US shareholders who had been excluded from a US class action under the WCAM based on a single argument.

unfairness of a settlement is written all over its face.[37] Unfair settlement terms may have many sources. Apart from the fact that the representative may simply be incompetent to negotiate a better settlement, courts must bear in mind the typical conflicts of interest that may have influenced the negotiations. Such conflicts may arise: (1) between the representative and the group or individual group members; (2) within the group; or (3) between the counsel and the group.[38] If we look at the potential shortcomings or unfair settlement terms, the categories developed in US law can also be helpful for the scrutiny of proposed settlements in Europe: courts will need to undertake a substantial fairness analysis and a procedural fairness analysis. The former refers to the settlement terms itself and the latter primarily to the negotiation process.

3.2.2 Typical risks involved in collective settlements

Examples of substantive unfairness may include cases in which the representative of the group has accepted a total amount of compensation that is too low compared to the likely litigated outcome; or, if there are sub-groups, where the amount for each group might be inadequate or might unfairly prefer one group over another.

Product liability or pharmaceutical cases may, for example, raise conflicts among the group members if some of the victims have already suffered injury, while others may develop health problems over time and have only 'future claims'. In US class actions, this type of conflict between actual and future

---

As none of the non-US shareholders had attempted to sue the defendant outside the United States after their exclusion from the US securities class action, the court concluded that they obviously faced severe problems in enforcing their claims in Europe. As a consequence, the court accepted the proposed settlement, although the amount of compensation offered to the non-US shareholders was much lower than the compensation paid by the defendant to US shareholders under a US class actions settlement; *Gerechtshof Amsterdam, beschikking* 17 January 2012 ECLI:NL:GHAMS:2012:BV1026 (Converium) No 6.4.1, 6.4.1.

37 In the United States, the famous *Kamilewicz v Bank of Boston Corp* case illustrates a clearly unfair settlement: Class members were entitled to a reimbursement of $2.19 by the bank for the miscalculation of a mortgage, but had to pay lawyer's fees of $91.33 in return (92 F3d 506, 508 [7th Cir 1996]). The Committee of the Judiciary of the US Senate reports another case in which class members had to sell real estate in order to recover damages from the settlement fund; Senate Rep No 109–14 (2005) 14.

38 As these conflicts of interest are likely to arise throughout a representative litigation, the ERCP provide a number of safeguards: Rule 214 (obligation of qualified claimant to act in the best interests of the group or sub-group); Rule 218(1)(a) (substitution of the qualified claimant, if necessary); Rule 218(1)(d) (establishing of sub-groups).

claimholders has often raised serious concerns.[39] Although it might be difficult to include future claims in a collective action in Europe, it will definitely be possible to include them in a settlement. The establishment of sub-groups will then be inevitable, as well as safeguards to ensure a sufficient amount of compensation for all group members; and expert opinion may be necessary to decide when, how and to what extent future claims can be expected.

Lawyers' fees may be excessive relative to the benefits for the group. The history of US class actions is full of examples of suspicious settlements which turned out to be an expected bonanza for class counsel, but left class member with dubious 'discount coupons' instead of money awards.

The court may also deny approval if the proposed method of distributing relief to the group is not appropriate. Eligibility criteria, payment calculation tools and requirements for proof may be inadequate; or the proposed fund administrator(s) may lack expertise, competence or neutrality.[40] One of the most difficult issues of distribution schemes is the calculation of the group members' loss or damages. In antitrust group actions or securities litigation, statistical analysis is often used to develop a model for calculating loss. Calculation of loss by the court itself when entering into a judgment can be more complex than in settlement distribution schemes.[41] Courts will often be bound by strict provisions of substantive law and be held to calculate the actual loss as exactly as possible. Settlements provide more flexibility, but they also

---

[39] John Coffee, 'The Corruption of the Class Action: The New Technology of Collusion' (1995) 80 *Cornell L Rev* 851; John Coffee, 'Class Wars: The Dilemma of the Mass Tort Class Action' (1995) 95 *Columbia L Rev* 1343, 1448 *et seq*. Settlements have been rejected by the US Supreme Court for not having taken into account conflicts of interest; *Anchem Products Inc. v Windsor*, 521 US 591 (1997); *Ortiz v Fibreboard Corp.*, 527 US 815 (1999).

[40] The *Deepwater Horizon* case illustrates the problem of neutral fund administrators, albeit not exactly a class action settlement case. In 2010, the Deepwater Horizon oil rig run by BP in the Gulf of Mexico exploded and approximately 5 million barrels of oil poured into the sea. On the initiative of President Obama, BP provided $20 billion to establish a compensation fund. Kenneth Feinberg, a very well-known claims administrator, was appointed to direct the fund and to decide on the claims of the victims with a team of more than 4,000 employees. The media raised concern about Feinberg's independence, because he was paid by BP. A dispute kicked off and finally a federal MDL court concluded that Feinberg could not be considered neutral and completely independent from BP. For details, see the case study by Byron Strier, 'The Promise and Peril of Media and Culture: The Toyota unintended Acceleration Litigation and the Gulf Coast Facility in the United States' in Deborah Hensler and Christopher Hodges and Ianika Tzankova (eds), *Class Actions in Context* (Edward Elgar Publishing 2016) 93 *et seq*.

[41] Therefore, Rule 228 of the ERCP does not require that the court calculate the damages suffered by each individual group member in detail.

should not operate on overly broad rules of thumb that ignore material differences in group members' claims and conflicts of interest within the group.

A procedural fairness analysis may take into account the adequacy of the settlement negotiations, and whether the representative made sufficient efforts to weigh the strengths and weakness of the claims or sought the assistance of a neutral mediator.[42] Particularly in the case of standalone settlements, it is crucial that the parties clearly define the group, and that the representative of the victims have done at least a summary examination of the claims involved.

3.2.3 Criteria for court approval applied in traditional class action jurisdictions

The experiences of courts in the United States and Australia suggest that judges need not and cannot scrutinize settlement contracts in detail; but they must at least be aware of the typical errors and potential deficiencies that might impair the interests of the group.[43] It is nevertheless vital to give the process of scrutinizing a proposed settlement a certain structure and ensure that courts have a checklist they can work with. In the United States, federal courts have developed lists of criteria which 'red-flag'[44] the risks typically involved in class settlements or list the 'hot-button indicators';[45] but the factors shortlisted vary from circuit to circuit.

In the Second Circuit, the so-called 'Grinnell' factors have been established since the 1970s.[46] They include: (1) the complexity, expense and likely duration of the litigation; (2) the reaction of the class to the settlement; (3) the stage of the proceedings and the amount of discovery completed; (4) the risks of establishing liability; (5) the risks of establishing damages; (6) the risks of maintaining the class action through trial; (7) the ability of the defendants to withstand a greater judgment; (8) the range of reasonableness of the settlement in light of the best possible recovery; and (9) the range of reasonableness of the settlement fund to a possible recovery in the light of all attendant risks of

---

[42] The involvement of a mediator can be a strong indication that there was no collusion between the parties to the settlement contract; for details and further references, see Alexander Eggers (n 32) 189.

[43] For a detailed study on court approval of mass settlements in the United States, the Netherlands and Germany, see Alexander Eggers (n 32).

[44] William Rubenstein, *Newberg on Class Actions,* vol 4 (5th edn, MN 2014) para 13.56.

[45] Barabara J. Rothstein and Thomas E. Willging, *Managing Class Action Litigation: A Pocket Guide for Judges* (Federal Judicial Center 2005) 12, www.uscourts.gov/sites/default/files/classgde.pdf.

[46] *City of Detroit v Grinnell Corp*, 356 F Supp 1380 (SDNY 1972), 495 F2d 448, 463 (2nd Cir 1974).

litigation.[47] In the Third Circuit, courts adopted the 'Grinnell' factors (under the name of 'Girsh' factors) and supplemented them with so-called 'prudential considerations', which are 'permissive and non-exhaustive, illustrating the additional inquiries that in many instances will be useful for a thoroughgoing analysis of the settlement's terms'.[48] The Ninth Circuit developed a slightly shorter list of eight factors[49] and the Tenth Circuit was satisfied with only four.[50] The American Law Institute also contented itself with four rather general factors in its Principles of Aggregate Litigation.[51] The list of ten factors that is provided by the Australian Federal Court Practice Manual CM 17 for court approval is in part almost identical to that of the Second Circuit in the United States.[52] Canadian authors have identified very similar factors for court approval in Canadian class actions.[53]

The US *Manual for Complex Litigation* also specifies a list of nine criteria to be applied when scrutinizing a proposed settlement for typically unfair settlement terms.[54] The 2018 amendments to Rule 23(e) of the FRCP now try to harmonize the standards applied by setting out specific factors to consider.

---

[47] For details, see Alexander Eggers (n 32) p 171 *et seq*.

[48] *In re Baby Products Antitrust Litigation*, 708 F3d, 163, 174 (3rd Cir 2013); also applied in *In re National Football Leage Players Concussion Injury Litigation*, 821 F3d 410, 437 (3rd Cir 2016).

[49] *Hanlon v Chrysler Corp*, 150 F3d 1011, 1026 (3rd Cir 1998); *Churchill Village, LL C v General Electric*, 361 F3d 566, 575 (9th Cir 2004).

[50] *Jones v Nuclear Pharmacy, Inc*, 741 F2d 322, 324 (10th Cir 1984).

[51] American Law Institute, *Principles of Aggregate Litigation* (2010) para 3.05.

[52] Practice Note CM 17 – Representative proceedings commenced under Part IVA of the Federal Court of Australia Act 1976 (Cth), No 11.2 (a)-(j).

[53] Catherine Piché, *Fairness in Class Action Settlements* (Carswell 2012) 179 *et seq*; an overview is provided by Jasminka Kalajdzic, 'Class actions and settlement culture in Canada' in Christopher Hodges and Astrid Stadler (eds) (n 3) and Jasminka Kalajdzic (n 12), Chapter 5, p 90 *et seq*.

[54] Examples of unfair settlement terms listed include granting class members illusory non-monetary benefits, such as discount coupons; imposing such strict eligibilty conditions or cumbersome claims procedures that many members will be unlikely to claim benefits, particulary if the settlement provides that unclaimed portions of the fund will revert to the defendant; treating similarly situated class members differently (eg, by settling objector's claims at significant higher rates than class members' claims); David F. Herr (n 31) para 21.61.

Rule 23 (e) FRCP 2019:

(2) Approval of the Proposal. If the proposal would bind class members, the court may approve it only after a hearing and only on finding that it is fair, reasonable, and adequate after considering whether:
- (A) the class representatives and class counsel have adequately represented the class;
- (B) the proposal was negotiated at arm's length;
- (C) the relief provided for the class is adequate, taking into account:
- (i) the costs, risks, and delay of trial and appeal;
- (ii) the effectiveness of any proposed method of distributing relief to the class, including the method of processing class-member claims;
- (iii) the terms of any proposed award of attorney's fees, including timing of payment; and
- (iv) any agreement required to be identified under Rule 23(e)(3); and
- (D) the proposal treats class members equitably relative to each other.

These criteria can, in principle, be a role model for European courts if one keeps in mind the differences between US class action settlements and European collective settlements. One should also not expect that such lists allow for a more or less mechanical process of 'calculating' the fairness of the settlement. The criteria are much too general to predict certain results. They nevertheless provide valuable orientation, make the overall assessment more transparent and prevent completely unacceptable settlements from being approved.[55] Whereas US courts are not required to explain why they have approved or disapproved a proposed settlement, European courts should be urged to do so.

In one respect, all of the lists developed provide no guidance, and probably for very good reasons. This concerns the question of how to weight the different criteria. The importance of these factors may change from case to case, as may the relative weight of one factor over another.[56] 'No one case fits neatly within some preconceived. . . category.'[57] Abstract specifications provide only pseudo clarity and may even distract courts from the need to consider the individual features of the settlement and case at hand.

---

[55] Alexander Eggers (n 32), 196 *et seq*.

[56] A good example of the importance of how to balance the criteria is offered by the California settlement in the *Volkswagen Dieselgate* case. The court emphasized that the strength of the individual claims on the merits and the likelihood of the outcome of the litigation must stand back against the fact that the settlement allowed a quick and environmentally friendly solution by withdrawing the diesel cars as soon as possible.

[57] Colson v Hilton Hotels Corp., 59 FRD 324, 326 No 9 (ND Ill 1972).

3.2.4 The Dutch experience

For settlement approval under the Dutch Act on Collective Settlement of Mass Claims (WCAM), Article 7:907(3) of the Dutch Civil Code lists the following criteria:

The court shall reject the request if:

a. the agreement does not comply with the provisions of paragraph 2;
b. the amount of the compensation awarded is not reasonable having regard, inter alia, to the extent of the damage, the ease and speed with which the compensation can be obtained and the possible causes of the damage;
c. it is insufficiently certain that the rights resulting from the agreement for persons on whose behalf the agreement has been concluded, can be followed up (performed);
d. the agreement does not provide in a possibility of an impartial settlement of disputes which may arise from the agreement by another than the judge or court that would have jurisdiction according to law;
e. the interests of the persons on whose behalf the agreement was concluded are otherwise not adequately safeguarded;
f. the foundations or associations referred to in paragraph 1 are not sufficiently representative with regard to the interests of persons on whose behalf the agreement has been concluded;
g. the group of persons on whose behalf the agreement was concluded is not large enough to justify a declaration by the court that the agreement is binding;
h. there is a legal person who will provide the compensation pursuant to the agreement and he is not a party to the agreement.

In particular, Dutch law requires that the foundation or association negotiating the settlement be sufficiently representative – an element which is of less or no importance in US class actions. For the Amsterdam Court of Appeal, the key element seems to be the amount of compensation awarded.[58] Although not explicitly listed in Article 7:907(3) of the Dutch Civil Code, the Amsterdam Court of Appeal emphasized in the *Dexia* case,[59] and also in later decisions,[60] the importance of comparing the amount offered in the settlement with the potential outcome of a litigation. Nevertheless, in the past, it did not go into details of legal or factual issues when assessing the possible recovery in litigation and often simply concluded that a settlement would be quicker, more efficient and less expensive than litigation.[61]

---

[58] Alexander Eggers (n 32) p 210 et seq.

[59] *Gerechtshof Amsterdam, beschikking* 25 January 2007, ECLI:NL:GHAMS:2007:AZ7033 (*Dexia*) No 6.6.

[60] *Gerechtshof Amsterdam, beschikking* 15 July 2009, ECLI:NL:GHAMS:2009:BJ2691 (*Vedior*) No 4.15; *Gerechtshof Amsterdam, beschikking* 29 May 2009; ECLI:NL:GHMAS:2009:BI5744 (Shell) No 6.17.

[61] *Gerechtshof Amsterdam, beschikking* 17 January 2012, ECLI:NL:GHMAS:2012:BV1016 (*Converium*) No 6.4.4.

In the *Fortis* case, the Amsterdam Court of Appeal for the first time rejected a proposed settlement and objected to the settlement distribution plan, which provided for a higher amount of damages for the sub-group of 'active claimants' (so-called 'incentive awards').[62] In contrast to the 'active claimants', 'non-active' claimants – free-riders – were entitled to a smaller amount according to the proposed settlement in the *Fortis* case. This distinction could have had vast implications for future WCAM settlements. Quite often, several foundations are competing to negotiate a settlement with the party potentially liable for a mass harm event and foundations try to unite as many victims as possible in order to strengthen their position. With the prospect of a higher amount of compensation for those who register with a foundation upfront, the competition would have intensified. The Amsterdam court held that such incentive awards were contrary to the principle of equal treatment of the group members.[63]

All in all, the criteria applied by the Amsterdam Court of Appeal are very similar to those used by US courts, but there is still no clear line of reasoning in the Netherlands – although the Amsterdam court has exclusive jurisdiction to hear WCAM cases.

3.3 European rules of civil procedure

Part XI ('Collective proceedings') of the ERCP provides only one rule (Rule 224) with respect to the approval of settlements:

> Rule 224. Settlement Approval Orders
> The court shall not make an order approving a settlement agreement where
> (a) the amount of compensation agreed for the group or any sub-group is manifestly unfair,
> (b) the terms of any other undertaking by a defendant are manifestly unfair,
> (c) the settlement is manifestly contrary to the public interest (*ordre public*) or
> (d) the terms, whether contained in the proposed settlement agreement or not, as to the payment of legal and other associated costs of the action are manifestly unreasonable.

---

62 In the United States, incentive awards are frequent in class action litigation. According to Theodore Eisenberg and Geoffrey Miller, 'Incentive Awards to Class Action Plaintiffs: An Empirical Study,' 53 *UCLA L Rev* 1303 (2006), 28 per cent of class action settlements between 1993 and 2002 included incentive awards to class representatives.

63 *Gerechtshof Amsterdam, beschikking* 13 July 2018 (final approval), ECLI:NL: GHAMS:2018:2422 (Fortis II) No 5.1.3.

Admittedly, the rule could be more detailed; but for the sake of clarity and flexibility of courts, it does not go into further detail. Rule 224 requires a 'fairness test' and emphasizes that only in case of 'manifestly' unfair settlement terms should approval be denied.[64] In this respect, the rule reflects practical knowledge from class action settlements that, whatever lists and criteria are developed, they can prevent court approval only where a settlement is distinctly and seriously contrary to the interests of the group. Compromise is the essence of a settlement and judges must resist the temptation to substitute the assessment of the parties to the settlement more or less completely with their own opinion.[65]

It was taken for granted that the overall assessment of court approval requires a structure, and that 'red-flagging' certain criteria will be helpful for courts. European courts will have to develop their own practice. Comparative insight from other jurisdictions can be useful, but only as a guideline. It did not seem necessary to make it part of the rules themselves. The text of the ERCP should not hamper the development in this respect. The text by implication allows courts to consider all factors they consider reasonable, including those traditionally used in US class actions. In particular, it seems more or less self-evident that the relief offered in the settlement must be balanced mainly against the risks, costs and delay of litigation. The assumption underlying Rule 224 is that whenever there is a conflict of interest, collusion or similar deficiencies during the negotiation process, these will predominantly be reflected in the amount of compensation or any other relief for the group members.[66]

Rule 224 does not aim to provide an exhaustive list of reasons for disapproving a proposed settlement and, for example, does not mention explicitly a procedural fairness test or shortcomings in the administration and distribution of compensation funds.[67] Nevertheless, if the proposed settlement is not fair and adequate with respect to the process of distributing the funds, approval can be denied – for example, if the terms of the settlement impose overly strict eligibility conditions or establish cumbersome claims procedures so that group members will be unlikely to claim compensation. In complex cases, settle-

---

[64] There is a kind of presumption that the settlement is fair; for Canada, see Jasminka Kalajdzic (n 12), p 99 *et seq*.

[65] Jasminka Kalajdzic (n 12), p 100: 'The corollary of the presumption of fairness is that judges will not substitute their judgment for that of the parties.'

[66] Alexander Eggers (n 32) 186 et seq shows that courts denied approval predominantly because they considered the amount to be recovered by class members too low. In Dutch WCAM proceedings, the adequacy of the amount of damage is also the core issue for court approval (Article 7:907(3) of the Dutch Civil Code).

[67] Applications which contain no terms on the administration of the compensation fund or its distribution are not approvable from the outset; ERCP Rules 222(2)(b) and (c).

ments should also provide for a dispute resolution mechanism for conflicts between fund administrators and group members.

Courts should in particular be alert when a proposed settlement contains *cy près*[68] solutions instead of offering compensation to the group members.[69] Such types of settlement terms are likely to appear in cases involving opt-out proceedings and small individual losses. *Cy près* can be an adequate solution where group members are unlikely to claim benefits from the fund, where there is a large group of victims and where the recovery per group member is so small that the costs of distribution and administration of a fund would exceed the individual benefits. Courts will have to examine the proximity or distance between the *cy près* recipients' activities and the interests of the group members.[70] Demanding statements from the recipients, public regulators and other experts can be helpful in this respect.

Settlement terms stipulating that unclaimed portions of the fund will revert to the defendant are also potentially unfair. Generally speaking, the defendant should not benefit from the apathy of the group members; it will be a better solution to pay out unclaimed portions of the fund to charity or other non-profit organizations. The European Parliament changed the European Commission's draft Directive on representative actions in the interests of consumers. It deleted the reference to *cy près* in the Commission's proposal and added instead a new paragraph 4a to Article 6 of the draft Directive:

> The redress measures aim to grant consumers concerned full compensation for their loss. In case of unclaimed amount left from the compensation, a court shall decide on the beneficiary of the remaining unclaimed amount. This unclaimed amount shall not go to the qualified representative entity nor to the trader.

This rule is intended to apply to court decisions, but it also indicates what kinds of solutions will be acceptable in a collective settlement. It also follows from the Parliament's text that compensation of consumers should be given priority over *cy près* even in case of trivial individual loss. The latest draft of 30 June 2020 merely states in Article 5b(6), sentence 2 that: 'Member States may lay down rules on the destination of any outstanding redress funds that were not recovered within the established time limits.' The ERCP aims to provide more flexibility in this respect and courts should decide on case-by-case basis whether settlement terms that completely exclude compensation for consumers or victims are adequate with respect to the type of mass harm and the type of *cy près* suggested.

---

[68] For a definition of *cy près*, see Chapter 6, n 4.

[69] Barabara J. Rothstein and Thomas E. Willging (n 45) 12.

[70] Barabara J. Rothstein and Thomas E. Willging (n 45) 13.

4. BASIS FOR COURT APPROVAL

4.1 Relevant inputs

The proposed settlement itself and – if existing – any side agreements are only a start for the review process. Courts will normally need further information and sources in order to apply the reasonableness test appropriately.[71] The necessary input will vary depending on the extent to which the court has already been involved in the dispute.[72]

Four categories of input may help the courts in assessing the fairness of a settlement: (1) facts and background information of various kinds and relevance; (2) comments by group members, other stakeholders and interest groups; (3) the estimation of the parties to the settlement on the procedural risks and prospects of (further) litigation; and (4) expert opinions on the economic, environmental or social impact of the settlement.

Rule 224(a) refers to manifestly unfair compensation of the whole group or sub-groups.

A good example to demonstrate that courts must get the full picture in order to assess settlement distribution schemes is the *Vioxx* case. In 2004, pharmaceutical company Merck withdrew its anti-inflammatory and painkiller drug Vioxx from the market in 80 countries after a clinical trial revealed that the drug might double the risk of strokes and heart attacks. Among other lawsuits, class actions in the United States and Australia followed. In 2013, the Australian Federal Court refused to approve a settlement in the *Vioxx* case because it ignored the strength of class members' claims and treated strong and weak claims alike. The settlement distribution scheme did not take into account that the class (persons who had suffered a heart attack or sudden cardiac death) also comprised patients with certain risk factors attributable to their personal health conditions (eg, hypertension, obesity, history of smoking). Accordingly, for these class members, the causal link between their death and the prescription of Vioxx was far from clear.[73] As the settlement itself was silent in this

---

71 US courts take care to confirm that there has been sufficient discovery before entering into a settlement, in order to avoid a situation where 'the unscrupulous are leading the blind'. For objections to settlements in Canada, see Jasminka Kalajdzic (n 12), p 101 *et seq*.

72 It goes without saying that, particularly in the case of standalone settlements, the court needs clear descriptions of the mass harm event, the group of victims to be bound by the settlement, the factual and legal basis of the claims, and the proposed settlement, including any side agreements.

73 *Peterson v Merck Sharp & Dohme (Australia) Pty Ltd [no 6]*, [2013] FCA 447 [9] –[20]; see also [2011] FCAFC 128; [2011] 196 FCR 145.

respect, it took objections from the group members and statements from other observers to address these inconsistencies.

Rules 224(b) and (c) allow disapproval of the settlement if any other undertaking by a defendant is manifestly unfair or if settlement terms violate a public interest. Defendants may, for example, promise (as a kind of *cy près* solution) to reduce prices for a certain period in order to compensate the loss that consumers have suffered due to cartels, unfair competition practices or any other violations.[74] This can have a negative or unknown impact on the market and can therefore be against the public interest. In the *Volkswagen Dieselgate* settlement before the MDL court in California, it was important in the public interest to protect the environment and to ensure that Volkswagen committed to repair or destroy the diesel cars repurchased from the owners, and not to export them to developing countries as they were.

4.2 Risk of further litigation – confidentiality

The merits of the claims and prospects of proving liability and damages will often be one of the most important benchmarks of courts when approving settlements. Where defendants have already admitted that they are liable in principle, the court's task is less complex in this respect. In the United States, the *Manual for Complex Litigation* suggests that class counsel must disclose all relevant information for assessing the fairness of the settlement.[75] The Advisory Committee on Civil Rules also proposed to impose an obligation on the parties to the settlement to provide an estimation of the prospects and risks of the litigation and the grounds on which they would prefer to settle the case.[76] In Australia, the Federal Courts Practice Notice CM 17 imposes on the parties to the settlement contract an obligation to address a number of factors in their application for court approval.[77] These include the complexity and likely

---

[74] Two famous US cases illustrate the use of *cy près*. In *Colson v Hilton Hotels Corp.*, 59 FRD 324, 326 (ND Ill 1972), the defendants had violated competition rules by overcharging hotel guests for telephone calls. As compensation, they promised to give a discount on telephone calls for future guests for a certain period. In *Daar v Yellow Cab Co*, 67 Cal 2d 695 (1967), a taxi company had also overcharged its customers illegally and offered lower taxi rates for a future period (and to future customers). For *cy près* in Australian class actions, see Fabian Stitz (n 30) 151 *et seq.*

[75] David F. Herr (n 31) para 21.641, particularly for settlement class actions 21.631.

[76] Advisory Committee on Civil Rules, Agenda Book 2017/04, www.uscourts.gov/sites/default/files/2017-04-civil-agenda_book.pdf 111. In practice, attorneys often submit comprehensive statements on the fairness of the settlement; Jed S. Rakoff, 'From the Bench: Are Settlements Sacrosanct?' (2011) 37 *Litigation Journal* 15.

[77] Practice Note CM 17 – Representative proceedings commenced under Part IVA of the Federal Court of Australia Act 1976 (Cth), No 11.2 (a)–(j).

duration of the litigation; the stage of proceedings; the risks of establishing liability; the risks of establishing loss or damage; the range of reasonableness of the settlement in the light of the best recovery; and the range of reasonableness of the settlement in light of all attendant risks of litigation.

Based on these examples, Rule 222(2)(d) of the ERCP stipulates that the application for approval shall include 'a concise statement of reasons showing why the terms of the settlement agreement are fair and adequate'. In practice, the application of Rule 222(2)(d) will require clear and open communication between the court and the parties, and transparency on what the court expects. Again, US and Australian class action practice can be helpful. In a first step, courts should develop a list of criteria that they intend to apply for court approval as discussed above and make this available for the parties (or as a practice guide on their websites). Moreover, it should be mandatory for parties to address these factors in their statements.[78]

This includes not only an estimation by the parties of the procedural risks of their claim or defence and the prospect of further litigation, but also – and especially in case of standalone proceedings – information on parallel proceedings and their state of affairs, which will be important for the court.

However, an individual assessment of the procedural risks by the qualified claimant and the defendant is sensitive information. None of the parties will be ready to disclose the strengths or weaknesses of its position as long as the settlement is not finally binding and it is unclear whether the litigation will proceed. Therefore, courts in Europe would also be well advised to learn from the Australian class action practice and allow the parties to treat these statements as confidential and not disclose them to the other party.[79]

Sometimes, courts will also have to accept settlements even though the claims of the group are weak on the merits. Court approval is an instrument for protecting the interests of the group members. Defendants will be able to pursue their own interests, and may have good cause to settle bad or dubious

---

[78] This is also the intention of Practice Note CM 17 – Representative proceedings commenced under Part IVA of the Federal Court of Australia Act 1976 (Cth), No 11.2. The factors listed subs (a)–(j) are not only a reminder for the court, but are explicitly listed to be addressed by the parties when applying for court approval of a settlement.

[79] Counsel in Australian class actions often include an application to their affidavits to treat documents disclosing the strengths and weaknesses of the parties' case confidential. Although courts are reluctant to allow such *in camera* proceedings, for obvious reasons, they are inclined to allow them with respect to these documents; Michael Legg, 'Class Action Settlements in Australia – The Need for Greater Scrutiny' (2014) 38 *Melbourne Univ L Rev* 590, 598–613. Courts may also inspect background information such as insurance policies of a party *in camera* in order to protect the legitimate interests of the party; for a similiar practice in the United States, see David F. Herr (n 31), para 21.631.

claims. The *Toyota Unintended Acceleration* case in the United States is a good example of a defendant that preferred to settle, even though liability was not clear at all, in order to end media coverage and save its reputation.[80]

As mentioned earlier, courts should not litigate the case further with the sole intention of assessing the adequacy of the settlement – for example, by taking evidence on the merits of the claims. Despite its broad wording, Rule 223(1)(a) of the ERCP – which allows the court to make any order necessary to obtain further information in order to assess the fairness of the proposed settlement – must not be misunderstood in this respect. It is one of the overarching principles of the ERCP that courts must ensure that the dispute process is proportionate (Rule 5)[81] and this principle of proportionality also applies to the procedure for approving settlements. In the context of the Swiss tentative draft for collective settlements, it was suggested that the court should not assess the overall prospect of success for the whole group. Instead, the court should select a couple of typical claims and do a summary examination on the merits.[82] The author describes this as walking a tightrope and his proposal does not advocate for the further taking of evidence, but only for a cursory review.

5. PROCEDURAL TOOLS FOR GATHERING INFORMATION

5.1 General considerations

Rule 223(1)(a) allows courts to 'make any order necessary to obtain further information in order to assess the fairness of the proposed settlement'. This offers a wide range of possibilities, including written statements by the parties and group members; production and inspection of relevant documents (eg, insurance policies); oral fairness hearings; and requests for *amicus curiae* (Rule 43) or statements by public regulators, authorities or any stakeholder or interest group which might provide additional input. Rule 223(1)(b) explicitly

---

[80] A very detailed study of the case, and particularly the influence of media coverage, is provided by Byron Strier, 'The promise and periol of media and culture: The Toyota unintended acceleration litigation and the Gulf Coast Facility in the United States' in Deborah Hensler and Christopher Hodges and Ianika Tzankova (eds), *Class Actions in Context* (Cheltenham 2016) 93.

[81] Rule 5: '(1) The Court must ensure that the dispute resolution process is proportionate. (2) In determining whether a process is proportionate the Court must take account of the nature, importance and complexity of the particular case and of the need to give effect to its general management duty in all proceedings with due regard for the proper administration of justice.'

[82] Matthis Peter, '*Kollektiver Rechtsschutz im Vorentwurf zur Änderung der ZPO*' [2019] ZZP 108, 117.

mentions the appointment of experts to assist the court, especially for the economic impact of settlements. Rule 223(1)(b) also takes into account the experience of common law class action jurisdictions, where expert opinions are often presented by the parties to the settlement and are therefore less neutral or reliable than statements by court-appointed experts.[83] According to Rule 223(1)(b), experts will be appointed by the court.

5.2 Comments by group members and second opt-out

Almost all class or group action regimes require that the class or group members to be bound by the settlement be given the opportunity to submit their comments[84] or to be heard during a fairness hearing. This is necessary – particularly in standalone settlement proceedings – to guarantee the right to be heard; but it is also an instrument for the court to receive input for its decision on approving or disapproving the settlement. Based on an 'exit and voice' principle,[85] some systems also allow or even require that class members have the chance of a (second)[86] opt-out of the settlement.[87] Where the applicants apply for court approval of a standalone settlement, the question of whether to opt in or opt out arises only once. We will address both issues in turn.

5.2.1 Group member comments

At first sight, group or class members seem to be the obvious source of information when it comes to the fairness of a proposed settlement. On second thoughts, however, courts should be extremely hesitant to rely too heavily on a lack of objections or on a small number of comments received. US courts apparently used to overemphasize the silence of the class members.[88]

---

[83] For Australian class action, Michael Legg explicitly advocated in favour of court-appointed experts to improve the settlement approval process (particularly when it comes to the assessment of the adequacy of lawyers' fees), Michael Legg (n 79) sub IV A, VI A.

[84] For example, Dutch WCAM Civil Procedure Code, Article 1013(5); Germany – KapMuG, Section 17(1) and Civil Procedure Code, Section 611 (4); FRCP, Rule 23(e)(1)(B).

[85] John Coffee, 'Class Action Accountability: Reconciling Exit, Voice, and Loyalty in Representative Litigation', 100 *Columbia L Rev* 370, 376 (2000); Samuel Issacharoff, 'Governance and Legitimacy in the Law of Class Actions' [1999] *Sup Ct Rev* 337, 366.

[86] Depending on whether the original collective redress action pending was based on an opt-in or opt-out mechanism.

[87] FRCP Rule 23(e)(4), with respect to class actions certified under Rule 23(b)(3).

[88] Christopher Leslie, 'The Significance of Silence: Collective Action Problems and Class Action Settlements' (2007) 59 *Florida L Rev* 71, 85; for example, *Wright v Stern*, 553 F Supp 2d 337, 345 (SDNY 2008): 'The fact that the vast majority of class

In Australia, Legg has rightly pointed out that silence may not equate to acquiescence, but might rather reflect the high cost of objecting compared to the benefit to be obtained; or the fact that group members are unware of the settlement, have insufficient information or have miscomprehended the settlement notice.[89] This observation is true regardless of the jurisdiction in which the representative action takes place and of any differences in the procedural tools of collective redress.[90] According to studies in the United States, only 1.1 per cent of class members object to proposed settlements.[91] Group members are always 'absent parties'; and despite any efforts to keep them posted on the ongoing litigation, the majority will neither be interested in details nor be able to finally assess whether the proposed settlement is a fair offer compared to the risk and prospects of further litigation – at least, not without consulting a lawyer. According to experience, comments by group members are often more likely to be submitted in case of a settlement providing for non-monetary relief instead of damages.[92]

In the United States, the fact that class members are invited to submit comments only once the court has granted preliminary approval of the settlement (Rule 23(e)(1)(B) of the FRCP) may also induce class members to stay passive and rely on the court's assessment, albeit a preliminary one. The ERCP attempts to avoid that risk. According to Rule 223(2), courts must advertise the proposed settlement and invite group members to comment; but in doing so, the court must make clear that it has not yet reached a conclusion on the fairness of the settlement. Group members must not be misled to conclude that the proposed settlement is fair and adequate from the court's perspective.

In securities cases, institutional investors with in-house counsel observing the litigation might be in a better position to object if they wish. Nevertheless, very often, they will not want to give up their relative anonymity as a group member and appear at a fairness hearing. General reputational concerns or the fear of being identified in public as having made wrong investment decisions

members neither objected nor opted out is a strong indication that the proposed settlement is fair, reasonable, and adequate'; in the same sense *in re Toys R US-Delaware, Inc - Fair and Accurate Credit Transactions Act (FACTA) Litigation*, 295 FRD 438, 456 (CD Cal 2014); *In re Processed Egg Products Antitrust Litigation*, 302 FRD 339, 356 (ED Pa 2014).

89 Michael Legg (n 79) sub III B; see also Fabian Stitz (n 30) 169 *et seq*.

90 David F. Herr (n 31) paras 21.61, 21.62, and William B Rubenstein, *Newberg on Class Actions,* vol 4 (5th edn, Eagan Minn 2011) 13.54, provide the same analysis with respect to US class actions.

91 Theodore Eisenberg and Geoffrey Miller, 'The Role of Opt-Outs and Objectors in Class Action Litigation: Theoretical and Empirical Issues' (2004) 57 *Vanderbilt L Rev*, 1529.

92 Alexander Eggers (n 32) p 245.

may come into play; but they may also prefer not to be identified as litigating against other companies with which they may have future or even current relationships.[93]

In the case of standalone settlements without previous litigation, taking of evidence and so on, comments by group members will be less helpful for the court, due to the lack of a solid basis for group members to estimate the prospects of success in case of individual or collective litigation. In the Dutch WCAM proceedings to date, hardly any group members filed objections to the settlement.[94] The reasons remain unclear.

If objections are submitted to the court, they will often be of poor quality and simply reflect the indignation of a single dissatisfied group member. In Australia, Canada and the United States, objections of class members seldom result in a settlement being rejected.[95] Nevertheless, it is important to encourage group members to comment on the proposed settlement, because they can provide at least hints from which the court may start to investigate further into the background of the settlement. Following the example given in Rule 23(e)(5)(A) of the FRCP, when advertising the proposed settlement and fixing a period for comments (Rule 223(2)(b) of the ERCP), the court should ask the group members to state 'with specificity the grounds for the objection'.

Courts should also be aware that the parties to the proposed settlement may be tempted to quieten objectors through extra payments or preferential treat-

---

[93] Michael Legg (n 79) sub III B.

[94] Alexander Eggers (n 32) p 246 fn 434 lists the following numbers: 12 objectors (size class not clear, 17,000 registered), *Gerechtshof* Amsterdam, *beschikking* 1 June 2006, ECLI:NL:GHAMS:2006:AX6440 (DES); zero objectors (size of class approx 11,000), *Gerechtshof* Amsterdam, *beschikking* 29 April 2009, ECLI:NL:GHAMS:2009:BI2717 (*Vie d'Or*); three objectors (size of class approx 500,000), *Gerechtshof* Amsterdam, *beschikking* 29 May 2009, ECLI:NL:GHAMS:2009:BI5744 (*Shell*); zero objectors (size of class approx 2000), *Gerechtshof* Amsterdam, *beschikking* 15 July 2009, ECLI:NL:GHAMS:2009:BJ2691 (*Vedior*); ten objectors (size of class approx 12,000), *Gerechtshof* Amsterdam, *beschikking* 17 January 2012, ECLI:NL:GHAMS:2012:BV1026 (*Converium*); four objectors (size of class approx 345,000; 300 persons opted out), *Gerechtshof* Amsterdam, *beschikking* 13 May 2014, ECLI:NL:GHAMS:2014:1690 (*DSB-Bank*); four objectors, *Gerechtshof* Amsterdam, *beschikking* 4 November 2014, ECLI:NL:GHAMS:2014:4560 (*DSB-Bank*); four natural persons and two groups of natural persons objected (size of class unknown), *Gerechtshof* Amsterdam, *beschikking* 16 June 2017, ECLI:NL:GHAMS:2017:2257 (*Fortis*). The *Dexia* case (class size approx 300,000) was an exception because even a couple of other foundations objected to the settlement and there was a high rate of opt-outs (25,000 persons = 8.3 per cent), *Gerechtshof* Amsterdam, *beschikking* 25 January 2007, ECLI:NL:GHAMS:2007:AZ7033.

[95] Michael Legg (n 79) sub III B refers to only one case in which half of the group members had opposed to the settlement. For Canada: Jasminka Kalajdzic (n 12), pp 103–06.

ment in the distribution process. If an objector withdraws his or her objections, the court will try to get to the bottom of the grounds, and should be able to take the objection raised into consideration when scrutinizing the settlement despite its withdrawal.

5.2.2 Opt-out of group members

5.2.2.1 Settlements negotiated during a pending collective action

Rules 225 and 226 explain the binding effect of an approved settlement. Where the pending action was based on an opt-in scheme (a decision to be made by the court when certifying the collective action – Rule 215), the settlement binds all group members who have opted in. In the case of opt-out proceedings, the settlement binds all group members unless they have opted out of the collective redress proceedings at the time the order approving the settlement is made. The idea of a second opt-out based on publication of the proposed settlement was discussed, but finally rejected. As the comments to Rule 226 specify, a second opt-out could jeopardize settlement negotiations. Defendants need a solid basis for calculating the amount to be paid for the compensation of the whole group and legal certainty with respect to the scope of claims settled. In the traditional class action world, the 'exit' option is deemed a strong indicator for the fairness of settlement and how satisfied group members are.[96]

Opt-out can be a safeguard against unfair settlements, but only if the following conditions are met: (1) group members have received information on the settlement and their right to opt out; (2) they are able to assess the pros and cons of opting out; and (3) there is a realistic alternative for them to enforce their claims in case they opt out.[97]

However, the very same reasons mentioned above to explain why group members do not come forward with objections to a settlement may apply to their not opting out. Statistics show that the rates of opt-outs of proposed settlement are low. Studies in the United States mention opt-out rates of only 0.1 per cent in the decade from 1995–2005. The rates clearly vary depending on the amount at stake for class members. In consumer cases with small individual loss (and almost no prospect of individually litigating the claims), class members tend not to opt out. Due to the lack of alternatives, not opting out might indicate consent; but not necessarily. Opt-out rates are likely to be

---

[96] US courts can take into consideration the opt-out rate when finally approving a proposed settlement, because the period for opting out starts to run with the notification of the proposed settlement that has obtained preliminary court approval.

[97] Christopher Hodges and Astrid Stadler, 'Introduction' in Christopher Hodges and Astrid Stadler (eds) (n 3) 16.

higher in case of mass tort, employment and commercial litigation, where damages are generally higher.[98]

All told, it seemed more appropriate for collective redress proceedings under the ERCP to require group members to make a general decision for or against participation at the beginning of the proceedings. Their opting in or not opting out gives the qualified claimant a mandate to conduct litigation and to negotiate a settlement for the group members. Taking into account, generally speaking, their lack of resources, motivation and knowledge with respect to assessing the fairness of the settlement, the interests of the group members are better protected by the need for court approval and a broad range of instruments which the court may use in gathering background information and comments on the proposed settlement.

5.2.2.2 Standalone settlements

Whereas the Dutch WCAM and other national procedures for obtaining court approval for a standalone settlement are all based on an opt-out mechanism,[99] the ERCP takes a more open stance. Rule 230 asks the applicants to specify in their application whether a binding settlement shall be reached on an opt-in or opt-out basis. As explained in Chapter 6, this allows the parties to the settlement to decide which mechanism they prefer and, in particular, whether they anticipate any problems with respect to the recognition of the approved settlement abroad. As the opt-out mechanism may raise (constitutional) concerns in some countries, parties may prefer to apply an opt-in mechanism. Their choice (and the question of whether the court will approve it) may also depend on notification issues. Where the group members are known by name and address, they can be notified personally and an opt-out mechanism can apply without great risk, because the group members will make an informed choice. There is no violation of their right to be heard. Where personal notification is not possible due to a group of unidentified group members, public announcements and an opt-out scheme may be problematic and imply the risk not to inform everybody; but this might also be the only way to include a large number of victims, investors or consumers in the settlement. Accordingly, a one-size-fits-all solution is not appropriate and parties and courts must make case-by-case decisions.

---

[98] Barabara J. Rothstein and Thomas E. Willging (n 45) 20.

[99] Dutch WCAM Civil Procedure Code, Article 1017(3) and Civil Code, Article 7-908(2). Under the WCAM rules, an opt-out is possible only after notification of the court-approved settlement; whereas in US class actions, class members can opt out upon preliminary court approval.

5.3 Fairness hearings

In addition to the tools already described, fairness hearings are a widespread instrument to discuss the fairness and adequacy of the proposed settlement with all persons involved. In some jurisdictions, it is even mandatory to hold a fairness hearing.[100] Such hearings may also play an important role in settlement approval procedures under the ERCP. In the case of standalone settlements, fairness hearings are of particular importance because they are the only 'day in court' for the parties to the settlement and for the group members.

US studies point out that only 'about a quarter to a half of the class representatives'[101] (not class members!) attend a fairness hearing. It is difficult to predict what will happen in European collective redress actions, but courts should make use of their case management powers and summon the parties to the settlement whenever necessary to ensure that they cooperate. Within the framework of the ERCP, Rule 2 (general rule on cooperation)[102] and Rules 47–49(10) (case management) allow them to do so, and to impose sanctions in case of non-compliance. With respect to the invitation of group members to the fairness hearing, the same problems may arise as described for written comments and objections.

6. EFFECTS OF COURT APPROVAL

6.1 Modifications of proposed settlement

If the court is not satisfied with a proposed settlement, Rule 232(a) allows the parties to renegotiate the settlement and file a new application.[103] Due to the parties' freedom of contract, the court may not *ex officio* modify the settlement

---

[100] United States – FRCP Rule 23(e)(2); Australia – Federal Court of Australia Act 1976 (Cth), Section 33 V; Michael Legg, 'Mass settlements in Australia' in Christopher Hodges and Astrid Stadler (n 3) 182; Netherlands – Civil Procedure Code, Article 1013(5); since 2013, the court may also schedule a pre-trial hearing to increase the parties' willingness to negotiate a settlement – Civil Procedure Code, Article 1018a; Slovenia – ZkoIT, Article 16(3); Switzerland – Tentative Draft Civil Procedure Code (March 2018), Article 352d(1).

[101] Barabara J. Rothstein and Thomas E. Willging (n 45) 20, citing a 1996 Federal Judicial Center study by Willging, Hooper and Niemic.

[102] Rule 2: 'Parties, their lawyers and the Court must cooperate to promote the fair, efficient and speedy resolution of the dispute.'

[103] According to the Dutch WCAM rules, the court may supplement or modify the settlement with the parties' consent or may give them the opportunity to change the settlement contract; Article 7:907(4) of the Dutch Civil Code.

terms. The court is, however, held to specify the grounds for refusal in order to allow for the submission of a revised version that can be approved.

6.2 Final decision on approval and its effects

Final approval of the settlement will be given by court judgment.[104] Rules 225 and 226 describe the extent of the binding effect, depending on whether the collective proceedings were opt-out or opt-in. For standalone settlements, a separate decision on the opt-in or opt-out mechanism must be made. The judgment is subject to appeal according to the general rules on appeal of the ERCP. As settlements will normally be fulfilled on a voluntary basis, the effects of the court judgment are mainly important when individual group members deny the binding effect of the settlement and sue the defendant individually before the courts of another jurisdiction. Recognition of the court decision is therefore crucial for the preclusive effect of the settlement and for a defendant that wants to 'buy global peace'. Cross-border issues are dealt with in Chapters 13 and 14.

7. CONCLUSIONS

European judges lack experience with court approval of collective settlements. The ERCP provides only a rough framework for the review process. European courts may benefit from the vast experience of judges in traditional class action jurisdictions to some extent and learn from their 'red-flag' policy; but at the end of the day, they will have to develop their own factors to be considered when scrutinizing proposed settlements and establish their own practice. This is a task for the future. Settlement approval orders (Rule 224) and any decision that dismisses an application for approval are judgments in the sense of Rule 131 of the ERCP, and courts must provide legal and factual grounds for their decisions.

It seems highly recommendable to develop practice manuals, handbooks and commentaries which reflect these decisions and provide comparative information and step-by-step guidance to develop a better basis for future decision making. As a start, jurisdictions which implement the ERCP (or any other set

---

[104] The same applies in the United States (consent decree, Charles A. Wright, Arthur R. Miller and Mary K. Kane, *Federal Practice and Procedure, Civil,* vol 7B (3rd edn, St Paul Minn 2005), Section 1797.1 with references; Germany, Section 23 of the KapMuG and Section 611 of the Civil Procedure Code; in the Netherlands, court approval is also given by a judgment and the settlement has the effect of a declaratory contract with a binding effect similar to *res judicata*; Article 7.900 of the Dutch Civil Code and Article 236 of the Civil Procedure Code.

of collective redress instruments) should also consider offering judges further training to improve their handling of this completely new and challenging task – ideally with the help of experienced colleagues from other jurisdictions. With respect to frivolous group actions, it has been observed that: 'European judges are used to playing an active role in litigation and will not be fooled by any attempts to set up predatory class suits whose only purpose is to blackmail corporate defendants.'[105] One cannot help but agree with this, and European judges will also master settlement approval proceedings. Nevertheless, they deserve support and need not reinvent the wheel.

[105] Elisabetta Silvestri, 'The difficult art of legal transplants: the case of class actions', (2010) 35 *Revista de Processo* 99.

12. Costs and funding of collective redress proceedings

Stefaan Voet

1. INTRODUCTION[1]

Any jurisdiction that wishes to introduce a collective redress mechanism must consider the same design options: will its scope be trans-substantive or restricted?[2] Who will have standing?[3] How will the class be notified?[4] Will the regime be opt-in or opt-out?[5] And what remedies will be available?[6] However, the question of how the mechanism will be funded and financed transcends all these issues – simply because without appropriate and clear funding rules, they will remain a dead letter. Funding rules are an essential precondition for the proper functioning of any civil justice system.[7] In that sense, the funding and financing issue goes to the heart of the collective redress mechanism.

This chapter will not assess what the optimal funding regime of a European collective redress mechanism should look like, as there are too many legal

---

[1] This chapter is largely based on (and is an update of) Stefaan Voet, 'The Crux of the Matter: Funding and Financing Collective Redress Mechanisms' in Burkhard Hess, Maria Bergström and Eva Storskrubb (eds), *EU Civil Justice: Current Issues & Future Outlook* (Hart Pub 2016) 201–22.

[2] Trans-substantive rules apply broadly to all civil lawsuits, regardless of the substantive law underlying the claims and regardless of the size of the litigation or the stakes involved.

[3] An individual class member, an (ad hoc) association (foundation) or governmental body. See Chapter 7.

[4] Individual notice or non-individual notice (eg, notice through television, newspaper advertisements, the Internet).

[5] 'Opt-in' means that the class includes only those individuals or legal persons who actively opt in to become part of the class. 'Opt-out' means that the class is composed of all individuals who belong to the defined class and claim to have been harmed by the same or similar infringement unless they actively opt out of the group.

[6] Injunctive, declaratory or damages relief. See Chapter 6.

[7] Mauro Cappelletti and Bryan Garth (eds), *Access to Justice: A World Survey* (Sijthoff/Giuffre 1978) 1.

and cultural differences to do so – both in the existing (and future) European collective redress mechanisms and in the one-on-one litigation funding rules.[8] The goal of this chapter is rather to map the various funding options and assess their pros and cons in a collective litigation context. These options will be juxtaposed with the European Law Institute/UNIDROIT European Rules of Civil Procedure (ERCP) (consolidated draft – 27 July 2019).

At the outset, it should be noted that the issue of funding and financing collective redress mechanisms is a complex one. It is challenging to embed this kind of procedure in the existing one-on-one litigation funding rules. In individual litigation, the costs and lawyer fees are (pre)financed by the identifiable plaintiff pursuing his or her individual claim, or by a third party (eg, a lawyer, a legal expenses insurer, a legal aid scheme or a third-party litigation fund) directly connected to the plaintiff. In collective redress litigation, and at least at the outset of the procedure, the plaintiff acts on behalf of a group of unquantifiable and unidentified class members. Rational apathy and free-rider problems minimize the incentive for those members to invest in the litigation, leaving the funding to be paid for or organized by their agent (ie, the class representative), who will in most cases be confronted with wealthy and sophisticated repeat players as counterparties in the litigation. This results in an investment asymmetry.[9]

The fees and costs in question are also substantial. Collective redress proceedings entail not only court costs and lawyer fees, but also specific class action-related costs connected to an intensive preparation stage; a complicated certification phase; multiple individual or non-individual notifications to class members; reaching a settlement; court-ordered investigations; a possible elaborate trial on the merits of the case; internal administration and communication processes; potential distribution procedures and so on. All these costs and fees must be pre-financed, irrespective of the outcome of the case.

In a one-on-one setting, there are two principal actors: the plaintiff pursuing his or her individual claim and his or her (representing) counsel. From the plaintiff's side, collective redress proceedings are characterized by a triangular structure. In addition to the class representative (qualified claimant) and the class lawyer, there are a number of unquantifiable and unidentified class members. Although they are not formal parties to the proceedings, it is their rights that are being adjudicated in a decisive manner, in the sense that they are directly bound by the *res judicata* effect of the decision, unless they have not

---

8 For an overview, see Christopher Hodges, Stefan Vogenauer and Magdalena Tulibacka (eds), *The Costs and Funding of Civil Litigation. A Comparative Perspective* (Hart Pub 2010).

9 Ianika Tzankova, 'Funding of Mass Disputes: Lessons from the Netherlands' (2012) 8 *JLEP* 549, 554.

opted in or have opted out. Therefore, the funding issue should first and foremost be approached from this triangular structure, and more specifically from the standpoint of the class representative and/or the class members (Section 3) and the class counsel (Section 4). Similarly, as in one-on-one litigation, class action litigation can be funded and financed by third parties (Section 5): legal expenses insurers, government funds, legal aid schemes and, most recently, third-party litigation funders.

2. LOSER PAYS RULE

At the outset, it should be reminded that the loser pays rule remains fully applicable. According to this rule, which is well entrenched in the European legal tradition,[10] the final outcome of the case will ultimately determine who must bear some or all of the costs and fees. That the loser pays rule should also apply in collective redress proceedings is suggested as the preferred European policy option: 'the Member States should ensure that the party that loses a collective redress action reimburses necessary legal costs borne by the winning party (loser pays principle), subject to the conditions provided for in the relevant national law.'[11]

This rule is viewed as a safeguard against abusive litigation.[12] All Member States with collective redress mechanisms follow the loser pays rule.[13]

Article 5(4a) of the 2019 Proposal of the Competitiveness Council for a Directive on Representative Actions states:

> Member States shall ensure that, within a representative action, consumers' interests are represented by qualified entities and that the entities have the rights and obli-

[10] Christopher Hodges, Stefan Vogenauer and Magdalena Tulibacka (eds), *The Costs and Funding of Civil Litigation. A Comparative Perspective* (Hart Pub 2010) 562.

[11] Recommendation (EU) 2013/396 on common principles for injunctive and compensatory collective redress mechanisms in the Member States concerning violations of rights granted under Union Law [2013] OJ L206/60, Article 13. See also European Commission Proposal for a Directive of the European Parliament and of the Council on representative actions for the protection of the collective interests of consumers, and repealing Directive 2009/22/EC, COM/2018/184 final, Article 7.1 ('[The qualified entity] shall demonstrate that it has sufficient financial resources to represent the best interests of the consumers concerned and to meet any adverse costs should the action fail'). For a summary of the Recommendation and the European Commission Proposal for a Directive on Representative Actions, see Stefaan Voet, 'Europe's Collective Redress Conundrum' (2018) 61 *JYIL* 205.

[12] Communication 'Towards a European Horizontal Framework for Collective Redress', COM(2013) 401, 9.

[13] Report on the implementation of the recommendation (COM(2018) 40 final) 7.

> gations of a party to the proceedings. The consumers concerned by the action shall be entitled to benefit from the measures referred to in paragraph 2. The consumers concerned by the action may bear costs of the proceedings only in exceptional circumstances in accordance with national law. . .[14]

Recital (13c) clarifies that the Directive should not affect national rules on recovery of procedural costs or on the loser pays rule. Only exceptionally should class members bear the costs of the proceedings (eg, when a class member has deliberately or negligently caused unnecessary legal costs by, for example, prolonging the proceedings through unlawful conduct). The costs of the proceedings should include, for example, any costs resulting from the fact that either party was represented by a lawyer or another legal professional, and any costs arising from the service or translation of documents.[15]

ERCP Rule 238(1) lays down the aforementioned loser pays rule: 'only a qualified claimant is liable for the costs and expenses of a collective redress proceeding if it is unsuccessful.'

Only the qualified claimant as a party will be liable for costs, and not the individual group members. On the other hand, if the qualified claimant wins the proceedings, the total amount of compensation that he or she will receive shall form a common fund. The qualified claimant's costs and expenses must be paid from this common fund before any distribution of compensation to group members.[16]

On the other hand, the general rules on costs – which do not strictly adhere to the loser pays rule – allow for some flexibility and discretion. According to Rule 241, in deciding on which party to impose the obligation to reimburse costs, the court shall take into account the circumstances of the specific proceedings – in particular, whether and to what extent the parties' claims were successful.[17] A collective action can be such a specific proceeding. Moreover, the court may also take into account the parties' conduct – in particular, whether and to what extent they acted in good faith and contributed to the fair, efficient and speedy resolution of the dispute.[18]

---

[14] Competitiveness Council Proposal for a Directive of the European Parliament and of the Council on representative actions for the protection of the collective interests of consumers, and repealing Directive 2009/22/EC, 14600/19.

[15] *Ibid.*

[16] ERCP Rules 238(2)-(3).

[17] ERCP Rule 241(1).

[18] ERCP Rule 241(2).

3. QUALIFIED CLAIMANT

The most obvious option is that the collective redress action is financed in the same manner as an individual action – namely, by the person or entity initiating the procedure: the class (or representative) plaintiff, or, according to the ERCP, the qualified claimant. This means that all fees and costs regarding the preparation, initiation, settlement and adjudication of the action must be pre-financed by him or her.

According to ERCP Rule 208,[19] a 'qualified claimant' is:

> (a) an organisation authorised, in accordance with national law, to bring collective redress proceedings and whose purpose has a direct relationship with the event giving rise to the mass harm,
> (b) an entity which is established solely for the purpose of obtaining redress for group members and which satisfied the requirements of Rule 209;
> (c) a person who is a group member and who meets the requirements of Rule 209(a)–(c).

According to the comments, standing is given to long-standing organizations representing the interests of consumers, investors or other potential victims (lit a). These include public regulators or public bodies, ad hoc organizations or private entities (lit b) which are established to represent the victims of a particular mass harm event; and natural persons who are themselves a member of the group of victims (lit c).

In other words, a collective redress procedure can be financed by an individual class member (Section 3.1) (Rule 208(c)), a governmental body (Section 3.2) (Rule 208(a)), or an association or foundation (Section 3.3) (Rules 208(a)–(b)).

3.1 Individual class member

If the qualified claimant is an individual class member, this means that there will be no funding at all. This will certainly be the case for small claims, but also for individually recoverable claims. In those cases, funding a collective redress procedure will boil down to a personal and unprofitable investment, which no one would wish to make. If, at the end of the proceedings, the qualified claimant also risked having to pay the costs of the defendant because of the loser pays rule,[20] there would be 'a disincentive to bringing grouped

---

19 As discussed in Chapter 7.

20 Garry D. Watson, 'Class Actions: The Canadian Experience' (2001) 11 *J Comp & Int'l L* 269, 274–77 ('the Ontario costs rule is problematic and causes difficulties

proceedings, and [this] might in fact create yet another barrier to access to legal remedies of the kind which the recommended procedure itself aims to overcome'.[21]

Theoretical methods for creating greater incentives or pooling class member resources seem unlikely to succeed. It would be possible to reward the class member who stood as a qualified claimant with a financial bonus, which would constitute an impetus to act. As Mulheron pertinently points out, however, this could lead to conflicts of interest:

> where a representative plaintiff benefits from the class proceeding to a greater extent than the class members, and such benefit is as a result of the extraneous compensation paid to the representative plaintiff rather than the damages suffered by him or her, there is undoubtedly an appearance of a conflict of interest between the representative plaintiff and the class members. This view holds that a class action should not be viewed as a method by which persons can seek to receive personal gain over and above any damages or other remedy to which they would otherwise be entitled on the merits of their claims.[22]

Allowing a class member with a greater interest than his or her fellow members (whose claims he or she alone is pursuing) to steer the litigation entails a real danger of conflict of interest. Moreover, this is at odds with the historical origin of an individual class member as class representative. In order to prevent abuses and conflicts, the class representative is required to have 'the same interest' as the other class members; their interests must be aligned.[23] This is hardly the case if one of them is eligible for a bonus.

---

because it raises the issue of who, properly advised, would agree to become a representative plaintiff').

[21] Australian Law Reform Commission, *Grouped Proceedings in the Federal Court* (Report No 46, 1988) 107.

[22] Rachel Mulheron, *The Class Action in Common Law Legal Systems: A Comparative Perspective* (Hart Pub 2004) 466. See also *In re Gould Sec Litig*, 727 F Supp 1201, 1209 (ND Ill 1989) ('if class representatives expect routinely to receive special awards in addition to their share of the recovery, the representative may be tempted to accept sub-optimal settlements at the expense of the class members whose interests they are appointed to guard'). Under the US Private Securities Litigation Reform Act, such awards are expressly prohibited (15 USC § 78u-4(a)(2)(A)(vi) (2012)).

[23] This is still a requirement in the US rule. See *Wal-Mart Stores, Inc v Dukes*, 131 S Ct 2541 (US 2011) (the class action is 'an exception to the usual rule that litigation is conducted by and on behalf of the individual named parties only. In order to justify a departure from that rule, a class representative must be part of the class and possess the same interest and suffer the same injury as the class members'). See also John C. Coffee Jr, 'Class Action Accountability: Reconciling Exit, Voice, and Loyalty in Representative Litigation' (2000) 100 *Columbia Law Rev* 370 (stating that the

It would also be conceivable to allow the qualified claimant to solicit other class members for financial contributions.[24] This is, for example, possible in British Columbia: 'with leave of the court, notice under this section may include a solicitation of contributions from class members to assist in paying solicitors' fees and disbursements.'[25]

The 2019 Proposal of the Competitiveness Council for a Directive on Representative Actions also leaves an opening for Member States to set out rules allowing for modest entry fees or similar participation charges from class members who have explicitly expressed their will to be represented by a qualified entity within a particular representative action for redress measures.[26]

Soliciting financial contributions from individual class members is a challenge, however, because the qualified claimant is acting on behalf of an unknown group of class members, who would be difficult to reach and sometimes even to identify. In small claims cases, it would be hard to persuade them to pay for the litigation. Therefore, this model:

> is unlikely to be much utilised because of the disincentive to class member participation which up-front funding would entail. In any event, the practicalities are that any potential benefit is surely a bit remote at the time that this request for contributions is normally made, at such an early stage of the proceedings.[27]

3.2 Governmental body

If the qualified claimant is a governmental body,[28] the collective redress action will be funded by the taxpayer. Due to limited resources, they will only finance

---

Supreme Court has accepted an implicit theory of representation: a representative is entitled to bind only those persons whose interests and legal positions match those of the representative). This also explains why the representative plaintiff must fairly and adequately protect the interests of the class (Rule 23(a)(4) US Federal Rules of Civil Procedure).

24 Vince Morabito, 'Federal Class Actions, Contingency Fees, and the Rules Governing Litigation Costs' (1995) 21 *Mon L Rev* 231, 236.

25 Section 19(7) of the Class Proceedings Act.

26 Competitiveness Council Proposal for a Directive of the European Parliament and of the Council on representative actions for the protection of the collective interests of consumers, and repealing Directive 2009/22/EC, 14600/19, Recital (13c) and Article 5(4a).

27 Rachel Mulheron, *The Class Action in Common Law Legal Systems: A Comparative Perspective* (Hart Pub 2004) 465.

28 For example, in Denmark, where the Consumer Ombudsman – which is a regulator – has exclusive standing to bring an opt-out class action. In Belgium, the Federal Consumer Ombudsman Service has collective redress standing, but only to conclude a collective settlement. See Stefaan Voet, 'European Collective Redress: A Status Quaestionis' (2014) 4 *IJPL* 97. See also Chapter 7.

meritorious cases that are in line with their policy. According to the European Commission, 'public authorities could be potential gatekeepers when funding collective redress, refusing to allocate resources to unmeritorious claims'.[29]

However, a possible danger is that they could be caught by political imperatives or the interests of particular stakeholder groups, which could raise concerns regarding access to justice.

3.3 Association or foundation

One may assume that funding would be easier, or at least less problematic, if the qualified claimant were an association or (ad hoc or special purpose) foundation than an individual member. It may be argued that at least the successful ones will have more financial resources, such as membership contributions, subsidies and other income.[30] The 2019 Proposal of the Competitiveness Council for a Directive on Representative Actions states that one of the criteria that qualified entities should meet in order to be designated to bring a cross-border representative action is that it have a non-profit making character and be in a sound and stable financial situation,[31] taking into account any revenues or assets they may have, for example.[32] This criterion guarantees their independence.

More importantly, associations and foundations will not pursue a personal interest, but only the interests of the class. Because class interests overlap with their statutory aim,[33] a collective redress action goes to the heart of their existence.[34] Just like governmental bodies, organizational plaintiffs will therefore act as gatekeepers, because it is unlikely that they would invest in frivolous or meritless cases with the objective of profit.

---

[29] European Commission, 'Green Paper on consumer collective redress', COM(2008) 794 final, 5.

[30] Samuel Issacharoff and Geoffrey P. Miller, 'Will Aggregate Litigation Come to Europe?' (2009) 62 *Vand L Rev* 179, 199.

[31] Competitiveness Council Proposal for a Directive of the European Parliament and of the Council on representative actions for the protection of the collective interests of consumers, and repealing Directive 2009/22/EC, 14600/19, Article 4a(3)(c) and (caa).

[32] *Ibid*, Recital (10).

[33] See Rule 208: 'a qualified claimant is (a) an organisation authorised, in accordance with national law, to bring collective redress proceedings *and whose purpose has a direct relationship with the event giving rise to the mass harm*, (b) an entity which is established *solely for the purpose of obtaining redress for group members* and which satisfied the requirements of Rule 209…' (emphasis added).

[34] Samuel Issacharoff and Geoffrey P. Miller, 'Will Aggregate Litigation Come to Europe?' (2009) 62 *Vand L Rev.* 179, 193–94.

That associations might be willing to finance this kind of litigation is illustrated by the Dutch *Dexia* case, one of the first actions under the Dutch Collective Settlements Act.[35] The representing consumer association (*Consumentenbond*) was able to concentrate the representation and aggregate claims by setting up a special purpose vehicle for the collective action, hiring one lawyer and law firm, and raising a substantial fund by requiring a modest contribution (€45) from each of its members.[36]

Another example is the Belgian *Lernout & Hauspie* case.[37] In 2001, Lernout & Hauspie Speech Products (L&H), a speech recognition technology company based in Ypres, went bankrupt due to overstated earnings, fictitious transactions and improper accounting methods. The major administrators of L&H and its financial and accounting partners (Dexia and KPMG) were indicted before a criminal court. According to Belgian law, crime victims are formal parties to the criminal proceedings, just as the public prosecutor and the defendant are formal parties. They can bring their civil claims during the criminal proceedings. After the criminal judge has dealt with the criminal aspect of the case and convicted the defendant, he or she is obliged to rule on the civil claims. This is the so-called 'piggyback', or *partie civile*, technique.[38] During the *L&H* criminal trial in 2007, it took several days for the more than 15 000 piggybacking victims to bring their civil claims. Most of them were represented by consumer or minority shareholder associations. One consumer association, acting on behalf of its 4000 members, did not charge anything. The members each paid an annual €150 contribution and were not charged an extra fee for the *L&H* case. The legal support in the case was offered pro bono. The only condition that the association imposed was that members retain their membership until the end of the proceedings – making this a perfect opportunity to improve customer relations.

Ideally, and to incentivize this, the direct funding and financing of collective redress actions by governmental bodies or associations could be coupled with

---

35 *Dexia, Gerechtshof Amsterdam,* 25 January 2007, ECLI:NL:GHAMS:2007:AZ7033.

36 Ianika Tzankova, 'Funding of Mass Disputes: Lessons from the Netherlands' (2012) 8 *JLEP* 549, 579.

37 Stefaan Voet, 'The L&H Case: Belgium's Internet Bubble Story' in Deborah R. Hensler, Christopher Hodges and Ianika Tzankova (eds), *Class Actions in Context. How Economics, Politics and Culture Shape Collective Litigation* (Edward Elgar Publishing 2016) 299–319.

38 Stefaan Voet, 'Public Enforcement and A(O)DR as Mechanisms for Resolving Mass Problems: A Belgian Perspective' in Christopher Hodges and Astrid Stadler (eds), *Resolving Mass Disputes* (Edward Elgar Publishing 2013) 279–84.

one-way cost shifting:[39] when the qualified claimant wins the procedure, the losing defendant must pay the qualified claimant's lawyer fees and costs. In case of a government fund,[40] these costs could be transferred back to the fund to finance future class action litigation. If the defendant wins the procedure, the governmental body or association would be exempted from paying lawyer fees and costs. This dispensation could be justified by the public interest in collective redress actions as a legal protection tool.

4. CLASS COUNSEL

A second option to address the issue of collective redress funding is allowing the class lawyer to fund and finance the litigation[41] on the basis of a contingency fee agreement, which is the default rule in the United States.[42] If the case is successful, the lawyer receives a contingency fee. If the case is lost, he or she receives nothing. The contingency fee is usually calculated on a lodestar or percentage of recovery basis. The lodestar method is a technique whereby

---

[39] See, on cost-shifting in a class action context: Laura Inglis, Kevin McCabe, Steve Rassenti, Daniel Simmons and Erik Tallroth, 'Experiments on the Effects of Cost-Shifting, Court Costs, and Discovery on the Efficient Settlement of Tort Claims' (2005) 33 *Fla St U L Rev* 89; Vince Morabito, 'Federal Class Actions, Contingency Fees, and the Rules Governing Litigation Costs' (1995) 21 *Mon L Rev* 231, 262; and Thomas D. Rowe Jr, 'Shift Happens: Pressure on Foreign Attorney-fee Paradigms from Class Actions' (2003) 13 *J Comp & Int'l L* 125.

[40] See *supra* section 3.2.

[41] Generally, class action lawyers use four funding mechanisms: (1) self-finance, which depends on the law firm's financial situation (ie, its cash flow) and the parameters of the case; (2) through a bank loan: most banks will only issue a loan based on the individual partners' collateral and personal credit; (3) a partnership with another law firm to share the cost burden; or (4) approaching a private financing company that specializes in funding contingency litigation through private financing. For an overview see Nora Frieman Engstrom, 'Re-Re-Financing Civil Litigation: How Lawyer Lending Might Remake the American Litigation Landscape, Again' (2013) 61 *UCLA L Rev Disc* 110.

[42] Janet C. Alexander, 'Contingent Fees and Class Actions' (1998) 47 *DePaul L Rev* 347; Lynn A. Baker, Michael A. Perino and Charles M. Silver, 'Setting Attorneys' Fees in Securities Class Actions: An Empirical Assessment' (2013) 66 *Vanderbilt Law Rev* 1677; Theodore Eisenberg and Geoffrey P. Miller, 'Attorney Fees and Expenses in Class Action Settlements: 1993-2008' (2010) 7 *J Empirical Legal Stud* 248; and Randal S. Jeffrey, 'Facilitating Welfare Rights Class Action Litigation: Putting Damages and Attorney's Fees to Work' (2003) 69 *Brook L Rev* 281. See generally on contingency fees: Lester Brickman, *Lawyer Barons: What Their Contingency Fees Really Cost America* (Cambridge University Press 2011); and Herbert M. Kritzer, *Risks, Reputations, and Awards. Contingency Fee Legal Practice in the United States* (Stanford University Press 2004).

the court multiplies a reasonable hourly rate by a reasonable number of hours expended.[43] The percentage of recovery method implies that the class counsel receives a fixed percentage (usually between 25 and 30 per cent)[44] of the awarded damages. Because contingency fees could be a major driving force behind a class counsel's motives to represent class members, and could lead to abuses or conflicts of interest, US courts assess and award reasonable lawyer fees and costs in certified class actions. Rule 23(h) of the US Federal Rules of Civil Procedure states: 'in a certified class action, the court may award reasonable attorney's fees and non-taxable costs that are authorized by law or by the parties' agreement. The following procedures apply. . .'

In Europe, contingency fees are considered to violate public order and to be incompatible with the ethics of the legal profession.[45]

The International Bar Association's 2011 International Principles on Conduct for the Legal Profession state that: 'a contingency fee or pactum de quota litis is permitted in certain jurisdictions provided certain requirements are met but prohibited as a matter of public policy in other jurisdictions.'[46]

The 2013 Charter of Core Principles of the European Legal Profession and Code of Conduct for European Lawyers of the Council of Bars and Law Societies of Europe goes further in prohibiting a *pactum de quota litis*:

> 3.3. Pactum de Quota Litis
>
> 3.3.1. A lawyer shall not be entitled to make a pactum de quota litis.

---

43 For a recent example, see 'Attorneys Win $43 Million From Meal, Rest Break Settlement', https://news.bloomberglaw.com/daily-labor-report/attorneys-win-43-million-from-meal-rest-break-settlement (last accessed 30 September 2020) ('the court used the lodestar-multiplier method to calculate the attorneys' fees award, ruling that a multiplier of 2.3x was justified given the skill and expertise of class counsel and the case's "long and extensive procedural history." The attorneys clocked 25,450 billable hours while working on the case, an amount Highberger deemed "reasonably necessary" to reach the settlement').

44 Lisa L. Casey, 'Reforming Securities Class Actions from the Bench: Judging Fiduciaries and Fiduciary Judging' (2003) 4 *BYU L Rev* 1239; and James L. Tuxbury, 'A Case for Competitive Bidding for Lead Counsel in Securities Class Actions' (2003) 1 *Colum Bus L Rev* 285.

45 Michael Faure, Fokke Fernhout and Niels Phillipsen, 'No Cure, No Pay, and Contingency Fees' in Mark Tuil and Louis Visscher (eds), *New Trends in Financing Civil Litigation in Europe: A Legal Empirical and Economic Analysis* (Edward Elgar Publishing 2010) 33–56. In Belgium, Article 446 of the Judicial Code explicitly forbids a fee arrangement linked to the outcome of the dispute.

46 International Bar Association, *International Principles on Conduct for the Legal Profession*, file:///C:/Users/u0103885/AppData/Local/Microsoft/Windows/INetCache/IE/2YQ1B76B/IBA-Int-Principles-on-Conduct-for-the-Legal-Profession.pdf (last accessed 30 September 2020), 32.

3.3.2. By "pactum de quota litis" is meant an agreement between a lawyer and the client entered into prior to final conclusion of a matter to which the client is a party, by virtue of which the client undertakes to pay the lawyer a share of the result regardless of whether this is represented by a sum of money or by any other benefit achieved by the client upon the conclusion of the matter.
3.3.3. "Pactum de quota litis" does not include an agreement that fees be charged in proportion to the value of a matter handled by the lawyer if this is in accordance with an officially approved fee scale or under the control of the Competent Authority having jurisdiction over the lawyer.

Commentary on Article 3.3 –Pactum de Quota Litis
These provisions reflect the common position in all Member States that an unregulated agreement for contingency fees (pactum de quota litis) is contrary to the proper administration of justice because it encourages speculative litigation and is liable to be abused. The provisions are not, however, intended to prevent the maintenance or introduction of arrangements under which lawyers are paid according to results or only if the action or matter is successful, provided that these arrangements are under sufficient regulation and control for the protection of the client and the proper administration of justice.[47]

Only intermediate forms of contingency fee arrangements are possible. An agreement by which the lawyer fees partially depend on the outcome of the case is allowed.[48] This comes down to a permissible enhancement of the lawyer fees based on success in the litigation.

Therefore, it is no surprise that the 2013 Recommendation rejects contingency fees. As a general rule, Member States should ensure that in collective redress proceedings, the lawyer's remuneration and the method by which it is calculated create no incentive to litigation that is unnecessary from the point of view of the interests of any of the parties.[49] Contingency fees create such an incentive. The rationale is clearly to avoid an abuse of the system or a conflict of interest.[50] Nevertheless, in its Recommendation, the European Commission has not entirely ruled out contingency fees as a policy option for collective redress cases. The Commission proposes that if Member States exceptionally

---

[47] Council of Bars and Law Societies of Europe, *Charter of Core Principles of the European Legal Profession and Code of Conduct for European lawyers*, https://www.ccbe.eu/NTCdocument/EN_CCBE_CoCpdf1_1382973057.pdf (last accessed 30 September 2020), 18–19 and 29.

[48] Michael Faure, Fokke Fernhout and Niels Phillipsen, 'No Cure, No Pay, and Contingency Fees' in Mark Tuil and Louis Visscher (eds), *New Trends in Financing Civil Litigation in Europe: A Legal Empirical and Economic Analysis* (Edward Elgar Publishing 2010) 42.

[49] Recommendation (EU) 2013/396 on common principles for injunctive and compensatory collective redress mechanisms in the Member States concerning violations of rights granted under Union Law [2013] OJ L206/60, Article 29.

[50] *Ibid*, Recital (19).

allow them, they should provide appropriate national regulation, taking into account the right to full compensation of the members of the claimant party.[51]

According to the 2018 Implementation Report, nine Member States allow some form of contingency fees. All of these Member States have specific provisions regarding their applicability in collective redress actions. Other Member States allow for performance fees – in the form of either a success fee or a reduction in remuneration if certain goals are not achieved.[52]

The fundamental problem with contingency and success fees in a collective redress context is that the class lawyer acquires a personal interest in the outcome of the litigation, which can be a breeding ground for conflicts of interest between the class and its counsel. This is the so-called 'agency problem,'[53] which primarily derives from the fact that the class lawyer represents a large number of unknown class members rather than an individual plaintiff. This problem can lead to 'sweetheart settlements' concluded by the class lawyer and the defendant with the goal of serving their own financial interests, instead of those of the class.[54] In one-on-one litigation, this 'personal interest in the outcome of the litigation' might no longer be an argument because the interests of the client and the lawyer are more aligned; but in collective redress litigation, it still is. This kind of procedure requires the mandatory intervention of a lawyer[55] – not only because of the procedural technicality and complexity, but especially because of the interests of the class members, who are absent from the procedure, but bound by its outcome.[56] Therefore, the adequacy (ie, expertise, knowledge and financial and human resources) of the qualified claimant,[57] and in particular of the class lawyer, is more than vital. The class members are forced to rely almost blindly on the way the class lawyer adminis-

---

[51] *Ibid*, Article 30.

[52] Report on the implementation of the recommendation (COM(2018) 40 final) 16.

[53] See Nancy J. Moore, 'Who Should Regulate Class Action Lawyers?' (2003) *U Ill L Rev* 1477 and Jasminka Kalajdzic, 'Self-Interest, Public-Interest and the Interests of the Absent Client: Legal Ethics and Class Action Praxis' (2011) 49 *Osgoode Hall Law J* 1.

[54] Ianika Tzankova, 'Funding of Mass Disputes: Lessons from the Netherlands' (2012) 8 JLEP 549, 554.

[55] See ERCP Rule 209(c): 'a person or entity shall not be a qualified claimant unless. . . c) they are legally represented.' The comments state: 'given that collective redress actions always have a certain level of complexity legal representation should be mandatory.' See also Rule 23(g)(1) US Federal Rules of Civil Procedure: 'unless a statute provides otherwise, a court that certifies a class must appoint class counsel'; and Article 1049 of the Code of Civil Procedure of Quebec: 'the representative or member who applies to act as such must be represented by an attorney.'

[56] Samuel Issacharoff and Geoffrey P. Miller, 'Will Aggregate Litigation Come to Europe?' (2009) 62 *Vand L Rev* 179, 206.

[57] See ERCP Rule 209(b).

ters, deals with and settles the case. The class counsel must also serve as a gatekeeper for the defendant, which must be protected against frivolous claims and blackmail settlements. In other words, the class lawyer serves a semi-public role. A personal financial interest in the outcome of the case can hinder, and even impede, this semi-public task.

As mentioned above, the Recommendation leaves an opening for contingency fees, as long as they are nationally regulated. It is indeed imperative to create safeguards. In order to avoid abuses and conflicts of interest, there should be oversight or monitoring of the class counsel. One option is to allow European judges – just like their American counterparts – to assess and award reasonable lawyer fees and costs in collective redress proceedings. Such judicial oversight and approval could prevent conflicts and abuses. In that regard, ERCP Rule 224 regarding settlement approval orders states that:

> the Court shall not make an order approving a settlement agreement where…
> (d) the terms, whether contained in the proposed settlement agreement or not, as to the payment of legal and other associated costs of the action are manifestly unreasonable.

However, contrary to, for example, common law judges, who are regarded as flexible case managers and who have no problem in ruling on lawyer fees, judges in some civil law jurisdictions will probably be more hesitant to delve into the lawyer fee issue. In some countries, such as Belgium, judges are already tremendously reluctant to rule on lawyer fees in one-on-one disputes. In most cases, they ask the local bar council for advice, with which they nearly always agree. Tzankova rightly observed the following:

> overall Dutch judges seem to feel uncomfortable and hesitate when they must invoke financial incentives and sanction parties for their conduct in the course of the litigation. Presumably, this is not an example of Dutch exceptionalism, but rather a feature of the judiciary system in civil law jurisdictions… Once could summarize the different attitudes towards costs and funding as civil law legal idealism and dogmatism versus common law legal realism and pragmatism.[58]

In this regard, it is significant that the Dutch Collective Settlements Act, although inspired by the US class action settlement regime, does not allow the Amsterdam Court of Appeal – which has exclusive jurisdiction to approve a collective settlement – to assess and review the lawyer fees directly. If these fees are paid out of the settlement fund, the court can review them indirectly as

---

[58] Ianika Tzankova, 'Funding of Mass Disputes: Lessons from the Netherlands' (2012) 8 *JLEP* 549, 553 (and referring to a Dutch empirical study: Paul Sluijter, *Sturen met proceskosten: wie betaalt de prijs van storend procesgedrag* (Kluwer 2011)).

part of its assessment of the general fairness of the settlement agreement.[59] For example, in the *Converium* case[60] – and to the surprise of many – the court had no problem with the contingency fee arrangement for the American lawyers, which involved up to 20 per cent of the settlement.[61] The court stated that it could rely on customary US fee practices as the legal services were largely provided in the United States by American law firms and on US court decisions approving American settlements. If, on the other hand, the lawyer fees are excluded from the settlement, the court will be unable to review them, making the fee level open to manipulation.

When the class lawyer acquires a personal interest in the outcome of the litigation, he or she can also be monitored and controlled by the client. Since the client represents the absent group of class members in this setting, this task can be entrusted to the latter in their capacity as possible objectors. However, not only is this considered to be costly and time consuming, but it is also doubtful whether individual class members have the capacity to discover possible collusion between defendants and class counsel.[62] It seems unfeasible for individual class members to exert optimal control. Therefore, it would be better to rely on governmental bodies and/or associations as qualified claimants to keep a watchful eye. Since they are more sophisticated interlocutors, they are in a much better position to stand up to the class counsel should a potential conflict or abuse situation arise.

5. THIRD PARTIES

5.1 Public funding and legal aid

Finally, third parties can fund and finance collective redress litigation. A first option is to provide public funding through a government fund.[63] The best

---

[59] Ianika Tzankova, 'Funding of Mass Disputes: Lessons from the Netherlands' (2012) 8 *JLEP* 549, 563.

[60] *Converium, Gerechtshof Amsterdam*, 17 January 2012, ECLI:NL:GHAMS:2012:BV1026.

[61] Stefaan Voet, 'Cultural Dimensions of Group Litigation: The Belgian Case' (2013) 41 *Ga J Int'l & Comp L* 433, 439.

[62] James D. Cox and Randall S. Thomas, 'Leaving Money on the Table: Do Institutional Investors Faill to File Claims in Securities Class Actions?' (2002) 80 *Wash U L Q* 855 and Alon Klement, 'Who Should Guard the Guardians? A New Approach for Monitoring Class Action Lawyers' (2002) 21 *Rev Litig* 25.

[63] Rachel Mulheron, *The Class Action in Common Law Legal Systems: A Comparative Perspective* (Hart Pub 2004) 454–59; and Jasmika Kalajdzic *et al*, 'Canada' (2009) 622 *Annals of the American Academy of Political and Social Science* 41.

example is the *Fonds d'aide aux actions collectives* in Quebec.[64] Under the auspices of the Ministry of Justice, the Fund helps to finance class action suits in the first instance or on appeal. Only natural persons and specific (statutory) associations can make an application, while (general) private associations cannot.[65] The Fund takes no particular criteria into account; it only verifies whether the class action would be initiated without its intervention. Where the Fund grants financial aid, it sets the terms of payment and reimbursement with the applicant and the applicant's counsel. If assistance is denied, the decision may be appealed before the *Tribunal administratif du Québec*. The latest annual report reveals that in 2018–19, the Fund received 30 new applications.[66] Of the 118 decisions made during that period, all applications were granted. Between 1 April 2018 and 31 March 2019, the Fund paid out C$3,556.109.96 in financial aid. In 2018–19, there were 560 class action proceedings pending in Quebec, of which 227 (41 per cent) were financed by the Fund. When a case that the Fund has financed succeeds, the Fund receives the legal costs paid by the defendant and a percentage of the damages awarded to the class.

A similar fund exists in Ontario: the Class Proceedings Fund.[67] It provides financial support to approved class action plaintiffs for legal disbursements and indemnifies plaintiffs for costs that may be awarded against them in proceedings it has funded. Just like the Quebec Fund, the Class Proceedings Fund is self-sustainable. It receives a levy amounting to 10 per cent of any awards or settlements issued in favour of the plaintiffs in proceedings it has funded, plus a return for any disbursements it has paid for. By the end of 2017, the Fund had received 246 applications and funded 146. The Fund provides funding for up to 10 per cent of the class actions commenced in Ontario.[68] According to the Law Foundation of Ontario, the cases that are funded by the Class Proceedings Fund 'provide access to justice, are in the public interest, and/or raise novel issues'.[69]

---

[64] www.faac.justice.gouv.qc.ca/ (last accessed 14 January 2020).

[65] Article 1049 of the Code of Civil Procedure of Quebec.

[66] *Fonds d'aide aux actions collectives*, *Rapport annuel 2018–2019*, file:///C:/Users/u0103885/AppData/Local/Microsoft/Windows/INetCache/IE/2DLO1OVW/906-20190925.pdf (last accessed 30 September 2020).

[67] https://lawfoundation.on.ca/for-lawyers-and-paralegals/class-proceedings-fund/ (last accessed 30 September 2020).

[68] The Law Foundation of Ontario, *Legal Help on the Frontlines. 2017 Annual Report*.

[69] *Ibid*, 30 with reference to *Edwards v the Law Society* [1994] 36 CPC (3d) 116: '[16]...Generally speaking, the committee would lean towards funding a case which raises issues of broad public importance or which is directed towards improving the situation of persons or groups who are historically disadvantaged in society. One of the central purposes of the Class Proceedings Fund is to provide access to justice for those

The 2019 Legislative Resolution of the European Parliament on the proposal for a Directive on representative actions explicitly permits Member States to allocate the revenues from fines for non-compliance with the final decisions on representative actions to a fund for financing representative actions.[70]

Another form of public funding is legal aid. Legal aid in a class action context is limited, since assistance is provided only to individual class members and not to entities, such as organizational plaintiffs. In EU Member States, legal aid is characterized by a free choice of legal counsel. Legal aid has been used in mass cases in the Netherlands and England and Wales. For example, in the *Dexia* case, the Dutch Legal Aid Board provided support to 4200 individual class members. Between 2002 and 2010, the Board spent about €3.3 million on lawyer fees.[71] Remarkably, about half of the *Dexia* class members who received legal aid opted out of the collective settlement, while the overall opt-out percentage was 10 per cent.[72]

Legal aid has also been provided in England and Wales.[73] One of the conditions for providing legal aid is that a case should have the potential to produce 'real benefits' for the public at large, in addition to benefits for the applicant. The Lord Chancellor's Guidance states that such benefits may include:

> potential financial benefit – this is usually the situation for most test cases or group actions or other cases seeking to establish a legal precedent. Success in such litigation will not usually guarantee compensation for those outside the litigation, who may still need to bring their own claims and prove their own issues on liability, causation and quantum.[74]

---

who would otherwise not be able to enforce their rights. It is in the public interest that the fund be administered so as to provide access to justice to those who otherwise would be unable to enforce their rights.'

[70] European Parliament legislative resolution of 26 March 2019 on the proposal for a directive of the European Parliament and of the Council on representative actions for the protection of the collective interests of consumers, and repealing Directive 2009/22/EC (COM(2018)0184 – C8-0149/2018 – 2018/0089(COD)), Article 14, 3 (at 92).

[71] Ianika Tzankova, 'Funding of Mass Disputes: Lessons from the Netherlands' (2012) 8 *JLEP* 549, 580.

[72] *Ibid.*

[73] Christopher Hodges, *Multi-party Actions* (Oxford University Press 2001) 177–202.

[74] Lord Chancellor's Guidance under Section 4 of the Legal Aid, Sentencing and Punishment of Offenders Act 2012, https://assets.publishing.service.gov.uk/government/uploads/system/uploads/attachment_data/file/885341/lord-chancellors-guidance-under-section_4-laspo_May_2020.pdf (last accessed 30 September 2020), 11.

The European Commission does not believe in public funding as a policy option, since it considers collective redress proceedings to be civil (private) proceedings, with deterrence merely a side effect:

> however, given that collective redress would be a procedure arising in the context of a civil dispute between two parties, even if one of them is composed of a number of claimants, and deterrence will be a side-effect of the proceedings, the Commission does not find it necessary to recommend direct support from public funds, since if the court finds that damage has been sustained, the party suffering that damage will obtain compensation from the losing party, including their legal costs.[75]

However, the 2018 Proposal of the European Commission for a Directive on Representative Actions states that Member States should take the necessary measures to ensure that procedural costs relating to representative actions do not constitute financial obstacles for qualified entities, such as limiting applicable court or administrative fees, granting them access to legal aid where necessary or providing them with public funding for this purpose.[76] The latter examples were abandoned in the 2019 Proposal of the Competitiveness Council for a Directive on Representative Actions.[77] Proposed Recital 39 clarifies:

> having regard to the fact that representative actions pursue a public interest by protecting the collective interests of consumers, Member States should maintain or aim to find means for the purpose of ensuring that qualified entities are not prevented from bringing representative actions under this Directive due to the costs involved with the procedures. These means *could* include limiting applicable court or administrative fees, granting the qualified entities access to legal aid where necessary or providing them with public funding for bringing representative actions as well as other means of support. *However, Member States should not be required to finance representative actions* (own emphasis added).

In times when public expenditure is under intense and increasing pressure, it is very uncertain whether European governments will provide resources for

---

[75] Communication 'Towards a European Horizontal Framework for Collective Redress', COM(2013) 401, 15.

[76] European Commission Proposal for a Directive of the European Parliament and of the Council on representative actions for the protection of the collective interests of consumers, and repealing Directive 2009/22/EC, COM/2018/184 final, Article 15.1.

[77] Competitiveness Council Proposal for a Directive of the European Parliament and of the Council on representative actions for the protection of the collective interests of consumers, and repealing Directive 2009/22/EC, 14600/19, Article 15.1: 'Member States shall take measures aiming to ensure that procedural costs related to representative actions do not become insurmountable obstacles preventing qualified entities from effectively exercising their right to seek the measures referred to in Article 5.'

a government collective redress fund or legal aid. If they are willing to do so, however, this public financial intervention will again work better with a governmental body or an association as qualified claimant than with an individual class member. As mentioned above,[78] the former does not pursue a personal interest, but rather the collective interests of the group. For a government fund or legal aid scheme, this can be a decisive and legitimizing factor in deciding whether to intervene. This intervention will have a public, and therefore more acceptable, dimension. On the other hand, legal aid will work only if the principles of party autonomy, the free choice of legal counsel and the right to determine one's litigation strategy are relaxed, or if the focus shifts to concentration:

> in the absence of a properly functioning concentration mechanism, the free choice of legal services provider that most EU Member States guarantee in mass disputes, weakens the finality of resolution and the effective use of public funds in mass claim disputes. In times of shrinking budgets for Legal Aid, it is difficult to find a convincing justification for spending disproportionate amounts of publicly available funds to resolve thousands of similar individual cases. Jointly resolving generic issues relevant for all members of the group is a more intelligent way to proceed, not only in terms of expected reductions in costs, but also in terms of improving the quality of legal representation and, therefore, outcomes. Furthermore, concentration reduces investment asymmetries between individual consumers and repeat corporate defendants. Moreover, reorganizing the Legal Aid system of mass dispute funding to facilitate concentration in dispute resolution and focus on generic, rather than individual issues, is expected to have advantages not only for individuals eligible for Legal Aid funding but for members of the group in general.[79]

5.2 Legal expenses insurance

In some cases, legal expenses insurance can fund class action litigation.[80] A distinction is made between before-the-event (BTE) and after-the-event (ATE) insurance.[81] BTE insurance is taken out by those wishing to protect themselves against potential litigation costs that could be incurred following

---

[78] See *supra* section 3.3.

[79] Ianika Tzankova, 'Funding of Mass Disputes: Lessons from the Netherlands' (2012) 8 *JLEP* 549, 584.

[80] Sean A. Smith, 'Too Much Risk: The Impact of Class Action Lawsuits on Claims Made Insurance Policies' (2009) 74 *Mo L Rev* 1171.

[81] Marco de Morpurgo, 'A Comparative Legal and Economic Approach to Third-Party Litigation Funding' (2011) 19 *Cardozo J Int'l & Comp L* 343, 353; and Francis Regan, 'The Swedish Legal Services Policy Remix: The Shift from Public Legal Aid to Private Legal Expense Insurance' (2003) 30 *J Law Soc* 49, 50, fn 4 (describing the two basic forms of legal expenses insurance: before the event and after the event).

a usually hypothetical future event. BTE insurance is generally paid on an annual basis to an insurance company. ATE insurance is taken out after an event to insure the policyholder against disbursements, as well as any costs should he or she lose the case. The focus in this context is on the instruction of a qualified lawyer by a legal expenses insurer when an insurance claim occurs. Another market is the 'in-kind' policy, where legal services are provided by in-house lawyers of the insurer. Legal expenses insurance in Europe is regulated by Directive 2009/138/EC of 25 November 2009 on the taking-up and pursuit of the business of Insurance and Reinsurance (the Solvency II Directive).[82] The Solvency II Directive lays down a series of requirements on fitness and propriety for managers of insurance and reinsurance undertakings, and responsible persons of independent control functions.

As with legal aid, in its present form, this funding mechanism provides assistance only to individual class members with legal expenses insurance. It also adheres to the principle of free choice of legal counsel. The Court of Justice of the European Union (CJEU) has ruled that where a large number of insured persons suffer a loss as a result of the same event, a legal expenses insurer cannot reserve the right to select the legal representative of all the insured persons concerned.[83] According to the CJEU, European law guarantees the policyholder the right to choose his or her own lawyer, even in a group action where several parties wish to pursue a claim against the same defendant. The policyholder has the right to instruct a legal representative of his or her choosing from the moment that he or she has a right to claim under the policy. That right is not limited to cases where proceedings have commenced, but exists from the time the potential claim arises for which the claimant has valid cover. This decision of the CJEU implies that legal expenses insurers cannot insist that the insured be represented by a class representative on the insurer's

---

[82] [2009] OJ L335/1. This Directive repealed Directive 87/344/EEC of 22 June 1987 on the coordination of laws, regulations and administrative provisions relating to legal expenses insurance. Articles 198 to 205 deal with legal expenses insurance.

[83] Case C–199/08 *Eschig v UNIQA Sachversicherung*, AG [2009] ECR 1-08295. See Catherine Paris, '*La Cour de justice réaffirme le droit de l'assuré en protection juridique de choisir librement son avocat*' (2010) 16 *JT* 272; Jason Rowley, 'Eschig v UNIQA Sachversicherung AG (C-199/08): Legal Expenses Insurance – Legal Expenses Insurance Regulations 1990' (2010) 1 *J Pers Inj Law* C32; Jules Stuyck, '*Assurance-protection juridique, action de groupe et libre choix de l'avocat*' (2010) 2 *Recueil Le Dal*loz 100 ; and Philip Woolfson, '*Assurance-protection juridique et libre choix de l'avocat: une victoire à la Pyrrhus pour le consommateur?*' (2009–10) 3 *Rev Aff Eur* 605. The case concerned an interpretation of old Article 4(1)(a) of Directive 87/344/EEC of 22 June 1987.

panel.[84] As with the previous funding mechanism, legal aid, the principles of party autonomy and the right to freely choose legal counsel thus have a negative impact on the funding of mass cases.

According to Tzankova, this European case law relates only to situations where the decision to hire an external lawyer has already been taken by the insurer. It does not apply to 'in-kind' policies, where the provider has decided to handle the case or where the proceedings have already been commenced by an in-house legal adviser who is not a qualified lawyer. At least according to Dutch law, the policyholder is restricted in his or her free choice prior to proceedings or in the context of collective settlement negotiations, allowing the legal expenses insurer to facilitate the concentration of representation to one or a limited number of lawyers.[85] In other institutional settings – such as in Germany, where most disputes are resolved through litigation and lawyers have a monopoly – this European case law would cause a different litigation funding dynamic.[86]

If the qualified claimant is an association, the insurer of the association will not cover the legal expenses of the collective redress action it initiates, for the simple reason that the association (ie, the policyholder) does not suffer personal losses that are covered. It acts on behalf of (unknown) victims who do not have a contractual relationship with the association's insurer and whose damages are not covered. When a class member requests the intervention of his or her own insurer, it will cover only the legal expenses of that member. For example, in the Dutch *Dexia* case, some legal expenses insurers reimbursed the €45 contribution that some of their policyholders had paid to the representing consumer association (*Consumentenbond*).[87] In other words, the success of legal expenses insurance in mass cases will depend on the number of class members that have such insurance, and on whether the legal infrastructure of the national legal system in question facilitates the concentration of measures through legal expenses insurance.[88]

5.3 Third-party litigation funding

5.3.1 Rise of third-party litigation funding

A new kind of funding that has come to the fore – both within and outside the context of collective redress, and especially in legal systems without con-

---

[84] Ianika Tzankova, 'Funding of Mass Disputes: Lessons from the Netherlands' (2012) 8 *JLEP* 549, 573.

[85] *Ibid*, 585.

[86] *Ibid*, 586–87.

[87] *Ibid*, 581. See *supra* section 3.3.

[88] *Ibid*, 583.

tingency fees – is (ATE) third-party litigation funding (TPLF).[89] Third-party funders[90] are private funders that enter into an agreement with one or more potential litigants. Funders usually assess the following criteria: (1) the chances of success of the case (including the likelihood of a settlement); (2) the estimate of the lawyer fees and the costs that the proceedings will entail; and (3) the financial solvency of the defendant. The agreement provides that the funder will meet some or all of the legal fees incurred by the law firm conducting the action; meet some or all of the out-of-pocket expenses incurred in the litigation; indemnify the funded party with respect to any cost orders made against that party if the litigation is unsuccessful; and pay any amount required to be provided by way of security for costs. In return, the funder will receive a percentage of the amount recovered by the persons or entities that have entered into a funding agreement in the event that they are successful in the litigation by way of either settlement or judgment. The percentage is usually in the range of 25 to 40 per cent, depending on the time taken and/or whether the case is appealed.[91]

---

[89] Marco de Morpurgo, 'A Comparative Legal and Economic Approach to Third-Party Litigation Funding' (2011) 19 *Cardozo J Int'l & Comp L* 343, 352; Gregory L. Fowler, Mark Shelley and Silvia Kim, 'Emerging Trends in International Litigation: Class Actions, Litigation Funding and Punitive Damages' (2009) 3 *Dispute Resolution International* 101; Deborah R. Hensler, 'The Future of Mass Litigation: Global Class Actions and Third-Party Litigation Funding' (2011) 79 *Geo Wash L Rev* 306; Jasminka Kalajdzic, Peter Cashman and Alana Longmoore, 'Justice for Profit: A Comparative Analysis of Australian, Canadian and U.S. Third Party Litigation Funding' (2013) 61 *Am J Comp L* 93; Michael Legg and Louisa Travers, 'Necessity is the Mother of Invention: The Adoption of Third-Party Litigation Funding and the Closed Class in Australian Class Actions' (2009) 38 *CLWR* 245; Jason Lyon, 'Revolution in Progress: Third-Party Funding of American Litigation' (2010) 58 *UCLA L Rev* 571; Rachel Mulheron and Peter Cashman, 'Third Party Funding: A Changing Landscape' (2008) 27 *CJQ* 312; Bernard Murphy and Camille Cameron, 'Access to Justice and the Evolution of Class Action Litigation in Australia' (2006) 30 *MULR* 434; Willem H. van Boom, 'Financing Civil Litigation by the European Insurance Industry' in Mark Tuil and Louis Visscher (eds), *New Trends in Financing Civil Litigation in Europe: A Legal Empirical and Economic Analysis* (Edward Elgar Publishing 2010) 99–104; and Willem H. van Boom (ed), *Litigation, Costs, Funding and Behaviour. Implications for the Law* (Routledge 2017). See also Gian Marco Solas, *Third Party Funding. Law, Economics and Policy* (Cambridge University Press 2019); and Ilja Tillema, *Entrepreneurial Mass Litigation. Balancing the Building Blocks* (Eleven International Pub 2019).

[90] For example, Juridica Capital, Burford Capital, Rembrandt IP Management, Coller IP Management, Counsel Financial, IMF, Allianz Prozess Finanz and IM Litigation Funding. The most frequent players are incorporated companies, listed on a stock exchange, obtaining funds from debt and equity sources.

[91] Jasminka Kalajdzic, Peter Cashman and Alana Longmoore, 'Justice for Profit: A Comparative Analysis of Australian, Canadian and U.S. Third Party Litigation Funding' (2013) 61 *Am J Comp L* 93, 100.

The TPLF industry has primarily emerged in common law jurisdictions. In the United States, TPLF has been used in low-value litigation, such as car accident and personal injury cases, but is gradually shifting to complex commercial litigation.[92] Since class actions in the United States are financed by lawyers on a contingency fee basis, private funders have not penetrated the US class action market.[93] According to Hensler:

> the entrance of third-party litigation funders into the US legal marketplace (firms that we would expect to contract with class action lawyers rather than class members) might increase the number of law firms willing to prosecute class actions, increase competition among firms for class counsel appointments, and increase investment by class counsel in pre-trial development of facts and law. The results might include increased numbers of class actions and higher-value settlements.[94]

Nevertheless, Marcus notes that some pressing legislative efforts have been made over the last years, mainly regarding the disclosure of TPLF.[95]

In England and Wales,[96] Lord Justice Jackson endorsed TPLF for collective litigation, along with contingency fees.[97] In November 2011, the Civil Justice Council published the Code of Conduct for Litigation Funders. The Association of Litigation Funders was charged with administering self-regulation of the

---

[92] Deborah R. Hensler, 'The Future of Mass Litigation: Global Class Actions and Third-Party Litigation Funding' (2011) 79 *Geo Wash L Rev* 306, 320.

[93] Jasminka Kalajdzic, Peter Cashman and Alana Longmoore, 'Justice for Profit: A Comparative Analysis of Australian, Canadian and U.S. Third Party Litigation Funding' (2013) 61 *Am J Comp L* 93, 127. See also Steven Garber, *Alternative Litigation Financing in the United States. Issues, Known, and Unknowns* (Rand Corporation 2010), https://www.rand.org/pubs/occasional_papers/OP306.html (last accessed 30 September 2020). Class actions in the United States are mainly funded by lawyers on a contingent fee basis.

[94] Deborah R. Hensler, 'The Future of Mass Litigation: Global Class Actions and Third-Party Litigation Funding' (2011) 79 *Geo Wash L Rev* 306, 322–23.

[95] Richard Marcus, 'Treading Water? Current Procedural Issues in America' (2018) 23 *ZZPInt* 183, 199–201 (referring to an amendment in that sense in the Litigation Funding Transparancy Act of 2019 and a proposal from the US Chamber Institute of Legal Reform calling for the addition to Rule 26(a)(1)(1) US Federal Rules of Civil Procedure of an additional disclosure requirement).

[96] For an overview, see Ilja Tillema, *Entrepreneurial Mass Litigation. Balancing the Building Blocks* (Eleven International Pub 2019) 195–238.

[97] Lord Justice Jackson, *Review of Civil Litigation Costs: Final Report*, December 2009, https://www.judiciary.uk/wp-content/uploads/JCO/Documents/Reports/jackson-final-report-140110.pdf (last accessed 30 September 2020), 334–35. The report also recommended experimentation with a public financing scheme funded by a tax against successful class actions, modelled after the Ontario Class Proceedings Fund (*ibid*, 131).

industry in line with the Code.[98] The Code sets out standards to be observed by all funders that are members of the Association of Litigation Funders of England and Wales. It largely focuses on capital adequacy, the withdrawal of funding and control over the litigation:

- Capital adequacy of funders: The Code requires funders to maintain adequate financial resources at all times in order to meet their obligations to fund all of the disputes they have agreed to fund, and to cover aggregate funding liabilities under all of their funding agreements for a minimum period of 36 months.
- Termination and approval of settlements: The Code provides that funders must behave reasonably and may withdraw from funding only in specific circumstances. Where there is a dispute about termination or settlement, a binding opinion must be obtained from an independent Queen's Counsel, who has been either instructed jointly or appointed by the Bar Council.
- Control: Under the Code, funders are prevented from taking control of litigation or settlement negotiations and from causing the litigant's lawyers to act in breach of their professional duties. This is in line with the practice, in England and Wales, of keeping the roles of funders, litigants and their lawyers separate. Because of their interest in the litigation, funders may ask to be kept informed of the progress of the case. Some funders may also have considerable litigation experience that could benefit the litigant and its legal team.

However, recent case law in England and Wales could (negatively) impact on future cases. In 2015, in *Arkin v Borchard Lines Ltd & Ors*, the English Court of Appeal held that a commercial litigation funder's liability for adverse costs is limited to the equivalent of the funding provided.[99] This so-called 'Arkin cap' was struck down in 2019 by the High Court of Justice. In *Davey v Money & Anor*,[100] the court refused to mechanically apply the 'Arkin cap', ruling

---

[98] https://lawfoundation.on.ca/for-lawyers-and-paralegals/class-proceedings-fund/ (last accessed 30 September 2020).

[99] *Arkin v Borchard Lines Ltd & Ors* [2005] 1 WLR 3055.

[100] *Davey v Money & Anor* [2019] EWHC 997. The 'Arkin cap' was criticized in 2009 by Jackon in his Review of Civil Litigation Costs Report: 'In my view, it is wrong in principle that a litigation funder, which stands to recover a share of damages in the event of success, should be able to escape part of the liability for costs in the event of defeat. This is unjust not only to the opposing party (who may be left with unrecovered costs) but also to the client (who may be exposed to costs liabilities which it cannot meet)' (Sir Rupert Jackson, *Review of Civil Litigation Costs: Final Report*, December 2009, https://www.judiciary.uk/wp-content/uploads/JCO/Documents/Reports/jackson-final-report-140110.pdf (last accessed 30 September 2020), 123.

that a commercial funder is liable for all of the defendants' indemnity costs incurred post the funding agreement in a successfully defended claim. The court stated that the 'Arkin cap' should be considered only as part of its overall discretion when considering how to achieve a just result.

In *Excalibur Ventures v Texas Keystone and others*, the English Court of Appeal held that a private funder is required to pay the defendants' costs on an indemnity basis even if the funder is not party to the misconduct that led to the award of indemnity costs. The court emphasized that third-party funders should seek to derive financial benefit from claims to the same extent as funded claimants, and that the 'derivative nature of a commercial funder's involvement should ordinarily lead to his being required to contribute to the costs' on the same basis as the funded claimant.[101]

In Australia, all large class actions are funded by private funders, of which Omni Bridgeway is the largest.[102] This is mainly explained by the Australian fee-shifting rules and the risk of adverse costs. If the class action is unsuccessful, class members have statutory immunity from paying any part of the costs and other expenses incurred by the winning party. These costs and expenses must be paid by the class representative. This creates a financial disincentive to take on this role. Therefore, and in the absence of contingency fees and lack of legal aid funding, TPLF has become the primary means of financing class action litigation in Australia.[103] However, TPLF in Australia has changed a key feature of the Australian class action rule. Because there is no certification phase that would result in an order binding the class members to the fee agreement between the representative plaintiff and the class lawyer or funder, third-party funders require all class members to sign individual litigation funding agreements entitling the funder to a share in the proceeds of the litigation if it is successful. This has converted the Australian opt-out scheme into an opt-in scheme. The use of so-called 'closed classes' was permitted by the Full Federal Court, given that the legislation expressly provides that a class action may be brought on behalf of 'some or all' of those affected.[104] According to

---

101 *Excalibur Ventures v Texas Keystone and others* [2016] EWCA Civ 1144.

102 See https://omnibridgeway.com/insights/blog/blog-posts/global/2019/11/13/imf-bentham-and-omni-bridgeway-complete-merger-becoming-a-global-leader-in-disputes-financing (last accessed 30 September 2020). The company is listed on the Australian Stock Exchange.

103 Jasminka Kalajdzic, Peter Cashman and Alana Longmoore, 'Justice for Profit: A Comparative Analysis of Australian, Canadian and U.S. Third Party Litigation Funding' (2013) 61 *Am J Comp L* 93, 100.

104 *Multiplex Funds Mgmt. Ltd. v P Dawson Nominees Pty Ltd.* [2007] 244 ALR 600. In 2009, the court held that litigation funding should be treated as a managed investment scheme (*Brookfield Multiplex Limited v International Litigation Funding Partners Pte Ltd* [2009] FCAFC 147). Since then, the Australian government has tried

some scholars, this undermines one of the key rationales for the class action regime: 'because "opt-in" classes restrict the ambit of beneficiaries to those who have agreed to enter into contractual litigation funding arrangements, access to justice by all those similarly affected has been curtailed.'[105]

TPLF as such is a purely contractual matter. Private third-party funders and the class members with whom they enter into an agreement are entirely free to agree on the conditions of the agreement, including the possible (partial) transfer of strategy-making power to the funder. However, some poignant problems can arise in a collective redress context. Besides the conversion of an opt-out scheme into an opt-in scheme, the triangular structure, as mentioned above,[106] turns into a complicated quadrangular structure. In addition to the qualified claimant, the class lawyer and the class members, a third-party funder enters into the equation. From the standpoint of the class lawyer, this can lead to ethical and fiduciary concerns about who the actual client is and whose instructions he or she must obey. Also, the agency problems in the relationship between the class lawyer and the class[107] are amplified with the presence of a third-party funder. Soft regulation,[108] judicial oversight or statutory provisions promoting transparency and good governance could tackle these problems.[109]

5.3.2 EU policy

In its Recommendation, the European Commission gives its support to TPLF as a policy option in collective redress litigation, but this support is condi-

---

to regulate TPLF. See Jasminka Kalajdzic, Peter Cashman and Alana Longmoore, 'Justice for Profit: A Comparative Analysis of Australian, Canadian and U.S. Third Party Litigation Funding' (2013) 61 *Am J Comp L* 93, 109–13; and Michael Legg, 'Reconciling Litigation Funding and the Opt Out Group Definition in Federal Court of Australia Class Actions. The Need for a Legislative Common Fund Approach' (2011) 30 *CJQ* 52.

105 Jasminka Kalajdzic, Peter Cashman and Alana Longmoore, 'Justice for Profit: A Comparative Analysis of Australian, Canadian and U.S. Third Party Litigation Funding' (2013) 61 *Am J Comp L* 93, 103, also pointing out other disadvantages of 'closed classes': satellite litigation, appeals, increase in transaction costs and barriers to settlement.

106 *Supra* Section 1.

107 *Supra* Section 4.

108 'Soft regulation should at least address (1) monitoring the conduct of third-party financiers prior to and in the course of the litigation, (2) the level of involvement of the financier with the litigation strategy, (3) the fiduciary duty of the class lawyer and (4) the award of the third-party litigation funder' (Ianika Tzankova, 'Funding of Mass Disputes: Lessons from the Netherlands' (2012) 8 *JLEP* 549, 588).

109 Rachel Mulheron and Peter Cashman, 'Third Party Funding: A Changing Landscape' (2008) 27 *CJQ* 312, 312.

tional. The Commission suggests a series of safeguards if TPLF is chosen as a funding option, in order to avoid abusive litigation.[110]

First of all, the 2013 Recommendation stipulates that the plaintiff – regardless of his or her capacity – should declare to the court at the outset of the proceedings the origin of the funds that he or she will use to support the legal action.[111] Although formulated in general terms, the provision clearly focuses on proceedings that are financed by third-party funders. This disclosure requirement was reiterated in Article 7.1 of the 2018 Proposal of the European Commission for a Directive on Representative Actions:

> the qualified entity seeking a redress order as referred in Article 6(1) shall declare at an early stage of the action the source of the funds used for its activity in general and the funds that it uses to support the action. It shall demonstrate that it has sufficient financial resources to represent the best interests of the consumers concerned and to meet any adverse costs should the action fail.[112]

The rationale behind this is, on the one hand, to ensure the necessary balance between access to justice and procedural safeguards against abusive litigation; and, on the other hand, to enable the courts to assess whether there may be a conflict of interest between the third-party funder and the qualified entity.[113]

However, the 2019 Proposal of the Competitiveness Council for a Directive on Representative Actions attenuated this requirement. First, the general provision of Article 7.1 was abandoned and replaced with a more specific provision.[114] In particular, the obligation to declare the source of the funds used to support the action was dropped. According to the 2019 Proposal, one of the criteria that qualified entities should meet in order to be designated to bring a cross-border representative action is that it 'disclose publicly by any appropriate means, in particular on its website, information. . . about the source of funding of its activity in general'.

---

[110] Communication 'Towards a European Horizontal Framework for Collective Redress', COM(2013) 401, 15.

[111] Recommendation (EU) 2013/396 on common principles for injunctive and compensatory collective redress mechanisms in the Member States concerning violations of rights granted under Union Law [2013] OJ L206/60, Article 14.

[112] European Commission Proposal for a Directive of the European Parliament and of the Council on representative actions for the protection of the collective interests of consumers, and repealing Directive 2009/22/EC, COM/2018/184 final, Article 7.1.

[113] *Ibid*, Recitals (4) and (25).

[114] Competitiveness Council Proposal for a Directive of the European Parliament and of the Council on representative actions for the protection of the collective interests of consumers, and repealing Directive 2009/22/EC, 14600/19, Article 4a(3)(cc).

Second, the Commission recommends that Member States ensure that, in cases where an action for collective redress is funded by a private third party, it is prohibited for the private third party:

(a) to seek to influence procedural decisions of the claimant party, including on settlements;
(b) to provide financing for a collective action against a defendant who is a competitor of the fund provider or against a defendant on whom the fund provider is dependent; and;
(c) to charge excessive interest on the funds provided.[115]

The 2019 Proposal of the Competitiveness Council for a Directive on Representative Actions states that one of the criteria that qualified entities should meet in order to be designated to bring a cross-border representative action is that:

> it is not influenced by persons, other than consumers, who have an economic interest in the bringing of any representative action, in particular by traders, including in case of funding by third parties, and it has procedures to prevent such an influence. ..[116]

Moreover, the Member States can set out additional rules on the basis of which they can reject the legal capacity of a qualified entity that wishes to bring a cross-border representative action if the action is funded by a third party that has an economic interest in the outcome of the action.[117]

---

[115] Recommendation (EU) 2013/396 on common principles for injunctive and compensatory collective redress mechanisms in the Member States concerning violations of rights granted under Union Law [2013] OJ L206/60, Article 16. This provision was largely copied in Article 7 of the European Commission Proposal for a Directive of the European Parliament and of the Council on representative actions for the protection of the collective interests of consumers, and repealing Directive 2009/22/EC, COM/2018/184 final.

[116] Competitiveness Council Proposal for a Directive of the European Parliament and of the Council on representative actions for the protection of the collective interests of consumers, and repealing Directive 2009/22/EC, 14600/19, Article 4a(3)(cb).

[117] *Ibid*, Article 4b(3) and Recital (11ea).

Finally, the Commission recommends that courts in the Member States be allowed to stay the proceedings where the financial resources are provided by a third party if:

(a) there is a conflict of interest between the third party and the claimant party and its members;
(b) the third party has insufficient resources in order to meet its financial commitments to the claimant party initiating the collective redress procedure; or;
(c) the claimant party has insufficient resources to meet any adverse costs should the collective redress procedure fail.[118]

In addition to these general principles of funding, the Commission proposes that Member States should ensure that in cases of private third-party funding of compensatory collective redress, it is prohibited to base remuneration given to or interest charged by the fund provider on the amount of the settlement reached or the compensation awarded, unless that funding arrangement is regulated by a public authority, to ensure the interests of the parties.[119]

According to the 2018 Implementation Report, the rules in the Recommendation pertaining to TPLF have not been implemented in any of the Member States.[120]

5.3.3 ERCP

ERCP Rule 237 deals with TPLF and collective redress proceedings. In line with the European policy as described above, TPLF is in principle allowed. Rule 237(1) states that a qualified claimant may use TPLF. Rule 237(2) refers to Rule 245, which is the general rule regarding TPLF (also applying outside the scope of collective redress proceedings): 'Rule 245 applies to any such third party funding agreement.'

However, Rule 237(2) adds that: 'A court may, however, require a qualified claimant to disclose the details of any such funding agreement relevant for the instance at stake to the court and, in so far as appropriate, to the parties.'

The comments clarify that details of the funding agreement are often confidential and should therefore be disclosed only upon the court's request, and should not be available to the public or the defendant.

---

[118] Recommendation (EU) 2013/396 on common principles for injunctive and compensatory collective redress mechanisms in the Member States concerning violations of rights granted under Union Law [2013] OJ L206/60, Article 15.

[119] *Ibid*, Article 32.

[120] Report on the implementation of the recommendation (COM(2018) 40 final) 9.

As mentioned above, this was echoed in Article 7.1 of the 2018 Proposal of the European Commission for a Directive on Representative Actions, but abandoned in the 2019 Proposal of the Competitiveness Council.[121]

Rule 245(1) – dealing with TPLF in general – states:

> a party who receives funding for the proceedings from a professional third-party funder or from a crowd-funder shall disclose this fact and the identity of the funder to the Court and the other party at the commencement of proceedings. The details of such a third-party funding arrangement are, however, not subject to this requirement.

This means that a qualified claimant whose collective redress procedure is funded by a third-party funder must disclose this fact and the identity of the funder to the court and the other party at the commencement of proceedings (Rule 245(1)). In principle, he or she need not disclose the details of the funding arrangement (Rule 245(1)), unless the court requires him or her to do so (Rule 237(2)).[122] Only where this is deemed appropriate can these details be disclosed to the other parties. In the context of collective redress proceedings, this seems to strike the right balance between the confidentiality of a funding arrangement on the one hand, and the risk of abuses and conflicts of interest on the other – which is exactly the purpose of the 2013 Recommendation.[123] The comments of Rule 245 clarify that the disclosure of the details of any funding agreement 'might be an adequate solution for collective redress cases; we believe that outside the scope of collective redress this internal information should simply be none of the opponent's and the court's business'.

Rules 245 (2)–(4) contain some other provisions regarding TPLF. However, these do not apply in collective redress proceedings. The comments state that 'the other aspects touched upon in the recommendation of 11 June 2013 and see Article 7 of the 11 April 2018 proposal should not be integrated into these rules'.

---

121 See *supra* Section 5.3.2.

122 Rule 245(5) states: 'except as provided in Rule 237, Rule 245 does not apply to proceedings on collective redress.' This is an unclear and confusing provision. Rule 237(2) trumps Rule 245(1). Both rules apply to collective redress proceedings, but the phrase of Rule 245(1) stating that the details are not disclosable can be overridden by the court in a collective redress proceeding.

123 *Supra* Section 5.3.2.

6. CONCLUSIONS[124]

Most European jurisdictions assume that collective redress procedures can and will be financed similar to individual procedures. As revealed above, this is simply not true. The funding and financing issue forms the core of any collective redress regime; it stands or falls with it. It therefore makes sense that in conceiving and designing such a regime, the funding question must be addressed ahead. All other procedural features rely on it. The standing question, for example, is inherently connected to this. If there is no solid regulatory framework regarding funding and financing, taking into account the various specificities of collective redress litigation, potential representatives will simply bring no cases.

The European legislature adopts another, less logical approach. Apart from reiterating the loser pays rule and (very) softly regulating TPLF, the Recommendation pays barely any attention to the funding and financing of collective redress proceedings. The idea appears to be aimed at addressing this issue *ex post* – that is, after the new Directive on Representative Actions has been introduced. The 2018 Implementation Report states that only in the future will the Commission:

> carry out further analysis for some aspects of the Recommendation which are key to preventing abuses and to ensuring safe use of collective redress mechanisms, such as regarding funding of collective actions, in order to get better a picture of the design and practical implementation.[125]

This is an unwise decision.

This view is echoed in the 2018 and 2019 Proposals of the European Commission and the Competitiveness Council for a Directive on Representative Actions. While in the Commission's Proposal, some guidance and safeguards were put forward – for example, regarding the disclosure requirement in Article 7 – these were as good as abandoned in the Competitiveness Council's Proposal.

Although the ERCP is silent on a lot of aspects of how to fund and finance a collective redress procedure efficiently, some clear and laudable choices were made: the loser pays rule; the fact that standing is given to established and ad hoc organizations and public bodies (as mentioned above, the standing and funding issues go hand in hand); the fact that the court can take into account

---

[124] Stefaan Voet, 'Europe's Collective Redress Conundrum' (2018) 61 *JYIL* 205, 221.

[125] Report on the implementation of the recommendation (COM(2018) 40 final) 20–21.

the payment of legal costs in approving a collective settlement; the allowance of TPLF; and a disclosure requirement similar to that in the 2018 Proposal of the European Commission for a Directive on Representative Actions. Hopefully, these Rules can serve as a beacon for future European and national legislative initiatives in light of the (probably) forthcoming new Directive on Representative Actions.

13. Cross-border issues

Michael Stürner

1. INTRODUCTION

From a historical perspective, collective actions are a comparatively new phenomenon in Europe. In recent decades, however, EU Member States have increasingly explored the extent to which the traditional binary focus of civil procedure should give way to a multi-party approach. When integrating collective elements, the core problem seems to lie in the clash between enhancing the efficiency of law enforcement and safeguarding fundamental procedural principles. The positions taken in this regard vary significantly. Hence, there is a broad spectrum of procedural diversity, which makes it difficult to keep track of the various models. To add further complexity, those proceedings often have a cross-border dimension. Indeed, the likelihood that collective proceedings will have cross-border implications increases with the number of participants.

Consequently, this chapter will focus on issues of jurisdiction of collective proceedings, and on the recognition and enforcement of the ensuing results. No attempt will be made to define the notion of collective proceedings.[1] Instead, a fairly broad approach will be adopted, which includes all types of proceedings with collective elements.[2] In a similar vein, Article 207 of the European Rules of Civil Procedure (ERCP) defines 'collective redress proceedings' as:

> proceedings brought by a qualified claimant on behalf of a group of persons who it is alleged are affected by an event giving rise to a mass harm, but where those persons, known as group members, are not parties to the action.

---

[1] See Astrid Stadler, '*Kollektiver Rechtsschutz und Revision der Brüssel I-Verordnung*' in Reinhold Geimer and Rolf A Schütze (eds), *Recht ohne Grenzen: Festschrift für Kaissis* (Otto Schmidt, 2012) 951, 960 *et seq*.

[2] Broadly, four different types of collective proceedings can be identified in the European Union: the representative model, the class action model, the test case model and the Dutch Act on Collective Settlement of Mass Claims (WCAM) model; see Alexia Pato, *Jurisdiction and Cross-Border Collective Redress. A European Private International Law Perspective* (Hart Publishing, 2019) 66 *et seq*.

I will not deal with the specificities of cross-border service of documents[3] or the taking of evidence in collective proceedings.[4]

2. JURISDICTION FOR COLLECTIVE REDRESS PROCEEDINGS

Any court seized may not proceed if its jurisdiction is not established. As this is an exercise of public authority, the determination of (international) jurisdiction also marks the limits of national sovereignty. Conflicts may arise if different states claim jurisdiction for the case at hand at the same time. Conversely, the functioning of collective proceedings is based on the premise that possibly all existing claims can be dealt with in one single forum. In EU law, the Brussels I *bis* Regulation contains rules on the allocation of cases to states and the priority in case of conflicts of jurisdiction. In this regard, the Brussels regime was designed with a view to individual proceedings only; there is no explicit mention of collective redress instruments and their particularities. This leads to a number of serious shortcomings in cross-border situations.

2.1 Applicability of the Brussels I *bis* Regulation

First, it seems clear that the Brussels I *bis* Regulation applies to all kinds of civil and commercial matters, including those with collective elements.[5] While some commentators argue that the exception in Article 1(2)(b) pertaining to 'bankruptcy, proceedings relating to the winding-up of insolvent companies or other legal persons, judicial arrangements, compositions *and analogous proceedings*' also excludes collective redress proceedings,[6] this seems flawed for a number of reasons. Such proceedings may indeed have collective elements, but they all presuppose a declaration of insolvency or similar. This involves, in the words of the Court of Justice of the European Union (CJEU) in *Gourdain/ Nadler*, 'the intervention of the courts culminating in the compulsory "liquidation des biens" in the interest of the general body of creditors of the person,

---

[3] ERCP Rules 68 to 81 apply in both domestic and cross-border cases. These rules are also applicable in collective redress proceedings (ERCP Part XI). Rules 82 to 86 provide only minor modifications for service of documents abroad.

[4] For details, see ERCP Rules 128 and 129, and Chapter 9 on the taking of evidence in collective redress proceedings.

[5] See Simon Horn, '*Grenzüberschreitende Musterfeststellungsklagen*' (2019) 118 *ZVglRWiss*, 315, 316; Astrid Stadler, '*Grenzüberschreitende Wirkung von Vergleichen und Urteilen im Musterfeststellungsverfahren*' [2020] *NJW*, 265, 268.

[6] See Herbert Woopen, '*Kollektiver Rechtsschutz*' [2018] IWRZ, 160, 163.

firm or company or at least in supervision by the courts'.[7] Clearly, this is by no means the aim of collective proceedings as referred to in this context.

Regarding some types of collective actions, however, the material scope of application of the Brussels I *bis* Regulation, which covers civil and commercial matters (Article 1(1) of the Brussels I *bis* Regulation), could give rise to difficulties. This pertains to associations vested with public authority or agencies similar to public authorities, such as the Competition and Markets Authority and the Financial Conduct Authority in the United Kingdom, or the Scandinavian ombudsman schemes. If such associations participate in the proceedings, mainly as claimants, the dispute may be considered not to be private in nature in the first place.[8] According to CJEU case law, the legal nature of the asserted claim, rather than the position of the parties, is primarily decisive.[9] If the claim is based on sovereign powers, it cannot be qualified as a civil law matter, as general private law rules deviate from those concerning claims based on sovereign powers.

However, the Brussels I *bis* Regulation remains applicable if a public authority does not claim such privileges. Consequently, it will be treated as a private party in the pertinent legal relationship, as may be the case regarding claims arising from the economic activity of public authorities.[10] On the other hand, actions brought by associations organized under private law and acting without sovereign power, such as the Austrian National Consumer Association, are usually qualified as civil or commercial matters.[11]

Rule 208 of the ERCP provides legal standing to individual group members, to ad hoc founded private entities and to organizations 'authorised, in accordance with national law, to bring collective redress proceedings and whose purpose has a direct relationship with the event giving rise to the mass harm'. These include public regulators, where authorized under national law, which will have the same power to bring a collective redress action as private entities or organizations. Thus, the Brussels I *bis* Regulation is applicable.

The qualification of a matter as civil remains correct if the beneficiary of the claim is the state – for example, in claims concerning the skimming off

---

7 Case C-133/78 *Gourdain v Nadler* EU:C:1979:49 no 735.

8 See Burkhard Hess, *Europäisches Zivilprozessrecht* [2010] Section 10 no 128 *et seq*; Astrid Stadler '*Grenzüberschreitender kollektive Rechtsschutz in Europa*', (2009) *Juristenzeitung* 121, 124 *et seq.*

9 Case C-29/76 *LTU v Eurocontrol* EU:C:1976:137 no 3, 5; Case C-343/*04 Land Oberösterreich v CEZ* [2006] ECR I-4558 no 22; Case C-292/05 *Lechouritou v Dimosio* EU:C:2007:102; Case C-406/09 *Realchemie Nederland BV v Bayer CropScience* AG EU:C:2011:668 no 41 *et seq.*

10 See Case C-172/91 *Sonntag v Waidmann* EU:C:1993:144 no 22.

11 Case C-167/00 *Verein für Konsumenteninformation v Karl Heinz Henkel* EU:C:2002:555.

of profits under Section 10 of the German Act against Unfair Competition (*Gesetz gegen unlauteren Wettbewerb*) or under Sections 33(2) and 34a of the German Competition Act (*Gesetz gegen Wettbewerbsbeschränkungen*).[12] In such cases, the state receives the illegal profit, rather than the association entitled to bring the action. The action is not punitive in nature; rather, it is a means of private law enforcement. For the same reason, the enforcement of contempt of court orders abroad pursuant to Section 890 of the German Code of Civil Procedure will fall within the scope of application of the Brussels I *bis* Regulation. While it is not the claimant that seeks an injunction, but rather the treasury of the forum state that is entitled to receive the fine, the CJEU has held in *Realchemie*[13] that such actions are considered to be civil or commercial matters.[14]

2.2 General jurisdiction

The main principle in the system of jurisdiction of the Brussels I *bis* Regulation, enshrined in Article 4(1), is the '*actor sequitur forum rei*' principle: that is, the claimant must sue at the defendant's forum. This rule aims to safeguard equality of arms. The claimant may decide when to sue and may determine the content of the action; the defendant, in turn, may need to answer the claim to avoid a default judgment and may even need to do so within a certain time-frame. Consequently, as a matter of procedural fairness, the defendant should in principle be allowed to defend the action at his or her place of residence. For collective proceedings, this means that all claims must be concentrated at the competent court in the state where the defendant has his or her domicile.[15]

This presupposes that the law of this state contains a suitable collective instrument in the first place. Moreover, it is for forum law to decide whether the claimant has standing to bring the action. As regards collective proceedings, many procedural systems allow only domestic associations to bring representative actions. Claims for the skimming off of unfair profits may only exceptionally be brought by foreign associations – for example, pursuant to Sections 10(1) and 8(3) no 3 of the German Act against Unfair Competition.[16] Foreign associations in particular have little incentive to bring such action, as the disgorged profits go to the federal treasury.

---

12 See Astrid Stadler (n 8) 124 *et seq.*

13 Case C-406/09 *Realchemie Nederland BV* v *Bayer CropScience* AG EU:C:2011: 668, NJW 2011, 3568 n 41 *et seq.*

14 BGHZ 185, 124; NJW 2010, 1883, 1884 *et seq.*

15 See Alexia Pato (n 2) 123 *et seq.*

16 See the references provided by Astrid Stadler (n 8), 126.

Group proceedings such as those recognized in Scandinavian jurisdictions, as well as under Spanish and Portuguese law, are also problematic. This is less true for opt-in models, where in general, foreigners affected by the claim can accede to the group litigation pending at the defendant's domicile. The situation is more complicated if the group proceedings adhere to the opt-out principle. In some jurisdictions – such as Portugal or, at the discretion of the courts, in Denmark – the collective action will switch to an opt-out model if the individual sum of damages in such actions is so low that the number of claimants will probably not be substantial.[17] The pertinent group as defined in the claim will also comprise claimants who are living abroad. Clearly, those claimants must be informed of the action and their procedural rights. It goes without saying that this process can prove to be difficult where some parties are domiciled abroad. Therefore, the court's discretion may be exercised in a way that restricts such proceedings to domestic parties. While this solution will not lead to the complete exclusion of foreign claimants at the defendant's forum – they can still bring individual actions for damages there – such a decision would severely curtail the procedural rights of foreign claimants.

The ERCP avoids this by conferring on the court discretion to decide whether collective redress proceedings should be based on an opt-in or an opt-out scheme (Rule 215). In any case, group members domiciled outside the forum state become part of the collective redress proceedings only based on an opt-in declaration (Rule 235).

2.3 Special heads of jurisdiction

Further to the general place of jurisdiction at the defendant's domicile, the Brussels I *bis* Regulation contains several special heads of jurisdiction. These may be of potential interest for claimants, particularly if collective redress is not available in the state where the defendant has his or her domicile.[18] Possible options include the special jurisdiction for torts according to Article 7(2) of the Brussels I *bis* Regulation; the special jurisdiction in contract according to Article 7(1) of the Brussels I *bis* Regulation; and the jurisdiction over consumer contracts according to Articles 17–19 of the Brussels I *bis* Regulation. At least in theory, jurisdiction for a collective action could also be based on the so-called *forum connexitatis* pursuant to Article 8(1) of the Brussels I *bis* Regulation.

17 See Astrid Stadler (n 8) 128 *et seq.*
18 See Alexia Pato (n 2) 127 *et seq.*

2.3.1 Jurisdiction for torts

The special jurisdiction for torts is of particular importance for collective proceedings. Pursuant to Article 7(2) of the Brussels I *bis* Regulation, jurisdiction lies with the courts at the place where the harmful event occurred. First, this refers to the relevant action that caused the harm. That place usually coincides with the liable party's domicile. Moreover, according to CJEU case law, Article 7(2) also includes the place where the damage occurred. Thus, jurisdiction rests with the courts of the place where the legal interests at stake were harmed.[19]

Under this head of jurisdiction, group proceedings can be brought for cases regarding cross-border product liability or violations of competition law even if the law applicable in the jurisdiction of the defendant's domicile does not recognize such a mechanism. For example, if breast implants made by a French manufacturer were purchased by consumers in Portugal who subsequently suffered harm as a result of the implants, group proceedings could be brought in Portugal. It is questionable whether all victims should be in a position to benefit from this forum and the type of action possible under the relevant procedural law. As only some of the victims were affected by the damage in this particular forum – in this case, Portugal – should all the foreign claimants be able to take advantage of such collective proceedings? At least from the tortfeasor's perspective, it would not seem justified to be subject to collective proceedings for the whole damage in a forum where only a fraction of the damage occurred. Some jurisdictions have introduced provisions which expressly stipulate that the opt-in possibility exists only for such claimants for whom international jurisdiction lies in the forum state.[20] In jurisdictions that do not have such provisions, the solution nevertheless must be the same: the Brussels regime requires that the conditions in Article 7(2) be met by all parties to the proceedings, irrespective of whether they are original claimants or join the proceedings through a declaration to opt in. Any other position would be viable only with the help of an extensive interpretation of Article 8(1) of the Brussels I *bis* Regulation, which will be analysed later.[21]

Article 7(2) of the Brussels I *bis* Regulation can also offer a forum for representative actions. The German Federal Court of Justice has held that the German courts have jurisdiction on this basis if a consumer association files an action for an injunction against a company domiciled in another Member State – in this case, a Latvian airline – because the company included unfair

---

19 Case C-21/76 *Bier BV v Mines de Potasse d'Alsace* EU:C:1976:166.
20 For references, see Astrid Stadler (n 8) 130.
21 See Section 2.3.4 below.

terms[22] in its terms and conditions.[23] However, by applying the CJEU's *Shevill* doctrine in this case, the court has jurisdiction to rule solely in respect of the harm caused in the state of the court seized.[24]

2.3.2 Jurisdiction in contract

Similar considerations apply *mutatis mutandis* to jurisdiction in contract according to Article 7(1) of the Brussels I *bis* Regulation. This head of jurisdiction applies, for example, if multiple violations of contractual stipulations have occurred to the detriment of capital investors.[25] However, jurisdiction arises only for such claimants in respect of whom the place of performance is situated in the prospective forum.

2.3.3 Jurisdiction over consumer contracts

In many cases, the jurisdiction over consumer contracts pursuant to Articles 17–19 of the Brussels I *bis* Regulation will apply. This head of jurisdiction takes precedence over the jurisdiction of the place of performance as spelled out in Article 17(1) of the Brussels I *bis* Regulation. If the trader directs his or her activities to the Member State of the consumer's domicile, this will give rise to a *forum actoris* to the benefit of the consumer pursuant to Article 18(2). This head of jurisdiction can be used only for claims arising from a contract between a consumer and a trader. Thus, if consumers residing in one Member State lodge a group action on the basis of Article 17 or 18 of the Brussels I *bis* Regulation in that state, other persons may join the action only if: (1) they are also consumers; and (2) they have their residence in that state. An assignment

---

22 A preventive action brought by a consumer protection organization for the purpose of preventing a trader from using terms considered to be unfair in contracts with private individuals is a matter relating to tort, delict or quasi-delict within the meaning of Article 7(2) of the Brussels I bis Regulation; see Case C-167/00 *Verein für Konsumenteninformation v Karl Heinz Henkel* EU:C:2002:555 no 40 *et seq.*

23 See *Bundesgerichtshof*, BGHZ 182, 24; on that decision, see Dietmar Baetge, '*Verbandsklagen im Europäischen Binnenmarkt und das nach den Rom-Verordnungen über Schuldverhältnisse anwendbare Recht*' [2011] ZEuP, 933; Astrid Stadler, '*Von den Tücken der grenzüberschreitenden Verbands-Unterlassungsklage, zugleich eine Besprechung von BGH, Urt. v. 09.07.2009*', Az: Xa ZR 19/08' [2010] VuR 83; Ansgar Staudinger and Paul Czaplinski, '*Anmerkung zur Entscheidung des Bundesgerichtshofes vom 09.07.2009, Xa ZR 19/08*' [2009] *NJW*, 3375. See also Kristin Kohler, *Die grenzüberschreitende Verbraucherverbandsklage nach dem Unterlassungsklagengesetz im Binnenmarkt* (Peter Lang, 2008).

24 In favour of an extension of the mosaic approach on all cases of unfair competition, see Jan Kropholler and Jan von Hein, *Europäisches Zivilprozessrecht* (9th edn) (Deutscher Fachverlag, 2011) Article 5 EuGVO no 85; Astrid Stadler (n 8) 128.

25 See Jan von Hein, '*Verstärkung des Kapitalanlegerschutzes: Das Europäische Zivilprozessrecht auf dem Prüfstand*' [2011] *EuZW*, 369.

of the claim to an assignee who has his or her domicile in the forum state does not help if the assignee is not a consumer, as he or she brings the action in the exercise of his or her commercial or professional activity.[26]

Another restriction exists with regard to representative actions: the jurisdiction over consumer contracts does not apply to consumer associations because, according to CJEU case law, they are not considered to be consumers.[27]

2.3.4 Pooling claims at the *forum connexitatis*

The restrictions on the special heads of jurisdictions of the Brussels I *bis* Regulation as described above beg the question of whether there are alternative ways to pool individual claims. One conceivable stepping stone may be seen in Article 8(1) of the Brussels I *bis* Regulation. Under this head of jurisdiction – the so-called *forum connexitatis* – it is possible to bring anchor claims: that is, claims which have such a close relationship to the action pending that the proceedings should be merged in order to avoid different outcomes as a result of separate proceedings. Article 8(1) applies only to cases in which various defendants have their residence in different Member States. However, looking at the cases concerned within the framework of collective interests, the plurality of potential participants is usually on the claimant's side. An analogous application of this head of jurisdiction is not viable, as the pertinent rule – being an exception to the general jurisdiction – must be interpreted in a restrictive manner.[28]

As a side note, Article 8(1) of the Brussels I *bis* Regulation has already been applied to collective proceedings. In the Netherlands, for example, there were proceedings regarding extra-judicial settlements concerning mass torts according to Articles 7:900 and following of the Dutch Civil Code (*Burgerlijk Wetboek)*.[29] In those proceedings, the Amsterdam Court of Appeal declared a settlement concluded between representatives of the victims and the defendant to be legally binding on the parties (*vaststellingsovereenkomst*). First, the applicability of the Brussels I *bis* Regulation to such a decision may be seen as problematic, as the parties to the settlement jointly submit the request for

---

26 Case C-89/91 *Shearson v TVB* EU:C:1993:15 no 14 *et seq.*

27 Case C-167/00 *Verein für Konsumenteninformation v Karl Heinz Henkel* EU:C:2002:555 no 33.

28 Case C-103/05 *Reisch Montage AG v Kiesel Baumaschinen Handels GmbH* EU:C:2006:471 no 23; Case C-98/06 *Freeport plc v Olle Arnoldsson* EU:C:2007:595 no 35.

29 On the WCAM proceedings, see Andreas Mom, *Kollektiver Rechtsschutz in den Niederlanden* (Mohr Siebeck, 2011) 311 *et seq*; Jan-Jaap Kuipers, 'Schemes of Arrangement and Voluntary Collective Redress: A Gap in the Brussels I Regulation' (2012) 8 *Journal of Private International Law* 225.

a court declaration. This does not fit neatly into the clear-cut dichotomy of claimants and defendants as set out in the Regulation.[30] From a functional perspective, the victims would assume the role of defendants, as the court declaration gives rise to the binding effect of the settlement on those persons who did not participate in the settlement procedure.[31] This point of view makes it plausible to apply Article 8(1) of the Brussels I *bis* Regulation. Consequently, jurisdiction lies with the Dutch courts if only one of the victims has his or her residence in the Netherlands.[32] However, this does not apply to consumer contracts, insurance and employment matters, as the specific rules at hand supersede Article 8.[33] Overall, apart from this particular case, the relevance of Article 8(1) to collective proceedings is currently marginal.

2.4 Party autonomy

It goes without saying that the principle of party autonomy remains unaffected by the Brussels I *bis* Regulation. It has sometimes been asked under what circumstances multiple claims can be pooled by way of assignment to one or more lead claimants, who then act as trustees in bringing the action.[34] Clearly, given the restrictions pertaining to special jurisdiction under the Brussels I *bis* Regulation described above – especially in relation to jurisdiction over consumer contracts – this 'surrogate collective action' offers protection only in very specific situations. Generally, when assigning the claim to the trustee, the favourable consumer forum will be stripped from the claim.[35] What remains is an agreement of jurisdiction according to Article 25 of the Brussels I *bis* Regulation[36] on the one hand, or entering an appearance of the defendant pursuant to Article 26 on the other. It seems likely that the tortfeasor may wish

---

[30] See Astrid Stadler (n 8) 125.

[31] Astrid Stadler (n 8) 125.

[32] See Andreas Mom (n 29) 380 *et seq*; in a similar vein, Astrid Stadler (n 8) 125 *et seq*; Astrid Stadler (n 1) 958 (n 35).

[33] See the references given by Jan Kropholler and Jan von Hein (n 24) Article 6 EuGVO no 3.

[34] See, for example, the German *EM.TV* case; see Jürgen Ellenberger, 'EM.TV' (2003) 9 EWiR 409; Burkhard Hess and Chrisoula Michailidou, '*Das Gesetz über Musterverfahren zu Schadensersatzklagen von Kapitalanlegern*' (2004) 30 ZIP 1381. On the test case proceedings, see Florian Jacoby, *Der Musterprozeßvertrag* (Mohr Siebeck, 2000).

[35] Case C-498/16 *Maximilian Schrems v Facebook Ireland Limited* EU:C:2018:37 no 45; Case C-89/91 *Shearson v TVB* EU:C:1993:15 no 14 *et seq*. See Michael Stürner and Christoph Wendelstein, '*Datenschutzrechtliche "Sammelklagen" im Zuständigkeitsregime der Brüssel Ia-VO*' (2018) *Juristenzeitung* 1083, 1090 *et seq*.

[36] Save for the exceptions provided by Article 25(4) of the Brussels I *bis* Regulation, which safeguards the interests of weaker parties as spelled out in Articles 15, 19 and 23;

to create a common forum for as many claimants as possible, to dispose of as many claims as possible at once, even though this forum is not at his or her seat.[37]

In conclusion, as the Brussels regime lacks an appropriate mechanism for the concentration of actions, collective proceedings can generally be initiated only at the general place of jurisdiction of the defendant or under agreements on jurisdiction or submission by the defendant.

2.5 Reform

When the Brussels I *bis* Regulation was revised, no efforts were made regarding collective proceedings. While the goal of the recast proposal published by the European Commission in December 2010[38] was to completely dispense with the exequatur procedure for decisions of courts in Member States, with the sole exception of an action for infringement of the right to a fair trial, such free circulation of judgments was not intended to apply to collective redress.[39] The rationale behind this dichotomy was the lack of mutual trust in the field of collective proceedings. At that time, the idea of a 'horizontal' European regulatory framework regarding collective redress, in which private international law and international procedural law issues alike would be regulated separately from the Brussels I framework, seemed not to be totally unrealistic. However, this separate framework has not yet materialized.

It is therefore unsurprising that the Commission Proposal concerning the revision of the Brussels I Regulation contained no rules on jurisdiction for collective proceedings. As under the current regime, it is generally possible to bring a collective action only at the defendant's domicile, some potential tortfeasors could be motivated to change their seat to a Member State in which collective proceedings are not recognized in order to escape potential actions against them.[40]

It has been suggested that the scope of application of Article 8(1) of the Brussels I *bis* Regulation should be extended to provide for a *forum connex-*

---

or if the courts whose jurisdiction such agreements purport to exclude have exclusive jurisdiction by virtue of Article 24.

[37] Astrid Stadler (n 8) 130 *et seq.*

[38] Proposal for a Regulation of the European Parliament and of the Council on jurisdiction and the recognition and enforcement of judgments in civil and commercial matters (Recast), COM(2010) 748 final.

[39] See Astrid Stadler (n 1) 951.

[40] See the cases of so-called 'insolvency tourism': a number of German traders have moved their seat to the United Kingdom at a pre-insolvency stage in order to benefit from the arguably more lenient insolvency regime there; see, with examples, Michael Stürner, '*Insolvenztourismus und Einzelgläubigeranfechtung*' (2017) 3 *KTS* 291.

itatis for collective actions.[41] Such a rule would have to balance the parties' interests: the head of jurisdiction should not be too far reaching in order to avoid forum shopping by the injured party. Jurisdiction could lie at the centre of the relevant harm.[42]

For representative actions, which are the most common type of collective action in EU Member States, it has been suggested that a special head of jurisdiction at the seat of the representative entity be introduced.[43] Such a forum would serve as a major incentive to bring collective proceedings.

For each area, it should be carefully considered to what extent deviation from the regular forum at the defendant's domicile is justified. Such an exception may apply to European collective proceedings rather than to purely domestic ones, as the European procedural framework prevents abusive forum shopping regardless of which court is competent. Equally, and especially if European collective proceedings were to be introduced, it would no longer be vital to establish a special head of jurisdiction for national collective proceedings.

3. RECOGNITION AND ENFORCEMENT OF COLLECTIVE SETTLEMENTS AND JUDGMENTS GIVEN IN COLLECTIVE REDRESS PROCEEDINGS

3.1 General considerations

If the losing party does not honour the enforceable claim, the aggrieved party may seek to enforce the judgment. This process may have a cross-border character – for example, if the defendant has financial assets in a state other than the forum state, or if a special head of jurisdiction is applicable, so that it is necessary to enforce the decision at the defendant's domicile.

When enforcing the judgments of courts of EU Member States, both the Brussels I *bis* Regulation and the Regulation Creating a European Enforcement Order for Uncontested Claims (EEO Regulation) may be applicable.[44] The

---

[41] See, for cartel damages claims, Jochen Bernhard, *Kartellrechtlicher Individualschutz durch Sammelklagen* (Mohr Siebeck 2010) 286 *et seq*; see also Burkhard Hess, 'Cross-border Collective Litigation and the Regulation Brussels I' [2010] IPRax 116, 118 *et seq*.

[42] A parallel can be drawn to actions pertaining to violations of personality rights over the Internet; see Case C-509/09 and Case C-161/10 *eDate Advertising GmbH v X and Olivier Martinez, Robert Martinez v MGN Limited* EU:C:2011:685, EuZw 2011, 962.

[43] See Alexia Pato (n 2) 223 *et seq*.

[44] See Astrid Stadler (n 8) 131 *et seq*.

difference between these enforcement mechanisms is that the EEO Regulation is applicable only to uncontested pecuniary claims; whereas the Brussels I *bis* Regulation covers all civil and commercial matters. According to both Regulations, enforcement in every Member State (except Denmark) is possible without further exequatur proceedings.[45] The creditor can choose between the Brussels I *bis* Regulation and the EEO Regulation.[46] This choice is also available if the requirements under the EEO Regulation are met.[47] However, as a general rule, this will not be the case within the framework of collective actions, as will be shown below.

3.2 Enforcement based on the Brussels I *bis* Regulation

Normally, the judgment creditor will proceed with enforcement according to the Brussels I *bis* Regulation. Pursuant to Article 2, lit a of the Regulation, only judgments rendered by courts of Member States can be enforced. This makes it difficult to enforce collective settlements under Dutch law, as the court only confirms them, but does not issue them. At the outset, Dutch law does not attach enforceability to the confirmation, so cross-border enforcement first requires an action for specific performance of the settlement.[48] Pursuant to Article 59 of the Regulation, a court settlement shall be enforced in other Member States only if it is enforceable in the Member State of origin.[49]

As regards collective proceedings that follow the opt-out model, the public policy exception of the state of enforcement (Article 45(1)(a) Brussels I *bis* Regulation) may come into play. This could prevent the recognition of such judgments where the law of the enforcement state does not recognize such collective proceedings because the rights of the group members are severely cur-

---

[45] See Michael Stürner, '*Die Vollstreckung aus ausländischen Zivilurteilen nach der Brüssel Ia-VO*' (2016) 11 *DGVZ* 215.

[46] Article 27 EEO Regulation. See Michael Stürner, 'Art. 27 EuVTVO' in Johann Kindl, Caroline Meller-Hannich and Hans-Joachim Wolf (eds), *Gesamtes Recht der Zwangsvollstreckung* (3rd edn) (Nomos 2015) para 2 *et seq*.

[47] Peter Mankowski, '*Wie viel Bedeutung verliert die EuGVVO durch den Europäischen Vollstreckungstitel?*' in Dietmar Baetge, Jan von Hein and Michael von Hinden (eds), *Die richtige Ordnung: Festschrift für Kropholler* (Mohr Siebeck 2008) 829, 833 *et seq*. See also BGH WM 2010, 433.

[48] See Andreas Mom (n 29) 370 *et seq*. However, the debtor will most probably honour the agreement on a voluntary basis; see Jan-Jaap Kuipers, 'Schemes of Arrangement and Voluntary Collective Redress: A Gap in the Brussels I Regulation' (2012) 8 *Journal of Private International Law* 225.

[49] See Astrid Stadler (n 5) 265.

tailed.[50] Likewise, there might be a violation of public policy if the collective proceedings end up with a decision that orders the defendant to pay punitive damages, such as are available under Greek law.[51]

3.3 Enforcement based on the EEO Regulation

Such difficulties would not exist from the outset if the party chose to enforce the decision based on the EEO Regulation. However, this is possible only if the claim was uncontested. Again, the Dutch collective settlements spring to mind. According to Article 3(1)(a) of the EEO Regulation, a claim shall be regarded as uncontested if the debtor has expressly agreed to it by means of a settlement which has been approved by a court or concluded before a court in the course of proceedings. However, such settlement will not be agreed upon during the course of the proceedings. Moreover, the EEO Regulation requires that all parties concerned have expressly accepted the settlement agreement – but this element is missing in opt-out proceedings. An analogy thus cannot be drawn with the passively uncontested claims which fall under the EEO Regulation, even though the defendant's consent is missing, because in this constellation it is ensured that information regarding both the action and its content has previously been formally delivered.[52]

3.4 Reform

With regard to the recognition and enforcement of decisions, according to the law as it stands, the main problems concern the public policy exception regarding opt-out proceedings. In a future recast of the Brussels I *bis* Regulation, a compromise will have to be found as to the types of collective actions for which recognition and enforcement should be possible. An enumeration of individual proceedings based on the model of the European Insolvency Regulation seems conceivable and would result in sufficient legal clarity. On the other hand, however, it could lead to petrification, as it would be cumbersome to revise this list. If European collective proceedings are to be established, it would be advisable to abolish the public policy exception following the example of the European Small Claims Regulation, but only under the

---

[50] See Astrid Stadler (n 8) 131 *et seq.* More openly, Axel Halfmeier, 'Recognition of a WCAM settlement in Germany' (2012) 2 *NIPR* 176; Axel Halfmeier and Philip Wimalasena, '*Rechtsstaatliche Anforderungen an Opt-out-Sammelverfahren: Anerkennung ausländischer Titel und rechtspolitischer Gestaltungsspielraum*' (2012) 13 *Juristenzeitung* 649, who argue against a violation of public policy.

[51] See Astrid Stadler (n 1) 957.

[52] Astrid Stadler (n 1) 962 *et seq.*

condition that the defendant's rights are safeguarded. As a matter of principle, this will be the case only for opt-in mechanisms.[53]

[53] See the list of procedural safeguards that need to be put in place, so as to guarantee fair court proceedings, in the Resolution of the European Parliament of 2 February 2012, at no 20 ('Towards a Coherent European Approach to Collective Redress', 2011/2089(INI)).

14. ERCP collective redress and the wider world

Astrid Stadler, Emmanuel Jeuland, Vincent Smith, Richard Marcus, Peter Cashman, Choong-soo Han and Hermes Zaneti Jr

1. FUTURE PROSPECTS FOR COLLECTIVE REDRESS[1]

1.1 Jurisdiction in European cross-border collective redress

The European Rules of Civil Procedure (ERCP) aim to provide a model for European countries to review and, where appropriate, amend their civil procedure codes. This is intended to enhance the consistency and effectiveness of civil and commercial law enforcement across the European legal landscape. However, the impact of the ERCP on national legislation remains to be seen.

A decade ago, the inclusion of a chapter in the ERCP on collective redress might have been controversial. At the time, fears of 'US-style' class action litigation dominated the debate on civil and commercial procedure in this area. But times change, and the need for procedures that enable redress for mass harms is now well recognized – albeit not (as yet) always well embedded in European civil procedure codes. Nevertheless, at the EU level, a harmonized overarching framework for collective actions seems readily achievable in the near future.[2]

Despite all previous efforts by the European Commission to implement a binding procedural instrument on collective redress, an important gap remains in private international law, as the Commission has not dared to touch on the Brussels I *bis* Regulation or the Rome Regulations in its collective

---

[1] By the editorial team.

[2] In particular, through the European Commission's proposal for a Directive on representative actions for the protection of the collective interests of consumers, 11 April 2018, 2018/0089 COD.

redress instruments.[3] In particular, collective actions will have to fit within the jurisdictional system of the Brussels I *bis* Regulation, even though the regulation does not provide a particular jurisdictional rule for mass litigation. However, the mere fact that all Member States must implement at least one harmonized instrument, as sketched by a new (proposed) Directive, will reduce the incentives and the need for forum shopping by qualified claimants in collective redress actions. Nevertheless, the Directive that may be enacted will aim only at a minimum harmonization of such procedural tools.

Member States that provide more effective instruments of collective redress in national law may therefore still be a preferred forum for litigation in case of mass harm events. Forum shopping cannot be completely avoided in cross-border collective redress situations, but there will be constraints due to the characteristic features of mass litigation, as discussed in the previous chapter.[4] In particular, the consolidation of all claims in a Member State in which only some group members have suffered a loss would not appear to be possible.

1.2 Consolidation of parallel collective actions from different Member States?

The *Volkswagen Dieselgate* case is a good example of parallel mass litigation in several Member States. Volkswagen AG is a defendant in mass tort actions in numerous Member States. However, the mechanism in Article 30 of the Brussels I *bis* Regulation which allows courts (other than the court first seized) to stay proceedings where related actions are pending in courts of different Member States was not applied in practice. Although the question of whether Volkswagen is liable for damages under tort law is at the 'core' of all these actions, and therefore the actions are 'related' in the sense of Article 30, the applicable tort law varies depending on the country in which the damage

---

3 Due to the existence of a well-established European system of international jurisdiction, jurisdiction was no part of the ERCP. See Regulation EU 1215/12 [2012] OJEU L 351/1.

4 In the United States, the Supreme Court decided that non-resident class members can be part of a class action, even if they lack minimum contacts to the forum state; *Phillips Petroleum Co. v Shutts*, 472 US 797, 808–12 (1985). The court pointed out that absent class members need less protection with respect to the due process clause than defendants. In recent years, the court has favoured a stricter interpretation of personal jurisdiction in class action cases – in particular, a direct link between the forum and the claims; see *Bristol-Myers Squibb Co. v Superior Court*, 137 S Ct 1773 (2017).

occurred (Article 4 of the Rome II Regulation). Therefore, courts hearing collective actions against Volkswagen apply different sets of tort rules.[5]

Nevertheless, there is a certain risk of contradictory judgments when it comes to questions of fact. All courts seized must decide more or less the same factual issues: did the board of directors of Volkswagen know about the use of the cheat device and when did they learn of it? Even with respect to legal issues, there are common question when it comes to deciding whether the use of the cheat software in diesel cars violated relevant directly applicable EU regulations. Similar situations will arise quite often in cross-border mass cases.

As discussed in Professor Marcus's contribution in the next section of this chapter, in the United States, multi-district litigation (MDL) is the prevailing mechanism for aggregation mass torts.[6] In the *Volkswagen* case, 63 class actions pending in federal US courts by the end of 2015 were consolidated before Justice Charles Breyer in the Federal District Court for the Northern District of California. As is well-known, all of these class actions were settled within less than a year.[7]

In its decision to transfer actions to the California court, the MDL panel noted:

> Since the filing of the motion, hundreds of cases, mostly class actions, have been filed on behalf of, inter alia, dealers, owners and lessees of affected vehicles. Centralization will eliminate duplicative discovery, avoid inconsistent pretrial

---

[5] Moreover, Article 30 of the Brussels I *bis* Regulation provides courts with discretion to decide whether to stay proceedings. By contrast, Article 29 of the Brussels I *bis* Regulation requires a mandatory stay of proceedings, but its scope of application is much narrower. It applies only if proceedings involve 'the same cause of action' and 'the same parties'. Collective actions pending in several Member States will often be filed by different qualified entities and therefore only Article 30 Brussels I *bis* Regulation will apply.

[6] Scott Dodson, 'Personal Jurisdiction and Aggregation', 113 *Northwestern Univ L Rec* 1, 14. According to Andrew D. Bradt and Theodore Rave, 'Aggregation of Defendants' Term: Bistol-Myers Squibb and the Federalization of Mass-Tort Litigation', 59 *Boston College L Rev*, 1251, 1254 (2018), approximately one-third of the federal docket consists of MDL cases; see also Andrew Bradt, 'The Long Arm of Multidistrict Litigation', 59 *William & Mary L Rev* 1165, 1169 (2018). See 28 USC § 1407, which allows consolidating actions before one court.

[7] After five months of negotiations, Judge Breyer issued an order granting preliminary approval of settlement for all consumers and resellers of 2.0 litre diesel cars in July 2016; www.cand.uscourts.gov/filelibrary/2808/Amended-Order-Granting-Preliminary-Approval.pdf (last accessed 12 August 2020). Settlements for the 3.0 litre diesel cars and the actions against Bosch followed.

> rulings (especially on issues relating to class certification), and conserve the resources of the parties, their counsel and the judiciary.[8]

Against the background of the US MDL mechanism, one may wonder whether we need an equivalent in Europe. Currently, existing European law does not provide any similar instrument or mechanism. The ERCP, however, includes a mechanism for consolidation in Rule 146[9] but it requires that the court to which actions pending in different courts will be transferred has jurisdiction to hear all actions. Similar rules can be found in national laws. As they respect jurisdictional rules, the transfer does not violate the defendant's rights.[10] Rule 146 of the ERCP will therefore not apply where actions are pending in courts of different Member States and if no single court has jurisdiction for all claims pending in the different courts.

The US MDL mechanism goes further and allows for the consolidation of actions irrespective of personal jurisdiction[11] but, in contrast to Rule 146 of the ERCP, cases can be transferred only for the limited purpose of pre-trial proceedings. The court before which the actions are consolidated will not be in a position to render a final court decision on the cases transferred; instead, these cases will be re-transferred to the courts originally seized. In practice, however, less than 3 per cent of MDL cases ever exit the MDL court because

---

[8] *United States Judicial Panel On Multidistrict Litigation in Re: Volkswagen 'Clean Diesel' Marketing, Sales Practices, And Products Liability Litigation* MDL 2672 Transfer Order Case NJ/2:15-cv-07012 Document 82 Filed 12/08/15, p 2; www.cand.uscourts.gov/filelibrary/1679/Transfer_Order_12-8-2015.pdf (last accessed 12 August 2020).

[9] Rule 146 – Consolidation of Proceedings: '(1) Where the jurisdiction of the Court first seised is established, it may, upon application of one of the parties, order the consolidation of several sets of proceedings under Rules 142 and 144. (2) The Court first seised may only consolidate proceedings when it has jurisdiction to hear them and when such parallel proceedings are pending at the first instance. (3) Before ordering consolidation the Court shall hear the parties and communicate with any other Courts seised. (4) When the Court first seised has assumed jurisdiction over the proceedings and has consolidated them, any other Court must decline jurisdiction. . .'

[10] For example, Section 145 of the German Code of Civil Procedure allows for the consolidation of proceedings pending before the same court. An equivalent in the United States is Rule 42 of the Federal Rules of Civil Procedure. For a detailed discussion of the topic, see Scott Dodson (n 6), 1–45.

[11] Andrew Bradt (n 6), 1165, 1169. § 1407 therefore deliberately goes beyond the rule in 28 USC § 1404 (a), which limits transfer to a district in which the case might have been brought from the beginning. One should keep in mind, however, that rather broad jurisdictional rules facilitate joinder of defendants in the United States compared to the situation in Europe; see the analysis of expansion of personal jurisdiction in the United States by Scott Dodson, (n 6), 15 *et seq.*

there is a settlement.[12] Nevertheless, defendants usually object to trial in the transferee forum because of the lack of personal jurisdiction of the transferee court.[13]

Given the current state of European law, there are good reasons why the consolidation of actions pending before the courts of different Member States is not permitted. In the United States, rules on pre-trial discovery as set forth in the Federal Rules of Civil Procedure (FRCP) are the same in all federal courts. In Europe, national procedural law still differs considerably between countries (and sometimes within them). Without EU harmonization or a Europe-wide adoption of the ERCP, claimants who have filed an action in a particular Member State (often based on a clear forum-shopping strategy) will not agree to see their case transferred to another Member State with completely different rules on pleadings, evidence, costs and so on. This is true at least for a complete and final transfer that would allow the court to which an action is transferred to finally decide the case.

One could, however, think of a model which follows the example of 28 USC § 1407 and allows for the consolidation of actions only for the taking of evidence. Again, in the absence of harmonization, one would have to bridge the differences in European evidence rules. Even if all Member States adopted the ERCP, the consolidation of proceedings for the purposes of evidence taking would be different from that provided by 28 USC § 1407. The US MDL rule allows for consolidation for the purpose of pre-trial discovery, which is (very often) completely different from the taking of evidence in a European sense.

The very broadly designed US pre-trial discovery rules aim to provide the parties with information and give them access to evidence in order to prepare for a trial or settlement negotiations. US courts are involved in pre-trial discovery proceedings only to a limited extent, particularly when the parties disagree on the scope or limits of discovery. Therefore, the US court before which actions are consolidated ('transferee court') will not have to make any decisions on the merits and will not even evaluate evidence, although it can make any pre-trial ruling including granting summary judgment.[14] The court to which actions are assigned does not have a general jurisdictional basis to hold a trial in the transferred cases.[15] Instead, originally it was not the primary goal

---

12 Andrew Bradt (n 6) 1169.

13 Andrew Bradt (n 6) 1170.

14 28 USC § 1407 (b) explicitly grants the transferee court all 'powers of a district judge in any district for the purpose of conducting pretrial depositions in such coordinated or consolidated pretrial proceedings'.

15 Therefore, there is also no legal basis for allowing plaintiffs to file claims directly into the MDL and thus bypassing § 1407, though often there are stipulations permitting such 'direct filing' without waiver of jurisdictional objections; see James M. Beck,

of the MDL mechanism to reduce the risk of contradictory court decisions – in contrast to the consolidation rules in the current EU jurisdiction Regulation – but rather to avoid repetitive and extremely expensive and burdensome evidence discovery proceedings.

In Europe, neither national civil procedural rules nor the ERCP includes pre-trial discovery proceedings similar to those in the United States. Nevertheless, it could be useful – particularly in complex collective redress actions – to avoid taking evidence on common factual issues before several courts. The hearing of witnesses or obtaining expert evidence or advice could theoretically be concentrated before one of the courts and the results could then be used in the other courts. However, one should bear in mind that the taking of evidence and fact finding are primary tasks of the courts that render a judgment based on that evidence. Few national procedural regimes allow for the taking of evidence in general to be delegated to a special master or other person who is not involved in making the final decision. This is also the position of the ERCP.[16] As is pointed out in the comments to Rule 97 of the ERCP, the presence of the whole court when receiving evidence is a basic procedural safeguard (the so-called 'immediacy principle'). This is also stressed by Rule 64(2) of the ERCP. The principle imposes limits on the consolidation of actions that are pending before different courts, even if these are limited to the gathering of evidence.

In the context of parallel potential collective redress actions, it may nevertheless be worth testing how far consolidation may go without interfering with jurisdictional rules and with any European civil court's right to hear and evaluate evidence on its own. Were there a legal basis, collective redress actions could be consolidated before one court for the hearing of witnesses and experts in order to save time and money. For example, a member of other courts before which collective actions are pending (and all parties of these actions) could be allowed to participate in the taking of evidence by being present and by being allowed to ask questions. Such European rules of cooperation already exist, for example, in Regulation (EC) No 1206/2001 on cooperation between the courts of the EU countries in the taking of evidence in civil and commercial matters. One may also assume that there is no need to engage another counsel for the taking of evidence before the transferee court. The videotaping of hearings will allow for the evaluation of testimony by all court members of the transferor

'MDL direct filing & personal jurisdiction', www.druganddevicelawblog.com/2017/10/mdl-direct-filing-personal-jurisdiction.html (last accessed 12 August 2020).

[16] 'Rule 97. Conduct of Hearings where evidence is to be adduced: (1) Whenever appropriate, the Court will hear and receive evidence directly at a hearing before the parties unless, exceptionally, it has authorised evidence to be taken by a delegate judge or at another location. . .'

courts at a later stage of the proceedings. The written reports of experts can also be shared easily by all transferor courts.

This scenario is definitely something for the future, but cross-border cooperation of courts in Europe in 'traditional' bilateral civil proceedings has already been established to some extent through European regulations and directives. Full consolidation goes beyond such cooperation and will also require a European institution similar to the US MDL panel, which has the power to decide on applications, verify whether common factual issues are indeed involved in different collective proceedings and select the court which will play the principal role.[17] In the long run, not only would such 'MDL' rules apply in mass harm situations or for collective redress actions, but collective litigation would be a primary field of application, as the amounts at stake are typically high and the taking of evidence is often expensive.

1.3 Benchmarking the ERCP collective redress framework

Having offered in this book a commentary on the ERCP collective redress rules from the standpoint of European legal experts, we also invited leading academics and practitioners from non-European countries in which various forms of collective redress are prominent features of the civil procedure landscape.

We start with comments from two of the most developed 'class action' regimes in the world: the United States and Australia. Many of the issues raised during the drafting of the collective redress chapter in the ERCP have been the subject of either, and often both, case law and legislation in those jurisdictions and the insights shared here by Professors Marcus and Cashman indicate that the solutions we proposed to most of the difficult issue have (at least) a fair chance of working in practice.

But the class action is not the only form of collective redress. Other countries have procedural mechanisms designed to provide an effective civil law remedy to victims of widely dispersed harm. We asked Professor Han of South Korea and Professor Zaneti of Brazil – both countries with longstanding traditions in collective redress – to give their reactions to the collective redress rules in the ERCP in light of their very different national traditions.

Our correspondents were invited to comment on the basis of a draft of the ERCP collective redress chapter as of July 2019. It is in substance the same as the Rules which were finally adopted by the European Law Institute (ELI) and UNIDROIT in September 2020.

---

[17] Electronic registers in which collective actions are published (ERCP Rule 211) will help courts and parties to overlook parallel proceedings in different Member States.

2. LEARNING FROM THE AMERICAN EXPERIENCE[18]

2.1 Introduction

The drafters of the ELI/UNIDROIT ERCP chapter on collective redress have built on experience from outside the European Union. The US experience with collective litigation has been developing for more than 50 years and is much more extensive than the experience of other countries (except perhaps Brazil; see the contribution of Professor Zaneti to this chapter). It began in the 1960s, with the adoption of extensive amendments to FRCP Rule 23 and the adoption of the MDL statute, permitting US federal courts to combine cases from across the country for management by a single judge, such as occurred with the *Volkswagen Dieselgate* litigation in the United States. These innovations of the 1960s were a leap into the unknown, so it seems useful to begin by noting what we now know from that half-century of experience.

2.2 Class certification is the biggest issue

In the 1960s, the drafters of the class action rule seemed to expect that class certification would involve a relatively modest effort, and that the main focus of class actions would be on litigating the substantive claims before the court. Indeed, for a time, class actions were certified on the basis of rather conclusory pleadings and US courts were forbidden to consider the merits until certification was resolved. Some courts even insisted that it be completed within

---

[18] By Richard Marcus. This section refers to Rule 23 of the American Federal Rules of Civil Procedure (FRCP), but does not otherwise provide full citations. Those interested in more detail may refer to other publications, including: Richard Marcus, 'Revolution v Evolution in Class Action Reform', 96 *NC L Rev* 903 (2018); Richard Marcus, E. Sherman and H. Erichson, *Complex Litigation* (6th ed 2015) (Chapters 4 and 6); Richard Marcus, 'The Big Bad Wolf: American Class Actions', in *Multi-Party Redress Mechanisms in Europe: Squeaking Mice?* (V. Harsagi and C.H. van Rhee, eds 2014) at 35; Richard Marcus, 'America's Dynamic and Extensive Experience With Collective Litigation', in *Resolving Mass Disputes* (C. Hodges and A. Stadler, eds, 2013), at 148; Richard Marcus, 'More Reform for the American Class Action?', 211 *Revista de Processo* 263 (Sao Paolo 2012); Richard Marcus, 'Reviving Judicial Gatekeeping of Aggregation: Scrutinizing the Merits on Class Certification', 79 *Geo Wash L Rev* 324 (2011); Richard Marcus, 'The American Class Action: Scourge or Savior?', 701 *Nat Bus Law* 15 (15 November 2000) (in Japanese). The author has, since 1996, served as associate reporter of the US Judicial Conference Advisory Committee on Civil Rules, which drafts amendments to Federal Rules of Civil Procedure, including Rule 23, the class action rule.

90 days. But more recently, the Supreme Court has emphasized that 'Rule 23 does not set forth a mere pleading standard'. Instead, serious attention to the legal and factual issues is critical to determining whether a case should be certified as a class action, and *most* of the parties' litigation activity – often involving expert witnesses and extensive discovery – is about whether the case is a proper class action. Class certification is often the only issue actually resolved by the US court, which never resolves the merits. Settlement usually follows class certification

A major reason why class certification is the biggest litigated issue is that, according to defendants, if the class is certified, the defendants feel they must settle rather than risk a 'bet the company' jury trial. So the US rules have repeatedly been revised to clarify and emphasize the responsibility of the judge to scrutinize proposed settlements in order to ensure they are fair to class members. ERCP Rules 222–24 resemble these US provisions. In the United States, this scrutiny of proposed class action settlements sometimes reveals that class counsel may have accepted a settlement that yields a large fee, but modest rewards for class members. Recently, there may have been an increase in the number of class action trials, but settlement remains very much the predominant outcome after certification.

2.3 Entrepreneurial lawyers are the lifeblood of US aggregate litigation

Almost unknown in the 1960s, entrepreneurial lawyers (sometimes called 'private attorneys general') have become central players in US class action litigation. To some extent, this reflects the US commitment to 'private enforcement' of public law via litigation initiated by private lawyers. The US rule makers have accordingly focused on the incentives for lawyers in regulating class actions and multi-district aggregate proceedings, sometimes emphasizing ways in which attorneys' fee awards can be tied to delivering relief to class members.

2.4 'Trans-substantive' aggregation rules can be put to inventive purposes

US procedural rules are mainly 'trans-substantive,' not sectoral or confined to certain types of claims. Indeed, although the framers of FRCP Rule 23 in the 1960s did not want class actions used for mass torts, they came to be important in that field by the late 1980s. In 1997, the US Supreme Court made class certification more difficult in mass tort litigation.[19] More recently, partly because class certification had become more difficult in mass tort litigation, resort was had to the MDL system to aggregate claims. As a result, at present, about 40 per cent of civil cases in the US federal court system are subject to an MDL transfer order, mostly in 'mega' mass tort MDL proceedings. Like the US approach, the ERCP applies to claims of all sorts, provided that they satisfy the requirements of Rule 212.

2.5 The ERCP in light of US experience

Against the background of this experience, here are some observations about the ERCP.

2.5.1 Certification and admissibility

ERCP Rules 212 and 213 contain the criteria for admissibility of collective actions and the details the court must address in an order admitting such an action. They look similar to the provisions of FRCP Rule 23(b)(3). ERCP Rules 204 and 205, meanwhile, authorize something like an FRCP Rule 23(b)(2) class action for injunctive or declaratory relief. An abiding issue for US courts has been the extent to which monetary relief can be added to a class action seeking an injunction. US lawyers have sought to expand 'injunctive' class actions to include monetary relief in order to avoid the greater demands of FRCP Rule 23(b)(3) certification, but the US Supreme Court has curtailed that activity.[20]

On another dimension, monetary relief can be an obstacle to certification of FRCP Rule 23(b)(3) class actions because they are allowed only when 'common questions predominate', and usually the amount of money damages is an individual matter. ERCP Rule 212(1) seems to have sufficient flexibility on this point.

ERCP Rule 215 offers a compromise on the question of whether class members must opt in to participate. In the United States, opting in is never required under FRCP Rule 23 and only some class actions even offer an opportunity to opt out. Thus, in FRCP Rule 23(b)(2) class actions for injunctions, there is no right to opt out because an injunction must apply equally to all

---

19 *Amchem Products, Inc. v Windsor*, 521 US 591 (1997) (rejecting settlement class certification in action for personal injuries due to workplace exposure to asbestos).

20 *Wal-Mart Stores, Inc. v. Dukes*, 131 S.Ct. 2541 (2011) (holding that Rule 23(b)(2) could not be used to certify a class seeking 'backpay' for employment discrimination because that would be 'individualized' relief not flowing automatically from a class-wide injunction, so that certification under Rule 23(b)(3) would be required for backpay claims).

members of the class. In that sense, the collective interest injunction authorized by ERCP Rule 204 appears to operate like FRCP Rule 23(b)(2) injunction class actions.

The opt-out procedure of FRCP Rule 23(b)(3) has drawn much criticism in the European Union, often on the grounds of individual autonomy. Perhaps those objections should also apply to the collective interest injunction under ERCP Rule 204: what if some members of the group oppose the injunctive remedy sought by an entity authorized pursuant to Rule 205(1) to pursue such relief? One might say that interest in money ought not be elevated (by the right to opt out) over matters of 'principle' that could bear on injunctive relief. But in the United States, it was thought that a class-wide injunction must apply equally to all in the class, while claims for money damages do support a right to opt out.

The drafters of ERCP Rule 215 recognize that interests of personal autonomy do not require a right to opt out in every collective action for monetary redress. The comment on Rule 215 acknowledges that 'rational apathy' would explain why those who have suffered 'minimal loss' would not bother to opt in. But from the US perspective, the comment sensibly goes on to recognize that the 'efficient enforcement of liability rules, which is a public good' calls for exceptions. This comment invokes the 'private enforcement' theme mentioned above. As the comment also notes, several Member States have already implemented opt-out systems without serious adverse results. So the ultimate decision whether to use an opt-in system is for the court's discretion, under the standards of Rule 215.

From the US experience, however, ERCP Rule 210 may require too much. It demands that the statement of claim include 'all relevant information available' concerning the requirements of Rule 212. In the United States, obtaining that information often depends on disclosure or discovery as part of the proceeding.

One feature of the US system that does not appear to be in the draft is an opportunity for an immediate appeal of the court's collective proceeding order under ERCP Rule 213. In 1998, US Rule 23(f) was added to the US procedure to permit either party to seek review of such an order. In part, that was based on the idea that a grant of class certification compelled the defendant to settle (waiving review of the class certification). It may well be that ERCP Rules 66(1) and 130(1)(d) would permit an appeal from an order under Rule 213 as a judgment on a 'preliminary procedural matter'. It would be useful for the draft to address that question explicitly. And it would also be useful to consider whether the appealability of a Rule 215 'judgment' should be entirely up to the first instance court; in the United States, the matter is within the discretion of the appellate court.

Finally, it is intriguing that ERCP Rule 210 commands the plaintiff to show that it has first tried to settle before commencing proceedings. If that effort is successful, the parties must presumably proceed under Rules 229 *et seq*, which appear to be based on the Dutch model. But it does not seem to include anything like the requirement in Rule 213(2) that the draft collective proceeding order be advertised with an invitation to others to apply to take up the litigation cudgel (under Rule 207). That requirement, incidentally, looks a great deal like the 1995 US Private Securities Litigation Act. Some might see this route as a 'back door' around the requirements of the collective redress rules, but it is perhaps a very useful back door. In the United States, we have seen 'pre-packaged' class actions filed as settlement class actions. In these cases, however, the US Supreme Court has warned that there should be heightened concern about adequacy of representation.

2.5.2 'Standing' and the qualifications of the representative

In the United States, there is effectively a very broad conception allowing any member of the proposed class to file the collective action – the sort of plaintiff that would satisfy ERCP Rule 208(c). This attitude ties in with the 'entrepreneurial' spirit of US class actions. Rule 208, on the other hand, relies heavily on entities authorized by national law to bring such actions, as they need not satisfy the standards of ERCP Rule 209.

In the United States, the question of governmental control of who may litigate is delicate. From the time of de Tocqueville, Americans have been joiners and there are now many organizations that litigate to pursue the goals of their members. To offer two such entities, consider the American Civil Liberties Union and the National Rifle Association. Presumably those would be within ERCP Rule 208(b). Though the 'private enforcement' model might invite government to deputize organizations to do that job, this intrusion into litigation might be questioned. In the United States, class actions are often brought *against* the government; allowing the government to decide who can bring them therefore seems odd.

One might ask how ERCP Rule 209 qualification standards connect to Rule 213(2)'s requirement that the court advertise for competing representatives. That implies that the court may sometimes have to select from among potential representatives. The standards of Rule 209 provide a starting point for that comparison; as does Rule 214 (requiring the claimant to act in the best interests of the group). But is there is subtle thumb on the scale in favour of governmentally approved organizations? Under Rule 208(a), they need not even satisfy Rule 209. Perhaps that means they should be recognized over any competing group relying on Rule 209(b) or 209(c). Even if that is so, it may be that more than one qualified claimant under Rule 208(a) may appear. Ultimately, again, it seems the court must exercise its wise discretion in this matter.

The more serious issue, from the US perspective, is why anyone would agree to be the claimant. The basic problem is money; as noted above, in the

United States, class actions are generally an entrepreneurial undertaking by lawyers who justify their actions as private enforcement of public law, but who pursue substantial attorneys' fee awards under US Rule 23(h) if they are successful. It does not appear that the same inducement exists for lawyers under the proposed rules. Perhaps the lawyers will be paid by the claimant, but the rules do not seem to entitle the lawyers to seek a court award for their fees. ERCP Rules 238(2) and (3) create a common fund to cover the claimant's costs; and Rule 240(1) covers the claimant's litigation costs if the case is successful. Technically, the US courts treat the award of attorneys' fees as belonging to the claimant, which may have a contractual obligation to pay the attorneys. But the court has a supervisory role.

The alternative outcome – the defendant wins – seems to erode any willingness of the claimant to pursue the action. ERCP Rule 238(1) makes it clear that only the claimant is liable for the costs of the prevailing defendant. The comment to ERCP Rule 215 takes comfort from the fact that unmeritorious actions will be deterred by the loser pays rule. In short, it appears that a qualified claimant must run the risk of bankruptcy if it loses, but may not gain much for itself by winning. This arrangement may be justified to avoid the 'misuse of collective redress actions' decried in the comment to Rule 209, but it leaves this US observer baffled as to why any organization would try to qualify under Rules 208 and 209.

2.5.3 Costs and funding of collective actions

As noted above, costs and funding are central to the viability of the collective redress system. ERCP Rule 209(b) says that the 'financial, human, and other resources available' should be considered whenever the person or entity seeking to represent the group is not authorized to do so under national law. ERCP Rule 243 authorizes the court to require a party to post security for costs.

The 'American Rule' is that each side bears its own costs. Out-of-pocket costs can be enormous. Party-appointed experts (see Rule 240(1)(c)) may be necessary to litigate class certification. Experts are also often essential to prove causation in mass tort litigation. US entrepreneurial lawyers sometimes shoulder million-dollar outlays for such costs of litigation without any assurance that they will recover those costs, much less be paid, unless they win their cases. But if they do win, they can expect a very handsome payoff.

There is much to be said for the loser pays rules that prevail in much of the rest of the world. But in collective actions, they do seem to erode the willingness of all but the most public- spirited organizations to undertake such suits. Maybe third-party funding – explicitly authorized by ERCP Rule 237 – will provide the necessary inducement or protection for organizations. And Rule 245 may provide sufficient inducement for funders to do that job. The United

States has only recently begun to deal with such third-party funding and its experience therefore cannot provide useful guidance to others.

But the US experience with cost awards, where authorized under US law, does provide a caution about ERCP Rule 241, which the comment tells us is the 'most important provision in these rules on costs'. The thrust of Rule 241 is sensible: the cost award should not be made mechanically, but take account of the particulars of the case, including both the amount of success and the conduct of the action. The United States has many specific attorney's fee shifting statutes, but determining who is the prevailing party can often be challenging in sprawling collective actions and assessing further whether the matter should be been settled much sooner can also be very difficult. Though the rule is sensible in emphasizing the court's discretion in addressing these issues, it is likely that litigating the cost issues can itself become highly expensive for the parties and quite exhausting for the court.

2.6 Conclusions

In conclusion, it must be emphasized that this draft is a stupendous achievement. The authors have built on US and other experience and produced a document that can be adapted to the circumstances in various European states. The probing questions above are not intended to detract from that achievement. And we can be confident that this document is not (as was the US venture of the 1960s) a leap into the unknown. It is solidly based on experience inside and outside the European Union. Accordingly (unlike the US situation in the 1960s), there is much reason for confidence that this draft will lead to the results its drafters are pursuing. Congratulations!

3. REFORM OF EUROPEAN COLLECTIVE REDRESS: SOME LESSONS FROM THE AUSTRALIAN EXPERIENCE WITH CLASS ACTIONS[21]

In considering proposals for reform of the ERCP, and in particular provisions for 'collective redress', there may be some important lessons from the Australian experience with class actions.

21 By Peter Cashman. A more comprehensive review of Australian class action developments is to be found in a chapter by the author entitled 'Enforcing Consumer and Capital Market Law in Australia' in *Enforcing Consumer and Capital Market Law* by Beate Gsell and Thomas Moellers (eds), to be published in 2020 by Intersentia.

Statutory class actions were first introduced in Australia on 4 March 1992 in the Federal Court as a result of Part IVA of the Federal Court of Australia Act 1976 (Cth) coming into operation. Statutory class action procedures are now available in the Federal Court of Australia and in the Supreme Courts of five states: Victoria, New South Wales (NSW), Queensland, Western Australia and Tasmania.[22]

The statutory regime in each Australian state is similar. The key features may be summarized as follows.

The threshold criteria for the commencement of a class action are minimalist (seven or more persons with claims against the same person, arising from the same, similar or related facts giving rise to a substantial common question of law or fact).

There is no certification. A class action can be commenced if the abovementioned criteria are satisfied, without judicial approval being required.

It is an 'opt-out' regime. Persons falling within the definition of the defined class are included whether or not they are aware or consent. They may be excluded by taking formal steps to 'opt out'.

The class action regime is available to those claiming financial or other loss, including both consumers and shareholders. It is being utilized by consumers, but in recent times it has been utilized more extensively by shareholders.

Commercial litigation funders may be able to take a percentage of the amount recovered by class members if the claim is successful. Historically, this was achieved by individual class members entering into litigation funding agreements with the commercial litigation funder.

Recently, Australian courts have made 'common fund' orders whereby the litigation funder may be entitled to recovery of a percentage from the class as a whole, if the case is successful, without individual contractual arrangements being entered into.[23] The court determines the reasonableness of the amount payable to the litigation funder at the conclusion of the proceedings.

Although both the Federal Court and the NSW Court of Appeal have held recently that Australian (federal and state) courts have power to make common fund orders in class action litigation, the High Court of Australia has recently determined that there is no power to make such an order (pursuant to Section 33ZF of the Federal Court of Australia Act 1976 (Cth)) at the outset or during

---

22 The Western Australian and Tasmanian reforms to introduce class actions in the Supreme Courts in those jurisdictions have only recently been introduced.

23 *Money Max Int Pty Ltd (Trustee) v QBE Insurance Group Limited* [2016] FCAFC 148 (Murphy, Gleeson and Beach JJ). All federal common fund orders made up to the end of 2018 are summarized in the empirical report available at https://ssrn.com/abstract=3326303 (last accessed 14 October 2019).

the course of the litigation.[24] At the time of writing, it remains a vexed question as to whether such an order can be made at the conclusion of the proceedings following a settlement or judgment.

Lawyers are not allowed to charge fees calculated as a percentage of the amount recovered. Normally, legal fees are calculated based on hourly rates, with a further 'uplift' (of up to 25 per cent of the hourly rate) if the fees are payable only in the event of success in the litigation. However, the Australian Law Reform Commission (ALRC) has recently recommended that the law be changed to permit percentage-based fees, subject to a number of specified conditions.[25]A similar recommendation was made by the Victorian Law Reform Commission (VLRC) and, as noted below, recent legislative reforms have been introduced in Victoria to permit this.

Although the courts have a general discretion in relation to the making of orders for costs at the conclusion of the proceedings, the successful party will usually obtain an order from the court that the losing party pay (most of) the legal costs incurred in conducting the litigation.

The lead applicant is personally liable for any adverse costs order,[26] whereas the class members are not liable for adverse costs.[27]

The limitation periods in respect of the causes of action relied upon by the class members are suspended upon filing of the action.

---

24 The New South Wales Court of Appeal decision is: *Brewster v BMW Australia Ltd* [2019] NSWCA 35 and the Full Federal Court of Australia decision is: *Lenthall v Westpac Life Insurance Services Limited* [2019] FCAFC 34. The High Court decisions are: *BMW Australia Ltd v Brewster* and *Westpac Banking Corporation v Lenthall* [2019] HCA 45 (4 December 2019).

25 On 24 January 2019, the attorney-general for Australia tabled in Parliament: Australian Law Reform Commission (ALRC), *Integrity, Fairness and Efficiency—An Inquiry into Class Action Proceedings and Third-Party Litigation Funders; Final Report 134* (Commonwealth of Australia 2018), www.alrc.gov.au/inquiry-categories/class-action-proceedings-and-third-party-litigation-funders (last accessed 14 October 2019).

26 Usually in a funded case the commercial litigation funder will indemnify the lead applicant in respect of any order for costs or security for costs. Often there will also be an after the event insurance policy taken out with a commercial insurer, whereby the insurer assumes liability to pay any such costs in consideration for the payment of a (substantial) premium. Often the premium is as high at one-third of the limit of indemnity required. Usually the majority of the premium amount is payable only upon a successful outcome.

27 In some limited circumstances a class member may become liable for certain costs – for example, if they become appointed as a sub-group representative or if they take steps in the litigation in connection with the resolution of individual issues in respect of their particular claim.

The advantage of the Australian 'opt-out' class action regime compared with jurisdictions which have an 'opt-in' requirement is starkly apparent from the experience to date in the *Volkswagen Dieselgate* litigation.

The class actions in the Australian litigation were commenced on behalf of the purchasers of *all* affected vehicles in Australia, comprising around 100,000 consumers. By way of contrast, the English group litigation scheme requires each claimant to commence an individual proceeding in the High Court. Proceedings have been commenced to date by approximately 95,000 UK consumers. Thus, the number of claimants in the Australian and UK proceedings are roughly similar. However, in the United Kingdom, there are approximately 1.2 million affected vehicles. Thus, the UK claimants comprise less than 8 per cent of affected consumers in the United Kingdom.

Similarly, in other European jurisdictions where those affected are required to take individual steps to commence proceedings (eg, Germany), or to have proceedings commenced on their behalf, the total number of those making claims is substantially less than the total population of persons with similar claims.

3.1 Doctrinal and procedural developments

In relatively recent decisions, Australian courts have resolved previously perplexing questions about: (1) whether class actions can be commenced on behalf of only *some* of those who may fall within the group affected by the conduct giving rise to class action proceedings; (2) whether, in cases involving multiple respondents, all class members must have an individual claim against *each* respondent; and (3) in the case of commercially funded proceedings, whether the funder may obtain an entitlement to a commission from *all* class members, not just those who may have entered into contractual litigation funding agreements.

To date, these questions have been answered: (1) yes; (2) no and (3) no, respectively.

However:

- the judicial determination of the first question is under attack on policy grounds and is the subject of proposals for legislative reform, discussed below;
- the judicial determination of the second question may not have finally determined the issue; and
- the judicial resolution of the third question is limited to interlocutory orders made at the outset or during the course of the proceeding; and as noted below, the court may have power to make such an order at the conclusion

of the proceedings in connection with settlement approval or following judgment.

3.1.1 Limited or open classes?

In *Multiplex*,[28] the Full Federal Court determined that limited or 'closed' classes were permissible under the class action regime provided for in Part IVA of the Federal Court of Australia Act 1976 (Cth), given that the legislation expressly provides that a class action may be commenced by or on behalf of 'some or all' who have 'claims'[29] as 'representing some or all of them'.[30] This issue was previously the subject of divided judicial views of members of both the Federal Court and the Victorian Supreme Court.

The Full Court resolution of this relatively straightforward matter of statutory interpretation has precipitated a policy debate about the relative merits of 'open' compared with 'closed' classes. This has been driven in part by the fact that in many instances – particularly before the decision of the Full Court in *Money Max* (discussed below) – many commercially funded class actions were commenced on behalf of classes limited to those who had entered into litigation funding arrangements, which in some cases comprised only those potential class members with the largest claims (eg, institutional shareholders in shareholder class actions).

The adverse policy consequence of this development is obvious. What was intended as an 'open' class action regime had, in the view of some, been subverted by the introduction of commercial litigation funding arrangements which – historically at least – were constrained by the commercial necessity to sign up persons with claims in order to obtain a legal entitlement (under contract law) to a share of the money recovered by funded class members.

Accordingly, there has been a policy move to amend the class action legislation to *require* that all class actions be commenced as open classes.[31] Although historically there appeared to be a notable transition from open to limited classes, with the introduction and expansion of commercial litigation funding, this appears to have been reversed – particularly following the decision of

---

28 *Multiplex Funds Management Ltd v P Dawson Nominees Pty Ltd* (2007) 164 FCR 275.

29 Section 33C requires that such 'claims' be 'against the same person'; be in respect of or arise from the same, similar or related circumstances; and give rise to a substantial common issue of law or fact.

30 *Federal Court of Australia Act 1976* (Cth), s 33C.

31 See: Australian Law Reform Commission, *Integrity, Fairness and Efficiency—An Inquiry into Class Action Proceedings and Third-Party Litigation Funders; Final Report 134* (Commonwealth of Australia 2018) 3.18, www.alrc.gov.au/inquiry-categories/class-action-proceedings-and-third-party-litigation-funders (last accessed 14 October 2019).

the Full Federal Court in *Money Max* to allow funders to obtain a (judicially approved) commission from class members as a whole, not just those who had individually entered into litigation funding arrangements (and thus without the onerous and expensive requirement to engage in 'book building'). However, in the aftermath of the recent High Court decision in *Brewster*, there may be a retreat to opt-in classes limited to claimants who have entered into litigation funding agreements with commercial funders.

Nevertheless, if it is judicially accepted that some form of 'common fund' order may be made at the conclusion of the proceedings, as is clearly suggested in recent amendments to the Federal Court Class Actions Practice Note,[32] funders may continue to finance open classes.

3.1.2 Common fund orders

In *Money Max*,[33] the Full Federal Court held that it had power to make an interlocutory order allowing a commercial funder of the litigation to obtain a commission or percentage of the successful recovery from all class members (ie, not just those who had entered into contractual litigation funding arrangements).

The judicial power to make such an order has been held to be derived from Sections 33ZF and 23 of the federal legislation. The former provides that the Federal Court may make 'any order the Court thinks appropriate or necessary to ensure justice is done in a proceeding'.[34]

The power to make such orders was the subject of appeals in two cases: one in the Federal Court (*Lenthall v Westpac Banking Corporation*) and one in the NSW Supreme Court (*Brewster v BMW Australia*). In the NSW Supreme Court, the question was remitted directly to the Court of Appeal by the docket judge (Sackar J) without having made any order in the proceeding before him (one of the many *Takata* airbag cases).[35] Both appeals were heard before a joint sitting of the Full Federal Court and the NSW Court of Appeal. The appellants contended, *inter alia*, that neither the Federal Court nor the Supreme Court is empowered by its respective federal and state class action legislation to make an interlocutory order of the type in question.

---

32 Issued on 20 December 2019. See para 15.4.

33 *Money Max Int Pty Ltd (Trustee) v QBE Insurance Group Limited* (2016) 245 FCR 191.

34 See generally, in addition to the decision in *Money Max: Pearson v State of Queensland* [2017] FCA 1096 (Murphy J); *Caason Investments Pty Limited v Cao* (No 2) [2018] FCA 527; *Lentall v Westpac Life Insurance Services Limited* [2018] FCA 1422.

35 *Owen Brewster v BMW Australia Ltd* [2018] NSWSC 1602.

In separate judgments, both the Full Court and the NSW Court of Appeal accepted that the respective courts were empowered to make common fund orders. Thus, it was accepted (subject to the decision of the High Court on appeal, discussed below) that, even if an order could be made early on an interlocutory basis, there is no certainty that (at the conclusion of the case), the order will not be varied in light of the ultimate outcome. Moreover, although Lee J specified a percentage amount (provisionally) payable to the funder in *Lenthall*, in *Money Max*, the Full Federal Court made it clear that court approval of a reasonable funding commission rate is to be left to a later stage, when more probative and more complete information is available to the court – which will likely be at the stage of settlement approval or the distribution of damages.[36]

The acceptance, prior to the High Court decision on appeal, that a common fund order can be made early in the proceedings appears to have led to the desirable policy result that open class actions have become more commercially attractive to litigation funders, with a consequential decrease in 'closed' class actions. However, this has led to one undesirable consequence. The attractiveness of common fund orders appears to have spurred an increase in duplicative and competing class actions instituted with financial support from a multiplicity of Australian and international funders. The Full Federal Court's prediction in *Money Max* that its decision would have the reverse effect[37] does not appear to have been borne out.

In any event, in its recent decision in the appeals from the Full Federal Court and the NSW Court of Appeal, the High Court held (by majority)[38] that the courts below had no power to make common fund orders on an interlocutory basis. As noted above, it remains unclear whether common fund orders are nor permissible *in any circumstances*, or whether such an order may still be made *at the conclusion of the proceeding* at the settlement or judgment stage (pursuant to Section 33V(2) or 33Z). This issue is presently under consideration in a number of cases, including the *Volkswagen Dieselgate* class action litigation.

3.1.3 Claims against each defendant?

In 2000 the Full Federal Court (Sackville J, with whom Spender and Hill JJ agreed) decided in *Nixon* that it is a requirement in class action proceedings

---

36 *Money Max Int Pty Ltd (Trustee) v QBE Insurance Group Limited* (2016) 245 FCR 191 [11].

37 *Money Max Int Pty Ltd (Trustee) v QBE Insurance Group Limited* (2016) 245 FCR 191 [14].

38 The majority judgments comprised the joint decision of Kiefel CJ, Bell and Keane JJ and the separate individual judgments of Nettle J and Gordon J. Gageler J and Edelman J each delivered separate dissenting judgments.

commenced in the Federal Court under the federal legislation that where there are multiple respondents, each class member must have an individual claim against each respondent.[39]

In *Bray v Hoffman-La Roche*,[40] the majority in a differently constituted Full Court disagreed with the decision in *Nixon*. The Full Federal Court subsequently held that there is no requirement in multi-respondent class actions for each class member to have a claim against every respondent. In *Cash Converters International Limited v Gray*,[41] the Full Federal Court determined that a proper construction of Section 33C(1) does *not* require that every group member have a claim against all respondents.

Thus, provided that at least seven group members have claims against each respondent, the class applicant has a claim against each respondent and the proceedings satisfy the other threshold requirements of Section 33C of the Federal Court of Australia Act 1976 (Cth).

At the state level, the NSW class action legislation was drafted so as to get around the impediment previously thought to arise from the decision in *Philip Morris*. Section 158(2) of the Civil Procedure Act provides that a 'person may commence representative proceedings on behalf of other persons against more than one defendant irrespective of whether or not the person and each of those persons have a claim against every defendant in the proceedings'. Although the NSW provisions state that it is not necessary for all group members to have claims against all defendants, the legislation is silent as to what the minimum requirements are. This may give rise to further controversy.

3.1.4 Some present controversial issues

Notwithstanding the substantial jurisprudence to date on the operation of the Australian class action regime, a number of issues remain controversial. A detailed consideration of these is outside the scope of the present analysis, but a number of such issues are referred to below.

3.1.4.1 Cy-près remedies

The issue of *cy-près* orders remains controversial in Australia.

In 2016, a class action was commenced against Reckitt Benckiser (RB), the manufacturer of pain relief pharmaceutical *Nurofen*.[42] The proceedings arose from allegedly misleading and deceptive conduct whereby RB had marketed

---

[39] *Philip Morris (Australia) Ltd v Nixon* (2000) 170 ALR 487. See generally Vince Morabito, 'Class Actions against Multiple Respondents' [2002] *FLR* 11.

[40] (2003) 130 FCR 317 (Carr and Finkelstein JJ; Branson J dissenting).

[41] (2014) 223 FCR 139 (Jacobson, Middleton and Gordon JJ).

[42] Along with Robert White, the author acted as counsel for the applicant and class members in this case.

a particular form of Nurofen as being targeted for effective action against specific types of pain. This product was sold, at a much higher price, alongside other types of Nurofen and generic products containing the same active ingredient (Ibuprofen). In fact, the higher priced product contained in effect the same active ingredient as the lower-priced product(s). Thus, consumers who paid the higher prices were paying more than they needed to pay, given that therapeutically equivalent products were available at lower prices. In addition to the class action proceedings, seeking compensation on behalf of those who paid the higher prices, penalty proceedings were brought against the company by the Australian Competition and Consumer Commission. The penalty imposed by the Federal Court[43] was increased on appeal.[44]

Although the case was brought for the obvious purpose of seeking to recover compensation for those who had paid the artificially high prices for the product(s), the losses of each consumer were relatively modest. It was considered unlikely that most consumers would take steps to make a formal claim following any judgment or settlement. Moreover, the transaction costs of processing claims might exceed the amounts of compensation sought in each individual case. Furthermore, if each class member was required to prove the nature and quantum of his or her purchases, this would likely lead to evidentiary complications, given that these were over-the-counter products and not pharmaceuticals available only on prescription (where there were likely to be reliable records of purchases).

With such difficulties in mind, the case was conceived and commenced as a test case to determine whether the Federal Court had power to award a *cy-près* remedy, by way of judgment following a determination of liability. In the *Nurofen* class action, it was contended that the existing powers of the Federal Court were wide enough to facilitate a *cy-près* order as part of a judgment (as distinct from settlement). This was vigorously contested by RB, which argued that the court had no such power and threatened a constitutional challenge to the purported statutory power of the court to make such an order.[45] However, such issues were not eventually judicially determined. After

---

[43] *Australian Competition and Consumer Commission v Reckitt Benckiser (Australia) Pty Ltd (No 5)* [2016] FCA 167 (29 February 2016) (Edelman J); *Australian Competition and Consumer Commission v Reckitt Benckiser (Australia) Pty Ltd (No 6)* [2016] FCA 355 (11 April 2016) (Edelman J).

[44] *Australian Competition and Consumer Commission v Reckitt Benckiser (Australia) Pty Ltd* [2016] FCAFC 181 (16 December 2016) (Jagot, Yates and Bromwich JJ); 340 ALR 25.

[45] More recently, the High Court has held that neither the Federal Court nor the NSW Supreme Court has the power to make common fund orders on an interlocutory basis pursuant to Section 33ZF of the Federal Court of Australia Act 2006 (Cth) or Section 183 of the Civil Procedure Act 2005 (NSW): *BMW Australia Ltd v*

considerable procedural skirmishing,[46] the class action proceeding was settled on the eve of trial.[47]

Recommendations by the Victorian Law Reform Commission[48] for conferral of an express judicial power to make *cy-près* orders were not implemented before the then Victorian government lost office. Inclusion of such provisions in the draft NSW class action reform proposals were removed after lobbying by the business community.[49] More recently, the power of the court to make *cy-près* orders in a settlement of a class action has been considered in detail in an incisive judgment of Justice Lee in the Federal Court.[50] The judge proceeded to approve a settlement which made provision for a *cy-près* distribution. However, the power of the court to make such an order by way of a judgment in the absence of a settlement remains a vexed issue.

3.1.4.2 Releases as part of a settlement

In many settlements, respondents understandably want 'global peace' and often seek releases of claims, including for the benefit of third parties not the subject of the class action proceedings. There is controversy as to the appropriateness and the power of the court to approve releases in respect of claims and parties not encompassed by the litigation.

Brewster; Westpac Banking Corporation v Lenthall [2019] HCA 45, by a five-to-two majority (Kiefel CJ, Bell and Keane J, with Gordon and Nettle JJ agreeing; Gageler and Edelman JJ dissenting). The decision leaves open the question of whether the courts have power to make such an order at the conclusion of the proceeding, either by way of judgment or in approving a settlement, pursuant to other statutory powers.

46 *Hardy v Reckitt Benckiser (Australia) Pty Limited* [2017] FCA 341 (31 March 2017) (Nicholas J); *Hardy v Reckitt Benckiser (Australia) Pty Limited (No 2)* [2017] FCA 785 (11 July 2017) (Nicholas J).

47 *Hardy v Reckitt Benckiser (Australia) Pty Limited (No 3)* [2017] FCA 1165 (20 September 2017) (Nicholas J).

48 See Chapter 8, 'Improving Remedies in Class Actions', in Victorian Law Reform Commission, *Civil Justice Review Report*, 2008. The author was the commissioner in charge of the civil justice review. The VLRC recommended that the Victorian Supreme Court should have express power to order *cy-près* remedies where: (1) there has been a proven contravention of the law; (2) a financial or other pecuniary advantage has accrued to the person or entity contravening the law as a result of such contravention; (3) the loss suffered by others, or the pecuniary gain by the person contravening the law, is capable of reasonably accurate assessment; and (4) it is not possible, reasonably practicable or cost effective to identify some or all of those who have suffered the loss.

49 See: Vince Morabito, 'Lessons from Australia on Class Action Reform in New Zealand' (2018) 24 *NZBLQ* 178 at 190–91.

50 *Simpson v Thorn Australia Pty Ltd trading as Radio Rentals (No 5)* [2019] FCA 2196.

3.1.4.3 Solicitors for the applicant also acting as claims administrators

In many class action settlements in Australia, the lawyers acting for the class members in the litigation have been appointed by the court as claims administrators to implement the settlement agreed to. This remains controversial and some judges have recently indicated a preference for a tendering process or independent claims administrators.

3.1.4.4 The appointment of contradictors at settlement hearings

In a number of cases, courts have required the appointment of an independent *contradictor* to appear at the settlement hearing and to assist the court in determining whether the proposed settlement is in the best interests of class members.

3.1.4.5 Independent review of legal fees and funders' commissions

Courts have also appointed an independent referee to examine the reasonableness of claims for legal fees and/or claims by funders for commission.

3.1.4.6 The power of the court to 'close' open classes

The question of whether courts have power, other than with the consent of the class representative, to make orders whose effect is to 'close' an open class by requiring members of the class to take affirmative steps in the action is presently the subject of a reserved decision of the NSW Court of Appeal in one of the *Takata* airbag class actions.[51] To date, both state and federal courts have made such orders, but usually where this is consented to by the lead applicant/plaintiff in the proceedings.

3.1.4.7 Concurrent conduct of regulatory and class action proceedings

Historically, many events have given rise to both regulatory proceedings, seeking a civil penalty, and class action proceedings seeking damages or compensation, against the same corporate entity. Often, these have been separately conducted by different judges of the same court. In some instances, such as the *Volkswagen Dieselgate* litigation, the same judge had the concurrent case management of all such proceedings. This may be more likely to occur in future cases, but the issue remains controversial where individual directors or corporate officers have been joined to the proceedings.

3.1.5 Findings from recent empirical research

Leaving aside doctrinal developments, there are some interesting implications from recent empirical research. A significant amount of empirical data is avail-

---

[51] *Haselhurst v Toyota*, Case 2019/00403346.

able in respect of the operation of the Australian class action regime(s). This has been compiled and analysed principally by Professor Vince Morabito of Monash University in Melbourne.[52] However, a detailed review of such empirical data is outside the scope of the present review. In a number of reports, Professor Morabito has published invaluable empirical data on the operation of the Australian class action regime.[53]

3.2 Policy developments

As noted above, both the VLRC and the ALRC have recently made various recommendations in relation to litigation funding and class actions. The VLRC report was tabled in the Victorian Parliament on 19 June 2018.[54] The report makes 31 recommendations for reform. The ALRC report was published on 24 January 2019.[55] The report makes 24 recommendations for reform.

---

[52] See, for example, the report Vince Morabito, 'An Evidence-Based Approach to Class Action Reform in Australia: Competing Class Actions and Comparative Perspectives on the Volume of Class Action Litigation in Australia', https://papers.ssrn.com/sol3/papers.cfm?abstract_id=3212527 (last accessed 21 October 2019).

[53] The reports published to date are as follows:

Vince Morabito, 'Common Fund Orders, Funding Fees and Reimbursement Payments (An Evidence-Based Approach to Class Action Reform in Australia' (January 2019), https://ssrn.com/abstract=3326303 (last accessed 12 August 2020); 'Closed Class Actions, Open Class Actions and Access to Justice (An Evidence-Based Approach to Class Action Reform in Australia' (November 2018), https://ssrn.com/abstract=3272089 (last accessed 12 August 2020); 'Competing Class Actions and Comparative Perspectives on the Volume of Class Action Litigation in Australia (An Evidence-Based Approach to Class Action Reform in Australia' (July 2018), https://ssrn.com/abstract=3212527 (last accessed 12 August 2020); *The First Twenty-Five Years of Class Actions in Australia* (Fifth Report; An Empirical Study of Australia's Class Action Regimes; July 2017), http://ssrn.com/abstract=3005901 (last accessed 12 August 2020); *Facts and Figures on Twenty-Four Years of Class Actions in Australia* (Fourth Report; An Empirical Study of Australia's Class Action Regimes; August 2016), http://ssrn.com/abstract=2815777 (last accessed 12 August 2020); *Class Action Facts and Figures – Five Years Later* (Third Report; An Empirical Study of Australia's Class Action Regimes; November 2014), http://ssrn.com/abstract=2523275 (last accessed 12 August 2020); *Litigation Funders, Competing Class Actions, Opt Out Rates, Victorian Class Actions and Class Representatives* (Second Report; An Empirical Study of Australia's Class Action Regimes; September 2010); *Class Action Facts and Figures* (First Report; An Empirical Study of Australia's Class Action Regimes; December 2009).

[54] Victorian Law Reform Commission (VLRC), *Access to Justice: Litigation Funding and Group Proceedings* (VLRC 2018), http://lawreform.vic.gov.au/sites/default/files/VLRC_Litigation_Funding_and_Group_Proceedings_Report_forweb.pdf (last accessed 21 October 2019).

[55] Australian Law Reform Commission (ALRC), *Integrity, Fairness and Efficiency—An Inquiry into Class Action Proceedings and Third-Party Litigation*

A detailed consideration of these reform proposals is beyond the scope of the present analysis. However, the Victorian government has recently introduced legislative reforms that would permit lawyers to act in class actions in that state on the basis of a fee calculated as a percentage of the amount recovered.

In considering proposals for reform of the ERCP, and in particular provisions for 'collective redress', the Australian class action regime and experience will no doubt provide some useful guidance.

4. KOREAN SITUATIONS IN COLLECTIVE REDRESS AND LESSONS FROM THE ELI/UNIDROIT COLLECTIVE REDRESS RULES[56]

4.1 Background and situation in Korea

Korea is one of the few countries in East Asia that has been most proactive in introducing various procedural solutions for collective disputes. In addition, these solutions have been adopted to be utilized in practice in several ways. First, although it is not a litigation-based system, an opt-in collective dispute mediation system was introduced in environmental cases in 1997 and a similar opt-in collective dispute mediation system was introduced in the consumer field in 2006; however, neither system is commonly used in practice. Therefore, it is difficult to see these as remedies for incidents of collective damage in Korea.

Since the late 1990s, many collective consumer damages cases have involved corporations that lacked business ethics in Korea. It was argued that US-based opt-out class actions should be introduced in a wider range of areas, including the consumer sector, despite strenuous opposition from the conglomerates. Ultimately, an opt-out class action, which was limited to the securities sector, was introduced in 2005[57] as the result of a compromise. During the debate on the introduction of class actions, the business sector

Funders; Final Report 134 (Commonwealth of Australia 2018), www.alrc.gov.au/inquiry-categories/class-action-proceedings-and-third-party-litigation-funders (last accessed 14 October 2019).

56 By Choong-soo Han.

57 Article 3 of the Korean Securities-Related Class Action Act (KSCAA) specifically provides the causes of actions on which the claims can be based as follows: (1) false representation (or omission) of any material fact in a registration statement or a prospectus; (2) false representation (or omission) of any material fact in an annual, bi-annual or quarterly report; (3) unfair securities practices, including insider trading or market manipulation; (4) and false representation in an audit report, all of which are causes of actions provided by the Financial Investment Services and Capital Market Act.

expressed concerns as to the possibility of vexatious or abusive lawsuits. In order to appease the business sector, excessive safeguards were put in place, which made it difficult for plaintiffs to avail of class actions in practice.

As of 2019, just 11 cases had been filed; only three of them ended with the distribution of compensation. The introduction of a class action system was also demanded in the consumer field. As a result, in 1996 an 'organization action' (a German-style '*Verbandsklage*') was introduced in the Korean Consumer Basic Act (KCBA), which allowed for cease-and-desist orders against defendants. In addition, in 2011 the same organization action mechanism was also introduced in the Korean Personal Information Protection Act.

Once again, however, the organization action mechanism has not been used as much as had been expected. To date, just seven such cases have been filed, which has caused scepticism about the value of this system. For example, if a firm suspends the sale of a misleading insurance product by itself or further to a sanction by a competent agency, the claimant lacks standing to sue and thus the court will dismiss the case without considering the merits of the claim.

The *Dieselgate* scandal was another event that led Korean consumers to realize that they have no appropriate means to respond to cases of mass harm. As of 2019, the only means for consumers to take countermeasures was to file an organization action under the KCBA seeking suspension and prohibition of misconduct by the business. No organization action was filed against Volkswagen when the scandal broke out, because administrative offices (eg, the Ministry of Land, Infrastructure and Transport) ordered that sales of the vehicle in question be suspended with a recall order, which left plaintiffs with nothing to gain from a collective lawsuit.

As a result, more than 5000 Korean consumers who bought Volkswagen diesel vehicles filed for damages against Volkswagen individually, dividing themselves into small groups using the joinder of party device under the Korean Civil Procedure Act (KCPA). The first judgment in these cases was rendered by the Seoul Central District Court on 7 July 2019 and awarded damages to the plaintiffs of 10 per cent of the car purchase price. This was far less than the remedy that the plaintiffs initially demanded, which was rescission of the contract and full repayment of the purchase price. Both parties were dissatisfied with the ruling and both have appealed.

Given this situation, an opt-out class action system would be an appropriate solution to these kinds of problems in the consumer field. There is little value in opt-in collective mediation systems and organization actions that seek to suspend or prohibit wrongdoing. Eight bills are currently pending in Korea's National Assembly relating to collective redress actions. Most of them propose the expansion of opt-out class actions to all areas, including consumer, environment and fair trade.

4.2 Lessons from the ERCP and some comments

Punitive damages and jury trials were traditionally unknown in Korea, because its jurisprudence is grounded on civil law. But today, statutory multiple damages (usually triple damages) are provided for in some statutes and a quasi-jury system is in use in criminal cases. On the other hand, as we have seen, the use of class actions in Korea is still in its infancy. At this point, there is a lot that Korea can learn from the ELI/UNIDROIT ERCP.

However, in this section, I would like to write a few comments on the ERCP collective action rules to provide a different perspective. I would also like to mention in advance that the issues I address here can be resolved by legislation in individual countries.

4.2.1 Mandatory settlement proposal before filing a suit

According to the ERCP, the qualified claimant must include in his or her claim all relevant information available, including evidence of the qualified claimant's attempt to settle the group members' claims.[58] In addition, except in case of emergency, a condition for the admissibility of a class action is that the plaintiff have allowed the defendant at least three months to answer the settlement proposal.[59] This position makes sense, as it is preferable to resolve a dispute through settlement rather than litigation. It would also be better if the Korean system made settlement attempts a mandatory procedural step, to improve its class action procedures.

However, before making a collective proceeding order under ERCP Rule 212, the court will publish a draft of the order and set a deadline for any other potential qualified claimants to apply under Rule 213(2). Only then shall the court select the qualified claimant from among the applicants based on the criteria in Rule 209.[60] In this situation, there will be a number of settlement proposals to the defendant from multiple, yet-to-be-determined claimants, which could lead to confusion.

4.2.2 The court's decision on the collective proceeding order

The ERCP sets out the conditions for the admissibility of a class action;[61] but it is not clear whether a separate oral plenary proceeding is required, whether full proof of those conditions is required or whether vindication (to the lower standard of *prima facie* evidence) is sufficient. In Korea, vindication, rather

---

58 Rule 210(1)(g).
59 Rule 212(1)(d).
60 Rule 213(3).
61 Rule 212(1).

than full proof, will suffice. To expedite the process, the admissibility proceedings are dealt with separately through interrogation procedures, rather than through plenary proceedings.[62]

According to the ERCP, a collective redress action is granted through a collective proceeding order issued under Rule 213. The question is whether the court's decision can be appealed. In Korea, an immediate 'miscellaneous' appeal can be made against a court's approval or disapproval order.[63] It may not be necessary to prescribe detailed appeal procedures in the ERCP, but as the admissibility proceeding plays an important role, it is essential to specify the possibility and method of appeal. It is also worth considering the speed of the process and allowing the plaintiff to appeal only against a 'disapproval' order. In Korea, the defendant will generally appeal an approval order, which delays the proceedings. For example, it took five years for the approval order to be confirmed (ie, final, conclusive and not subject to appeal) in the *Royal Bank of Canada* case and four years in the *Deutsche Bank* case.[64]

The ERCP states that the court may order any action to continue as a collective redress action upon application, even if the proceedings were commenced by the joinder of parties from the beginning.[65] I fully understand this position. Due to unavoidable circumstances during the lawsuit, it may be necessary to switch from the joinder of parties to a collective redress action. However, I am concerned that converting existing joinder of party procedures to collective redress actions could be more difficult than simply filing a new collective redress action. Moreover, it is unclear to me whether the qualified claimant should be selected through an admissibility proceeding, or through an opt-in or opt-out procedure.

4.2.3 Does the admissibility proceeding require regulation of the lawyer?

The ERCP states that a qualified claimant must be represented by a lawyer,[66] but it does not regulate the qualifications of the lawyer or his or her retainer ceiling. However, according to the comments on Rule 214, conflicts may be expected between the group or the qualified claimant on the one side and the

---

62 KSCAA Article 13(2).

63 KCPA Articles 15(4) and 17(1).

64 *Royal Bank of Canada* (Seoul Appeal Court, 17 November 2015, Case 15Ra656/15Ra657; *Deutsche Bank* (Seoul Central District Court, 28 June 2016, Case 12Kahap17061). The Korean Supreme Court's website confirms that everyone is allowed to access the details of notices of the complaints and the permission decisions for securities class action; www.scourt.go.kr/portal/notice/securities/securities.jsp.

65 Rule 212(2).

66 Rule 209(c).

lawyer who represents the claimants on the other. They also suggest that such conflicts must be addressed by the general rules on costs (eg, by a prohibition on contingency fee arrangements) and by the need for court approval of a proposed settlement (including the costs arrangements in the settlement). In the case of Korea, the court controls the lawyer from appointment to resignation, including his or her retainers. In other words, there are a number of matters that must be immediately notified to the group members once the admissibility order is finalized: the statement of the plaintiff's lawyer and the agreement on the lawyer's legal fee.[67] However, in Korea, contingency fees are allowed in civil cases only. In class actions, it is common to pay 15 to 20 per cent of the total amount of money recovered as a contingency fee.

The lack of provisions regarding plaintiff's attorneys in the ERCP collective redress chapter seems to arise from the fact that the responsibility for initiating and conducting the collective redress lies with the qualified claimant. In Korea, however, the attorney of the lead plaintiff administers the litigation. The plaintiff's attorney must be someone who can represent the interests of the class in a fair and appropriate manner. No one who has been involved in at least three securities-related class actions as a representative party or a representative party's attorney in the preceding three years may serve as a representative party to any securities-related class action or as the plaintiff's attorney, respectively.[68] It is necessary at least to define the qualifications and conditions of the attorney of the qualified claimant in the class action lawsuit.

4.2.4 Overlapping class action suits

Where multiple class actions with the same cause of action are filed with the same court in Korea, the court is required by law to consolidate them. Similarly, where such multiple class actions are filed with the different district courts, the higher court with common jurisdiction over the district courts will determine which court should preside over the case and the designated court must consolidate the case. When class actions are filed, information about such filing is posted on the website of the Supreme Court and thus anyone can find information on filed class actions.[69]

However, the ERCP has implemented rules which exclude parallel or subsequent collective redress proceedings against the same defendant based on the same mass harm event.[70]

---

67 KCPA, Articles 18(1)1 and 2 and Article 10.
68 KSCAA, Article 11(3).
69 For example, *supra* n 63.
70 Rule 211(2).

4.2.5 Dual structure of class action and evaluation

4.2.5.1 Opt-in as a general rule: the Korean experience

The ERCP adopts an opt-in mechanism as the principal system and adopts an opt-out mechanism as an exception.[71] In Korea, there have long been provisions for an opt-in type of collective dispute mediation system, as this is the collective dispute mediation process under the Korean Environmental Dispute Resolution Act and the KCBA. However, this opt-in mediation system has rarely been used, so there are doubts as to the practical use of opt-in systems in Korea.

In addition, plaintiffs who request an opt-out mechanism in practice bear the burden of proving the validity of the opt-out mechanism. I am not sure whether this is appropriate, as they may experience difficulties in showing that their compensation would be limited[72] or that the number of opt-in participants would be small.[73] It is possible that the procedure of the lawsuit might be delayed because the court must decide which mechanism is most suitable for the case: opt-in or opt-out.

On the other hand, the opt-in mechanism is not very different from the existing joinder of group members' individual claims. This is because registering a lawsuit in a collective redress action is no different from filing a suit as joinder of parties. In addition, one reason for admitting an opt-out class action is to serve as a deterrent on the business which intentionally committed the illegal act, so that similar illicit activities can be prevented in the future. The opt-in mechanism, on the other hand, has been empirically proven to be a difficult method for private enforcement.

4.2.5.2 Misuse and abuse of opt-out class action

As regards the opt-out class action, there was much alarm over 'abusive' cases in the United States. However, in Korea, which has used this method since 2005, abuse of the system has not been an issue; rather, it is necessary to encourage people to utilize the system. This is primarily because the court manages and supervises the loser pays rule, the appointment and resignation of lawyers and even the amount of the legal fees. In the three completed cases in Korea to date, the attorneys' success fee was recognized by the court as 15 to 20 per cent of the total amount of compensation.

According to ERCP Rule 245(3), parties may enter into success fee arrangements with counsel or a third-party funder if such arrangements are consistent

---

[71] Rule 215(1).

[72] Rule 215(2)(a).

[73] Rule 215(2)(b).

with applicable law, the parties' access to fair legal representation and the integrity of the proceedings. Details of the success fee system will be established according to the applicable law; but I wonder what would happen if the ERCP applied a higher standard? For example, what would be the effect if the adequacy of the compensation was subject to the court's review, instead of the lower intervention in Rule 245(4)?

4.2.6 Expansion of opt-out class action in Korea

Since the inauguration of the new Moon administration in 2017, the authorities have been trying to expand the areas in which class actions can be filed. Some lawmakers went even further and submitted a bill that would allow class actions to be filed not only in relation to antitrust and consumer protection, but also to the environment and personal information disclosure breaches. It is generally agreed that the expansion of class actions is inevitable in view of the increase in collective disputes, despite vigorous opposition from business.

4.2.7 Modification of loser pays rule in class action

In the Korean legal system, plaintiffs must pay in advance a filing fee calculated by reference to the projected damages;[74] and once the action is complete, the loser bear the legal fees, including the attorneys' fees incurred by the winning party.[75] Similarly, in securities-related class actions, the leading plaintiff must pay the legal fees of the other party if it loses, regardless of whether the case was meritorious or frivolous. In the case of opt-out class actions, it is necessary to revise the loser pays rule and establish the principle that each party will bear his or her own litigation costs.

4.2.8 Third-party funding

Third-party litigation funding is not available in Korea. Third-party litigation funding has been criticized, as it allows someone with no direct interest in the actual dispute to conduct and control the litigation but it has the advantage of allowing plaintiffs to file suit without the burden of considerable legal costs. The Korean Lawyers Act provides that fees and other profits earned through services that may be provided by attorneys only should not be shared with a non-attorney.[76] However, class actions cost more than a general lawsuit, so third-party litigation funding should be allowed to promote access to justice. The problem is how best to manage the side effects of allowing third-party funding. It might be preferable to say that, like a success fee, third-party

---

[74] KCPA, Article 116.

[75] KCPA, Article 98.

[76] Korean Lawyers Act, Article 34(5).

funding should be subject to the court's review, instead of what Rule 245(4) provides.

4.2.9 *Cy-près* outcomes

Once the amount of damages has been determined by the Korean court and the damages award has been paid by the defendant, the amount will be distributed to class members, after deducting litigation costs.[77] After the distribution, the remaining balance will be returned to the defendant.[78]

Under the ERCP, according to Rule 224 and its comments, if settlement is made, the *cy-près* solution seems to be assumed as a possibility. However, in Korea, it is unclear whether the distribution plan through settlement can include contributions to a charity or consumer group instead of group members. Of course, this problem can be solved by an express stipulation in the Korean Securities-Related Class Action Act. In the meantime, however, it is essential to make provision for the donation of the remaining balance to the related non-profit association by mutual consent. Thanks to the ERCP, I expect that this issue will be robustly debated in Korean legal circles.

5. THE BRAZILIAN EXPERIENCE FROM OVER 40 YEARS OF COLLECTIVE REDRESS: SOME COMMENTS ON THE ERCP COLLECTIVE REDRESS RULES FROM A BRAZILIAN PERSPECTIVE[79]

5.1 The Brazilian experience with class actions

The Brazilian experience with class actions is one of the richest in the civil law world. It is a success story, but not an unmitigated one. After a long period of wide access to justice by way of opt-out class actions, the number of such actions reached levels that called for adjustments and the introduction of new tools to secure collective judicial protection. This section will present the traditional Brazilian approach to class actions and address some of the recent developments. The aim is to propose a holistic approach to collective redress that builds on Brazil's experience with class actions, fitting the new tools into a coherent system of collective redress that guarantees both effective judicial protection of the individual group members and public interests involved and due process of law, as required in a constitutional democracy. In doing so, the

---

77 KSCAA, Article 39.

78 KSCAA, Article 55.

79 By Hermes Zaneti Jr.

text will take into consideration the ERCP collective redress rules, especially regarding aspects of standing (qualified entity), opt-in/opt-out mechanisms and the destination of damages, costs and funding.

It is submitted that the only way to deal with the risk of an overly narrow approach of the techniques of protection is to understand collective redress as a *sui generis* genre of procedural law, composed of distinct elements, but nevertheless to be understood as an integrated system to secure effective collective protection through procedures that offer adequate procedural safeguards.

The Brazilian model of collective redress is based on the view that it is wrong to think that only opt-out class actions can serve society's need for collective protection. Rather, the better approach is one that combines opt-out and opt-in techniques – including aggregated litigation (which should be considered as a form of opt-in collective redress) – and then adds stimulus to self-regulation (both before and during the judicial process), as well as administrative redress through regulatory agencies and various kinds of ombudsmen. An approach that combines all these means of collective redress lives up to the insights of contemporary economics, which suggest that an institutional design with an architecture of choices (market design) would allow for the most efficient use of resources in different categories of cases.[80]

This section aims to explain, with a particular view to non-Brazilian readers, how the Brazilian system of collective redress is currently configured and how it has brought about, and dealt with, the almost 300,000 class actions filed between 2014 and 2018.[81]

5.2 The origins and development of class actions to pursue a public good (damages, costs and funding)

Brazil has more than 40 years of experience with class actions. The Brazilian doctrine on collective redress evolved considerably between 1977 and 1981, inspired by Italian studies of US class actions. Detailed statutory law followed in 1977 (expansion of the *actio popularis* from 1965 to protect historic, touristic, aesthetic environmental and cultural goods); in 1981 ('environmental law protection' – class actions to protect environmental rights); in 1985 ('*ação civil pública*' – a trans-sectoral class action) and 1988 (constitutional guarantees). However, it is in particular in the Consumer Defence Code of 1990 (CDC) that

---

[80] A. Roth, *Who Gets What – And Why. The New Economics of Matchmaking and Market Design* (Mariner Books, 2016); R.H. Thaler and C.R. Sunstein, *Nudge. Improving Decisions about Health, Wealth, and Happiness* (Penguin Books, 2008).

[81] See the data in Portuguese at https://bit.ly/2YVRhmM (last accessed 17 December 2019, searching for '*ação civil pública*', '*ação coletiva*', '*ação popular*' and '*ação de improbidade administrative*').

the Brazilian model of collective redress really expresses itself. The necessary coherence of the law of collective redress was secured by the doctrine and the courts considering the various rules as part of a coherent system – a procedural 'microsystem' for collective redress.

The US inspiration is clear; but the Brazilian experience and the cultural public values attributed to the *actio popularis* resulted in a different and quite unique development. Brazil does not have punitive damages by jury trial, entrepreneurial lawyering or contingency fees. Furthermore, the initiators of the proceedings are not themselves members of the group (representative members), but rather various private and public entities (see below). Another important feature is that, due to Brazilian *res judicata secundum eventum litis* (see below), there is no risk to the party autonomy that governs in civil law procedure countries, because every individual can still bring his or her own individual claim.

In the CDC, new categories of rights were created by statutory law in order to protect collective interests in a broad sense. Article 81 of the CDC establishes three categories of collective *lato sensu* rights: (1) 'diffuse rights' (trans-individual rights of an indivisible nature in which the parties involved are indeterminate persons connected by circumstances of fact – for example, living in the same area); (2) strictly collective rights (trans-individual rights of an indivisible nature, in which the involved party is a group, category or class of people connected among each other or with the defending party through a legal relationship); and (3) 'homogeneous individual rights' (individual rights of a common origin). The most complex category is the latter, as this entails the joinder of individual rights originating *ex post facto* from the same material facts. Taken together, these three categories should allow every kind of right of a group of people to be protected by the courts.

The procedural microsystem for collective redress ensures that awarded damages can be directed to, for instance, a fund. As an example, the Diffuse Rights Fund was established by law[82] to receive damages awarded in successful class actions based on diffuse rights and strictly collective rights, as well as a kind of *cy-près* fund for cases where insufficient individually harmed people claim their awards after a money judgment in a class action to protect individual homogeneous rights.[83]

There are no costs or attorneys' fees for the plaintiffs. The loser pays rule applies only for the defendant, or in case of frivolous or bad-faith litigation.

---

[82] Article 13, '*ação civil pública*', Law 7.347/1985.

[83] Article 100, CDC 1990.

The state covers the costs if the plaintiffs lose the case.[84] This risk-free gratuity is one of the features that explain the high volume of cases in Brazil.

Based on the Constitution, statute law and Brazilian legal procedural tradition, and some of the collective redress actions that have reached the higher courts in Brazil over the years, such actions can result in, among other things, orders to compensate consumers; to take, desist or refrain from any given action in order to protect the environment (eg, the installation of technical equipment to reduce emissions, the closure of a factory or the shelving of plans of expansion); to recover degraded areas and return the natural environment to the *status quo ante*; to carry out facility enhancement works in prisons, hospitals or schools; to change practices in such institutions under the supervision of the public prosecutor or the courts; to supply beds to hospitals; and to provide vacancies for certain groups of children in pre-school day care centres. Brazil protects group and diffuse rights in a broad, trans-sectoral (trans-substantive) way, and is open to new emerging rights. Environmental protection is one of the largest spaces for collective litigation. In some cases, the climate change argument has been expressly quoted in the higher courts.[85]

Regarding the effectiveness of the Brazilian system, it should be noted that Brazil adheres to the Multi-Door Court House movement, with the new Civil Procedure Code providing for a general duty to encourage alternative dispute resolution. As far as collective redress is concerned, Brazilian law has encouraged collective settlements since 1985.[86] As a result, many cases are resolved through conduct adjustment agreements. Furthermore, the Brazilian system of collective redress has allowed for the evolution of self-regulation, even after the filing of an action.

The key institution in the indispensable coordination of the various mechanisms of collective redress is the Office of the Public Prosecutor. Its importance is demonstrated particularly well by the fact that, even if collective redress is sought by class actions brought by others, the public prosecutor has the duty to intervene in the proceedings and act as *custos legis*. If we look at the period 2014–17, more than 80 per cent of class actions were filed by public prosecu-

---

[84] Article 18, Law 7.347/1985.

[85] REsp 1000731/RO, Justice Herman Benjamin, 25 August 2009; AREsp 837.218/SP, Justice Og Fernandes, 14/05/2019; REsp 1782692/PB, Justice Herman Benjamin 13 August 2019.

[86] Article 5, § 6, Law 7.347/1985, altered by the CDC 1990. See the survey 'Public Prosecution: A Portrait'. The 'winning consumer' website, linked to the Office of the Public Prosecutor, which exists in the various state and federal units, has reported more than 400 occurrences of consumer conduct adjustment agreements, many with national coverage. The website give access for more than 2000 decisions and national conduct adjustment agreements for the benefit of Brazilian consumers; see https://bit.ly/2Nv7ZUo (last accessed 12 August 2020).

tors, totalling 173,137 such actions (including 57,514 collective settlements). Moreover, data from public prosecutors shows that 256,678 preparatory procedures and (civil) investigations were initiated in matters relating to diffuse, collective rights or group rights in 2017 alone. The system of collective redress that has produced these results was praised by Mauro Cappelletti in 1994, in an analysis that highlighted the role of the Brazilian public prosecutor: 'Clearly, *independence* and *specialization* are two absolutely necessary conditions for the success of the solution considered here.'[87]

To give one last example, it is appropriate to present some of the results in Brazil of the global *Dieselgate* case. In Brazil, an action filed by a consumer association resulted in an award of BRL 1 million (about €215,000) in collective damages for the diffuse rights of Brazilian consumers (non-pecuniary losses) and BRL 64,000 (about €14,000) in individual damages to each of the 17,057 buyers of the Amarok Diesel 2011/2012 vehicle (BRL 54,000 for material damages and BRL 10,000 for non-pecuniary losses). The Office of the Public Prosecutor intervened as *custos legis* in the action and appealed the judgment in an attempt to increase the award, albeit without success. The case is still pending at the Superior Court of Justice.[88]

5.3 Fair and effective collective redress in a combined model

5.3.1 Opt-out or opt-in?

In the analysis of the contemporary Brazilian system of collective redress, due account should be taken of the fact that a new Civil Procedure Code was introduced in 2015. The new code left the pre-existing rules on class actions in various statutes untouched, but it nevertheless engages much more directly with such actions than the previous code of 1973. Under the previous regime, the necessary coherence was assured by the procedural 'microsystem' for collective redress. To a certain extent, this systematic approach served as a shield against the rather individualist approach of the CPC of 1973.

With the new CPC of 2015, the relationship between the CPC and the microsystem for the law of collective redress has completely changed. First, the CPC introduced a new rule on aggregate litigation (repetitive cases; opt-in) that interacts with the class action model (opt-out). Second, the code entails fundamental norms that serve as benchmarks for the assessment of the Brazilian system of collective redress – in particular, with a view to what a fair

---

87 M. Cappelletti, *Dimensione della Giustizia nella Società Contemporanee* (Il Mulino, 1994), pp 109–10.

88 TJRJ – APC no 041231820.2015.8.19.0001.

collective process entails. The microsystem of collective redress remains, but the new CPC is very much part of that microsystem.

With the CPC's introduction of new procedures to deal with multiple claims on the same point of law (repetitive cases), the Brazilian system of collective judicial redress has become a system with two different branches: (1) the 40-year-old traditional class action through opt-out, as described in the previous sections and below; and (2) the class action through opt-in, aggregate litigation (repetitive cases).

A fair and effective system for collective redress must guarantee: (1) adequacy of representation of the stakeholders (in most cases, members or groups in the procedure who are absent – that is, absent members); (2) the right to be heard by appropriate representatives of the group and the duty of the judge to discuss the factual and legal grounds in the case, including the participation of interest groups as *amici curiae* or through public hearings for the reinforcement of argumentative representativeness; and (3) that the outcome of the process deals with the public interests involved, in addition to individual pretensions.

For these reasons, it is necessary to strike the right balance between the various forms of collective redress available, especially between the use of class actions and aggregate litigation. Due to the importance that the Brazilian system attaches to the public interest, a guideline to strike this balance is the view that the existence of a class action ought to lead to the suspension, even *ex officio*, of individual cases (see below).

The ERCP offers an interesting mix of opt-in and opt-out, with a preference for the former. The opt-out model is limited to small claims and actions where significant numbers of group members are unlikely to opt in. It is respectfully submitted that an additional category of opt-out class actions should have been added to the list: namely, class actions that protect a public interest (eg, claims that result from environmental disasters or public policies), and where the opt-out model is arguably needed to guarantee a proper solution.

One of the important new rules in the Brazilian CPC is the cooperative certification, as a typical consequence of the general duty of cooperation (Article 6°). If the case reveals complexities on points of fact or of law, the judge must schedule a hearing for the clarification of these points, to be carried out with the cooperation of all parties.[89] The hearing is the correct moment to discuss the certification of the proceedings as opt-in or opt-out; and to identify the groups and subgroups allowed in the case and, if necessary, whether to have group opt-ins and group opt-outs (as in the case of cross-border issues). The combination of the opt-in and opt-out model is still new in Brazil and, although

[89] Article 357 § 3° of the CPC.

it has been widely criticized, some agreements have been proposed with the opt-in method.

5.3.2 Standing

The Office of the Public Prosecutor is not the only public body that plays a role in class actions in Brazil: the federal government, member states of the federation, municipalities and numerous other public institutions and bodies have standing to bring class actions. So too do several civil law organizations and associations, such as the abovementioned consumer association in the *Dieselgate* case. In all cases brought by bodies other than the Office of the Public Prosecutor, however, the public prosecutor will intervene to protect the public interest (*custos legis*). Failure to include the Office of the Public Prosecutor in the proceedings will result in the annulment of the procedure if the public prosecutor considers that this has harmed the public interest (*pas nullité sans grief*).

This very liberal approach to legal standing in class actions with many potential co-plaintiffs is a distinctive feature of the Brazilian model for collective redress. The right to bring an action is *autonomous* (not dependent on any administrative authorization of the class members); *exclusive* (only those authorized by law can bring such actions); *concurrent* (the actions can be filed in an active joinder of parties – for example, between public prosecutors and associations); and *disjunctive* or *simple* (the action can be filed by just one plaintiff). It ought to be understood as a form of procedural substitution (as pointed out by Emmanuel Jeuland, a more technical term for civil law countries than 'representative proceeding' used in English), in which the group (the holder of the right) is replaced by the authorized party by statutory law (*ope legis*), and where standing (adequacy of representation) can be judicially controlled only after this first phase – that is, later in the concrete case (*ope judicis*).

From a Brazilian perspective, the ERCP could be clearer on the important role played by independent public bodies – whether public prosecutors, ombudsmen or other independent bodies – in order to protect public interests. Public bodies with financial and political independence can provide for far better supervision of these actions and their outcomes than the models with private parties only, as in the case of 'entrepreneurial lawyering' in the United States.

5.3.3 *Res judicata erga omnes secundum eventum litis*

Another characteristic element of Brazilian class actions is the *res judicata erga omnes secundum eventum litis*. The legal basis is Article 103 of the CDC, which states that a class action judgment produces *erga omnes* and *ultra partes* effects, but without prejudicing the interests or individual rights of the people forming part of the collective, group, category or class. In short, if a class action is successful, all absent members of the class benefit from the ruling. If unsuccessful, however, the principle of *res judicata* prevents any other class action on the same claim(s), but it does not prevent the holders of individual rights from going to court to pursue their individual rights in individual actions. For the same reasons, there is no *lis pendens* between individual action and class action.

This approach to *res judicata* in class action litigation has always been controversial. That is particularly so because the US version of opt-out class actions is characterized by *pro et contra* binding effect, even against the holders of individual rights. However, recent developments in Brazilian law have considerably reduced the practical effect of this difference between Brazilian and US law. New rules on claim preclusion – that is, new ways to prevent the discussion of the same issue/claim again – in individual or class action cases include: (1) rules on the effect of the legal interpretation adopted in a test case to all other identical cases (aggregate litigation, applicable in both individual and collective cases); and (2) general rules on binding precedents (applicable to both individual and collective cases).[90] The list is complemented by recent judge-made rules for so-called 'macro' litigation generating multitudinous cases, allowing for the stay of individual claims related to the class action, as mentioned previously. In a binding precedent, the Superior Court of Justice ordered the stay of all individual actions related to a class action for one year.[91] If the class action is successful, affected individual actions can be converted into liquidation and enforcement proceedings. On the other hand, if the class action fails, the detrimental effect thereof could also affect the individual actions.

---

90 Articles 985, I and II, and 927 of the CPC. F. Didier Jr and H. Zaneti Jr, *Curso de Direito Processual Civil. Processo Coletivo,* 13ª ed, Vol 4 (Salvador 2019).

91 F. Didier Jr and H. Zaneti Jr (n 90), pp 101–05. In the decision, which discussed inflationary purges and consumer law in the face of bank conduct, the stay of the individual cases was granted by analogous application of Article 313 Va of the CPC. A judgment on the merits in the individual cases was deemed to depend on the judgment in the class action, in order to prevent contradictory decisions. REsp. n 1.110.549-RS, Rel Min Sidnei Beneti, j, 28 October 2009. The decision is a clear example of judge-made case management rule, which has since been applied many times by the courts (REsp 1353801/RS, Rel Ministro Mauro Campbell Marques, Primeira Seção, julgado, 14 August 2013, DJe 23/08/2013). In the case in which this precedent was established, the individual actions were deemed to have arisen and converted from cognitive proceedings into liquidation and execution proceedings (REsp 1189679/RS, Rel Ministra Nancy Andrighi, Segunda Seção, julgado, 24 November 2010, DJe 17 December 2010).

In the terms of the binding precedent: 'As a result of collective action concerning the macro litigation that generates multitudinous litigations, individual actions are suspended, awaiting the judgment of collective action.'[92] As provided in ERCP Rule 217(2), there is no *lis pendens* between individual action and collective action opt-out in Brazil. However, the individual claimant must be notified of the existence of the class action to opt out or stay the claim.

5.4 Conclusions

The ERCP rules on collective redress are a very valuable contribution. They address the most important issues and also have the potential to influence jurisdictions outside Europe. The broad concept of collective redress adopted allows for both opt-in and opt-out solutions, trans-substantive protection of rights (non-sectoral approach) and a choice between different remedies (eg, mass joinder, group litigation, test cases).

The opt-in preference is in line with the European tradition. The choice of an opt-out solution for small claims cases and cases where a significant number of group members would be expected not to opt in represent important exceptions with the potential to make such class actions more effective.

Still, based on the Brazilian experience of more than 40 years of collective redress, it is respectfully submitted that more room for *flexibility* and *case management* during the proceedings is needed. This includes the possibility to modify a certification/admissibility court order, and to choose more freely between *opt-in* and *opt-out* actions. To some extent, this solution is already stipulated: as the same collective redress action can result in groups and subgroups, it is possible to have one group using the *opt-out* system (eg, forum state members) and a subgroup using the *opt-in* system (eg, foreign residents' subgroup). This rule can thus apply case by case and should not be restricted to cross-border issues.

A default opt-out system should be introduced for public interest actions and where specific funds (eg, *cy-près*) are required, to avoid the 'profit benefit' of the mass wrongdoer. The Brazilian experience is that the best solution to protect group rights is a combined model with collective redress actions (opt-out and opt-in), incentives for settlement through collective dispute resolution and online dispute resolution systems. The ERCP provides valuable guidance in the right direction.

---

[92] REsp 1110549/RS, Justice Sidnei Beneti 28 October 2009). This approach was already applied in other situations (REsp 1353801/RS, Justice Mauro Campbell Marques, 14 August 2013).

6. CONCLUSIONS: ERCP COLLECTIVE REDRESS RULES AS A MODEL[93]

The contributions to this chapter show both that the ERCP collective redress rules adopt the latest thinking from advanced class action jurisdictions as appropriate to the European context and that they can also serve as a model, not only within Europe but also more widely – in particular, in those countries with a civil law tradition which are less familiar with common law class action mechanisms. The ERCP collective redress rules seek to strike a balance between access to justice (effectiveness) and concerns over the principle of party autonomy, which underpins civil procedure in much of Europe and beyond.

In the first part of this book, we considered the civil procedure foundation for collective redress – multi-party proceedings – and examined how the ERCP seeks to balance between the procedural approaches to civil litigation across the various legal traditions in Europe. The use of 'gathering' techniques, such as joinder and consolidation, for multi-party litigation is present in most European civil procedure systems but the way in which these are articulated in practice varies greatly from country to country. The ERCP seeks to reduce, as far as possible, the variations in civil procedure relating to multiple parties – although it cannot, of course, eliminate them entirely.

Collective redress – which has become an increasingly prominent feature of European civil procedure since the European Commission began to consider changes in this area in 2004 – has increased significantly in profile since the Commission's Recommendation on collective redress of 2013. As the commentary in Chapters 4 to 11 indicates, the drafting of the collective procedure Part of the ERCP was not always straightforward. It is based both on the current practice in Europe – and therefore seeks to reflect fully the principles set out in the Recommendation – and (as discussed in this chapter) on best practice in non-European countries.

The need for a degree of consistency in collective redress procedures in Europe is obvious, and is highlighted by major actual or potential cross-border claims, such as *Dieselgate* and the current 'trucks' cartel litigation. The European Commission continues to look to address the 'redress gap' for victims of breaches of directly applicable EU law. The draft Directive on representative actions for the protection of the collective interests of consumers[94] will, if the relevant provisions remain in the final instrument, require EU Member States to introduce a form of representative action (both opt-in

[93] By the editorial team.

[94] 11 April 2018, COM (2018) 184.

and, probably, opt-out). The need for civil procedure rules to accompany the implementation of this Directive may mean that the collective redress Part of the ERCP could form the model for new civil procedure rules across Europe.

Appendix (ERCP Rules)

ELI – UNIDROIT

European Rules of Civil Procedure

Reproduced with the kind permission of the European Law Institute and UNIDROIT

PART XI – COLLECTIVE PROCEEDINGS

SECTION 1 – COLLECTIVE INTEREST INJUNCTIONS

Rule 204. Scope of Application

(1) The Rules in Part XI, Section 1 apply to orders, known as collective interest injunction, made by a court, which direct any person to cease any conduct or behaviour that is infringing the law.
(2) A collective interest injunction cannot be made on an interim basis under Part X of these Rules.

Rule 205. Entitlement to apply for a Collective Interest Injunction

(1) Any entity authorised under national law to bring actions in the collective interest may apply for a collective interest injunction that requires the cessation of any infringement of the law.
(2) Where appropriate the court may order additional measures such as the publication of its decision with a view to eliminating the continuing effects of the infringement.

Rule 206. Effect of collective interest injunctions
A collective interest injunction binds the defendant in all future proceedings.

SECTION 2 – COLLECTIVE PROCEEDINGS

A. General Part

Rule 207. Collective Proceedings
Collective proceedings are proceedings brought by a qualified claimant on behalf of a group of persons who it is alleged are affected by an event giving rise to a mass harm, but where those persons, known as group members, are not parties to the action.

Rule 208. Claimants Qualified to Bring Collective Proceedings
A qualified claimant is:

(a) an organisation authorised, in accordance with national law, to bring collective proceedings and whose purpose has a direct relationship with the event giving rise to the mass harm,
(b) an entity which is established solely for the purpose of obtaining redress for group members and which satisfied the requirements of Rule 209; or
(c) a person who is a group member and who meets the requirements of Rule 209(a)–(c).

Rule 209. Requirements for qualified claimants
A person or entity shall not be a qualified claimant unless:

(a) they have no conflict of interest with any group member,
(b) they have sufficient capability to conduct the collective proceeding. In assessing this issue, the court shall take account of the financial, human and other resources available to putative qualified claimant. If appropriate, the court may require security for costs (see Rule 243),
(c) they are legally represented, and
(d) they are neither a lawyer nor exercising any legal profession.

Rule 210. Collective Proceedings – Statement of Claim

(1) A statement of claim in collective proceedings must include all relevant information available concerning

    (a) the event giving rise to the mass harm,
    (b) the group,
    (c) the causal connection between the event of mass harm and the loss suffered by the group members,
    (d) the similarity of the claims of the group members in law and fact,
    (e) whether compensation or other collective remedies are sought,

   (f) the financial and other resources available to the qualified claimant to pursue the collective proceeding,
   (g) evidence of the qualified claimant's attempt to settle the group members' claims.

(2) Before commencing collective proceedings and upon the application a qualified claimant, the court may issue an order preventing a potential defendant from bringing an action with respect to the event of mass harm.

Rule 211. Registration of Collective Proceedings

(1) Upon the qualified claimant submitting a collective proceedings statement of claim to the court, the court must enter the proceedings into a publicly accessible electronic register.
(2) After registration any other court must dismiss any collective proceedings against the same defendant(s) in respect of the same mass harm.

B. Admissibility of Collective Proceedings

Rule 212. Conditions of Admissibility

(1) The court may admit a collective proceeding if

   (a) it will resolve the dispute more efficiently than joinder of the group members' individual claims,
   (b) all of the claims for relief made in the proceeding arise from the same event or series of related events causing mass harm to the group members,
   (c) the claims are similar in law and fact, and
   (d) except in cases of urgency, the qualified claimant has allowed the defendant or defendants at least three months to respond to a settlement proposal.

(2) Upon application, the court may order any proceeding to continue as a collective proceeding.

Rule 213. Collective Proceeding Order

(1) An order made under Rule 212 must include the following information:

   (a) the name and address, and other relevant contact details of the qualified claimant;

(b) a concise description of the event of mass harm giving rise to the collective proceeding;
(c) the names or a description of all of the persons allegedly affected by the mass harm. The description must contain sufficient detail to enable any person allegedly affected by the event causing mass harm to know if they are within the group or not;
(d) the type of collective proceeding under Rule 215.

(2) Before making an order under this Rule the court shall advertise a draft of the order and set a deadline for any other potential qualified claimants to apply under Rule 207.
(3) The court shall determine which of several potential qualified claimants, if any, shall become the qualified claimant in the proceedings. It shall do so on the basis of the criteria set out in, among others, Rule 209. Where more than one qualified claimant is selected they must act jointly.
(4) The collective proceeding order shall be advertised in a manner which the court considers will best bring it to the attention of any person likely to be affected by the event causing mass harm on which the proceeding is based. The advertisement shall invite such persons to opt-in to the proceeding and shall give information on how to do so.
(5) The collective proceeding order or the refusal to grant such an order are subject to appeal by the qualified claimant and the defendant.

Rule 214. Obligation of Qualified Claimant
A qualified claimant must at all times act in the best interests of the whole group or sub-group, if a qualified claimant for a sub-group.

Rule 215. Types of Collective Proceeding

(1) Collective proceedings shall operate on an opt-in basis unless the court makes an order under Rule 215(2).
(2) The court may order that the proceedings will include all group members who have not opted-out of the proceedings under Rule 215(3) where it concludes that:

(a) the group members' claims cannot be made in individual actions because of their small size; and
(b) a significant number of group members would not opt-in to the collective proceeding.

(3) Where the court makes an order under Rule 215(2) it must set a deadline for group members to notify the court that they wish to opt-out. In excep-

tional circumstances the court may permit group members to opt-out after the deadline has expired.

(4) The court shall decide to whom and how notification under Rule 215(3) shall be given.

Rule 216. Opt-in Proceedings

(1) Where collective proceedings operate on an opt-in basis, group members must notify the court if they wish to join the proceedings in the manner specified by the court.

(2) The court shall ensure that group member notifications are properly recorded in a public register, which may be established in accordance with Rule 220.

Rule 217. Individual Actions

(1) Group members who have opted-in under Rule 216 or who have not opted-out under Rule 215(3) cannot bring an individual court action in respect of the same event of mass harm against a defendant to the collective proceeding.

(2) In cases under Rule 215(2) any group member who brings an individual action against a defendant to collective proceedings during the opt-out period shall be treated as having opted-out of the proceedings.

(3) Any time limit provided in national law for individual actions to be brought by a group member in respect of loss caused by the event of mass harm shall be suspended from the date of commencement of the collective proceeding. The period of suspension shall end when

  (a) the collective proceeding is withdrawn or dismissed; or
  (b) the group member opts-out under Rule 215(2)–(4).

(4) Where Rule 217(3)(a) or (b) apply, the remaining limitation period for individual claims will start six months after the withdrawal, dismissal or the date on which the opt-out was effected.

C. Case Management of Collective Proceedings

Rule 218. Case Management Powers

(1) In collective proceedings, the court has additional case management powers, including the power

(a) to remove a qualified claimant of a group or any sub-group if they no longer satisfy the conditions in Rule 208 and Rule 209 or fails to act in the interests of all group members,
(b) to authorise, with their consent, a new qualified claimant,
(c) to modify the description of the group,
(d) to divide a group into sub-groups and to authorise, with their consent, a qualified claimant for each sub-group,
(e) to dismiss the collective proceeding or to order it to continue as individual proceedings if there is no longer a qualified claimant
(f) to direct the correction of the group register (Rules 216(2) and 220).

(2) The court may hear any person it considers has an interest in the management of the case before making any case management order under this Rule.

Rule 219. Advertisements

(1) In collective proceedings the court shall advertise or shall require advertisement

(a) when a qualified claimant is removed or authorised,
(b) when the description of the group is modified or the group is divided into sub-groups,
(c) when a collective settlement is offered,
(d) when any order or judgment is made,
(e) of information about the secure electronic platform under Rule 220; and
(f) if the collective proceeding is dismissed or withdrawn.

(2) The advertisement shall be made in a manner which the court considers will best attract the attention of any person likely to be affected by the event causing mass harm and in sufficient time to allow affected persons a reasonable opportunity to participate as they see fit in the proceedings.

Rule 220. Communication – Secure Electronic Platform
The court must create or authorise the creation of a secure electronic platform for the efficient management of the collective proceeding.

D. Settlements in Commenced Collective Proceedings

Rule 221. Court Approval

A group member will not be bound by any agreement settling a collective proceeding in whole or in part unless that agreement is approved by the court.

Rule 222. Application for the approval of a settlement agreement

(1) A party to a proposed settlement agreement may apply to the court for approval under Rule 221.
(2) The application for approval shall include:

 (a) the description of the group whose members will the bound by the settlement,
 (b) a copy of the proposed settlement agreement. In a collective proceeding for compensation, the proposed agreement shall include the total amount of compensation payable, and the criteria for distributing the compensation to each group member;
 (c) the proposed administration of the compensation fund and method of distributing the compensation payment to group members, and
 (d) a concise statement of reasons showing why the terms of the settlement agreement are fair and adequate.

Rule 223. Procedure for Approving Settlements

(1) Before approving a settlement the court may

 (a) make any order necessary to obtain further information in order to assess the fairness and adequacy of the proposed settlement,
 (b) appoint an expert to assist the court.

(2) The court must

 (a) advertise the proposed settlement according to Rule 219, ensuring that it is clear that the court has not reached a conclusion on the fairness of the settlement,
 (b) fix a period within which any comments may be made, and
 (c) consider all comments made by the group members and the parties.

(3) The court may consider all other relevant comments received.

Rule 224. Settlement Approval Orders
The court shall not make an order approving a settlement agreement where

(a) the amount of compensation agreed for the group or any sub-group is manifestly unfair,
(b) the terms of any other undertaking by a defendant are manifestly unfair,

(c) the settlement is manifestly contrary to the public interest (ordre public), or
(d) the terms, whether contained in the proposed settlement agreement or not, as to the payment of legal and other associated costs of the action are manifestly unreasonable.

Rule 225. Approved Settlements in Opt-in Actions
An approved settlement binds all group members who have opted-in at the time the order approving the settlement is made.

Rule 226. Approved Settlements in Opt-out Proceedings
An approved settlement binds all group members unless they have opted-out of the collective proceedings at the time the order approving the settlement is made.

E. Judgments in Collective Proceedings

Rule 227. Effect of Final Judgments

(1) A final judgment of the court in collective proceedings binds

   (a) all of the parties, and all group members who have opted-in to the proceedings; or
   (b) all of the parties, and all of the group members resident in the forum state who have not opted-out of the proceedings within the period set by the court in Rule 215(3).

(2) No other collective proceeding may be commenced in respect of any claims for relief determined in a final judgment.
(3) A final judgment may be enforced by the qualified claimant. If the qualified claimant does not enforce the final judgment within a reasonable time any group member, with the court's permission, may enforce the final judgment.

Rule 228. Amount of Compensation
A final judgment that sets the amount of compensation in a collective proceeding shall include

(a) the total amount of compensation payable in respect of the group or any sub-group. If an exact calculation of this amount is impossible or excessively difficult, the court may estimate the amount,
(b) the criteria for distributing the compensation to each group member, and the method of administration of the compensation fund.

F. Collective Settlements outside Collective Proceedings

Rule 229. Standing to Reach Settlement

(1) Any entity fulfilling the requirements in Rule 208 (a) and (b) to be a qualified claimant may reach a collective settlement agreement for a group even where a collective proceeding order has not been made.
(2) Any such collective settlement agreement shall be negotiated in good faith for the benefit of all group members.

Rule 230. Application for Approval of Collective Settlement

(1) An application to the court for approval of a collective settlement agreement in accordance with Rule 229 must be made by all of the parties to it.
(2) The application shall include all of the information required under Rule 222(2). It shall also specify whether a binding settlement shall be reached on an opt-in or an opt-out basis.

Rule 231. Approval Procedure
The procedure for approval of collective settlements in Rule 223 applies to any application to approve a collective settlement following an application under Rule 230.

Rule 232. Approval Order and Opt-in/Opt-out Procedure
The court must approve the proposed collective settlement on the basis of Rule 224.

(a) If the court does not approve the proposed collective settlement it must give its reasons for refusing to aprove it, and must remit the agreement to the parties.
(b) The court must advertise the approved settlement in accordance with Rule 219(2), give information on whether the settlement shall become binding based on an opt-in or opt-out procedure, and fix a period of at least three months for the group members to opt-in or opt-out. The court shall decide to whom and how the notification to opt-in or to opt-out shall be given. If the terms of the settlement require a fixed number or percentage of group members to accept the settlement this must also be communicated clearly.
(c) After the period fixed for opt-in or opt-out notifications and, where applicable, if the necessary number or percentage of group members have opted-in or have not opted-out, the court shall declare the approved

settlement binding. Otherwise the court shall declare that the approval proceedings have been terminated without a binding settlement.

(d) An approved settlement shall bind all of the persons who have opted-in to the settlement or who have not who have not opted-out of the settlement.

SECTION 3 – CROSS BORDER ISSUES

Within the European Union

Rule 233. Recognition of Qualified Claimant

The recognition of a claimant as a qualified claimant by a court in an order made under Rule 213(1)(a) binds every other court in European Union member states without the need for further application for recognition in relation to actions arising from the same event of mass harm.

Rule 234. Judicial Co-ordination

(1) When a mass harm has cross-border effects, the registry entries for each collective proceeding shall be made available on the European e-justice platform or any similiarly effective platform.

(2) European Union member state's courts must use their best effort to co-ordinate collective proceedings in different member states in order to avoid irreconcilable judgments or settlement approvals.

Rule 235. Group Members outside the Forum State

(1) The court shall ensure that group members outside the forum state are informed of the collective proceeding in accordance with Rule 219.

(2) No order made under Rule 215(2) binds group members outside the forum state.

(3) Group members outside the forum state must, if they choose, be allowed to opt-in.

(4) Rule 235(1)–(3) also apply to collective settlement proceedings under Rules 229–232.

Rule 236. Multiple Substantive Laws

(1) Group members shall not be prevented from participating in a single collective proceeding if they are subject to different substantive laws.

(2) In any case where group members are subject to different substantive law, the court may divide the group into sub-groups under Rule 218(1)(d).

SECTION 4 – COSTS, EXPENSES AND FUNDING

Rule 237. Third Party Funding

(1) A qualified claimant may use third-party litigation funding.
(2) Rule 245 applies to any such third-party funding agreement. A court may, however, require a qualified claimant to disclose the details of any such funding agreement relevant for the instance at stake to the court and, in so far as appropriate, to the parties.

Rule 238. Costs and Expenses of Collective Proceedings

(1) Only a qualified claimant is liable for the costs and expenses of a collective proceeding if it is unsuccessful.
(2) If the proceeding is successful, the total amount of compensation received by the qualified claimant shall form a common fund.
(3) The qualified claimant's costs and expenses incurred in bringing the proceeding must be paid from the common fund before any distribution of compensation to group members in accordance with Rule 228. Rule 245(4) applies accordingly.

Index